# Lecture Notes in Computer Science 2804

Edited by G. Goos, J. Hartmanis, and J. van Leeuwen

# Springer

*Berlin*
*Heidelberg*
*New York*
*Hong Kong*
*London*
*Milan*
*Paris*
*Tokyo*

Marco Bernardo   Paola Inverardi (Eds.)

# Formal Methods for Software Architectures

Third International School on Formal Methods
for the Design of Computer, Communication
and Software Systems: Software Architectures, SFM 2003
Bertinoro, Italy, September 22-27, 2003
Advanced Lectures

Springer

Series Editors

Gerhard Goos, Karlsruhe University, Germany
Juris Hartmanis, Cornell University, NY, USA
Jan van Leeuwen, Utrecht University, The Netherlands

Volume Editors

Marco Bernardo
Università degli Studi di Urbino "Carlo Bo"
Istituto di Scienze e Tecnologie dell'Informazione
Piazza della Repubblica 13, 61029 Urbino (PU), Italy
E-mail: bernardo@sti.uniurb.it

Paola Inverardi
Università degli Studi di L'Aquila
Dipartimento di Informatica
Via Vetoio 1, 67010 Coppito (AQ), Italy
E-mail: inverard@di.univaq.it

Cataloging-in-Publication Data applied for

Bibliographic information published by Die Deutsche Bibliothek
Die Deutsche Bibliothek lists this publication in the Deutsche Nationalbibliografie;
detailed bibliographic data is available in the Internet at <http://dnb.ddb.de>.

CR Subject Classification (1998): D.2, F.3, D.3

ISSN 0302-9743
ISBN 3-540-20083-5 Springer-Verlag Berlin Heidelberg New York

This work is subject to copyright. All rights are reserved, whether the whole or part of the material is
concerned, specifically the rights of translation, reprinting, re-use of illustrations, recitation, broadcasting,
reproduction on microfilms or in any other way, and storage in data banks. Duplication of this publication
or parts thereof is permitted only under the provisions of the German Copyright Law of September 9, 1965,
in its current version, and permission for use must always be obtained from Springer-Verlag. Violations are
liable for prosecution under the German Copyright Law.

Springer-Verlag Berlin Heidelberg New York
a member of BertelsmannSpringer Science+Business Media GmbH

http://www.springer.de

© Springer-Verlag Berlin Heidelberg 2003
Printed in Germany

Typesetting: Camera-ready by author, data conversion by Boller Mediendesign
Printed on acid-free paper      SPIN: 10949788      06/3142      5 4 3 2 1 0

# Preface

In the last decade *software architecture (SA)* has emerged as a central notion in the software development of large complex systems. SA main feature resides in being a manageable but meaningful abstraction of the system under development. In the software life cycle, SA is the first system representation that encompasses a description of both the system structure and the system behavior. The static, structural view describes how the system is made up of interconnected subsystems called components. The dynamic, behavioral view specifies how these components interact at execution time to achieve the system's goals. SA abstractions allow for the early validation of basic design choices with respect to both functional and nonfunctional requirements. Moreover SA plays a significant role throughout the software development life cycle, from requirements analysis and validation, to design, and down to code and execution level. Due to the importance of the SA level of abstraction, in the past years there has been much research activity in the use of formal methods in SA for analysis and validation purposes.

This volume collects the set of papers accompanying the lectures given at the third *International School on Formal Methods for the Design of Computer, Communication and Software Systems (SFM)*. The school addresses the use of formal methods in computer science as a prominent approach to the rigorous design of computer, communication and software systems. The main aim of the SFM series is to offer a good spectrum of current research in foundations as well as applications of formal methods, which can be of help for graduate students and young researchers intending to approach the field.

SFM 2003:SA is devoted to software architectures and covers architectural description languages and tools as well as architecture-level analysis and synthesis techniques for an architecture-centric software development process that encompasses system requirements, design, testing, and evolution. The school also includes lectures concerned with mobility, performance, and dependability at the architectural level of design. The ordering of the papers in this volume follows the order of the lectures and reflects the software life cycle.

The opening paper by David Garlan introduces the problem of formally describing SA, which is preliminary to any SA investigation-based activity. Axel van Lamsweerde addresses the problem of bridging requirements and SA and proposes a goal-oriented approach to architectural design based on a framework for modeling, specifying, and analyzing requirements. Jeff Kramer, Jeff Magee, and Sebastian Uchitel's paper outlines their tool-supported approach to the design and analysis of complex systems at the architectural level, which can also be used as an initial basis for validating requirements. The analysis of SAs in themselves, as independent software artifacts, is the theme of Alex Wolf, Judy Stafford, and Mauro Caporuscio's paper, which illustrates the application of dependence analysis to architectural descriptions of software systems.

At the design level, component-based design techniques are gaining popularity, and in this context SA plays a key role since it represents the reference skeleton component-based applications are based on. The two papers by Nima Kaveh and Wolfgang Emmerich and by Paola Inverardi and Massimo Tivoli describe how analysis and verification of such systems can be carried out by taking advantage of the architectural/middleware supporting infrastructure. The role of SA for the validation of the implemented systems is addressed in Antonia Bertolino, Henry Muccini, and Paola Inverardi's paper. There an approach for SA-based conformance testing is described: architectural tests are selected from a labelled transition system representing the SA behavior and are then refined into concrete tests to be executed on the implemented system. José Luiz Fiadeiro and Luis Filipe Andrade devise in their paper the use of SA for evolutionary purposes, that is as a means to cope with system changes throughout the system's life time. The architectural support for mobile applications is addressed in Amy Murphy, Gian Pietro Picco, and Gruia-Catalin Roman's paper, where the role of formal middleware modeling is exploited to develop mobile applications. The last two papers deal with SA and nonfunctional system attributes. The paper by Simonetta Balsamo, Marco Bernardo, and Marta Simeoni proposes a methodology based on the combined use of stochastic process algebras and queueing networks for predicting, improving, and comparing the performance of alternative architectural designs. The paper by Valérie Issarny and Apostolos Zarras focuses on dependability issues and presents an approach, supported by suitable tools, to depict what needs to be specified at the architectural level to enable the automated generation of models for dependability analysis.

We believe that this book offers a comprehensive view of what has been done and what is going on at present in terms of SA description languages and analysis and testing support in the international community. We wish to thank all the lecturers and all the participants for a lively and fruitful school.

September 2003

Marco Bernardo and Paola Inverardi
SFM 2003:SA Directors

# Table of Contents

# Formal Modeling and Analysis of Software Architecture: Components, Connectors, and Events

David Garlan

Carnegie Mellon University, Pittsburgh PA 15213, USA,
garlan@cs.cmu.edu

**Abstract.** Developing a good software architecture for a complex system is a critically important step for insuring that the system will satisfy its principal objectives. Unfortunately, today descriptions of software architecture are largely based on informal "box-and-line" drawings that are often ambiguous, incomplete, inconsistent, and unanalyzable. This need not be the case. Over the past decade a number of researchers have developed formal languages and associated analysis tools for software architecture. In this paper I describe a number of the representative results from this body of work.

## 1 Introduction

The field of software architecture is concerned with the design and modeling of systems at a level of abstraction that reveals their gross structure and allows one to reason about key system properties, such as performance, reliability, and security. Typically architectural modeling is done by describing a system as a set of interacting components, where low-level implementation details are hidden, and relevant high-level system level properties (such as expected throughputs, latencies, and reliabilities) are exposed [29, 32].

Software architecture can be viewed as a level of design and system modeling that forms a bridge between requirements and code. By providing a high-level model of system structure it permits one to understand a system in much simpler terms than is afforded by code level structures, such as classes, variables, methods, and the like. Moreover, if characterized properly an architectural description should in principle allow one to argue that a system's design satisfies key requirements by appealing to abstract reasoning over the structure. Finally, an architecture forms a blueprint for implementations, indicating what are the principle loci of computation and data storage, the channels of communication, and the interfaces through which communication takes place.

To illustrate with a simple example, consider a simple pipelined dataflow architecture, in which streams of data are processed in linear fashion by a sequence of stream transformations, or "filters." When annotated with properties such as rates of processing, buffering capabilities of the channels, and expected input rates, one can typically reason about expected throughput and latency of

M. Bernardo and P. Inverardi (Eds.): SFM 2003, LNCS 2804, pp. 1–24, 2003.
© Springer-Verlag Berlin Heidelberg 2003

the overall system. Additionally, the architectural structure likely mirrors the implementation structures For example, each filter might be implemented as a separate process communicating over buffered, asynchronous channels provided by the operating system.

Software architecture consequently plays a critical role in almost all aspects of the software development lifecycle.

**Requirements specification:** Architectural design allows one to determine what one can build, and what requirements are reasonable. Often an architectural sketch is necessary to assess product viability. For example, a preliminary architectural design might tell one whether subsecond response time is a feasible requirement on a new client-server system.

**System design:** Software architecture is a form of high-level system design. It typically determines the first, and most critical, system decomposition. A system without a well-conceived architecture is doomed to failure.

**Implementation:** As noted, an architecture is often the blueprint for low-level design and implementation. The components in an architectural description typically represent subsystems in the implementation, where the architectural interfaces correspond to the interfaces provided by an implementation.

**Reuse:** Most systems exhibit regular structures that represent instances of reusable idioms. For example signal processing systems are often designed as stream processing systems. Data-centric information systems are often designed as 3-tiered client-server systems. More generally, software architectures are a key component of *product lines* and *frameworks*. Those systems exploit architectural (and coding) regularities across a family of systems to make it possible to design and create new systems at low cost by specializing a general framework to create a particular product.

**Maintenance:** Software architectures facilitate maintenance by clarifying the system design, and enabling maintainers to understand the impact of changes. Since maintenance can account for well over half of a system's lifetime costs, and a substantial portion of maintenance is simply understanding a system in order to make a desired change, software architectures can be play a significant role in maintenance.

**Run time adaptation:** Increasingly systems are expected to operate continuously. Automated mechanisms for detecting and repairing system faults while a system is running will likely become essential capabilities in future systems. Software architecture can play an key role in supporting self adaptation, by providing a reflective model that can be used as a basis for automated repair.

Unfortunately, the potential uses of software architecture are thwarted by today's relatively informal approaches to architectural representation, documentation, and analysis. Architectural designs are, more often than not, simply informal "box-and-line" diagrams accompanied by prose. While these representations remain useful to practitioners [31] they suffer from their imprecision. Generally, it is not possible to use them for analysis, to determine with confidence whether some property holds of a system, whether a design is complete or consistent, whether an implementation conforms to an architectural design, or whether a proposed change violates an architectural principle.

In an effort to improve this situation many researchers have proposed formal notations and tools to set architectural design on a more solid engineering footing. Indeed, over the past decade dozens of architectural description languages (ADLs), numerous architectural evaluation methods, and many architectural analysis tools have been proposed by researchers [14, 23].

In the remainder of this paper, we outline some of the ways in which formal methods and notations can be brought to bear on software architecture. We begin with a brief introduction to software architecture. Next we consider various formal approaches to modeling and analyzing architectures. Then we briefly consider automated support, and conclude by listing some of the more interesting open research problems.

## 2   Software Architecture

Before characterizing ways in which we can apply formal modeling and analysis to software architecture, it is important to be clear about what we mean by the term. Definitions of software architecture abound. (The Software Engineering Institute's Web site catalogs more than 90 definitions [8].) A typical one is the following:

> The structure or structures of the system, which comprise software components, the externally visible properties of those components, and the relationships among them [6].

Unfortunately, as with most definitions of software architecture, this one begs the questions: What structures? What is a component? What kinds of relationships are relevant? What is an externally visible property?

In practice there are a number of kinds of structural decompositions of a system [8, 18]. Each of these has a legitimate place in the design and description of a complex software system, and each has its associated uses with respect to modeling and analysis.

One of these is a code decomposition, in which the primary elements are code modules (classes, packages, etc.). Relationships between these elements typically determine code usage and functionality relationships (imports, calls, inherits-from, etc.). Typical analyses include dependency analysis, portability analysis, reuse analysis.

A second class of decomposition characterizes the run-time structures of a system. Elements in such descriptions include the principal components of a system that exist as a system is running (clients, servers, databases, etc.). Also important in such descriptions are the communication channels that determine how the components interact. Relationships between these elements determine which components can communicate with each other and how they do so. Analyses of these structures address run-time properties, such as potential for deadlocks and race conditions, reliability, performance, and security. Whether a particular analysis can be performed will usually depend on the kind of system. For example, a queueing theoretic analysis might only be valid for a system composed of components that process streams of requests submitted by clients. Or, a schedulability analysis might only be valid for a system in which each component is treated as a periodic process.

Other structural representations might emphasize the physical context in which a system is deployed (processors, networks etc.), or developed (organizational teams or business units).

In this paper we focus on the second of these classes of structure: run-time decompositions emphasizing the principal computational elements and their communication channels. Sometimes this is referred to as the "component and connector" viewtype [8]. Indeed, in what follows, unless otherwise indicated, when we refer to the software architecture a system, we will mean a component and connector architectural view of it.

While systems can in principle be described as arbitrary compositions of components and connectors, in practice there are a number of benefits to constraining the design space for architectures by associating an *architectural style* with the architecture. An architectural style typically defines a vocabulary of types for components, connectors, interfaces, and properties together with rules that govern how elements of those types may be composed.

Requiring a system to conform to a style has many benefits, including support for analysis, reuse, code generation, and system evolution [11, 34, 7]. Moreover, the notion of style often maps well to widely-used component integration infrastructures (such as EJB, HLA, CORBA), which prescribe the kinds of components allowed and the kinds of interactions that may take place between them.

## 3    Formal Approaches to Software Architecture

Since architectural description is a multi-faceted problem, it is helpful to classify the properties of interest into several broad categories:

**Structure:** What are the principal components and the connectors that allow those components to communicate? What kinds of interfaces do components provide? What are the boundaries of subsystem encapsulation? Do the structures conform to any constraints on topology? Is the design complete?

**Design Constraints:** What design decisions should not change over time? What assumptions are being made that should be preserved in the face of future modification, or dynamically evolving architectures?

**Style:** What are the constraints implied by the architectural style? Does a given system conform to constraints of a given architectural style? What analyses are appropriate for a particular architectural style. What are the relationships between different architectural styles? Is it possible to combine two styles to produce a third one?

**Behavior:** What is the abstract behavior of each of the components? What are the protocols of communication that are required for two components to interact? Are the components behaviorally compatible? How does a system evolve structurally over time? Can we guarantee that all possible structures that emerge at run time will satisfy some property?

**Refinement:** Does a more detailed representation, and in particular a concrete implementation, respect the structure and properties of an architectural design?

Let us now consider how formal representations of software architecture can address many of these questions.

## 3.1    Formalizing Architectural Structure

Over the past decade there has been considerable research devoted to the problem of providing more precise ways to characterize the structure of software architectures, and to derive properties of those structures. Indeed, more than a dozen Architecture Description Languages (or *ADLs*) have been proposed. These notations usually provide both a conceptual framework and a concrete syntax for modeling software architectures. They also typically provide tools for parsing, unparsing, displaying, compiling, analyzing, or simulating architectural descriptions written in their associated language.

Examples of ADLs include Aesop [11], Adage [9], C2 [22], Darwin [20], Rapide [19], SADL [26], UniCon [30], Meta-H [7], and Wright [4]. While all of these languages are concerned with architectural design, each provides certain distinctive capabilities: Adage supports the description of architectural frameworks for avionics navigation and guidance; Aesop supports the use of architectural styles; C2 supports the description of user interface systems using an event-based style; Darwin supports the analysis of distributed message-passing systems; Meta-H provides guidance for designers of real-time avionics control software; Rapide allows architectural designs to be simulated, and has tools for analyzing the results of those simulations; SADL provides a formal basis for architectural refinement; UniCon has a high-level compiler for architectural designs that support a mixture of heterogeneous component and connector types; Wright supports the formal specification and analysis of interactions between architectural components.

Although there is considerable diversity in the capabilities of different ADLs, all share a similar conceptual basis [23], that determines a common foundation for architectural description. The main elements are:

- *Components* represent the primary computational elements and data stores of a system. Intuitively, they correspond to the boxes in box-and-line descriptions of software architectures. Typical examples of components include such things as clients, servers, filters, objects, blackboards, and databases. In most ADLs components may have multiple interfaces, each interface defining a point of interaction between a component and its environment.
- *Connectors* represent interactions among components. Computationally speaking, connectors mediate the communication and coordination activities among components. That is, they provide the "glue" for architectural

designs, and intuitively, they correspond to the lines in box-and-line descriptions. Examples include simple forms of interaction, such as pipes, procedure call, and event broadcast. But connectors may also represent more complex interactions, such as a client-server protocol or a SQL link between a database and an application. Connectors also have interfaces that define the roles played by the various participants in the interaction represented by the connector.

– *Systems* represent configurations (graphs) of components and connectors. In modern ADLs a key property of system descriptions is that the overall topology of a system is defined independently from the components and connectors that make up the system. (This is in contrast to most programming language module systems where dependencies are wired into components via import clauses.) Systems may also be hierarchical: components and connectors may represent subsystems that have "internal" architectures.

– *Properties* represent semantic information about a system and its components that goes beyond structure. As noted earlier, different ADLs focus on different properties, but virtually all provide *some* way to define one or more extra-functional properties together with tools for analyzing those properties. For example, some ADLs allow one to calculate overall system throughput and latency based on performance estimates of each component and connector [33].

– *Constraints* represent claims about an architectural design that should remain true even as it evolves over time. Typical constraints include restrictions on allowable values of properties, topology, and design vocabulary. For example, an architecture might constrain its design so that the number of clients of a particular server is less than some maximum value.

– *Styles* represent families of related systems. An architectural *style* typically defines a vocabulary of design element types and rules for composing them [32]. Examples include dataflow architectures based on graphs of pipes and filters, blackboard architectures based on shared data space and a set of knowledge sources, and layered systems. Some architectural styles additionally prescribe a framework[1] as a set of structural forms that specific applications can specialize. Examples include the traditional multistage compiler framework, 3-tiered client-server systems, the OSI protocol stack, and user interface management systems.

As a very simple illustrative example, consider a simple containing a client and server component connected by a RPC connector. The server itself might be represented by a subarchitecture. Properties of the connector might include the protocol of interaction that it requires. Properties of the server might include the

---

[1] Terminology distinguishing different kinds of families of architectures is far from standard. Among the terms used are "product-line frameworks," "component integration standards," "kits," "architectural patterns," "styles," "idioms," and others. For the purposes of this paper, the distinctions between these kinds of architectural families is less important than the fact that they all represent a set of architectural instances.

average response time for requests. Constraints on the system might stipulate that no more than five clients can ever be connected to this server and that servers may not initiate communication with a client. The style of the system might be a "client-server" style in which the vocabulary of design includes clients, servers, and RPC connectors.

This conceptual basis of ADLs provides a natural way to model the runtime architectures of systems. First, ADLs allow one to describe compositions of components precisely, making explicit the ways in which those components communicate. Second, they support hierarchical descriptions and encapsulation of subsystems as components in a larger system. Third, they support the specification and analysis of non-functional properties. Fourth, many ADLs provide an explicit home for describing the detailed semantics of communication infrastructure (through specification of connector types). Fifth, ADLs allow one to define constraints on system composition that make clear what kinds of compositions are allowed. Finally, architectural styles allow one to make precise the differences between kinds of component integration standards.

To be concrete, we now describe a representative ADL, called Acme [13] Acme supports the definition of four distinct aspects of architecture. First is structure—the organization of a system as a set of interacting parts. Second is properties of interest—information about a system or its parts that allow one to reason abstractly about overall behavior (both functional and extra-functional). Third is constraints—guidelines for how the architecture can change over time. Fourth is types and styles—defining classes and families of architecture.

**Structure**  Architectural structure is defined in Acme using seven core types of entities: *components, connectors, systems, ports, roles, representations, and rep-maps.* Consistent with the vocabulary outlined earlier, Acme *components* represent computational elements and data stores of a system. A component may have multiple interfaces, each of which is termed a *port.* A port identifies a point of interaction between the component and its environment, and can represent an interface as simple as a single procedure signature. Alternatively, a port can define a more complex interface, such as a collection of procedure calls that must be invoked in certain specified orders, or an event multicast interface.

Acme *connectors* represent interactions among components. Connectors also have interfaces that are defined by a set of *roles.* Each role of a connector defines a participant of the interaction represented by the connector. Binary connectors have two roles such as the *caller* and *callee* roles of an RPC connector, the *reading* and *writing* roles of a pipe, or the *sender* and *receiver* roles of a message passing connector. Other kinds of connectors may have more than two roles. For example an event broadcast connector might have a single *event-announcer* role and an arbitrary number of *event-receiver* roles.

Acme *systems* are defined as graphs in which the nodes represent components and the arcs represent connectors. This is done by identifying which component ports are *attached* to which connector roles.

Figure 1 contains an Acme description of the simple architecture described above. A *client* component is declared to have a single *send-request* port, and the server has a single *receive-request* port. The connector has two roles designated *caller* and *callee*. The topology of this system is defined by listing a set of *attachments* that bind component ports to connector roles. In this case, the client's requesting port is bound to the rpc's caller role, and the servers's request-handling port is bound to the rpc's callee role.

```
System simple_cs = {
   Component client = { Port sendRequest }
   Component server = { Port receiveRequest }
   Connector rpc  = { Roles {caller, callee} }
   Attachments : {
       client.sendRequest to rpc.caller ;
       server.receiveRequest to rpc.callee }
}
```

**Fig. 1.** Simple Client-Server System in Acme.

To support hierarchical descriptions of architectures, Acme permits any component or connector to be represented by one or more detailed, lower-level descriptions. Each such description is termed a *representation*.

When a component or connector has an architectural representation there must be some way to indicate the correspondence between the internal system representation and the external interface of the component or connector that is being represented. A *rep-map* (short for "representation map") defines this correspondence. In the simplest case a rep-map provides an association between internal ports and external ports (or, for connectors, internal roles, and external roles).[2] In other cases the map may be considerably more complex.

Figures 2 illustrates the use of representations in elaborating the simple client-server example. In this case, the *server* component is elaborated by a more detailed architectural representation.

**Properties** The seven classes of design element outlined above are sufficient for defining the *structure* of an architecture as a graph of components and connectors. However, there is more to architectural description than structure. But what exactly? Looking at the range of ADLs, each typically has its own forms of auxiliary information that determines such things as the run-time semantics of the system, protocols of interaction, scheduling constraints, and resource consumption. Clearly, the needs for documenting extra-structural properties of a system's architecture depend on the nature of the system, the kinds of analyses required, the tools at hand, and the level of detail included in the description.

---

[2] Note that rep-maps are not connectors: connectors define paths of interaction, while rep-maps identify an abstraction relationship between sets of interface points.

```
System simpleCS = {
  Component client = { ... }
  Component server = {
        Port receiveRequest;
        Representation serverDetails = {
          System serverDetailsSys = {

            Component connectionManager = {
               Ports { externalSocket; securityCheckIntf; dbQueryIntf } }

            Component securityManager = {
               Ports { securityAuthorization; credentialQuery; } }

            Component database = {
               Ports { securityManagementIntf; queryIntf; } }

            Connector SQLQuery = { Roles { caller; callee } }
            Connector clearanceRequest = { Roles { requestor; grantor } }
            Connector securityQuery = {
               Roles { securityManager; requestor } }
            Attachments {
               connectionManager.securityCheckIntf to clearanceRequest.requestor;
               securityManager.securityAuthorization to clearanceRequest.grantor;
               connectionManager.dbQueryIntf to SQLQuery.caller;
               database.queryIntf to SQLQuery.callee;
               securityManager.credentialQuery to securityQuery.securityManager;
               database.securityManagementIntf to securityQuery.requestor; }

         }
       Bindings { connectionManager.externalSocket to server.receiveRequest }
   }
 }
 Connector rpc  = { ... }
 Attachments { client.send-request to rpc.caller ;
                 server.receive-request to rpc.callee }
```

**Fig. 2.** Client-Server System with Representation.

To accommodate the open-ended requirements for specification of auxiliary information, Acme supports annotation of architectural structure with arbitrary lists of properties. Figure 3 shows the simple client-server system elaborated with several properties. In the figure, properties document such things as the client's expected request rate and the location of its source code. For the *rpc* connector, properties document the protocol of interaction described as a Wright specification [4] (described in Section 3.4).

Properties serve to document details of an architecture relevant to its design and analysis. However, from Acme's point of view properties are uninterpreted values—that is, they have no intrinsic semantics. Properties become useful, however, when tools use them for analysis, translation, display, and manipulation.

```
System simple_cs = {
  Component client = {
        Port sendRequest;
        Properties { requestRate : float = 17.0;
                     sourceCode : externalFile = "CODE-LIB/client.c" }}

  Component server = {
        Port receiveRequest;
        Properties { idempotent : boolean = true;
                     maxConcurrentClients : integer = 1;
                     multithreaded : boolean = false;
                     sourceCode : externalFile = "CODE-LIB/server.c" }}

  Connector rpc  = {
        Role caller;
        Role callee;
        Properties { synchronous : boolean = true;
                     maxRoles : integer = 2;
                     protocol : WrightSpec = "..." }}

  Attachments {
     client.send-request to rpc.caller ;
     server.receive-request to rpc.callee }
}
```

**Fig. 3.** Client-Server System with Properties.

## 3.2 Formalizing Architectural Design Constraints

One of the key ingredients of an architecture model is a set of design constraints that determine how an architectural design is permitted to evolve over time. Acme uses a constraint language based on first order predicate logic. That is, design constraints are expressed as predicates over architectural specifications. The constraint language includes the standard set of logical constructs (conjunction, disjunction, implication, quantification, and others). It also includes a number of special functions that refer to architecture-specific aspects of a system. For example, there are predicates to determine if two components are connected, and if a component has a particular property. Other functions return the set of components in a given system, the set of ports of a given component, the set of representations of a connector, and so forth. Figure 4 lists a representative set of example functions. (For a detailed description see [25].)

Constraints can be associated with any design element of an architectural model. The scope of the constraint is determined by that association. For example, if a constraint is attached to a system then it can refer to any of the design elements contained within it (components, connectors, and their parts). On the other hand, a constraint attached to a component can only refer to that compo-

| | |
|---|---|
| Connected(comp1, comp2) | True if component comp1 is connected to component comp2 by at least one connector |
| Reachable(comp1, comp2) | True if component comp2 is in the transitive closure of Connected(comp1, *) |
| HasProperty(elt, propName) | True if element elt has a property called propName |
| HasType(elt, typeName) | True if element elt has type typeName |
| SystemName.Connectors | The set of connectors in system SystemName |
| ConnectorName.Roles | The set of the roles in connector ConnectorName |

**Fig. 4.** Sample Functions for Constraint Expressions.

nent (using the special keyword *self*, and its parts (that is, its ports, properties, and representations).

To give a few examples, consider the following constraints that might be associated with a system:

*connected(client, server)*

will be true if the components named *client* and *server* are connected directly by a connector.

*Forall conn : connector in systemInstance.Connectors @ size(conn.roles)*
*= 2*

will be true of a system in which all of the connectors are binary connectors.

*Forall conn : connector in systemInstance.Connectors @*
        *Forall r : role in conn.Roles @*
                *Exists comp : component in systemInstance.Components @*
                        *Exists p : port in comp.Ports @ attached(p,r) and (p.protocol*
*= r.protocol)*

will be true when all connectors in the system are attached to a port, and the attached (port, role) pair share the same protocol. Here the port and role protocol values are represented as properties of the port and role design elements.

Constraints can also define the range of legal property values, as in

*self.throughputRate >= 3095*

and indicate relationships between properties, as in

*comp.totalLatency =*
        *(comp.readLatency + comp.processingLatency + comp.writeLatency)*

Constraints may be attached to design elements in one of two ways: as an *invariant* or a *heuristic*. In the first case, the constraint is taken to be a rule that cannot be violated. In the second case, the constraint is taken to be a rule that should be observed, but may be selectively violated. Tools that check for consistency will naturally treat these differently. A violation of an invariant makes the architectural specification invalid, while a violation of a heuristic is treated as a warning.

Figure 5 illustrates how constraints might be used for a hypothetical *MessagePath* connector. In this example an invariant prescribes the range of legal buffer sizes, while a heuristic prescribes a maximum value for the expected throughput.

```
System messagePathSystem = {
   ...
   Connector MessagePath = {
      Roles {source; sink;}
      Property expectedThroughput : float =  512;
      Invariant (queueBufferSize >= 512) and (queueBufferSize <= 4096);
      Heuristic expectedThroughput <= (queueBufferSize / 2);
   }
}
```

**Fig. 5.** *MessagePath* Connector with Invariants and Heuristics.

### 3.3   Formalizing Architectural Style

An important general capability for the description of architectures is the ability to define styles—or families—of systems. Styles allow one to define a domain-specific or application-specific design vocabulary, together with constraints on how that vocabulary can be used. This in turn supports packaging of domain-specific design expertise, use of special-purpose analysis and code-generation tools, simplification of the design process, and the ability to check for conformance to architectural standards.

The basic building block for defining styles in Acme is a type system that can be used to encapsulate recurring structures and relationships. Using Acme one can define types of components, connectors, ports, and roles. Each such type provides a type name and a list of required substructure, properties, and constraints.

Figure 6 illustrates the definition of a *Client* component type. The type definition specifies that any component that is an instance of type *Client* must have at least one port called *Request* and a property called *request-rate* of type float. Further, the invariants associated with the type require that all ports of a *Client* component have a *protocol* property whose value is *rpc-client*, that no client more than 5 ports, that a component's request rate is larger greater than 0. Finally, there is a heuristic indicating that the request-rate should be less than 100.

```
Component Type Client = {
    Port Request = {Property protocol: CSPprotocolT};
    Property request-rate: Float;
    Invariant Forall p in self.Ports @ p.protocol = rpc-client;
    Invariant size(self.Ports) <= 5;
    Invariant request-rate >= 0;
    Heuristic request-rate < 100;
}
```

**Fig. 6.** Component Type "Client."

An Acme style, or *family*[3] is defined by specifying a set of types and a set of constraints. The types provide the design vocabulary for the style. The constraints determine how instances of those types can be used.

Figure 7 illustrates the definition of a "Pipe and Filter" style, together with a sample system declaration using the style. The style defines two component types, one connector type, and one property type. The single invariant of this family prescribes that all connectors must be pipes. The system *simplePF* is then defined as an instance of the style. This declaration allows the system to make use of any of the types in the style, and it must satisfy all of the style's invariants.

But what does it mean for an instance to satisfy a type? In Acme, types are interpreted as predicates, and asserting that an instance satisfies a type is the same as asserting that it satisfies the predicate denoted by the type. The predicate associated with a type is constructed by viewing declared structure as asserting the *existence* of that structure in each instance. In other words, a type defines the *minimal* structure of its instances.[4] (Hence, in the example of Figure 7 it is essential to include the invariant asserting that all connectors have type *pipe*.)

The use of a predicate-based type system has several important consequences. First, design elements (and systems) can have an arbitrary number of types. For example, the fact that a structural element is declared to be of a particular type, does not preclude it from satisfying other type specifications. This is an important property since it permits, for example, a system to be considered a valid instance of a style, even though it was not explicitly declared as such.

Second, the use of invariants fits smoothly within the type system. Adding a invariant to a structural type or family simply conjoins that predicate with the others in the type. This means that the type system becomes quite expressive – essentially harnessing predicate logic to create useful type distinctions.

---

[3] For historical reasons a "style" in Acme is termed a "family."

[4] The semantics of the Acme type system is similar to – but considerably simpler than – that of other predicate-based type systems, such as the one used by PVS [28]. For a formal treatment of the semantics, see [25].

```
Family PipeFilterFam = {

   Component Type FilterT = {
        Ports { stdin; stdout; };
        Property throughput : int;
   };
   Component Type UnixFilterT extends FilterT with {
        Port stderr;
        Property implementationFile : String;
   };
   Connector Type PipeT = {
        Roles { source; sink; };
        Property bufferSize : int;
   };
   Property Type StringMsgFormatT = Record [ size:int; msg:String; ];
   Invariant Forall c in self.Connectors @ HasType(c, PipeT);

}


System simplePF : PipeFilterFam = {

    Component smooth : FilterT = new FilterT
    Component detectErrors : FilterT;
    Component showTracks : UnixFilterT = new UnixFilterT extended with {
        Property implementationFile : String = "IMPL_HOME/showTracks.c";
    };

    // Declare the system's connectors
    Connector firstPipe : PipeT;
    Connector secondPipe : PipeT;

    // Define the system's topology
    Attachments { smooth.stdout to firstPipe.source;
                  detectErrors.stdin to firstPipe.sink;
                  detectErrors.stdout to secondPipe.source;
                  showTracks.stdin to secondPipe.sink; }
}
```

**Fig. 7.** Definition of a Pipe-Filter Family.

Third, the process of type checking becomes one of checking satisfaction of a set of predicates over declared structures. Hence, types play two useful roles: (a) they encapsulate common, reusable structures and properties, and (b) they support a powerful form of checkable redundancy.

The use of predicates does, however, raise the issue that, in general, checking for satisfaction of predicates is not decidable. Therefore, systems that rely on predicate-based type systems usually do so with the aid of a theorem prover (for example, PVS [28]). In Acme, however, we constrain the expressiveness of types so that type checking remains decidable by ensuring that quantification is only over finite sets of elements. (Finiteness comes from the fact that Acme structures can only declare a finite number of subparts – components, ports, representations, and others.)

## 3.4   Formalizing Architectural Behavior

In addition to formal modeling of architectural structure, properties, constraints and styles, it is also useful to be able to model and analyze architectural behavior. By associating behavior with architectures, we are able to express much richer semantic models, capturing things such as the fact that a pipe provides buffered, order-preserving data transmission, or that a given component will call the services of another component in some particular order. This in turn allows us to attach analyze important properties, such as system deadlocks, race conditions, and interface incompatibilities.

In principle there are many possible ways one might specify behavior of the elements in an architectural model. Indeed, almost any formalism can be used, and researchers have experimented with formal techniques ranging from pre-post conditions [1], process algebras [4, 20], statecharts [5], POSets [19], rewrite rules [17], and many others.

However, all of these have a similar flavor: (1) they document the individual elements with behavior characterized in terms of abstract events, states and transitions, and (2) they then perform various composition checks or simulations to test for aggregate behavior, mismatches, deadlocks, and other anomalies.

**Wright.** To illustrate how this can be done, consider the Wright architecture specification language [4]. Wright adopts an approach based on the process algebra CSP [16]. Specifically it associates a CSP-like process with each component, each component interface (port), each connector, and each connector interface (role). The overall behavior is then a set of interacting protocols.

The notation used is a subset of CSP, containing the following elements:

– **Processes and Events:** A process describes an entity that can engage in communication events.[5] Events may be primitive or they can have associated data (as in e?x and e!x, representing input and output of data, respectively). The simplest process, STOP, is one that engages in no events. The event $\sqrt{}$ is used represent the "success" event. The set of events that a process, P, understands is termed the "alphabet of P," or $\alpha P$.
– **Prefixing:** A process that engages in event e and then becomes process P is denoted $e \rightarrow P$.

---

[5] It should be clear that by using the term "process" we do not mean that the implementation of the protocol would actually be carried out by a separate operating system process. That is to say, processes are logical entities used to specify the components and connectors of a software architecture.

- **Alternative:** ("deterministic choice") A process that can behave like P or Q, where the choice is made by the environment, is denoted $P \,\square\, Q$. ( "Environment" refers to the other processes that interact with the process.)
- **Decision:** ("non-deterministic choice") A process that can behave like P or Q, where the choice is made (non-deterministically) by the process itself, is denoted $P \sqcap Q$.
- **Named Processes:** Process names can be associated with a (possibly recursive) process expression. Unlike CSP, however, we restrict the syntax so that only a finite number of process names can be introduced. We do not permit, for example, names of the form $Name_i$, where $i$ can range over the positive numbers.

In process expressions $\rightarrow$ associates to the right and binds tighter than either $\square$ or $\sqcap$. So $e \rightarrow f \rightarrow P \,\square\, g \rightarrow Q$ is equivalent to $(e \rightarrow (f \rightarrow P)) \,\square\, (g \rightarrow Q)$.

In addition to this standard notation from CSP we introduce three notational conventions. First, we use the symbol § to represent a successfully terminating process. This is the process that engages in the success event, $\sqrt{}$, and then stops. (In CSP, this process is called SKIP.) Formally, $\S \stackrel{\text{def}}{=} \sqrt{} \rightarrow STOP$. Second, we allow the introduction of scoped process names, as follows: **let** $Q = expr1$ **in** $R$. Third, as in CSP, we allow events and processes to be labeled. The event $e$ labeled with $l$ is denoted $l.e$. The operator ":" allows us to label all of the events in a process, so that $l : P$ is the same process as $P$, but with each of its events labeled. For our purposes we use the variant of this operator that does not label $\sqrt{}$. We use the symbol $\Sigma$ to represent the set of all unlabeled events.

This subset of CSP defines processes that are essentially finite state. It provides sequencing, alternation, and repetition, together with deterministic and non-deterministic event transitions.

**Connector Description.** To see how this is used let us consider first how a connector is specified. A connector type is specified by a set of *roles* processes and a *glue* process. The roles describe the expected local behavior of each of the interacting parties. For example, the client-server connector illustrated earlier would have a client role and a server role. The client role process might describe the client's behavior as a sequence of alternating requests for service and receipts of the results. The server role might describe the server's behavior as the alternate handling of requests and return of results. The glue specification describes how the activities of the client and server roles are coordinated. It would say that the activities must be sequenced in the order: client requests service, server handles request, server provides result, client gets result.

This is how it would be written using the notation just outlined.

**connector** Service =
    **role** Client = request!x→ result?y → Client $\sqcap$ §
    **role** Server = invoke?x→ return!y → Server $\square$ §
    **glue** = Client.request?x→ Service.invoke!x
        →Service.return?y→Client.result!y→**glue**
      $\square$ §

The Server role describes the communication behavior of the server. It is defined as a process that repeatedly accepts an invocation and then returns; or it can terminate with success instead of being invoked. Because we use the alternative operator ( [] ), the choice of invoke or $\sqrt{}$ is determined by the environment of that role (which, as we will see, consists of the other roles and the glue).

The Client role describes the communication behavior of the user of the service. Similar to Server, it is a process that can call the service and then receive the result repeatedly, or terminate. However, because we use the decision operator ($\sqcap$) in this case, the choice of whether to call the service or to terminate is determined by the role process itself. Comparing the two roles, note that the two choice operators allow us to distinguish formally between situations in which a given role is *obliged* to provide some services – the case of Server – and the situation where it may take advantage of some services if it chooses to do so – the case of Client.

The **glue** process coordinates the behavior of the two roles by indicating how the events of the roles work together. Here **glue** allows the Client role to decide whether to call or terminate and then sequences the remaining three events and their data.

The example above illustrates that the connector description language is capable of expressing the traditional notion of providing and using a set of services – the kind of connection supported by import/export clauses of module interconnection.

As another illustration, consider two examples of a shared data connector.

**connector** Shared Data$_1$ =
    **role** User$_1$ = set$\rightarrow$User$_1$ $\sqcap$ get$\rightarrow$User$_1$ $\sqcap$ §
    **role** User$_2$ = set$\rightarrow$User$_2$ $\sqcap$ get$\rightarrow$User$_2$ $\sqcap$ §
    **glue** = User$_1$.set$\rightarrow$**glue** [] User$_2$.set$\rightarrow$**glue**
            [] User$_1$.get$\rightarrow$**glue** [] User$_2$.get$\rightarrow$**glue** [] §

**connector** Shared Data$_2$ =
    **role** Initializer =
        **let** A = set$\rightarrow$A $\sqcap$ get$\rightarrow$A $\sqcap$ §
        **in** set$\rightarrow$A
    **role** User = set$\rightarrow$User $\sqcap$ get$\rightarrow$User $\sqcap$ §
    **glue** = **let** Continue = Initializer.set$\rightarrow$Continue
                      [] User.set$\rightarrow$Continue
                      [] Initializer.get$\rightarrow$Continue
                      [] User.get$\rightarrow$Continue [] §
           **in** Initializer.set$\rightarrow$Continue [] §

The first, Shared Data$_1$, indicates that the data does not require an explicit initialization value. The second, Shared Data$_2$, indicates that there is a distinguished role Initializer that must supply the initial value.

To take a more complex example, consider the following specification of a pipe connector.

**connector** Pipe =
    **role** Writer = write→Writer ⊓ close→§
    **role** Reader =
      **let** ExitOnly = close→§
      **in let** DoRead = (read→Reader
                      [] read-eof→ExitOnly)
      **in** DoRead ⊓ ExitOnly
    **glue** = **let** ReadOnly = Reader.read→ReadOnly
                     [] Reader.read-eof
                       →Reader.close →§
                     [] Reader.close→§
         **in let** WriteOnly = Writer.write→WriteOnly
                       [] Writer.close→§
         **in** Writer.write→**glue**
          [] Reader.read→**glue**
         [] Writer.close→ReadOnly
         [] Reader.close→WriteOnly

It might appear to be a simple matter to define a pipe: both the writer and the reader decide when and how many times they will write or read, after which they will each close their side of the pipe. In fact, the writer role is just that simple. The reader, on the other hand, must take other considerations into account. There must be a way to inform the reader that there will be no more data.

**Connector Semantics.** The intuition behind a connector description is that the roles are treated as independent processes, constrained only by the glue, which serves to coordinate and interleave the events. To make this idea precise we use the CSP parallel composition operator, ∥, for interacting processes. The process $P_1 \| P_2$ is one whose behavior is permitted by both $P_1$ and $P_2$. That is, for the events in the intersection of the processes' alphabets, both processes must agree to engage in the event. We can then take the meaning of a connector description to be the parallel interaction of the glue and the roles, where the alphabets of the roles and glue are arranged so that the desired coordination occurs.

Hence, the *meaning of a connector description* with roles $R_1$, $R_2$, ..., $R_n$, and glue *Glue* is the process:

$$Glue \parallel (R_1{:}R_1 \parallel R_2{:}R_2 \parallel \ldots \parallel R_n{:}R_n)$$

where $R_i$ is the (distinct) name of role $R_i$, and

$$\alpha Glue = R_1{:}\Sigma \cup R_2{:}\Sigma \cup \ldots \cup R_n{:}\Sigma \cup \{\surd\}.$$

In this definition we arrange for the glue's alphabet to be the union of all possible events labeled by the respective role names (*e.g.* Client, Server), together with the $\sqrt{}$ event. This allows the glue to interact with each role. In contrast, (except for $\sqrt{}$) the role alphabets are disjoint and so each role can only interact with the glue. Because $\sqrt{}$ is not relabeled, all of the roles and glue can (and must) agree on $\sqrt{}$ for it to occur. In this way we ensure that successful termination of a connector becomes the joint responsibility of all the parties involved.

**Describing Components.** Thus far we have concerned ourselves with the definition of connector types. To complete the picture we must also describe the ports of components and how those ports are attached to specific connector roles in a complete software architecture.

In Wright, component ports are also specified by processes: The port process defines the expected behavior of the component at that particular point of interaction. For example, a component that uses a shared data item only for reading might be partially specified as follows:

**component** DataUser =
  **port** DataRead = get$\rightarrow$DataRead $\sqcap$ §
  *other ports...*

Since the port protocols define the actual behavior of the components when those ports are associated with the roles, the port protocol takes the place of the role protocol in the actual system. Thus, an attached connector is defined by the protocol that results from the replacement of the role processes with the associated port processes. More formally, the meaning of attaching ports $P_1 \ldots P_n$ as roles $R_1 \ldots R_n$ of a connector with glue *Glue* is the process:

$$Glue \parallel (R_1{:}P_1 \parallel R_2{:}P_2 \parallel \ldots \parallel R_n{:}P_n).$$

Note that this definition of attachment implies that port protocols need not be identical to the role protocols that they replace. This is advantageous because it allows greater opportunities for reuse. For instance, in the above example, the DataUser component should be able to interact with another component (via a shared data connector) even though it never needs to **set**. As another example, we would expect to be able to attach a File port as the Reader role of a pipe (as is commonly done in Unix when directing the output of a pipe to a file).

But this raises an important question: when is a port "compatible" with a role? For example, it would be reasonable to forbid DataRead to be used as the Initializer role for the Shared Data$_2$ connectors, since it requires an initial **set**; clearly DataRead will never provide this event.

**Analyzing Architectural Behavior.** Once one has a formal definition of behavior there are a number of analyses that one can perform. The most obvious one is checking that a connector is well-formed. That is to say, that the Glue in combination with the roles does not lead to deadlock. Another useful check is to investigate race conditions. This can be done by checking whether certain events can ever occur out of order.

Yet another check is to answer questions like "what ports may be used in this role?" At first glance it might seem that the answer is obvious: simply check that the port and role protocols are equivalent. But as illustrated earlier, it is important to be able to attach a port that is not identical to the role. On the other hand, we would like to make sure that the port fulfills its obligations to the interaction. For example, if a role requires an initialization as the first operation (*cf.*, the shared data example), we would like to guarantee that any port actually performs it.

Informally, we would like to be able to guarantee that an attached port process always acts in a way that the corresponding role process is capable of acting. This can be recast as follows: When in a situation predicted by the protocol, the port must always continue the protocol in a way that the role could have.

In CSP this intuitive notion is captured by the concept of refinement. Roughly, process $P_2$ refines $P_1$ (written $P_1 \sqsubseteq P_2$) if the behaviors of $P_1$ include those of $P_2$. Technically, the definition is given in terms of the failures/divergences model of CSP [16, Chapter 3]. For various technical reasons, however, the actual definition of compatibility is a little more complex to define, although it captures the same essential idea of refinement. (See [4] for details.)

As another check, one can investigate whether a port can be left unattached. This can be done by seeing if the port will deadlock when connected to a "do nothing" connector. Other checks are described in detail in [2].

**Analyzing Reconfigurable Architectures** Thus far the analysis has assumed a *static* architecture: that is, the structure of the architecture does not change during the execution of a system. While this is often a useful approximation to systems, clearly in the general case systems do evolve structurally. At the very least, during initialization the system must be created, and this is not likely to be an atomic operation.

As another example, consider a simple client-server system, such as the one illustrated earlier, but that allows for the possibility that a server may crash. In such cases the system might reconfigure itself so that the client uses a backup server. This can be done by adding a new connector during run time. One of the things we would like to guarantee for such a system is that no client requests are lost. This requires some constraints on when reconfiguration can happen.

Some work has been done to address these issues, although comparatively that work is relatively sparse. In our own work we showed how to extend Wright to handle dynamically changing topologies [3]. Others have looked at ways to use the Pi Calculus to specify such things [20]. Others have looked at graph grammars [24] and category-theoretic approaches [35]. Unfortunately, in all of these cases the complexity of the specification becomes drastically higher, and the models become much less tractable for static analysis.

# 4    Automated Support

For all of the formal approaches outlined earlier, researchers have developed numerous tools to aid in the modeling and analysis process for architects. Broadly speaking there are three general categories of tools:

1. **Design Assistants:** These tools tend to focus on providing a graphical front end to allow architects to develop designs. Typically they provide a pallet of component and connector types that can be instantiated to create system descriptions. Typical examples are environments such as C2 [22], MetaH [7], Aesop [11], and Darwin [20].
2. **Design Checkers:** While automated support for architectural creation and browsing is valuable, to be effective one must also provide analysis capabilities. Hence, a number of tools have been created to perform various checks. For example AcmeStudio [25] checks for violations of design constraints. Wright provides a tool for performing the checks outlined earlier. Those checks are based on the use of the FDR [10] model checker for CSP. Kramer and Magee demonstrate how to use their LTSA tool to check specifications written in their process algebra, FSP [21].
3. **Code Generators:** In many cases a formal definition of an architecture can be used to generate system code. For example, the UniCon system handles the generation of connector code for a wide variety of connector types [30]. Similarly C2 can generate partial implementations in using various infrastructures to handle component interaction.

# 5    Conclusion and Future Prospects

As we have tried to illustrate, software architecture is a field in which formal modeling and analysis can have a major impact. While the state of practice continues to rely on informal and semi-formal descriptions, considerable research has been done to develop good formal models and associated tools for analyzing them.

But the story is far from complete and there a number of areas in which further research is needed. Here are a few.

– Scalability: Although some large case studies have been carried out (e.g., [5]), there are relatively few demonstrated success stories for large, complex industrial systems. When systems have thousands of components, it is not clear how well the representation techniques (particularly graphical ones) scale. Nor is it clear whether analyses remain tractable. For example, many analysis tools are based on model checkers, which have significant limitation on the size of the model that can be checked.
– Dynamism: As noted earlier a key issue is modeling systems whose structure changes at run time.
– Code conformance: One of the big problems is guaranteeing that an implementation conforms to its architectural specification. In situations where a

code generator is used it is often possible to guarantee conformance by construction. But more generally, given an architecture and body of code, there has been very little work on finding ways to make sure they are consistent. The main problem is that architectures (as we have discussed them) represent run-time models, whereas code is obviously a design-time artifact. In general it is undecidable whether a given body of code will generate a given architecture.

There are also some intriguing new directions being explored in the area of self-adaptive systems. Increasingly systems are required to run continuously. Moreover they must often do this in the context of environments whose resources are constantly changing (e.g., wireless bandwidth), or whose components may be changing dynamically (e.g., web services). One approach that is being investigated by a number of researchers is the incorporation of self-adaptation or self-healing into a system. The interesting question is how should one do this?

One approach is to use architectural models as the basis for system monitoring and repair [12, 15, 27]. The idea is that the architectural model becomes available at run-time in order to understand whether a system is performing optimally, and if not it can be used model to reason about reasonable repair strategies at a high level of abstraction. While work is just beginning in this area, it appears to be a promising avenue for future research.

# References

[1] Gregory Abowd, Robert Allen, and David Garlan. Formalizing style to understand descriptions of software architecture. *ACM Transactions on Software Engineering and Methodology*, October 1995.

[2] Robert Allen. *A Formal Approach to Software Architecture*. PhD thesis, Carnegie Mellon, School of Computer Science, January 1997. Issued as CMU Technical Report CMU-CS-97-144.

[3] Robert Allen, Rémi Douence, and David Garlan. Specifying and analyzing dynamic software architectures. In *Proceedings of the 1998 Conference on Fundamental Approaches to Software Engineering (FASE'98)*, Lisbon, Portugal, March 1998.

[4] Robert Allen and David Garlan. A formal basis for architectural connection. *ACM Transactions on Software Engineering and Methodology*, July 1997.

[5] Robert Allen, David Garlan, and James Ivers. Formal modeling and analysis of the HLA component integration standard. In *Proceedings of of the 6th International Symposium on the Foundations of Software Engineering (FSE-6)*, Lake Buena Vista, Florida, November 1998. ACM Press.

[6] L. Bass, P. Clements, and R. Kazman. *Software Architecture in Practice*. Addison Wesley, 1998. ISBN 0-201-19930-0.

[7] Pam Binns and Steve Vestal. Formal real-time architecture specification and analysis. In *Tenth IEEE Workshop on Real-Time Operating Systems and Software*, New York, NY, May 1993.

[8] Paul Clements, Felix Bachmann, Len Bass, David GArlan, James Ivers, Reed Little, Robert Nord, and Judith Stafford. *Documenting Software Architectures: Views and Beyond*. Addison Wesley, 2002.

[9] L. Coglianese and R. Szymanski. DSSA-ADAGE: An Environment for Architecture-based Avionics Development. In *Proceedings of AGARD'93*, May 1993.

[10] *Failures Divergence Refinement: User Manual and Tutorial.* Formal Systems (Europe) Ltd., Oxford, England, 1.2$\beta$ edition, October 1992.

[11] David Garlan, Robert Allen, and John Ockerbloom. Exploiting style in architectural design environments. In *Proceedings of SIGSOFT'94: The Second ACM SIGSOFT Symposium on the Foundations of Software Engineering*, pages 179–185. ACM Press, December 1994.

[12] David Garlan, Shang-Wen Cheng, and Bradley Schmerl. Increasing system dependability through architecture-based self-repair. In A. Romanovsky R. de Lemos, C. Gacek, editor, *Architecting Dependable Systems*. Springer-Verlag, 2003.

[13] David Garlan, Robert T. Monroe, and David Wile. Acme: Architectural description of component-based systems. In Gary T. Leavens and Murali Sitaraman, editors, *Foundations of Component-Based Systems*, page 47. Cambridge University Press, 2000.

[14] David Garlan and Dewayne Perry. Introduction to the special issue on software architecture. *IEEE Transactions on Software Engineering*, 21(4), April 1995.

[15] Ioannis Georgiadis, Jeff Magee, and Jeff Kramer. Self-organising software architectures for distributed systems. In *Proceedings of the First ACM SIGSOFT Workshop on Self-Healing Systems (WOSS '02)*, 2002.

[16] C.A.R. Hoare. *Communicating Sequential Processes.* Prentice Hall, 1985.

[17] Paola Inverardi and Alex Wolf. Formal specification and analysis of software architectures using the chemical, abstract machine model. *IEEE Transactions on Software Engineering, Special Issue on Software Architecture*, 21(4):373–386, April 1995.

[18] P. B. Kruchten. The 4+1 view model of architecture. *IEEE Software*, pages 42–50, November 1995.

[19] David C Luckham, Lary M. Augustin, John J. Kenney, James Veera, Doug Bryan, and Walter Mann. Specification and analysis of system architecture using Rapide. *IEEE Transactions on Software Engineering, Special Issue on Software Architecture*, 21(4):336–355, April 1995.

[20] J. Magee, N. Dulay, S. Eisenbach, and J. Kramer. Specifying distributed software architectures. In *Proceedings of the Fifth European Software Engineering Conference, ESEC'95*, September 1995.

[21] Jeff Magee and Jeff Kramer. *Concurrency: State Models and Java Programs.* Wiley, 1999.

[22] Nenad Medvidovic, Peyman Oreizy, Jason E. Robbins, and Richard N. Taylor. Using object-oriented typing to support architectural design in the C2 style. In *SIGSOFT'96: Proceedings of the Fourth ACM Symposium on the Foundations of Software Engineering*. ACM Press, October 1996.

[23] Nenad Medvidovic and Richard N. Taylor. Architecture description languages. In *Software Engineering – ESEC/FSE'97*, volume 1301 of *Lecture Notes in Computer Science*, Zurich, Switzerland, September 1997. Springer.

[24] Daniel Le Metayer. Software architecture styles as graph grammars. In *Proceedings of the Fourth ACM Symposium on the Foundations of Software Engineering*. ACM SIGSOFT, October 1996.

[25] Robert T. Monroe. *Rapid Develpomentof Custom Software Design Environments.* PhD thesis, Carnegie Mellon University, July 1999.

[26] M. Moriconi, X. Qian, and R. Riemenschneider. Correct architecture refinement. *IEEE Transactions on Software Engineering, Special Issue on Software Architecture*, 21(4):356–372, April 1995.

[27] P. Oriezy et al. An architecture-based approach to self-adaptive software. *IEEE Intelligent Systems*, 14(3):54–62, 1999.

[28] S. Owre, J. M. Rushby, and N. Shankar. PVS: A prototype verification system. In Deepak Kapur, editor, *11th International Conference on Automated Deduction (CADE)*, volume 607 of *Lecture Notes in Artificial Intelligence*, pages 748–752. Springer-Verlag, June 1992.

[29] Dewayne E. Perry and Alexander L. Wolf. Foundations for the study of software architecture. *ACM SIGSOFT Software Engineering Notes*, 17(4):40–52, October 1992.

[30] Mary Shaw, Robert DeLine, Daniel V. Klein, Theodore L. Ross, David M. Young, and Gregory Zelesnik. Abstractions for software architecture and tools to support them. *IEEE Transactions on Software Engineering, Special Issue on Software Architecture*, 21(4):314–335, April 1995.

[31] Mary Shaw and David Garlan. Formulations and formalisms in software architecture. In Jan van Leeuwen, editor, *Computer Science Today: Recent Trends and Developments*, Lecture Notes in Computer Science, Volume 1000. Springer-Verlag, 1995.

[32] Mary Shaw and David Garlan. *Software Architecture: Perspectives on an Emerging Discipline*. Prentice Hall, 1996.

[33] Bridget Spitznagel and David Garlan. Architecture-based performance analysis. In *Tenth International Conference on Software Engineering and Knowledge Engineering (SEKE'98)*, San Francisco, CA, June 1998.

[34] Richard N. Taylor, Nenad Medvidovic, Kenneth M. Anderson, Jr. E. James Whitehead, Jason E. Robbins, Kari A. Nies, Peyman Oreizy, and Deborah L. Dubrow. A component- and message-based architectural style for gui software. *IEEE Transactions on Software Engineering*, 22(6):390–406, June 1996.

[35] Michel Wermelinger. Formal specification and analysis of dynamic reconfiguration of software architecture. In *Proceedings of the 20th International Conference on Software Engineering*, volume 2, pages 178–179. IEEE Computer Society Press, 1998.

# From System Goals to Software Architecture

Axel van Lamsweerde

Université catholique de Louvain, Département d'Ingénierie Informatique
B-1348 Louvain-la-Neuve (Belgium)
avl@info.ucl.ac.be

**Abstract**. Requirements and architecture are two essential inter-related products in the software lifecycle. Software architecture has long been recognized to have a profound impact on non-functional requirements about security, fault tolerance, performance, evolvability, and so forth. In spite of this, very few techniques are available to date for systematically building software architectures from functional and non-functional requirements so that such requirements are guaranteed by construction. The paper addresses this challenge and proposes a goal-oriented approach to architectural design based on the KAOS framework for modeling, specifying and analyzing requirements. After reviewing some global architectural decisions that are already involved in the requirements engineering process, we discuss our architecture derivation process. Software specifications are first derived from requirements. An abstract architectural draft is then derived from functional specifications. This draft is refined to meet domain-specific architectural constraints. The resulting architecture is then recursively refined to meet the various non-functional goals modelled and analyzed during the requirements engineering process.

## 1 Introduction

Requirements engineering (RE) is concerned with the elicitation of the goals to be achieved by the system envisioned (WHY issues), the operationalization of such goals into specifications of services and constraints (WHAT issues), and the assignment of responsibilities for the resulting requirements to agents such as humans, devices and software available or to be developed (WHO issues) [Lam00a].

Architectural design (AD) is concerned with the organization of the software-to-be into main components and interactions between them [Sha96, Bos00].

It has long been recognized that architectural design has a major impact on non-functional requirements about security, fault tolerance, performance, interoperability and maintainability [Per92, Sha96]. The problem of building an architecture which satisfies the software requirements is obviously central to software engineering. By and large, such building is however an ad hoc, largely informal and unsystematic process to date.

As a very first step, a rigorous architectural design process should rely on the use of precise descriptions of the software components and their interactions. Many architecture description languages (ADLs) have been proposed for this purpose, e.g., [All97, Gar97, Luc95, Mag95, Mor95, Med96]. An ADL captures the information

M. Bernardo and P. Inverardi (Eds.): SFM 2003, LNCS 2804, pp. 25-43, 2003.
© Springer-Verlag Berlin Heidelberg 2003

required to guarantee desired properties related to the interaction of its components, as opposed to detailed design issues such as the choice of specific algorithms and data structures. ADLs provide support for explicitly modeling software components, connectors, their configurations, and constraints on the components, connectors and configurations. One may thereby define a limited vocabulary of components and connectors, and rules by which they can be legally composed or legally interact. Some ADLs support architecture-level analysis to examine whether properties of interest are satisfied (e.g., absence of deadlocks). Other ADLs constrain component composition and run-time interactions so as to enforce the desired properties. ADL-based tools can then check conformance to rules of interaction and composition. Other tools can generate monitoring systems able to check at run-time whether the interaction rules are followed. Preliminary experience with ADLs suggest that architectural design based on such notations can be beneficial to the development, validation, maintenance, and reuse of software [Sha96]. For example, analysis at the architecture level has revealed anomalies and errors in a software integration framework for distributed simulation applications [All98]; new architecture-based integration tools have been successful at rapidly generating code for complex applications [Sha95].

Yet the key issue of constructing a software architecture that meets the elaborated requirements remains largely open. Very little work has been reported since Parnas' seminal work on heuristics for identifying components and dependencies among them [Par79]. In [Mor95], a formal framework is proposed in which correctness-preserving transformations can be applied to refine abstract architectures into concrete ones. Refinement patterns are also proposed there which are proved formally correct once for all and can be reused in matching situations. Bosch and Molin suggest an informal, iterative process for architecture elaboration based on successive evaluations and transformations of architectural drafts to meet non-functional concerns [Bos99]. Gross and Yu show how the NFR goal-oriented qualitative framework from [Myl92, Chu00] can be used to document design patterns for selection during the architectural design process [Gro01]. In [Lam00a], an oversimplified procedure is just outlined by which components and dataflow connectors are derived first from functional requirements and then refined to meet non-functional goals through other types of refining connectors.

This paper presents some ongoing work on goal-oriented architecture derivation that goes far beyond our preliminary efforts. We put the following ideal (meta)requirements on our derivation process:

- the derivation should be systematic so as to provide active guidance to achitects,
- it should be incremental and allow for reasoning on partial models,
- it should lead to (at best) provably or (at least) arguably "correct" and "good" architectures –that is, meeting functional requirements and achieving non-functional ones,
- it should allow different architectural views to be highlighted, e.g., a security view, a fault tolerance view, etc.

At present stage, what we come up with is a systematic, goal-oriented process that partially intertwines requirements and architecture elaboration and at places allows for incremental, formal analysis of partial models through animation or checking against upstream, higher-level goal formulations.

Section 2 introduces some necessary background on goal-oriented model elaboration [Lam01]; it briefly recalls how software requirements can be incrementally derived from system goals and how high-level architectural choices are already made during that process. Section 3 shows how software specifications can be derived from requirements. The derivation of abstract dataflow architectures from functional software specifications is discussed in Section 4. The resulting architectural draft is refined first by imposing architectural styles on parts of it to meet domain-specific architectural constraints (Section 5). The next, iterative step then consists in refining this global, style-based architectural draft through local, pattern-directed refinement of components and connectors so as to meet the non-functional goals that emerged from the goal elaboration process (Section 6).

Throughout the exposition we will use the Meeting Scheduler benchmark as a running example [MOD]. The reader may refer to [Fea97] for a full problem statement.

## 2    Background

We introduce some basic concepts and terminology before recalling how goal, object, agent and operation  models can be built systematically.

### 2.1    Goals, Agents, Objects, and Operations

A *goal* is a prescriptive statement of intent about some system (existing or to-be) whose satisfaction in general requires the cooperation of some of the agents forming that system. *Agents* are active components such as humans, devices, legacy software or software-to-be components that play some *role* towards goal satisfaction. Some agents thus define the software whereas the others define its environment; the word "system" refers to the software under consideration *and* its environment. Unlike goals, *domain properties* are descriptive statements about the environment –e.g., physical laws, organizational norms, etc.

Goals may refer to a wide variety of prescriptive assertions.

- *Functional goals* refer to services the system is expected to provide. For example, SatisfactionGoals are functional goals concerned with satisfying agent requests; InformationGoals are goals concerned with keeping agents informed about object states.

- *Non-functional goals* refer to quality of service, development objectives or architectural constraints.

   -*quality-of-service* goals capture application-specific concerns about safety, security, usability, performance, interoperability, accuracy of software information with respect to what it represents in the environment, etc.;

*-development* goals refer to standard software quality criteria such as maintainability, reusability, etc.;

*-architectural constraints* refer to domain-specific features of environment agents and relationships among them to be taken into account during architectural design –such as the distribution of human agents, organization data or physical devices in the environment.

Goals are organized into AND/OR *refinement-abstraction structures* where higher-level goals are in general strategic, coarse-grained and involve multiple agents whereas lower-level goals are in general technical, fine-grained and involve less agents [Dar93, Dar96]. In such structures, *AND-refinement* links relate a goal to a set of subgoals (called refinemen*t*) possibly conjoined with domain properties; this means that satisfying all subgoals in the refinement is a sufficient condition in the domain for satisfying the goal. *OR-refinement* links relate a goal to an alternative set of refinements; this means that satisfying one of the refinements is a sufficient condition in the domain for satisfying the goal.

Goal refinement ends up when every subgoal is *realizable* by some individual agent assigned to it, that is, expressible in terms of conditions that are *monitorable* and *controllable* by the agent [Let02a]. A *requirement* is a realizable goal under responsibility of an agent in the software-to-be; an *expectation* is a realizable goal under responsibility of an agent in the environment (unlike requirements, expectations cannot be enforced by the software-to-be).

Goals prescribe *intended* behaviors; they can be formalized in a real-time linear temporal logic [Man92, Koy92, Dar93]. For example, one goal for a meeting scheduling system might assert that the date constraints of people expected to attend a meeting shall be known to the scheduler within $M$ days after the meeting is requested:

**Goal** Achieve [ParticipantsConstraintsKnown]
  **FormalSpec** $\forall$m: Meeting, p: Participant
    Requested (m) $\wedge$ Invited (p, m) $\wedge$ Scheduling (s, m) $\Rightarrow$ $\Diamond_{\leq Md}$ Knows (s, p.Constraints)

(Semi-formal keywords such as Achieve, Avoid, Maintain are used for lightweight reference to goals according to the temporal behavior pattern they prescribe.)

*SoftGoals* prescribe *preferred* behaviors; they are used to select preferred alternatives in an AND/OR goal refinement graph through qualitative reasoning [Myl92, Chu00]. SoftGoals can be refined but are in general hard to formalize.

The state of the system is defined by aggregation of the states of its objects. An *object* can be an entity, an association, an event or an agent (active object). Objects are characterized by attributes and domain properties (invariants). An *object model* is represented by a UML class diagram.

The *agent model* captures responsibility links between agents and goals together with monitoring/control links between agents and object attributes. The object attributes monitored and controlled by an agent define its *interface* to other agents [Let02a].

A goal assigned to some agent in the software-to-be is *operationalized* in functional services, called operations, to be performed by that agent. An *operation* is an input-output relation over objects; operation applications define state transitions. When specifying an operation, a distinction is made between domain pre/postconditions and additional pre-, post- and trigger conditions required for achieving some underlying goal. A pair *(domain precondition, domain postcondition)* captures the elementary state transitions defined by operation applications in the domain. A *required precondition* for some goal captures a permission to perform the operation when the condition is true. A *required trigger conditio*n for some goal captures an obligation to perform the operation when the condition becomes true provided the domain precondition is true. A *required postcondition* defines some additional condition that any application of the operation must establish to achieve the corresponding goal.

## 2.2     From System Goals to Software Requirements

Operational software requirements are derived gradually from the underlying system goals. The derivation proceeds according to the following steps [Lam01].

- *Goal modeling:* A goal refinement graph is elaborated first by identifying relevant goals from input material (such as interview transcripts and available documents) –typically, by looking for intentional keywords in natural language statements and by asking *why* and *how* questions about such statements;

- *Object modeling:* UML classes, attributes and associations are derived systematically from goal specifications refering to them;

- *Agent modeling:* agents are identified, their monitoring/control capabilities are elicited from goal formulations, and alternative assignments of goals to agents are explored (alternative agent assignments define alternative system proposals and software/environment boundaries where more or less is automated);

- *Operationalization:* operations and their domain pre- and postconditions are identified from goal specifications; additional required pre-, post- and trigger conditions are derived so as to ensure the corresponding goals.

The above steps are ordered by data dependencies and, of course, intertwined. Each step is guided by heuristics and derivation patterns associated with specific tactics [Dar96, Let02a, Let02b]. Additional parallel steps of the method handle goal mining from scenarios [Lam98b], the management of conflicts between goals [Lam98a] and the management of obstacles to goal satisfaction [Lam00c], respectively.

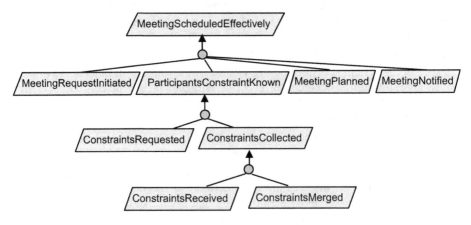

**Fig. 1 –** Portion of a goal refinement graph

Fig. 1 shows a portion of the goal model for our meeting scheduling system that includes the goal Achieve [ParticipantsConstraintsKnown] formalized above. This goal was formally refined using the formal **Refine-by-Milestone** pattern twice (see Fig. 2). The goal Achieve [ConstraintsRequested] is formally operationalized into an operation RequestConstraintsToParticipants using the formal **Bounded-Achieve** pattern (see Fig. 3 where **S** denotes the *Since* temporal operator over past states [Man92]).

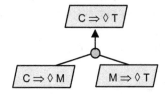

**Fig. 2** – Refinement-by-milestone pattern

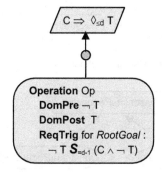

**Fig. 3** – Bounded-Achieve operationalization pattern

## 2.3    On the Invitable Intertwining between Requirements and Architecture

It has long been recognized that specification and implementation are often intertwined in practice [Swa82]. More abstractly, problem and solution spaces are intertwined due to the recursive nature of problem solving –a problem is solved by specifying sub-problems and solving them. This observation has been remade recently in the context of requirements and architecture [Nus01].

In our framework, such intertwining appears at places where decisions have to be made among multiple alternatives being raised.

- A goal may be refined into several alternative AND-combinations of subgoals [Dar96];

- An obstacle obstructing a goal may be resolved through several alternative obstruction resolution tactics [Lam00c];

- A conflict among multiple goals may be resolved through several alternative conflict resolution tactics [Lam98];

- A "terminal" goal realizable by multiple agents may be assigned to several alternative candidate agents [Let02a]. When a software agent is being considered

for assignment, there are alternative choices on the *granularity* of that agent –
from a fine-grained agent entirely dedicated to that goal to a global, coarse-
grained "software-to-be" agent (see Section 4).

For each type of alternative, decisions have to be made which in the end will produce
different architectures. A specific refinement, resolution or assignment is selected
based on qualitative preferences dictated by positive contributions to high-priority
softgoals [Myl92, Chu00, Lam00a] and/or resolution of other critical obstacles and
conflicts [Lam00c, Lam98a]. Such early choices may have a global impact on the
architecture.

Fig. 4 and 5 illustrate the point in the case of alternative refinements and assignments,
respectively.

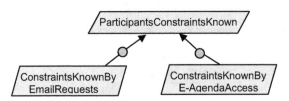

**Fig. 4 –** Alternative goal refinements

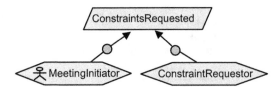

**Fig. 5 –** Alternative agent assignments

The global architecture of a meeting scheduler based on e-mail communication for
getting participants constraints will be different from one based on the participant
electronic agendas. There will be architectural differences between a version where
meeting initiators are taking responsibility for handling constraint requests and a more
automated version where a software component ConstraintRequestor will be responsible
for this. [Lam00a] shows an example where two alternative goal refinements for a
train control system lead to completely different architectures –from centralized to
fully distributed.

## 3    From Software Requirements to Software Specifications

Requirements are formulated in terms of objects in the real world, in a vocabulary
accessible to stakeholders [Jac95]; they capture required relations between objects in
the environment that are monitored and controlled by the software, respectively
[Par95].

*Software specifications* are formulated in terms of objects manipulated by the software, in a vocabulary accessible to programmers; they capture required relations between input and output software objects.

In our meeting scheduling example, consider the following requirement assignable to some component of the meeting scheduler software:

**Requirement** Achieve [ConstraintsRequested]
**FormalSpec** ∀m: Meeting, p: Participant:
         Requested (m) ∧ Invited (p, m) ⇒ ◊$_{≤Rd}$ ConstrRequested (p)

In this formulation, the associations Requested, Invited and ConstrRequested correspond to phenomena that are observable in the environment. They need to be mapped to software input-ouput variables to produce, e.g., the following target software specification:

         ∀m: MeetingClass, p: ParticipantClass
         MeetRequest (m) ∧ p **in** InviteeList (m) ⇒ ◊$_{≤Rd}$ ConstrReqSent (p)

Software specifications may be derived from requirements systematically as follows.

1.  Translate all goals assigned to software agents into the vocabulary of the software-to-be by introduction of software input-output variables;

2.  Map relevant elements of the (domain) object model to their images in the software's object model;

3.  Introduce (non-functional) accuracy goals requiring the mapping to be consistent, that is, the state of software variables and database elements must accurately reflect the state of the corresponding monitored/controlled objects they represent [Dar93];

4.  Introduce input/output agents to be responsible for such accuracy goals – typically, sensors, actuators or other environment agents.

For our above example, the accuracy goals will be

         ∀m: Meeting, m': MeetingClass, p: Participant, p': ParticipantClass
         Mapping (m, m') ∧ Mapping (p, p') ⇒
            MeetRequest (m) ⇔ Requested (m)
            p' **in** InviteeList (m') ⇔ Invited (p, m)
            ConstrReqSent (p) ⇔ ConstrRequested (p)

The first two equivalences will be assigned as expectations, e.g., to the MeetingInitiator agent (she has to include p' in the software input variable InviteeList iff that person is really among those expected to attend the meeting) whereas the third equivalence will be assigned as expectation, e.g., to the CommunicationInfrastructure agent.

Serious system failures are often caused by accuracy goal violations arising from environment agents not filling their expectations [Jac95, Lam00c]. If *Req* denotes the set of requirements assigned to software agents, *Exp* the set of expectations assigned to environment agents, *Dom* the set of domain properties, *Soft* the set of software specifications, *Acc* the set of accuracy goals, and *G* the set of goals under consideration, the following satisfaction relations must hold for every requirement *req* in *Req* and goal *g* in *G*:

         Soft, Acc, Dom |= req     with  Soft, Acc, Dom |≠ **false**
         Req, Exp, Dom |= g        with  Req, Exp, Dom |≠ **false**

## 4     From Software Specs to Abstract Dataflow Architectures

From now on all the elaborated requirements and derived software specifications will be assumed to be non-conflicting as conflicts have been managed upstream in the requirements engineering process [Lam98a].

A first architectural draft is obtained from data dependencies among the software agents assigned to functional requirements. These agents become architectural components statically linked through dataflow connectors; there is no other "interaction" among the agents. In the transformation, the alternative of fine-grained components *C* associated with specific functional goals is preferred so as to address the non-functional softgoal *Maximize* [Cohesion (C)].

The procedure for deriving a dataflow architectural draft from our goal, agent and operation models is as follows.

1.  For each functional goal assigned to the software-to-be, define one component regrouping a software agent dedicated to the goal together with the various operations operationalizing the goal and performed by the agent. The agent's interface is defined by the sets of variables the agent monitors and controls, respectively; such variables are derived from the goal assertion [Let02a] reformulated in terms of software variables according to the mapping defined in the previous step (see Section 3).

2.  For each pair of components *C1* and *C2*, derive a dataflow connector from *C1* to *C2* labelled with variable *d* iff *d* is among *C1*'s controlled variables and *C2*'s monitored variables:

$$\text{DataFlow (d, C1, C2)} \iff \text{Controls (C1, d)} \wedge \text{Monitors (C2, d)}$$

Fig. 6 shows a partial result of step 1 for a portion of the goal graph in Fig.1; Fig. 7 shows the dataflow architectural draft resulting from step 2.

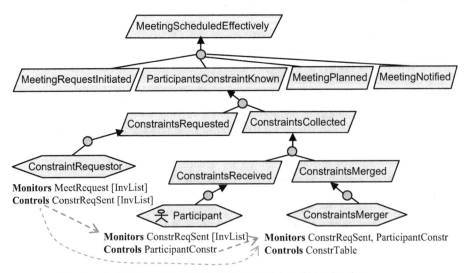

**Fig. 6 –** Assigned agents, their interfaces and data dependencies

The arrows in Fig. 7 denote dataflow connectors; they are labelled with corresponding data. Note that the ConstraintRequestor agent's interface in Fig. 6 was derived from the monitored and controlled conditions in the functional spec of the goal ConstraintRequested given in Section 3 and assigned to that agent.

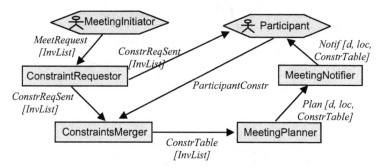

**Fig. 7 –** Derived dataflow architecture

In the dataflow architecture derived, each component is specified by the specification of the goal assigned to it together with the pre/trigger/post-conditions of the various operations operationalizing that goal.

When these specifications are formalized, our FAUST tools on top of the GRAIL environment [Dar98] can check at this abstract architecture level that the components together achieve higher-level goals from the goal graph, with counter-example scenarios being generated if this is not the case (we currently use bounded SAT solvers to do this). It can also generate state machines from the pre/trigger/post-condition specifications and animate them to vizualize whether the components behave as expected.

## 5    Style-Based Architecture Refinement to Meet Architectural Constraints

The initial abstract architecture obtained in Section 4 defines our refinement space. Before exploring alternative ways of refining components and connectors locally, this space may need to be globally constrained by architectural requirements. The latter typically arise from domain-specific features of environment agents or relationships among them, e.g., the distribution of human agents, organizational data or physical devices the software is controlling (see Section 2.1).

Our proposal here is to refine the dataflow architecture by imposing "suitable" architectural styles, that is, styles whose underlying (soft)goals match the architectural constraints. This requires such styles to be documented by applicability conditions (such as domain properties and the softgoals they are addressing [Gro01]) and effect conditions on the resulting architecture.

This step is currently fairly qualitative but can be made systematic through the use of transformation rules.

Fig. 8 shows a transformation rule for the introduction of the *event-based* style.

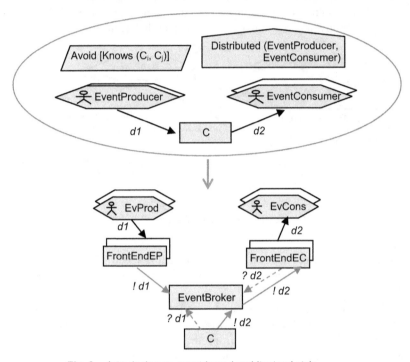

**Fig. 8 –** Introducing an event-based architectural style

The "home" notation is used there to denote a domain property. Standard arrows still denote dataflow connectors; a grey dashed arrow labelled by *?d* means that the source component *registers interest* to the target component for events corresponding to productions of *d*; a grey arrow labelled by *!d* means that the source component *notifies* the interested target component of events corresponding to productions of *d*. The latter events carry corresponding value for *d*.

Fig. 9 outlines a portion of the result of applying the style-based transformation in Fig. 8 to the abstract dataflow architecture in Fig. 7.

Note that there are still data flowing through the gray event notification arrows as the events carry the corresponding data among their attributes. There is in fact a proof obligation that *refinements must preserve the properties of more abstract connectors and components*. In this case, an abstract dataflow channel between two components must be preserved either directly or indirectly through intermediate components (e.g., the EventBroker here).

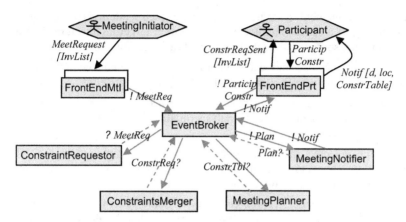

**Fig. 9 –** Style-based architecture to meet architectural constraints

# 6 Pattern-Based Architecture Refinement to Achieve Non-functional Requirements

Once an abstract dataflow architecture has been refined to meet architectural constraints it needs to be refined further in order to achieve the other types of non-functional goals, that is, quality-of-service goals and development goals. For example, the event broker in Fig. 9 should be split up into several brokers handling different kinds of events if the development goal *Maximize*[Cohesion(EventBroker)] is to be achieved. This is the next step of our derivation process.

Many quality-of-service goals impose constraints on component interaction. For example, security goals restrict interactions to limit information flows along channels; accuracy goals impose interactions to maintain a consistent state between related objects; usability requirements put constraints on information presentation and dialogs. Development goals such as *Minimize*[Coupling(C1,C2)] or InformationHidden(C1,C2) also impose specific constraints on the way the corresponding components may interact. On another hand, some non-functional goals impose constraints on single components only, e.g., *Maximize*[Cohesion(C)].

The next refinement step works on a more local basis than the previous one to "inject" quality-of-service and development goals within pairs of components (connector refinement) or single components (component refinement). The procedure is as follows. (We use NFG as an abbreviation for "quality-of-service or development goal".)

1. For each terminal NFG in the goal refinement graph $G$,
   - identify all specific connectors and components $G$ may constrain;
   - instantiate $G$ to those connectors and components (if necessary).

2. For each NFG-constrained connector or component, refine it to meet the instantiated NFGs associated with it; use *architectural refinement patterns* to drive the refinement as follows:

- access a refinement pattern catalog where each pattern is a rewrite rule consisting of a source architectural fragment, a target architectural fragment refining that source, and a set of NFG goals achieved by the target,
- select patterns whose source and NFG goals match the connector/components and the instantiated NFGs associated with them, respectively;
- if there are several matching patterns, select a most preferred one based on NFG prioritization and tradeoff analysis (qualitative reasoning may be used to support this [Gro01]);
- apply the selected matching refinement pattern instantiated to the NFG-constrained connector or component to produce a new architectural fragment replacing the connector and connected components.

As a first example, consider the NoReadUpNoWriteDown pattern for confidentiality goals based on the Bell-LaPadula multi-level security model [Rie99]. Fig. 10 shows a formal representation of it. Note that the required postcondition of the refining component SecurityFilter is derived formally from the confidentiality goal specification using our formal operationalization patterns [Let00b].

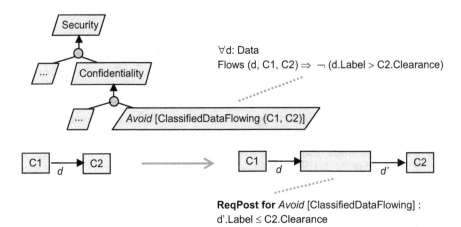

Fig. 10 – The NoReadUpNoWriteDown pattern for confidentiality goals

Let us now illustrate a pattern-based architectural refinement of the architectural draft for our meeting scheduling software obtained in Fig. 9.

Step 1 above results in localizing the impact of the confidentiality goal

Avoid [ParticipantConstraintsKnownToNonInitiatorParticipants]

from the full goal graph on the dataflow connector between the MeetingPlanner component and the MeetingNotifier component via the EventBroker component (see Figs. 7 and 9). In step 2 the NoReadUpNoWriteDown pattern is seen to be matching by considering two disclosure levels: one for meeting initiators, the other for normal participants.

The application of the intantiated pattern results in the introduction of a new component between the EventBroker and the MeetingNotifier:

ParticipantConstraintsFilter

that will ensure that participants constraints are filtered for normal participants from the data PlanningDetails attached to the event Notif transmitted from the MeetingPlanner to the MeetingNotifier via the EventBroker.

Fig. 11 and Fig. 12 suggest a sample of architectural patterns for quality-of-service and development goals, respectively. For our meeting scheduling software, the first pattern in Fig. 12 might be used to introduce a ConstraintsTable abstract data type component for use by the ConstraintsMerger and Planner components.

# 7   Conclusion

We presented a systematic, incremental approach to deriving software architecture from system goals. The approach is grounded on the KAOS goal-oriented method for requirements engineering with the intent of exporting the virtues of goal orientation for constructive guidance of software architects in their design task. It mixes qualitative and formal reasoning towards the attainment of software architectures that meet both functional and non-functional requirements.

The architectural refinement of connectors and components is explicitly linked to the non-functional goals the refinement aims to achieve. This means that *architectural views* according to corresponding non-functional features (e.g., security views or fault tolerance views) are easily extracted through query systems such as the one provided by the GRAIL environment [Dar98].

This approach leaves a lot of questions open for further investigation though.

Up to what extent can the qualitative reasoning involved in architectural refinement be made more formal is an issue to be clarified if more sophisticated tool support is to be provided during the derivation process. In particular, the current style-based way of introducing architectural constraints leaves a lot of room for further improvement.

The proposed approach is purely refinement-based. This is clearly insufficient in a number of situations where architectural features need to be propagated bottom-up, e.g., from middleware requirements. A complementary, dual approach based on abstraction patterns might be worth investigating to address this problem.

In its current form, our approach does not reach the point where interaction protocols are detailed precisely. Our intent is to integrate previous, good-old-time results to formally derive such protocols, in particular through fixpoint computation of deadlock-free and starvation-free synchronizing schemes that achieve the goals [Lam79].

**Acknowledgement.** Insightful discussions on architectural refinement with R. Riemenschneider and D. Perry are gratefully acknowledged. Thanks are also due to members of the IFIP Working Group WG2.9 for feedback and criticism on earlier versions of this work.

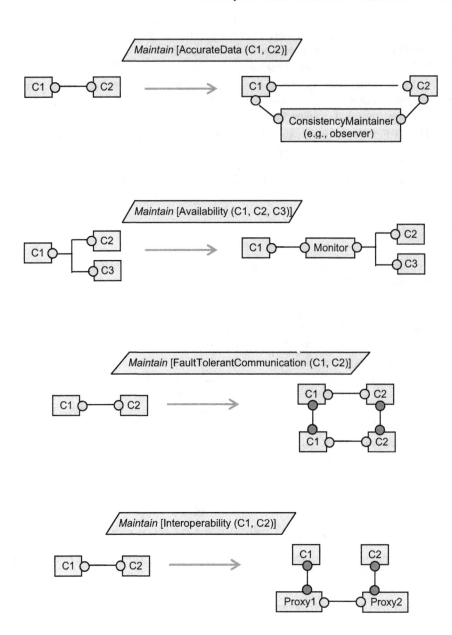

**Fig. 11** – Architectural refinement patterns for quality-of-service goals

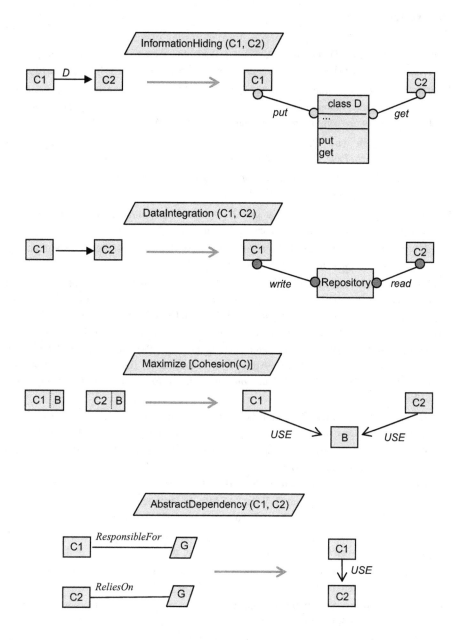

**Fig. 12 –** Architectural refinement patterns for development goals

# References

[All97] R. Allen and D. Garlan, "A Formal Basis for Architectural Connection", *ACM Transctions on Software Engineering and Methodology*, Vol. 6 No. 3, July 1997, 213-249.

[All98] R. Allen, D. Garlan and J. Ivers, "Formal Modeling and Analysis of the HLA Component Integration Framework", *Proc. FSE-6 - 6th Intl Symposium on the Foundations of Software Engineering*, Lake Buena Vista, ACM, November 1998.

[Bos99] J. Bosch and P. Molin, "Software Architecture Design: Evaluation and Transformation", *Proc. IEEE Symp. On Engineering of Computer-Based Systems*, 1999.

[Bos00] J. Bosch, *Design and Use of Software Architectures – Adopting and Evolving a Product Line Approach*. Addison-Wesley, 2000.

[Chu00] L. Chung, B. Nixon, E. Yu and J. Mylopoulos, *Non-functional requirements in software engineering*. Kluwer Academic, Boston, 2000.

[Dar93] A. Dardenne, A. van Lamsweerde and S. Fickas, "Goal-Directed Requirements Acquisition", *Science of Computer Programming*, Vol. 20, 1993, 3-50.

[Dar96] R. Darimont and A. van Lamsweerde, "Formal Refinement Patterns for Goal-Driven Requirements Elaboration", *Proc. FSE'4 - Fourth ACM SIGSOFT Symposium on the Foundations of Software Engineering*, San Francisco, October 1996, 179-190.

[Dar98] R. Darimont, E. Delor, P. Massonet, and A. van Lamsweerde, "GRAIL/KAOS: An Environment for Goal-Driven Requirements Engineering", *Proc. ICSE'98 - 20th Intl. Conf. on Software Engineering,* Kyoto, April 1998, vol. 2, 58-62. (Earlier and shorter version found in *Proc. ICSE'97 - 19th Intl. Conf. on Software Engineering*, Boston, May 1997, 612-613.

[Fea97] M. Feather, S. Fickas, A. Finkelstein, and A. van Lamsweerde, "Requirements and Specification Exemplars", Automated Software Engineering Vol. 4, 1997, 419-438.

[Fea98] M. Feather, S. Fickas, A. van Lamsweerde, and C. Ponsard, "Reconciling System Requirements and Runtime Behaviour", *Proc. IWSSD'98 - 9th International Workshop on Software Specification and Design*, Isobe, IEEE CS Press, April 1998.

[Gar97] D. Garlan, R. Monroe and D. Wile, "ACME: An Architecture Description Interchange Language", *Proceedings CASCON'97*, Toronto, Nov. 1997, 169-183.

[Gro01] D. Gross and E. Yu, "From Non-Functional Requirements to Design Through Patterns", *Requirements Engineering Journal* Vol. 6, 2001, 18-36.

[Jac95] M. Jackson, *Software Requirements & Specifications - A Lexicon of Practice, Principles and Pejudices*. ACM Press, Addison-Wesley, 1995.

[Koy92] R. Koymans, Specifying message passing and time-critical systems with temporal logic, *LNCS 651*, Springer-Verlag, 1992.

[Lam79] A. van Lamsweerde and M. Sintzoff, "Formal Derivation of Strongly Correct Concurrent Programs", *Acta Informatica* Vol. 12, 1979, 1-31.

[Lam95] A. van Lamsweerde, R. Darimont and P. Massonet, "Goal-Directed Elaboration of Requirements for a Meeting Scheduler: Problems and Lessons Learned", *Proc. RE'95 - 2nd Int. Symp. on Requirements Engineering*, York, IEEE, 1995.

[Lam98a] A. van Lamsweerde, R. Darimont and E. Letier, "Managing Conflicts in Goal-Driven Requirements Engineering", *IEEE Trans. on Sofware. Engineering*, Special Issue on Inconsistency Management in Software Development, November 1998.

[Lam98b] A. van Lamsweerde and L. Willemet, "Inferring Declarative Requirements Specifications from Operational Scenarios", *IEEE Trans. on Sofware. Engineering*, Special Issue on Scenario Management, December 1998, 1089-1114.

[Lam00a] A. van Lamsweerde, "Requirements Engineering in the Year 00: A Research Perspective", Keynote paper, *Proc. ICSE'2000 - 22$^{nd}$ Intl. Conference on Software Engineering,* IEEE Press, June 2000.

[Lam00b] A. van Lamsweerde, "Formal Specification: a Roadmap". In *The Future of Software Engineering*, A. Finkelstein (ed.), ACM Press, 2000.

[Lam00c] A. van Lamsweerde and E. Letier, "Handling Obstacles in Goal-Oriented Requirements Engineering", *IEEE Transactions on Software Engineering*, Special Issue on Exception Handling, October 2000.

[Lam01] A. van Lamsweerde , "Goal-Oriented Requirements Engineering: A Guided Tour", *Invited Minitutorial, Proc. RE'01 - 5$^{th}$ Intl. Symp. Requirements Engineering*, Toronto, August 2001, pp. 249-263.

[Let02a] E. Letier and A. van Lamsweerde, "Agent-Based Tactics for Goal-Oriented Requirements Elaboration", *Proc. ICSE'02: 24$^{th}$ Intl. Conf. on Software Engineering*, Orlando, IEEE Computer Society Press, May 2002.

[Let02b] E. Letier and A. van Lamsweerde, "Deriving Operational Software Specifications from System Goals", *Proc. FSE'10:* 10$^{th}$ *ACM SIGSOFT Symp. on the Foundations of Software Engineering*, Charleston, November 2002.

[Luc95] D. Luckham and J. Vera, "An Event-Based Architecture Definition Language", *IEEE Transactions on Software Engineering*, Vol. 21 No. 9, Sept. 1995, 717-734.

[Mag95] J. Magee, N Dulay, S. Eisenbach and J Kramer, "Specifying Distributed Software Architectures", *Proceedings ESEC'95 - 5th European Software Engineering Conference*, Sitges, LNCS 989, Springer-Verlag, Sept. 1995, 137-153.

[Man92] Z. Manna and A. Pnueli, *The Temporal Logic of Reactive and Concurrent Systems,* Springer-Verlag, 1992.

[Med96] N. Medvidovic, P. Oreizy, J. Robbins, and R. Taylor, "Using Object-Oriented Typing to Support Architectural Design in the C2 Style", *Proc. FSE'4 - Fourth ACM SIGSOFT Symposium on the Foundations of Software Engineering*, San Francisco, October 1996.

[MOD] Model Problems for Software Architecture, http://www-2.cs.cmu.edu/People/ModProb/.

[Mor95] M. Moriconi, X. Qian, and R. Riemenschneider, "Correct Architecture Refinement", *IEEE Transactions on Software Engineering*, Vol. 21 No. 4, Apr. 1995, 356-372.

[Myl92] Mylopoulos, J., Chung, L., Nixon, B., "Representing and Using Nonfunctional Requirements: A Process-Oriented Approach", *IEEE Trans. on Sofware. Engineering*, Vol. 18 No. 6, June 1992, pp. 483-497.

[Nus01] B. Nuseibeh, "Weaving Together Requirements and Architecture", IEEE Computer, Vol. 34 No. 3, March 2001, 115-117.

[Par79] D.L. Parnas, "Designing Software for Ease of Extension and Contraction", *IEEE Transactions on Software Engineering* SE-5 No. 2, March 1979.

[Par95] D.L. Parnas and J. Madey, "Functional Documents for Computer Systems", *Science of Computer Programming,* Vol. 25, 1995, 41-61.

[Per92] D. Perry and A. Wolf, "Foundations for the Study of Software Architecture", *ACM Software Engineering Notes*, Vol. 17 No. 4, October 1992,40-52.

[Rie99] R.A. Riemenschneider, "Checking the Correctness of Architectural Transformation Steps via Proof-Carrying Architectures", *Proc. W1CSA1 - First IFIP Conference on Software Architecture*, San Antonio, February 1999.

[Rum99] J. Rumbaugh, I. Jacobson and G Booch, *The Unified Modeling Language Reference Manual.* Addison-Wesley, Object Technology Series, 1999.

[Sha95] M. Shaw R. DeLine D. Klein, T. Ross, D. Young, and G. Zelesnick, "Abstractions for Software Architecture and Tools to Support Them", *IEEE Transactions on Software Engineering*, Vol.21, No.4, April 1995, 314-335.

[Sha96] M. Shaw and D. Garlan, *Software Architecture: Perspectives on an Emerging Discipline.* Prentice-Hall, 1996.

[Sta95] The Standish Group, "Software Chaos", http:// www.standishgroup.com/chaos.html.

[Swa82] W. Swartout and R. Balzer, "On the Inevitable Intertwining of Specification and Implementation", *Communications of the ACM*, Vol. 25 No. 7, July 1982, 438-440.

[Yue87] K. Yue, "What Does It Mean to Say that a Specification is Complete?", *Proc. IWSSD-4, Fourth International Workshop on Software Specification and Design*, IEEE, 1987.

# Software Architecture Modeling & Analysis: A Rigorous Approach

Jeff Kramer, Jeff Magee, and Sebastian Uchitel

Department of Computing, Imperial College London
{j.kramer,j.magee,s.uchitel}@imperial.ac.uk

**Abstract.** In this overview paper, we outline a tool supported approach to the design and analysis of complex systems at the architectural level. The foundations of this approach are the use of the architectural description language Darwin to capture structural information about components and their interconnection and the use of a process algebra FSP to describe the behaviour of individual components. These descriptions are combined to construct a system behavioural model that can be animated to validate requirements and model checked against properties specified in Linear Temporal Logic. Recently, this foundation has been extended with work on the synthesis of behavioural models from scenarios captured as message sequence charts (MSC). Models described in this way can be used as an initial basis for validating requirements and as a specification that must be satisfied by more detailed models. The approach we outline is supported by the Labelled Transition system Analyser (LTSA) tool, which has been extended to deal with MSCs.

## 1  Introduction

Design at the Software Architecture level is intended to bridge the gap between requirements and implementations in the design of complex systems. Software Architecture describes the gross organization of a system in terms of its components and their interactions. Our initial emphasis in Software Architecture description was to capture system structure. The authors have published work on the use of the architecture description language Darwin for specifying the structure of distributed systems[5] and subsequently directing the construction of those systems[6]. A commercial version of Darwin called Koala has been used in the development of a family of television products[12]. Darwin describes a system in terms of components that manage the implementation of services. Interconnection structure is specified by bindings between the services required and provided by component instances. Darwin has both a graphical and a textual form with appropriate tool support [9].

Here we focus on the use of Darwin structural descriptions as a framework for behavior analysis rather than system construction. Darwin has been designed to be sufficiently abstract to support multiple views, two of which are the behavioral view (for behavior analysis) and the service view (for construction) Each view is an elaboration of the basic structural view: the skeleton upon which we hang the flesh of behavior specification or service implementation [4]. A further view is that of

M. Bernardo and P. Inverardi  (Eds.): SFM 2003, LNCS 2804, pp. 44-51, 2003.
© Springer-Verlag Berlin Heidelberg 2003

performance modeling and analysis which is developed by annotating the behavioral specification with stochastic delays and probabilistic choice.

Here we focus on the behavioral view initially using a simple process algebra - Finite State Processes (FSP) - to specify behavior. These specifications are translated into Labeled transition Systems (LTS) for analysis purposes. Analysis is supported by the Labeled Transition Analyzer (LTSA) tool [7]. This supports a range of analysis techniques which include Compositional Reachability Analysis and Linear Temporal Logic model-checking with partial order reduction [2]. The LTSA tool also supports the synthesis of behavioral models from Message Sequence Charts (MSC)[11]. In the following, we first describe the relationship between components and their behavioral specifications and then show how these are combined into system models. We illustrate how these models can be analyzed with respect to safety and liveness properties and conclude by illustrating the role of MSC specifications in the architectural setting.

## 2  Primitive Components

A primitive component is one with no substructure of components. In the service view of architecture, a primitive component has an implementation defined by an object or objects programmed in a programming language. In the behavioural view, a primitive component is defined by a finite state LTS. The example of figure 1 depicts the Darwin graphical and textual description of a primitive component with two required interfaces.

```
                        interface Wallet
   CLIENT                  {authorise; invoice; confirm; default;}
      service           interface Service
      wallet              {request; reply; abort; }

                        component CLIENT {
                          require
                            wallet:Wallet;
                            service:Service;
                        /%
                        CLIENT =
                          (wallet.authorise ->service.request->
                            (service.reply -> CLIENT
                            |service.abort -> CLIENT
                            )
                           ).%/
                        }
```

**Fig. 1.** CLIENT component with embedded FSP behavior description.

The component forms part of a simple Ecommerce system in which a client uses a *wallet* service to pay for services acquired using the *service* interface. These services are specified as sets of actions, which may be reified in an implementation as method calls. The behavior of the CLIENT component is specified by FSP embedded between /% %/ braces in the Darwin component description.

Primitive component behavior is defined in FSP using action prefix "->" and choice "|". If x is an action and P a process then (x->P) describes a process that initially engages in the action x and then behaves exactly as described by P. If x and y are actions then (x->P|y->Q) describes a process which initially engages in either of the actions x or y. After the first action has occurred, the subsequent behavior is described by P if the first action was x and Q if the first action was y. The CLIENT component of Figure 1 thus authorizes payment for a service, requests the service and then waits for either the service to be successfully delivered or for it to be aborted. The model for a SERVER component in the Ecommerce system is depicted in Figure 2.

```
component SERVER {
  provide
    service:Service;
  require
    wallet:Wallet;
/%
SERVER
  = (service.request -> wallet.invoice
     -> (wallet.confirm -> service.reply ->SERVER
        |wallet.default -> service.abort ->SERVER
        )
    ).
%/
}
```

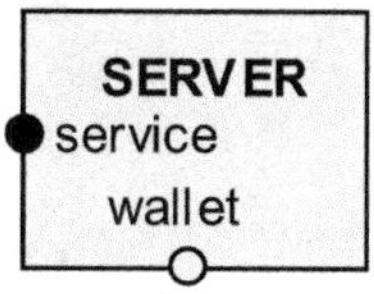

| | SERVER |
|---|---|
| ● | service |
| | wallet |
| | ○ |

**Fig. 2.** SERVER component with embedded FSP behavior description.

The SERVER component requires a wallet and provides a service. Provided services are denoted in the Darwin graphical notation by filled in circles. When the server receives a request for a service, it invoices its wallet for payment and supplies the service if the wallet confirms payment, otherwise it aborts the service.

## 3   Composite Components

A composite component is constructed from interconnecting instances of more primitive components. A composite component defines a structure and no additional behavior. Interconnections between components are formed by binding required interfaces to provided interfaces as shown in Figure 3 for the Ecommerce system.

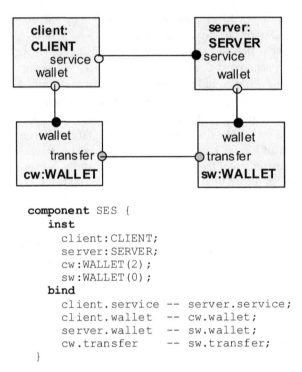

```
component SES {
    inst
        client:CLIENT;
        server:SERVER;
        cw:WALLET(2);
        sw:WALLET(0);
    bind
        client.service -- server.service;
        client.wallet  -- cw.wallet;
        server.wallet  -- sw.wallet;
        cw.transfer    -- sw.transfer;
}
```

**Fig. 3.** Ecommerce composite component

Whereas the behavior of primitive components is defined by using FSP's dynamic combinators, the behavior of a composite component is defined using the static combinators of parallel composition ""‖" and relabelling "/". The FSP corresponding to a composite component is compiled directly from the Darwin description. For Figure 3, the FSP is shown below:

```
||SES =
    (client:CLIENT
     ‖ server:SERVER
     ‖ cw:WALLET(2)
     ‖ sw:WALLET(0)
    )
    /{client.service/server.service,
      client.wallet/cw.wallet,
      server.wallet/sw.wallet,
      cw.transfer/sw.transfer
    }.
```

In this brief introduction to Darwin and FSP, we have illustrated the basic approach to associating behavior description with architectural descriptions. Both Darwin and FSP have many additional features that facilitate the description of large complex models. In particular, we have not dealt with hierarchical component structures, with parameterized interfaces and components, with replicated services and components and with *portals* that delay the decision as to which component provides a component as opposed to implements it. For example, the wallet-to-wallet interface in the example is specified as a portal (greyed in circle) since at this level of design we have chosen to represent the transfer as a completely symmetric atomic transfer. An implementation would need to reify this as a more complex protocol. Darwin does not have a separate connector construct. Connectors can be represented by a distinguished class of components. They are modeled in exactly the same way as components.

## 4  Model Analysis & Animation

The behavior of a model can be interactively explored using the LTSA tool. The output of such an execution is essentially a trace of action names. Each action is the abstract representation in the model of an input or output of the proposed system. In addition, the LTSA supports safety property [1] and progress property [3] checks. For example, the following safety property for the simple Ecommerce system (SES) asserts that if a payment transfer occurs the service should be delivered otherwise no payment results in no service.

```
property HONEST
        = (transfer.unit -> service.reply -> HONEST
          |transfer.null -> service.abort -> HONEST
          ).
```

In common with other model checking tools, the LTSA produces counter examples when it discovers a safety property or progress property violation in a model. A difficulty can arise in interpreting the meaning of traces in relation to the original problem domain. Even when the meaning is clear to the model designer, the problem of communicating model behavior and the results of analysis to non-technical stakeholders of a system remains. We advocate the use of graphic animation in validating behavioral models against requirements and in communicating the results of model analysis. Animation does not interfere with the process of model development, specification and analysis – it is treated as an annotation to the model [8]. Multiple animations can be attached to the same model reflecting different user perspectives. The semantics of animation are soundly based in Timed Automata, and the execution uses a JavaBean based animation engine, called SceneBeans, generated from XML documents.

## 5  Requirements Scenarios to Models

Scenario-based specifications, such as Message Sequence Charts (MSCs), are a useful part of a requirements specification. Scenarios describe how system components and users interact in order to provide system level functionality. Each scenario is a partial story which, when combined with other scenarios, should conform to provide a consistent, but usually partial, system description. Thus stakeholders may develop descriptions independently, contributing their own view of the system to those of other stakeholders. As an example, Figure 4 depicts the messages sequence for successfully requesting a service in the simple Ecommerce system and Figure 5 in which the client has no funds in its associated wallet and consequently, the service is not supplied.

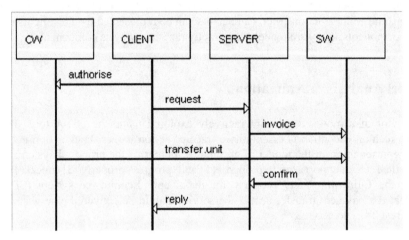

**Fig. 4.** MSC for CLIENT with credit

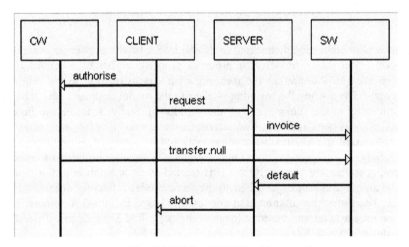

**Fig. 5.** MSC for CLIENT with no credit

The LTSA tool can synthesize a behavioral model from a set of message sequence charts such as those of Figures 4 & 5. The tool permits the user to check for implied scenarios[10]. These are scenarios that the user has not specified directly but are message sequences that can occur in the architectural behavioral model. The user may then choose to include these as possible scenarios or exclude them as negative scenarios. This is an iterative process that supports elicitation of behavior. Models synthesized from MSCs can be used as an initial specification for validation purposes and can be used subsequently as a check for more detailed models such as those specified in Darwin/FSP above.

# 6 Conclusion

This paper has give a brief overview of our approach to using models in software architecture design. This involves building behavior analysis models early in the software lifecycle. These models are developed in conjunction with architecture development and requirements capture. The objective is to provide early feedback on the operation of a proposed system that can be fed back to customers and to highlight potential design problems early in the design process.

We have tried to ameliorate some of the difficulties that users suffer in employing formal models. We have adopted notations that, while not as simple as many might prefer, do reflect the complexity of the task at hand and are based on a familiar formalism, state machines. From our experience, we are encouraged by the ability of both industrial and student software engineers to learn and use FSP and LTS. There is no doubt that the provision of an automated light-weight tool, such as the LTSA, for drawing LTS diagrams and exploring and analyzing models, is an essential element in making the learning process easier and the result more rewarding.

By using a model-based design process early in the software lifecycle we hope that users gain the greatest benefit from model building and analysis. By providing techniques to generate models from scenarios and by associating the models with the proposed software architecture, we intend to embed modeling into the software process. The ability to associate animation with models provides an accessible means for interpreting both model behavior and misbehavior to users. Analysis and animation can be carried out at any level of the architecture. Consequently, component models can be designed and debugged before composing them into larger systems. The analysis results are easily related to the architectural model of interconnected components.

A more detailed account of our work may be found in the references below. The LTSA application package that supports MSCs is available from:

http://www.doc.ic.ac.uk/ltsa/

# References

1.  S. C. Cheung and J. Kramer, *Checking Safety Properties Using Compositional Reachability Analysis*, ACM Transactions on Software Engineering and Methodology, Vol. 8, No. 1, pp. 49-78, 99.
2.  D. Giannakopoulou and J. Magee, *Fluent Model-checking for Event-based Systems*, ESEC/FSE, Helsinki, Sept. 2003.
3.  D. Giannakopoulou, J. Magee and J. Kramer, *Checking Progress with Action Priority: Is it Fair?*, 7th European Software Engineering Conference held jointly with the 7th ACM SIGSOFT Symposium on the Foundations of Software Engineering (ESEC/FSE'99), Toulouse, France, 1687, pp. 511-527, September 1999.
4.  J. Kramer and J. Magee, *Exposing the Skeleton in the Coordination Closet*, Coordination'97, Second International Conference on Coordination Models and Languages, Berlin, Germany, 1282, pp. 18-31, September 1997.
5.  J. Magee, N. Dulay, S. Eisenbach and J. Kramer, *Specifying Distributed Software Architectures*, 5th European Software Engineering Conference (ESEC'95), Sitges, Spain, 989, pp. 137-153, September 1995.

6.  J. Magee, N. Dulay and J. Kramer, *Regis: A Constructive Development Environment for Parallel and Distributed Programs*, Distributed Systems Engineering Journal, Special Issue on Configurable Distributed Systems, Vol. 1, No. 5, pp. 304-312, 94.

7.  J. Magee and J. Kramer, *Concurrency - State Models & Java Programs*, Chichester, John Wiley & Sons, 1999.

8.  J. Magee, J. Kramer, D. Giannakopoulou and N. Pryce, *Graphical Animation of Behavior Models*, 22nd International Conference on Software Engineering (ICSE'00), Limerick, pp. 499-508, June 2000.

9.  K. Ng, J. Kramer and J. Magee, *Automated Support for the Design of Distributed Systems*, Journal of Automated Software Engineering (JASE), Vol. 3, No. 4, pp. 261-284, 1996.

10. S. Uchitel, J. Kramer and J. Magee, *Detecting Implied Scenarios in Message Sequence Chart Specifications*, Joint 8th European Software Engineering Conference (ESEC'01) and 9th ACM SIGSOFT Symposium on the Foundations of Software Engineering (FSE'01), Vienna, pp. 74-82.

11. S. Uchitel, J. Kramer and J. Magee, *Synthesis of Behavioural Models from Scenarios*, IEEE Transactions on Software Engineering, Vol. 29, No. 2, pp. 99-115, 2003.

12. R. vanOmmering, *Koala, a Component Model for Consumer Electronics Product Software*, Second International ESPRIT ARES Workshop, Las Palmas de Gran Canaria, Spain, 1429, pp. 76-85, February 26-27, 1998.

# The Application of Dependence Analysis to Software Architecture Descriptions

Judith A. Stafford[1], Alexander L. Wolf[2], and Mauro Caporuscio[3]

[1] Department of Computer Science
Tufts University
Medford, MA 02155 USA
jas@cs.tufts.edu

[2] Department of Computer Science
University of Colorado
Boulder, Colorado 80309-0430 USA
alw@cs.colorado.edu

[3] Dipartimento di Informatica
Università dell'Aquila
I-67010 L'Aquila, Italy
caporusc@univaq.it

**Abstract.** As the focus of software design shifts increasingly toward the architectural level, so too are its analysis techniques. Dependence analysis is one such technique that shows promise at this level. In this paper we briefly describe and illustrate the application of dependence analysis to architectural descriptions of software systems.

## 1 Introduction

Traditionally, software architectures are described using informal, natural-language documents. Box and arrow diagrams are often used to bring more precision to the descriptions, but while they can reveal some ambiguous and missing properties, they are not capable of modeling all the information provided in the natural-language specification, such as system behavior. Formalization, as applied to software development at the architectural level, involves the application of mathematically based modeling languages to capture structural and behavioral properties of the components of a system. Above all, these languages provide support for rigorous analysis of a system early in the life cycle and/or at high levels of abstraction. Additionally, a formally described software architecture can serve as a vehicle for precise and unambiguous communication among the stakeholders in a system, and can provide a means to accurately capture domain-specific properties in ways that support domain-specific architectural generalizations.

The goal of formally describing and analyzing the structure and behavior of a software system is not new. Formal approaches have been proposed and used in various phases of software development and maintenance for as long as people have recognized the challenges of software engineering. Formal design notations

M. Bernardo and P. Inverardi (Eds.): SFM 2003, LNCS 2804, pp. 52–62, 2003.
© Springer-Verlag Berlin Heidelberg 2003

and their associated analyses, in particular, were a major focus of research in the 1970s and early 1980s. Results ranged from techniques for describing and analyzing module interconnection, which were intended to address static properties of component structure and import/export relationships, to techniques for describing and analyzing concurrent processes, which were intended to address dynamic properties of component interaction behavior.

Software architecture is but the latest framework within which researchers are trying to attain the goal of formal system description and analysis. Its emphasis is on unifying and extending earlier techniques for description and analysis, and in applying the resulting new techniques in the context of modern-day software practice. Unification is coming about from considering how the component structure of a system can be used to modularize the description and analysis of behavioral properties such that those descriptions and analyses can be performed in a more tractable, compositional manner. Extensions are being explored that are enhancing the typing of components and their interfaces to account for dynamic interaction behaviors. And, finally, the application of formal approaches is benefiting from the rapidly growing industry interest in system development based on large-grain component assembly rather than on small-grain component programming.

## 2  Formal Architectural Analysis

Research in architectural analysis centers on determining which specific properties are appropriate for this level of analysis, and on developing techniques to carry out those analyses. The premise underlying this work is that the confidence gained through analysis at an architectural level will translate into confidence in other levels of the system.

Many techniques for analyzing software systems have been developed over the past decades. Most, however, are ineffective for analyzing large systems. This is particularly true for techniques aimed at analyzing concurrent systems, where state explosion problems are especially acute. To make techniques for these situations more tractable, traditional specification and analysis techniques have been enhanced in a variety of ways. Software architecture can be seen as another approach to attacking the problem by providing a particular method for abstraction and modularization.

Automated analysis techniques can differ in the levels of assurance they provide. In general, the techniques trade off efficiency and tractability against precision and completeness. For instance, it may be possible to guarantee some properties only under certain assumptions or conditions. Carefully chosen, those assumptions and conditions can match well with the context in which the system is anticipated to operate, and thus the analysis can provide useful information.

A desirable characteristic of any imprecise or incomplete analysis technique used to examine a property is that it give no false positive results concerning that property. In other words, it should never indicate the absence of a problem when, in fact, there is a problem. On the other hand, it is reasonable to allow a technique to indicate the possible presence of a problem, even if none truly exists, and defer further analysis to some other automated analysis technique or to the human. This characteristic is commonly referred to as *conservatism*. Clearly, the most conservative analysis technique is one that indicates the possible presence of an error in all situations. Such an absurd technique, while highly efficient (it can be implemented using a constant function), is not of use. One goal of analysis research is to increase the precision of conservative techniques such that they are both efficient and useful.

## 3   Dependence Analysis

Dependence analysis involves the identification of interdependent elements of a system. It is referred to as a "reduction" technique, since the interdependent elements induced by a given inter-element relationship forms a subset of the system. It has been widely studied for purposes such as code restructuring during optimization, automatic program parallelization, test-case generation, and debugging. Dependencies can be identified based on syntactic information readily available in a formal specification. This type of analysis generally ignores state information, but may incorporate some knowledge of the semantics of a language to improve the precision of the results [6].

Dependence analysis as applied to program code is based on the relationships among statements and variables in a program. Techniques for identifying and exploiting dependence relations at the architectural level have also been developed [8,13,14,15]. Dependence relationships at the architectural level arise from the connections among components and the constraints on their interactions. These relationships may involve some form of control or data flow, but more generally involve source structure and behavior. Source structure (or structure, for short) has to do with system dependencies such as "imports", while behavior has to do with dynamic interaction dependencies such as "causes". Structural dependencies allow one to locate source specifications that contribute to the description of some state or interaction. Behavioral dependencies allow one to relate states or interactions to other states or interactions. Both structural and behavioral dependencies are important to capture and understand when analyzing an architecture.

## 4   Example: Aladdin

Aladdin [9] is a tool that identifies dependencies in software architectures. It was designed to be easily adapted for use with a variety of architectural description languages and has been demonstrated on the languages Acme [4] and Rapide [10].

If one thinks of an architectural description as a set of boxes and arrows in a diagram, where the arrows represent the ability for a box, or some port into or out of that box, to communicate with another box in the diagram, then one can think about Aladdin as walking forwards or backwards from a given box, traversing arrows either from heads to tails or vice versa. In Aladdin, the arrows are called *links* and the process of walking (i.e., performing a transitive closure) over the links is called *chaining*.

If there is no knowledge about how a box's input ports behaviorally relate to it output ports, then a forward (backward) walk must include leaps from each input (output) port that is reached to all output (input) ports. In that case, the analysis is essentially being performed in a conservative manor at the component level, which can lead to a high degree of false dependencies. If, instead, the designer makes a precise statement about how input and output ports are related, presumably using an appropriately rich architecture description language, then Aladdin can take advantage of this information to produce a more precise reduction set.

The behavioral relationship among the input and output ports of a component define the interaction behavior of that component. It is important to note that the interaction behavior is not intended to capture the functional behavior of the component. For example, the description of how a server interacts with its clients is independent of the computation carried out by the server on behalf of its clients. Aladdin uses a summarization algorithm operating on the description of a component's interaction behavior to identify possible relationships between pairs of input and output ports. The resulting connections are called *transitional connections*.

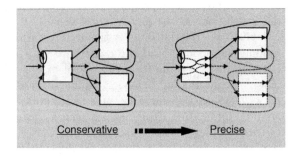

**Fig. 1.** Increasing Precision of Dependence Analysis.

Figure 1 illustrates the improvement in precision that can be gained when transitional connections are included in the information used to determine possible dependencies. The solid arcs in this figure denote arcs that must be traversed in order to identify a conservative set of dependencies. In the view of the system shown on the left, the transitional connections are unknown. Therefore, when tracing back from the circled port, one must assume that any stimulus applied to input port could have contributed to a response on any output port. The lack of information on the interaction behavior of the component forces the analysis to include all components of the system in the dependency set. The existence of the transitional connections in the view of the system on the right provides information that allows the analysis to eliminate the component connected only by the dashed arcs.

Rather than constructing a complete dependence graph, Aladdin's analysis is performed on demand in response to an analyst's query. The query might request information about the existence of certain specific kinds of anomalous dependence relationships, or might request information about the parts of the system that could affect or be affected by a specific port in the architecture. A view of Aladdin's interface is shown in Figure 2. A file containing a Rapide architectural specification is selected using the file menu. In this figure a specification for a variant of the familiar gas station example was selected. The specification is displayed in the left pane of the main Aladdin window. The right pane displays the list of component ports that have been identified from the architectural description.

Rapide is a high-level, event-based simulation language that provides support for the dynamic addition and deletion of predeclared components. Rapide descriptions are composed of type specifications for component interfaces and architecture specifications for permissible connections among the components of a system.

System behavior is described through architectural connection rules, state transition rules, and patterns of events required to generate events that activate the rules. System behavior can be simulated through execution of the Rapide description. The results of a simulation of system behavior can be studied using a representation called a *poset*. A poset is a partially ordered set of events captured during a single simulation of a system.

Components are defined in terms of their interfaces. Three types of components are described in Figure 3, which is the Rapide description of the gas station problem. The component types are a pump, a customer, and an operator. In this simple example we see that interfaces specify several aspects of the component's interactions with other components. The declaration of *in* and *out* actions specify the component's ability to observe or emit particular events. Implicitly declared actions represent events generated in the environment of the system that are emitted by or watched for in an interface; the event `start` in the first transition rule of the customer interface in Figure 3 is an example. Behaviors, which may involve local variables, describe the computation performed by the component, including how the component reacts to *in* actions and generates *out* actions. Computations are defined in an event pattern language [12], where a pattern is a set of events together with their partial ordering. The partial order of events is represented as a poset.

The analyst can instruct Aladdin to perform any of several queries. The queries window shown at the top left in the figure appears when the analyst selects the "Queries" menu item. The analyst can choose to see a list of ports with no source or those with no target, which are two kinds of port-related anomalies. The small window to the right of the window "Queries" contains a list of all the ports in the specification that do not have targets. Ports with no

**Fig. 2.** Use of Aladdin to Identify Anomalies and Perform Port-Based Queries.

source or no target may indicate an unspecified connection or they may indicate a function of the component that is not used in this particular architecture.

The analyst can also choose to create a chain. If "Create chain..." is selected, then the window "Get Query" appears. The analyst selects a query, in this case the analyst wanted to see a chain of all the ports in the architecture that could causally affect port R.ON. Dotty [3], a graph layout tool, is used to display the

```
type Dollars is integer; -- enum 0, 1, 2, 3 end enum;
type Gallons is integer; -- enum 0, 1, 2, 3 end enum;

type Pump is interface
action in  O(), Off(), Activate(Cost : Dollars);
       out Report(Amount : Gallons, Cost : Dollars);
behavior
    Free : var Boolean := True;
    Reading, Limit : var Dollars := 0;
    action In_Use(), Done();
begin
    (?X : Dollars)(On ~ Activate(?X)) where
    $Free ||> Free := False; Limit := ?X; In_Use;;
    In_Use ||> Reading := $Limit; Done;;
    Off or Done ||> Free := True; Report($Reading);;
end Pump;


type Customer is interface
action in  Okay(), Change(Cost : Dollars);
       out Pre_Pay(Cost : Dollars)Okay(), Turn_On(), Walk(), Turn_Off();
behavior
       D : Dollars is 10;
begin
       start ||> Pre_Pay(D);;
       Okay ||> Walk;;
       Walk ||> Turn_On;;
end Customer;


type Operator is interface
action in  Request(Cost : Dollars), Result(Cost : Dollars);
       out Schedule(Cost : Dollars), Remit(Change : Dollars);
behavior
       Payment : var Dollars := 0;
begin
       (?X : Dollars)Request(?X) ||> Payment := ?X; Schedule(?X);;
       (?X : Dollars)Result(?X) ||> Remit($Payment - ?X);;
end;


architecture gas_station() return root is
    O : Operator; P : Pump; C1, C2 : Customer;
connect
    (?C : Customer; ?X : Dollars) ?C.Pre_Pay(?X) ||> O.Request(?X);
    (?X : Dollars) O.Schedule(?X) ||> P.Activate(?X);
    (?X : Dollars) O.Schedule(?X) ||> C1.Okay;
    (?C : Customer) ?C.Turn_On ||> P.On;
    (?C : Customer) ?C.Turn_Off ||> P.Off;
    (?X : Gallons; ?Y : Dollars)P.Report(?X, ?Y) ||> O.Result(?Y);
end gas_station;
```

**Fig. 3.** Rapide Description of the Gas Station Example [11].

resultant chain, which appears in the window "Dotty". The chain is displayed as a directed graph rooted at the node representing the specified port of interest, in this case the node R.ON at the bottom of the graph. The arcs are labeled with a relationship type and represent direct (or perhaps summarized) dependence relationships between pairs of ports. The nodes of the graph represent all ports that could cause, directly or indirectly, the port of interest, the event R.ON, to be triggered.

This query was performed in order to help identify the cause of a failure in a Rapide simulation of the gas station. In the simulation it was discovered that A2 was never allowed to refuel. The cause of this is apparent from viewing the chain, and in fact could have been discovered through running an anomaly check prior to simulation, since the event A2.OKAY has no source. Through examination of the chain, the analyst determines that the problem occurs because O.REQUEST must record the source of a request so that the appropriate OKAY can be triggered.

Aladdin takes advantage of the behavior section of Rapide interface definitions. Aladdin applies a summarization algorithm to the behavioral description in order to identify the transitional connections in the Rapide description. Aladdin can also be used in conjunction with Rapide's simulation tools. If a specification error is detected during a simulation, Aladdin can be used to identify a reduced set of description elements.

As another example, consider the architecture depicted in Figure 4. The components and relationships shown in this figure represent the architecture of a software system called MobiKit [1], which supports the mobility of clients of a distributed publish/subscribe service. Clients of the system first "move out" from one location and then "move in" to a new location. Figure 5 shows a portion of a forward chain resulting from this architecture. The analysis reveals a lack of coordination in the architecture. For example, a mobile client can perform a *moveIn* operation before the *moveOut* is completed.

Aladdin can also be used independently of any particular architecture description language. The analyst can manually define links by using, for example, an informal graphical notation. When all the connections have been identified, the analyst can make queries about the relationship of specific ports to other ports in the architecture, as described above. In this way it supports Jackson and Wing's notion of "lightweight formal methods" [5] in a manner similar to Feather's use of a database [2].

## 5   Conclusion

As the focus of software design shifts increasingly toward the architectural level, so too are its analysis techniques. Dependence analysis is one such technique that shows promise at this level. For dependence analysis to most effective, however, designers must employ sophisticated, behavior-oriented architectural description languages. As it turns out, the model underlying these languages tends to be that of concurrent, compositional, event-based computation, not the traditional

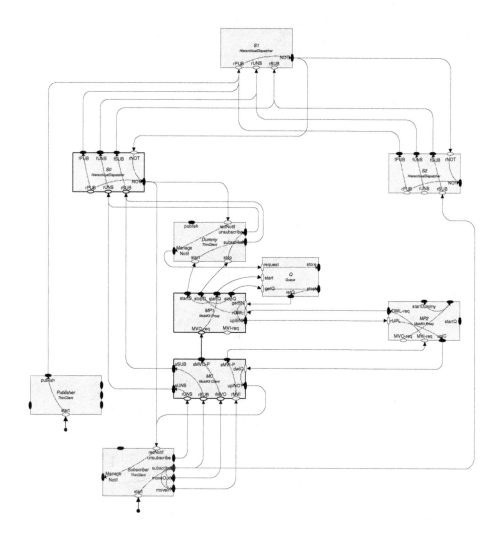

**Fig. 4.** Architecture of MobiKit.

basis for dependence analysis. Early work is beginning to emerge to extend the theoretical foundation of dependence analysis [7], but much remains to be done.

## Acknowledgments

The work of J.A. Stafford was sponsored in part by the Software Engineering Institute, a federally funded research and development center sponsored by the U.S. Department of Defense. The work of A.L. Wolf was supported in part by

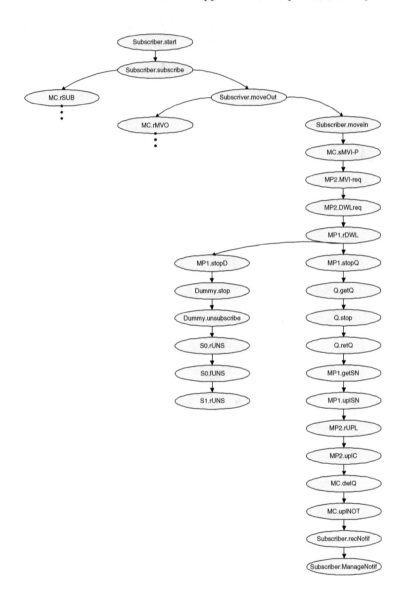

**Fig. 5.** Portion of a Chain Derived from the MobiKit Architecture.

the Air Force Material Command, Rome Laboratory, and the Defense Advanced Research Projects Agency under Contract Number F30602-00-2-0608. The content of the information does not necessarily reflect the position or the policy of the U.S. Government and no official endorsement should be inferred. The work of M. Caporuscio was supported in part by the MIUR National Research Project SAHARA.

# References

1. M. Caporuscio, A. Carzaniga, and A.L. Wolf. Design and Evaluation of a Support Service for Mobile, Wireless Publish/Subscribe Applications. *IEEE Transactions on Software Engineering.* To appear.
2. M.S. Feather. Rapid Application of Lightweight Formal Methods for Consistency Analyses. *IEEE Transactions on Software Engineering*, 24(11):949–959, November 1998.
3. E.R. Gansner, E. Koutsofios, S.C. North, and K.-P. Vo. A Technique for Drawing Directed Graphs. *IEEE Transactions on Software Engineering*, 19(3):214–230, March 1993.
4. D. Garlan, R. Monroe, and D. Wile. ACME: An Architecture Description Interchange Language. In *Proceedings of CASCON '97*, pages 169–183. IBM Center for Advanced Studies, November 1997.
5. D. Jackson and J.M. Wing. Lightweight Formal Methods. *Computer*, 29(4):21–22, April 1996.
6. A. Podgurski and L.A. Clarke. A Formal Model of Program Dependences and its Implications for Software Testing, Debugging, and Maintenance. *IEEE Transactions on Software Engineering*, 16(9):965–979, September 1990.
7. J.A. Stafford. *A Formal, Language-Independent, and Compositional Approach to Control Dependence Analysis.* PhD thesis, University of Colorado, Boulder, Colorado, USA, August 2000.
8. J.A. Stafford and A.L. Wolf. Architecture-Level Dependence Analysis in Support of Software Maintenance. In *Proceedings of the Third International Software Architecture Workshop*, pages 129–132, November 1998.
9. J.A. Stafford and A.L. Wolf. Architecture-Level Dependence Analysis for Software Systems. *International Journal of Software Engineering and Knowledge Engineering*, 11(4):431–452, August 2001.
10. RAPIDE Design Team. Draft: Guide to the Rapide 1.0 Language Reference Manuals. July 1997.
11. RAPIDE Design Team. Draft: Rapide 1.0 Architecture Language Reference Manual. July 1997.
12. RAPIDE Design Team. Draft: Rapide 1.0 Pattern Language Reference Manual. July 1997.
13. S. Vestal. *MetaH Programmer's Manual Version 1.27.* Honeywell, Inc., Minneapolis, MN, 1998.
14. M.E.R. Vieira, M.S. Dias, and D.J. Richardson. Analyzing Software Architectures with Argus-I. In *Proceedings of the 2000 International Conference on Software Engineering*, pages 758–761. Association for Computer Machinery, June 2000.
15. J. Zhao. Using Dependence Analysis to Support Software Architecture Understanding. *New Technologies on Computer Software*, pages 135–142, September 1997.

# Validating Distributed Object and Component Designs⋆

Nima Kaveh and Wolfgang Emmerich

Department of Computer Science
University College London
Gower Street, London WC1E 6BT, UK
{N.Kaveh|W.Emmerich}@cs.ucl.ac.uk

**Abstract.** Distributed systems are increasingly built using distributed object or component middleware. The dynamic behaviour of those distributed systems is influenced by the particular combination of middleware synchronisation and threading primitives used for communication amongst distributed objects. A designer may accidentally choose combinations that cause a distributed application to enter undesirable states or violate liveness properties. We exploit the fact that modern object and component middleware offer only a small number of underlying synchronisation primitives and threading policies. For each of these we define a UML stereotype and a formal process algebra specification of the stereotype semantics. We devise a means to specify safety and liveness properties in UML and again map those to process algebra safety and liveness properties. We can thus apply model checking techniques to verify that a given design does indeed meet the desired properties. We propose how to reduce the state space that needs to be model checked by exploiting middleware characteristics. We finally show how model checking results can be related back to the input UML models. In this way we can hide the formalism and the model checking process entirely from UML designers, which we regard as critical for the industrial exploitation of this research.

## 1    Introduction

Distributed software architectures prescribe the composition of software components intended to be deployed on a distributed system. There is an increasing trend of developing software applications based on distributed architectures. Increased overall system availability through better fault tolerance, parallel execution of an application and a simplification of scalability are some of the key motivators behind the popularisation of distributed architectures.

The direct use of networking primitives or proprietary technologies for the development of distributed applications is no longer a viable option. Such approaches stifle application maintainability and ease of interoperability with other applications developed with proprietary technologies. Instead, open object and

---

⋆ This work is partially funded through EU project TAPAS (IST-2001-34069).

M. Bernardo and P. Inverardi (Eds.): SFM 2003, LNCS 2804, pp. 63–91, 2003.
© Springer-Verlag Berlin Heidelberg 2003

component middleware technologies, such as CORBA [26] and Enterprise Java Beans [22], are rapidly becoming the preferred approach for the development of distributed systems.

These middleware approaches attempt to hide the complexity of distribution and aspire to provide developers with the ability to invoke operations on remote hosts in the same way as they would invoke local methods. While they succeed in many respects, there are some fundamental differences between local and remote method invocations [2]. One such difference is the inherent parallel execution of objects or components that reside on different machines. A local method call can recursively call itself, possibly indirectly via some other methods, and will not cause any problems as long as the recursion terminates at some stage. Recursion of distributed objects may however cause deadlocks. Due to the non-determinism introduced by components that execute in parallel, it is considerably more complicated to develop safe distributed applications than centralised applications.

Software engineers can now use these powerful middleware technologies for the implementation of distributed systems. The implementation support, however, needs to be complemented with appropriate architecture and design methods that address the new challenges that are introduced by the use of distributed object and component middleware. In particular, software engineers need support for reasoning about the correctness of a distributed object design that goes beyond the diagram drawing capabilities offered by current CASE tools.

In this paper we show that the use of particular combinations of client-side synchronisation primitives and server-side threading policies provided by most distributed object middleware may cause deadlocks as well as safety and liveness problems. We discuss a method to support the software engineer in detecting violations of desired system properties in their distributed object designs. We exploit the fact that object and component middleware standards and implementations only offer a fixed number of client-side synchronisation primitives and server-side threading policies. We suggest the use of UML stereotypes to represent each of these primitives in distributed object designs. We define the semantics of the stereotypes using a process algebra. We use that semantics to translate UML models and properties into behaviourally equivalent process algebra representations and can then use model checking techniques to detect any violations of the properties. Finally, we demonstrate how model checking results can be related back to the original UML design model. We present the tools that we have built in support of this method and evaluate the scalability of our validation technique.

In the next section, we discuss a scenario that we use throughout this paper to exemplify the problems that we address, as well as our solutions. Section 3 gives details of how UML stereotypes are used to model the identified synchronisation characteristics of a given system and includes UML models of the example scenario. Section 4 shows how designers can express desired safety and liveness properties in UML for the design models to adhere to. Sections 5 and 6 use a process algebra to define the semantics for the identified synchronisation primitives and threading policies as well as user-defined safety and progress properties. In Section 7, we demonstrate the importance of tackling the state explosion problem and outline our efforts in that area. In Section 8, we show how deadlocks and safety property violations can be detected using reachability analysis as well as the use of efficient graph algorithms on the underlying state space for the detection of a restricted form of liveness properties. Section 9 shows the mechanism by which designers receive feedback from the verification process. We discuss the scalability of our approach in Section 10. Section 11 introduces the tool that we have built to support our approach, with focus on its design and architecture. Section 12 puts our work in context with related research in the field. Finally, we conclude in Section 13 and present future goals for this research.

## 2   Motivating Scenario

To aid the demonstration of this work, we discuss an example of a distributed software architecture, which we assume is implemented using object middleware technology. We refer to this scenario throughout the paper to demonstrate the key steps of our approach.

The example that we use is a stock trading system, which in practice is often distributed as different market participants interact from different locations with servers that are hosted by a stock exchange. In particular, traders need to interact with a component that executes orders when a transaction is completed. Every completed transaction at the same time determines a new price for a stock that needs to be communicated to all interested market participants.

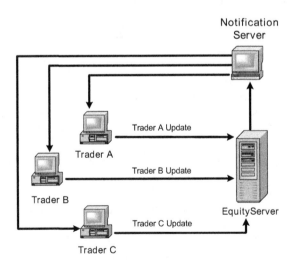

**Fig. 1.** Market Trading Scenario

Fig. 1 depicts the main components of the stock trading system and the communication channels between them. To keep the scenario simple, we only concentrate on the three types of entities responsible for communicating trade information, since it is these entities that determine the dynamic synchronisation behaviour of the application. We do not make any assumption about the infrastructure of the system, except that their hosts are connected by a network and that they communicate via object-oriented middleware.

Market traders carry out transactions and monitor fluctuations in various stock prices. Triggered by changes in prices or external requests from customers to deal in particular stock, a Trader will enter a new transaction and send its results to the EquityServer. Fig. 1 shows three traders sending updates to the EquityServer. Note that the Trader entity could in reality consist of multiple components but for all intents and purposes of this scenario it is viewed as a simple entity that can send and receive information.

Upon receipt of trading information the EquityServer will carry out specific computations based on the received data and other sources, such as stock profiles stored in a database. At a certain point the EquityServer will complete processing the transaction results and use this data to feed new price information to all traders. To do so, the EquityServer sends an updated price to the NotificationServer, which, in turn, publishes the price to registered traders. The delegation of the task to the notification server simplifies the EquityServer and minimises coupling. We assume that all traders have registered with the NotificationServer during initialisation and that communication channels are already established.

Communication between all entities in the system follows the push model. In this model information flows in one direction and is initiated by the source. In our example the sink end always reacts by forwarding information to the next entity. This creates recursion, whereby a Trader component calls an operation from the EquityServer, which calls an operation from the NotificationServer and this, in turn eventually calls back the Trader to notify it of a new price. If all these operations are called in a synchronous manner and servers are single threaded, we will reach a situation where all the components are blocked waiting the reception of information from one another, thus entering a deadlock.

Additionally, there are several domain specific properties that the designer may want the trading system to adhere to for the successful execution of the application. If we consider a closed market, prices are not changed in any other way than traders completing a transaction. This means that prior to any new prices being sent by the NotificationServer, traders need to send trade results to the EquityServer entity. Another desirable property is the guarantee that traders will be able to deal in stocks, no matter what the state of other components. Devising a means of representing these properties in a suitable notation and being able to verify a design model for such properties is the main theme of this paper.

# 3   Distributed Object Design

We use the Unified Modelling Language [29] for designing the static export inter-faces of distributed object types and their dynamic object interactions. UML is widely accepted and deployed in industry and we hope to leverage its popularity to bring our research results into industrial practice. UML is a self-descriptive notation, in that its entities are defined via meta-model expressed in UML. The consequence of this approach is a lack of formal semantics for the notation, which is needed for rigorous verification of a design model. The UML standard also provides extension-mechanisms by which new semantics can be introduced into a model, whilst still remaining within the UML framework. This section describes how our approach uses the stereotype extension mechanism for em-bodying middleware specific information into UML design models.

Initially we chose UML class and interaction diagrams to model a given system [16]. This resulted in the system being represented at a type level of abstraction through class diagrams and an instance level of abstraction through interaction diagrams. The use of interaction diagrams limited us in obtaining only one specific interleaving of interactions between objects. This clearly did not take full advantage of the exhaustive search powers of model checking techniques. In this paper, we use UML state diagrams [10] rather than interaction diagrams to model the dynamic behaviour of distributed objects. Statecharts maintain the ability to model dynamic behaviour but because they model the behaviour at a type-level of abstraction they also hold all possible interleaving of object interactions in a given system.

The behaviour of distributed object interactions is governed by synchronisa-tion and threading policies. We note that current distributed object and com-ponent middleware systems support a fixed number of such synchronisation and threading primitives. OMG's CORBA, Microsoft's Component Object Model (COM) and Java Remote Method Invocation (RMI) all support synchronous in-vocations, which block the client until the server returns the result. CORBA also supports deferred synchronous, oneway and asynchronous invocations. Server objects, similarly, only support a small number of threading models. CORBA's Portable Object Adapter defines single-threaded behaviour, which would force a client to wait while a server object is busy processing another request and multi-threaded behaviour, which is often implemented by spawning new threads for requests or by selecting a thread from a thread pool. RMI only directly supports single threaded behaviour, but server programmers can use Java's threading primitives to construct multi-threaded behaviour on top of this.

As the synchronisation and threading behaviour is of great importance for the overall design of a distributed object system, we believe that they should be captured in static and dynamic design diagrams. CORBA provides a superset of the synchronisation primitives and threading policies of COM and RMI. We subsequently define stereotypes for all the primitives that CORBA provides. These primitives can then be used during the design of applications based on other distributed object and component technologies too. Our approach therefore caters for design and property violation detection of all applications based on mainstream object and component middleware.

Recent advances in middleware technology have brought about component middleware technologies such as Enterprise Java Beans and the CORBA Component Model (CCM). Components representing business logic are hosted in the middleware's container. Component middleware technologies use existing object middlewares for establishing communication between components. For example EJB communication is achieved via RMI and CCM communication is done through CORBA. Therefore by providing semantics for the primitives of the underlying object middleware technologies we cater for the component middleware technologies as well.

The ⟨⟨synchronous⟩⟩ stereotype represents a synchronous request primitive, while the ⟨⟨deferredsynchronous⟩⟩ stereotype is used to indicate a deferred-synchronous request being made on a server object. The ⟨⟨asynchronous⟩⟩ stereotype is used to indicate an asynchronous client request, and a ⟨⟨oneway⟩⟩ stereotype represents a oneway request. Similarly on the server-side, we define the ⟨⟨singleThreaded⟩⟩ stereotype to indicate that a particular server object uses a single threaded policy to deal with incoming service requests and the ⟨⟨multiThreaded⟩⟩ stereotype shows that the server object handles multiple concurrent service requests by using multiple threads. We will specify the semantics of these stereotypes formally in Section 5.

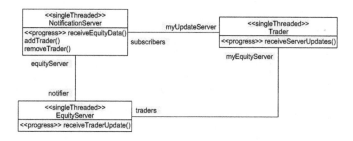

**Fig. 2.** Class diagram of Market Trading Scenario

Server-side threading policies are defined statically for object types. We therefore model those in the class diagrams that capture the export interfaces of object types. As an example, Fig. 2 shows a class diagram of the equity trading system. Each of the classes correspond to one of the three entities in the example scenario of Section 2. Each class is annotated with the ⟨⟨singleThreaded⟩⟩ stereotype, indicating that they handle one incoming request at a time. As previously mentioned, this is the default threading policy in all mainstream middleware. Each class has a method responsible for receiving stock related information. This method is remotely invoked by an object of another class in order to push information to the recipient. Method `receiveTraderUpdate()` in the `EquityServer` class, for instance, is invoked remotely by an instance of the `Trader` class in order to pass any trading activity reports. Likewise, method `receiveServerUpdates()` of `Trader` is invoked by an object of type `NotificationServer` to pass the `EquityServer` updates.

Synchronisation of remote operation invocations is a dynamic aspect and as such we define them in state diagrams. We use the synchronisation stereotypes mentioned above in those transitions of statecharts whose actions correspond to remote operation invocations. The statechart of the `EquityServer` in Fig. 3 initially starts in the `idle` state. After receiving a request for its exported `receiveTraderUpdate` method, it moves to state `update`. The action `notifier.receiveEquityData` that takes place whilst moving from `update` to `updates completed` is marked with a ⟨⟨synchronous⟩⟩ stereotype. This corresponds to a request invocation upon the `receiveEquityData` method of the `NotificationServer` class in Fig. 2. Notice that the action name contains the name of the association-end used in the class diagram. From this information we can deduct that an `EquityServer` object requests a remote synchronous operation from a single-threaded `NotificationServer` server object. Finally, the `EquityServer` goes back to the `idle` state causing a reply to be sent back to the `Trader` instance who sent the updates. If a state diagram contains actions indicating receiving an operation request then the designer must also indicate the point at which a reply is sent back to the client object. An example of this is the `receiveEquityData` and `receiveEquityData_reply` actions in Fig. 3.

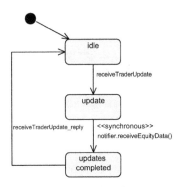

**Fig. 3.** EquityServer Statechart

Fig. 4 shows how the `NotificationServer` can register and unregister traders whilst in the `idle` state. Requests to be added or removed from the subscription list is replied to immediately via the `addTrader_reply` and `removeTrader_reply` methods respectively. Upon reception of update instructions from the `EquityServer` it moves into the `sending` state. It then continually sends updates via the `traders.receiveServerUpdates` action, until all traders have been notified. This action is marked with the ⟨⟨synchronous⟩⟩ stereotype. Similarly to the `EquityServer` case, we can deduct that instances of the `NotificationServer` class invoke the remote synchronous method `receiveServerUpdates` on `Trader` objects. The object re-enters the `idle` state upon updating all traders.

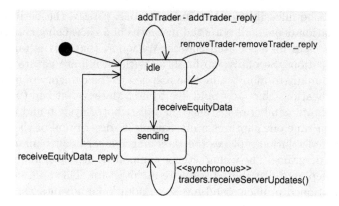

**Fig. 4.** NotificationServer Statechart

Fig. 5 shows the statechart for the `Trader` class. A trader processes a new transactions whilst in the `trading` state. It then sends the results of the trade to the `EquityServer` using the `myEquityServer.receiveTraderUpdate` action. This action is marked with a ⟨⟨synchronous⟩⟩ stereotype, indicating that invocations made to instances of type `EquityServer` are synchronous. After replying to the `receiveTraderUpdate` event the object returns to state `idle`.

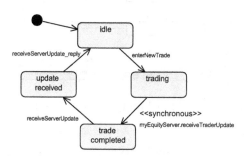

**Fig. 5.** Trader Statechart

Although class diagrams and state diagrams depict the static and dynamic characteristics of a system respectively, they both operate at a type-level of abstraction. In the case of distributed software architecture, it is often necessary to include instance-level designs as well. This is because the wide ranging dynamic behaviour of a distributed system depends on deployment configuration of an application and its environment. This also explains the need for component instantiation primitives in popular Architecture Description Languages such as Darwin [19].

Our initial solution for the inclusion of instance-level information was to derive it from the cardinality of association ends in class diagrams. This method was found to be infeasible for two main reasons. Firstly, the derived instance-level information depicts all potential instances of a class being connected to all other instances of its associated classes. We found that this is rarely the case in real applications. Secondly, cardinalities with an infinite nature such as one-to-many and many-to-many cannot be mapped to the category of finite-natured formal specifications that we would like to use. Moreover at run-time there will only exist a finite number of instances in a distributed system and by specifying this at design time one captures a more accurate description of the system.

Our revised solution replaces the class diagram cardinality information with UML object diagrams. These characterise component instances and their connec-tors in the deployed distributed software architecture. This approach addresses the two mentioned problems and has some additional advantages: UML object diagrams allow designers to model different run-time configurations of an ap-plication, which can be automatically verified against a given set of safety and liveness properties. Moreover, designers gain flexibility as they can verify differ-ent run-time configurations of an application without any modifications to the state or class diagrams. Deployment diagrams were not considered for this pur-pose as they force designers to indicate matters such as location and different types of resources, which are of no use to our approach and furthermore break some of the transparencies that middleware technologies aim to provide.

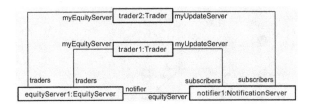

**Fig. 6.** Distributed Equity Trading System

Fig. 6 shows the deployment of the Distributed Equity Trading System Archi-tecture using an object diagram. The run-time configuration of the application consists of two distributed **Trader** objects and one distributed **EquityServer** and **NotificationServer** object. The connectors are shown as links in the object dia-gram and reflect the association instances that exist between objects. Each link holds the names of the association-ends of its respective association. This is done to prevent any ambiguities in the case of having multiple associations between classes. In distributed object programs, these connectors would be implemented using distributed object references, which a client needs to request a remote operation execution.

In order to reconfigure the architecture to reflect, for example, that two equity markets work in conjunction with each other, we could reconfigure this architecture by sharing the same **NotificationServer** object but include a second **EquityServer** object. This would then be achieved by connecting **notifier1** in

Fig. 6 with the new `EquityServer` object (`equityServer2`) and having new `Trader` objects linked to the `equityServer2` instance.

# 4   Property Specification

Our prior work in the area of reasoning about distributed object architectures concentrated on the detection of potential deadlocks [17]. Deadlocks are a common source of errors in distributed applications. The absence of deadlocks is a necessary, but not sufficient criterion for the behavioural correctness of a distributed software architecture. Designers might want to specify more general safety and liveness properties. A *safety property* defines that no undesirable behaviour will be exhibited during the execution of a system, while a *liveness property* determines the desirable actions that will eventually be executed.

Unlike for absence of deadlocks, designers need to provide the assertions for safety and liveness properties, as they are specific to a particular distributed application. Traditionally notations such as Linear Temporal Logic [28] have been used to express these properties. The main drawback of this logic is the high level of expertise and fluency in formal notations that is required from a designer. Thus, such an option would break the formal specification transparency that our approach offers to designers. For these reasons we provide the designer with a technique of expressing desired properties in UML notation. There has been some research [23] carried out in order to create new categorisations of properties. However, for the purposes of our approach and the properties that we would like to offer the traditional safety and liveness classifications are sufficient and as we cannot benefit from different categorisation, we have based our work on well-understood conceptual foundations.

## 4.1   Safety Properties

We support the specification of safety properties for distributed object designs based on action orderings as these are more intuitive for the distributed system designer than the reachability of states. This is because the parallel execution of objects and components causes a large number of potential states many of which are implicit and not directly evident to designers. Moreover the notion of actions map nicely to operation invocations, which are the means of interaction in object middleware.

As was discussed above, the designer provides a UML state diagram for each object type in order to model the behaviour of instances of that type. Thus the order and occurrence of actions within a single UML state diagram govern the behaviour of individual instances. Using safety properties, we can determine whether the behaviour that is modelled locally in objects respects global correctness criteria.

We define safety properties by asserting global constraints on the order in which remote operation invocations may occur. We propose the use of state diagrams to determine these action ordering. We refer to these diagrams as *safety state diagrams* in order to distinguish them from those that determine object behaviour.

In order to define the intuitive meaning of these safety statecharts, we need to introduce the notion of traces and alphabets. A *trace* is a sequence of distributed operation invocations that is permitted by the state diagrams that govern the behaviour of individual distributed objects. A single element of a trace is an *action*, which we label with the name of the invoked operation. The set of operation names used in the union of all possible traces is called the *alphabet* of the distributed object system. Given a subset $S$ of a distributed object system's alphabet $A$, we may *restrict* a trace of the system with $S$ by deleting any actions that denote operations that are not in $S$.

The union of operation names that annotate transitions in a safety state diagram will be a subset of the system's alphabet. When checking for a safety property, we would like to ascertain that any trace of the distributed system restricted to the alphabet used in the safety state diagram is identical to the one described in the safety state diagram.

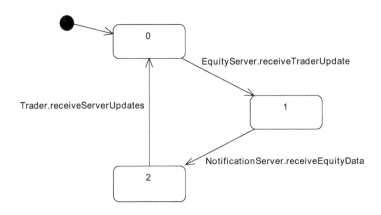

**Fig. 7.** Safety Property with Types

Fig. 7 shows a safety property for the scenario example discussed in Section 2. The purpose of the property is to ensure that trade activity is generated before any updates are sent to the traders. This property states that all possible execution traces of the application should respect the below recurring pattern in the given order:

1. An instance of the `EquityServer` class must receive a `receiveTraderUpdate` request
2. Next an instance of the `NotificationServer` class must receive a `receiveEquityData` request
3. Next an instance of the `Trader` class must receive a `receiveServerUpdates` request. Back to step 1.

The alphabet of the Trading system is the union of traces obtained from the interaction between all instances of the `EquityServer`, `NotificationServer` and `Trader` classes. In the case of the above safety property we have introduced a subset of the alphabet which needs to be matched by all traces obtained from any interaction. This safety alphabet consists of the actions shown in Fig. 7 enumerated over the instances of the corresponding types, obtained from the object diagram of Fig. 6.

In Fig. 7, the operation names are preceded by class names. The meaning of that construct is that we offer a non-deterministic choice of any objects that are instances of that class. There may be situations, however, where designers want to express safety properties for particular objects. Thus, we also support the enumeration of sets of object names from the object diagram that describes the distributed system architecture.

Fig. 8 demonstrates this by specialising the safety property in Fig. 7 by only including the `trader1` object. In general, designers simply wrap a comma separated list of objects in curly braces to indicate that the property targets certain instances instead of all instances associated with a class.

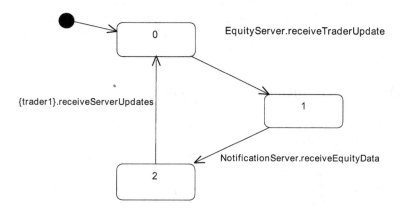

**Fig. 8.** Safety Property with Objects

By supporting the safety properties using action ordering we enable designers to express various higher level properties specific to a distributed application, such as mutual exclusion.

## 4.2   Liveness Properties

The focus of liveness properties is on the continuity of the execution of an application i.e. that a specific set of actions eventually happen. We currently support the progress property as defined by Magee and Kramer [20]. Intuitively, progress means that that it is always the case that an action from a given set will eventually be executed. Progress evaluates to the temporal logic property of "always eventually" Using progress properties, we can detect livelocks in application designs.

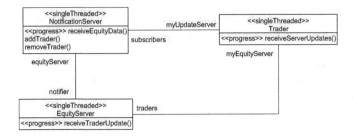

**Fig. 9.** Trading Order Liveness Property

We support the specification of progress properties by defining a ⟨⟨**progress**⟩⟩ stereotype that can be attached to operations of classes crucial to the progress of the application. Fig. 9 depicts an example that adds progress properties to the example scenario discussed in Section 2. In this case, we have identified that the respective methods of each class responsible for circulating new and update trade information are vital for the continuity of our application.

## 5   Formal Semantics of Stereotypes

Section 3 demonstrated our approach in producing annotated UML models of a distributed application. In order to make firm and accurate deductions about the dynamic behaviour of such an application, our approach prescribes a mapping of the design model into a formal specification. The formal specification is a description of when and in what way do parallel executing objects synchronise with one another. The point of synchronisation is found by analysing the state diagram of each object type. The method of synchronisation is derived by detecting the client-side synchronisation primitive and the server-side threading policy stereotypes specified for each interaction.

Process algebras represent mathematically rigorous frameworks for modelling concurrent systems of interacting processes. We have chosen process algebras for defining a formal semantics of our stereotypes over alternatives such as denotational and axiomatic models due to their more powerful model of concurrency. Process algebras allow for hierarchical description of processes, a valuable feature for compositional reasoning, verification and analysis. The particular algebra that we have chosen for defining the semantics of the stereotypes are Finite State Processes [20] (FSP). We chose FSP because it is well-supported by a model checking tool.

In our approach we have derived FSP specifications for all combinations of client-side synchronisation primitives and server-side threading policies discussed in Section 3. By analysing the input annotated UML model we obtain the specific combination of synchronisation primitives and threading policies specified by the designer. By mapping each detected combination with its corresponding formal semantic and by finally composing all the formal specification fragments together, we obtain a formal specification of the overall application design.

There are two concepts that we commonly use across specifications of primitives and threading policies. Firstly we insert into the system specification, middleware-specific actions relating to the mediation of requests and results between a client and a server object. This is required for the correct modelling of the system's synchronisation behaviour. Secondly we directly support the notion of instance-level modelling in the formal domain by reflecting the specification from the object diagrams discussed in Section 3.

At a notation level there are two techniques that we use for the generation of FSP specifications, namely synchronised actions and parallel composition. Each FSP process is composed of a set of actions that occur in a specified and fixed order. Parallel composition is used to describe a system with multiple concurrent processes, whereby the actions of the processes are interleaved. Therefore, whilst the actions of individual processes still occur in a fixed order, we obtain many different execution traces of the composite process. Note, that this directly reflects the concept of concurrent states in UML statecharts. Processes can be forced to perform actions simultaneously in a lock-step fashion via synchronised/shared actions. Actions with the same name are executed at the same time; this achieves synchronisation between concurrent processes. Actions with different names can be synchronised using the FSP relabelling mechanism. This Section discusses these specifications in detail.

## 5.1   Synchronisation Primitives

A *synchronous* request blocks the client object until the server object processes the request and returns the results of the requested operation. This is the default synchronisation primitive not only in CORBA, but also in RMI and COM. Fig. 10 shows the FSP specification for a *synchronous* call. A central component of any object middleware system is an Object Adapter(OA). The Object Adapter is the key entity in middleware technology, in terms of orchestrating the synchronisation between server objects and client requests. It is possible for an object adaptor to be responsible for handling more than one server object. However since there is no way of knowing this, our formalisation assumes the extreme case of appointing an object adapter for each server object. The role of an object adapter is directly mapped to the OA FSP process, which forms the synchronisation between Client and Server processes. The OA process receives requests sent by the Client process and relays them onto the Server process. SynchInvocation is a composite process made up of the parallel composition of the Client, Server and OA processes. It uses relabelling to synchronise the four actions of the OA process with the relevant actions in the Client and Server process. For example the sendRequest action of the Client process is synchronised with OA's receiveRequest action, similarly the OA's relayReply is synchronised with the `Server`'s `sendReply` action. This simply indicates that a client must have sent a request before the server sends back a reply. The overall execution of the composite process follows the order set in the `OA` process, therefore implementing a *synchronous* call.

```
Client=(sendRequest-> receiveReply-> Client).

OA=(receiveRequest->relayRequest->
    receiveReply->relayReply->OA).

Server=(receiveRequest->processRequest->
        sendReply->Server).

||SynchInvocation=(client:Client || serverOA:OA
                    ||server:Server)
/{client.sendRequest/serverOA.receiveRequest,
  client.receiveReply/serverOA.relayReply,
  server.receiveRequest/serverOA.relayRequest,
  server.sendReply/serverOA.receiveReply}.
```

**Fig. 10.** Synchronous Stereotype Semantics

With an *asynchronous* request control is returned to the client as soon as the invocation has been sent. Results of the invocation are returned to the client by a call-back mechanism invoked by the server. This means that the onus of directing the results to the client is now on the server. Fig. 11 shows the FSP specification for the *asynchronous* invocation method. Similarly to the previous case the `OA` process mediates the synchronisation of the `Client` and `Server` actions. However, in this case the client can engage in other actions infinitely often before it receives a call-back invocation from the server, via the OA. This is indicated by the "..." in the process, `otherExecutions`. This is made possible by the FSP choice operator "|", which introduces a non-deterministic method of executing alternate actions.

A *oneway* method invocation does not block because there is no reply by the server. This offers an inexpensive way of invoking methods but offers no guarantees or indications as to whether the request has been received or processed by the server.

## 5.2   Threading Policies

The primitives described in Section 5.1 were demonstrated in combination with a single threaded policy. The multi-threaded policy, expressed using the `<<multiThreaded>>` stereotype, allows for handling multiple requests simultaneously. There are several different methods of implementing this policy but all use the common principle of delegating the request handling to threads. Threadpools are a common implementation method, whereby new requests are delegated to

```
Client=(sendRequest->OtherExecutions),
OtherExecutions=(...->OtherExecutions |
                 callBack->receiveReply->Client).

OA=(receiveRequest->relayRequest->
    receiveReply->relayReply->OA).

Server=(receiveRequest->processRequest->
        sendReply->Server).

||ASyncInvocation=(client:Client || serverOA:OA
                  ||server:Server)
/{client.sendRequest/serverOA.receiveRequest,
  client.callBack/serverOA.relayReply,
  server.receiveRequest/serverOA.relayRequest,
  server.sendReply/serverOA.receiveReply}.
```

**Fig. 11.** Asynchronous Stereotype Semantics

threads drawn from a threadpool. Once the request has been processed the thread is returned to the threadpool and is declared available again. If all threads are busy at the time of a request arrival the request is put into a queue. In the situation where the queue is also full the request is discarded. If the client is expecting a reply from its operation request it will receive a generated system-level exception. Fig. 12 defines the semantics of a server that uses a thread pool policy. The total number of slave threads and queue slots are specified as constants at the beginning. The server-side is composed of four processes, representing the thread, threadpool, queue and the server. All server-side processes are composed with the same label so as to synchronise their action. The Server process uses two variables to keep track of the current size of the queue and the number of threads currently in use. The server ReceiveRequest action indicates the arrival of a client request. If there are any available threads the synchronised action getFreeThread is taken which starts the ThreadPool process. This further causes the Thread process to be initiated using the shared delegateTask action. Once the request has been serviced the responsible Thread process engages in a ReceiveReply. If the number of used threads has not reached the maximum the server attempts to add the message to the queue. This addToQueue succeeds if there are free queue slots left, otherwise the message is being rejected.

## 6   Formal Semantics of Properties

In order to automatically verify the generated formal specification of a system against user-provided properties, we need to translate the expressed safety and liveness properties into the process algebra domain. The property specifications

```
const PoolSize=16
const QueueSize = 10
range T=0..PoolSize
range Q=0..QueueSize

OA=(receiveRequest->relayRequest->
    receiveReply->sendReply->OA).

Thread=(delegateTask->taskExecuted->sendBackReply->Thread).

ThreadPool = ThreadPool[0],
ThreadPool[i:T]=
 if (i<PoolSize) then
     (getFreeThread->delegateTask->ThreadPool[i+1]
   | taskExecuted -> ThreadPool[i-1])
 else (noFreeThreads -> ThreadPool[i]).

Queue = Queue[0],
Queue[j:Q]=
 if(j<QueueSize)then(inspectQueue->
  if(j>0) then (dequeueMessage->Queue[j-1]
             | addToQueue[j]->Queue[j+1])
  else(addToQueue[j]->Queue[j+1]))
 else (rejectMessage -> Queue[j]).

Server = Server[0][0],
Server[i:T][j:Q]=(receiveNewRequest->
 if(i<PoolSize) then
   (getFreeThread->Server[i+1][j])
 else (noFreeThreads->
  if(j<QueueSize)then
     (addToQueue[j]->Server[i][j+1])
  else (rejectMessage->Server[i][j]))).

||MTSystem=(oa:OA||server:Server||
            server:ThreadPool||server:Thread||
            server:Queue)
   /{server.receiveNewRequest/oa.relayRequest,
     server.sendBackReply/oa.receiveReply}.
```

**Fig. 12.** Semantics of Multi-Threaded Stereotype

need to be in the same notation as the system specification. In this section we discuss the generation and integration of property specifications expressed in Section 4.

## 6.1  Safety Property Semantics

In order to generate FSP to model the system at an object level of granularity we must refer to the object diagram. Fig. 13 shows the corresponding generated FSP process algebra for the safety property specified in Fig. 7. The class names in the transitions are replaced by a list of instance names obtained from the object diagram.

For example the server class name on the first transition is EquityServer. Consulting the object diagram shows that the list of instances of this class contains only one element, equityServer1. By further consulting the state and object diagrams we determine the list of client objects that are linked to and invoke operations from equityServer1 – trader1 and trader2. We can now construct the FSP action by combining the names of the clients, the server and the operation.

```
property SFY= ({trader1,trader2}.equityServer1.receivetraderupdate->S1),
S1=({equityServer1}.notifier1.receiveequitydata->S2),
S2=({notifier1}.trader1.receiveserverupdates->SFY
    |{notifier1}.trader2.receiveserverupdates->SFY).
```

**Fig. 13.** Safety Property Semantics Example

The above specification is composed of three sections, each section corresponding to each transition action of Fig. 7. As introduced in Section 4.1, the complete set of traces generated from the formal specification of the Trading scenario need to comply with the traces generated from the above safety property.

## 6.2  Liveness Property Semantics

Fig. 14 shows the generated FSP specification for the progress property example of Fig. 9. Similarly to the safety property example discussed in previous subsection, we make use of the object diagram to generate object-level specifications. Each annotated method is prefixed with the object names of the class type and further prefixed with the object name of instances linked to them in the object diagram. For example the progress property EQUITYSERVER_PROGRESS0 addresses the source instance equityServer1 as well as instances that can potentially invoke the operation receiveTraderUpdate, namely trader1 and trader2.

# 7  Minimisation

The main challenge of verification of system properties using model checking techniques is the potential for state explosion [11]. There has been a growing trend of applying model checking techniques to more complex fields, such as software engineering, than its original field of use, hardware and protocol design. This growing complexity has turned this problem into a pivotal factor for

```
progress EQUITYSERVER_PROGRESS0=
  { trader1.equityServer1.receivetraderupdate,
    trader2.equityServer1.receivetraderupdate }

progress NOTIFICATIONSERVER_PROGRESS0 =
  { equityServer1.notifier1.receiveequitydata }

progress TRADER_PROGRESS0 =
  { notifier1.trader1.receiveserverupdates,
    notifier1.trader2.receiveserverupdates }
```

**Fig. 14.** Progress Property Semantics Example

deploying finite-state verification techniques. Attempting to verify distributed object systems amplifies this problem. This is due to the high degree of autonomy present between objects executing in parallel, giving way to a very large number of possible execution traces. As a consequence, the model's state space grows exponentially with respect to the number of objects involved, rendering naive brute force approaches unusable.

We tackle the state space explosion problem from a number of different angles. Our work concentrates on exploiting middleware characteristics for state reduction and the generated process algebra only takes into account a small finite number of synchronisation primitives and threading policies.

The insight of knowing our problem domain is further reflected in the underlying process algebra specification that we generate. The behaviour of each distributed object is described in one FSP process. However, only the actions that deal with making or receiving remote method requests, as described in the UML state diagram, are exposed. The execution of local method calls, the interaction between a possibly large number of local objects, as well as the operation parameter and return values have no implications on the emergent synchronisation behaviour of a distributed application and can therefore be ignored. Abstracting from these details reduces the state space significantly. We can achieve further reductions by considering the way in which middleware implements distributed interactions.

In all object and component-oriented middleware systems there is a middleware component that is responsible for receiving all incoming requests for a server objects and for delivering them to the appropriate object implementation for servicing. In CORBA, this component is called the Object Adapter, COM provides a Service Control Module that has this function and Java/RMI uses the activation interfaces that are contained in the RMI daemon. We subsume these components under the notion of *object adapters* below.

An object adapter decouples client from server objects. All operation invocation requests are initially received by the object adapter on the server object's hosts and the adapter then forwards them to the server objects as exemplified in Fig. 15. Likewise any reply of the server object will be transmitted via the object adapter. Since the object adapter has a fixed interface of only two actions – for receiving and replying to requests – and the client objects can only interact with server objects through these two actions, we can achieve further minimisation of the state space: In a scenario of $n$ clients invoking $m$ different server methods, we can reduce the combination of interactions from $n \times m$ to $n \times 2$. This means that the final state space will be independent of the number of methods that a server object type exports. As the final state space is the product of the size of the component states during parallel composition, this reduction will greatly reduce the final state space.

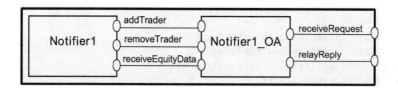

**Fig. 15.** Middleware Aware Minimisation

# 8   Model Checking

Model checking provides a means of automatically verifying input process algebra for a given set of properties. This is achieved by building a state space representation of the specification and exhaustively searching this space to ensure that all states are valid with respect to the desired properties. Model checking tools vary in features such as the data structures they use to hold the state space and the algorithm they use for searching the state space. Whilst such features may affect the performance of the model checking performance by a given factor, they are quite similar in the way they approach the problem.

The FSP process algebra is provided with the Labelled Transition System Analyser(LTSA) model checker. The LTSA model checker generates a Labelled Transition System(LTS) for each of the generated FSP processes and applies our minimisation methods. These LTSs are then composed together into one large LTS, taking into account the required synchronisation between the objects as specified in the FSP processes. This final LTS represents the state space of the application model. Subsequently the LTSA carries out an exhaustive search of the state space for verification purposes. It is the exhaustive nature of the search that gives formal verification methods their rigorous powers and high reliability in finding the most subtle of errors. In case of a property violation detected the LTSA outputs the shortest trace of actions that causing the violation.

A deadlock situation is detected when a state with no outgoing transition is found. This indicates that there is no further states that the modelled application can enter, causing the system to halt and deadlock. Fig. 16 shows the trace of actions leading to a potential deadlock in the Trading scenario we have been discussing. The trace shows how initially `trader1` sends the results of an equity transaction to the `equitysever1` instance. The instance `equityserver1` receives this and successfully requests the object `notifier1` to send equity price updates to the traders. The deadlock occurs when `trader1` again sends new transaction information to `equityserver1`, but `notifier1` immediately follows this up by sending another update to `trader1`. At this stage both `trader1` and `notifier1` are blocked and any further synchronous invocations to these two objects would block the caller for ever. Thus when this does happen the system enter a deadlock status.

```
Trace to DEADLOCK:
 trader1.equityServer1.receivetraderupdate
 equityServer1.receivetraderupdate
 equityServer1.notifier1.receiveequitydata
 notifier1.receiveequitydata
 notifier1.trader1.receiveserverupdate
 trader1.receiveserverupdate
 trader1.receiveserverupdates_reply
 notifier1.receiveequitydata_reply
 equityServer1.receivetraderupdate_reply
 trader1.equityServer1.receivetraderupdate
 equityServer1.receivetraderupdate
 notifier1.trader1.receiveserverupdate
 equityServer1.notifier1.receiveequitydata
 trader2.equityServer1.receivetraderupdate
```

**Fig. 16.** LTSA Deadlock Trace

A safety property violations is detected when the model checker finds a trace of actions containing one or more actions of the safety property, where the safety property's action ordering is not followed. Fig. 17 shows an example of the safety property violation depicted in Fig. 8. This safety property stated that out of all active traders only the instance, `trader1` should be informed of new equity updates via instances of the `NotificationServer` class. The property is violated in our distributed object model as the `NotificationServer` object might send notifications to both trader objects (refer to Fig. 6). In this case an update was sent to the instance `trader2`.

Progress violations are detected by looking for any set of actions that form an infinite cycle in which one or more of the progress actions are not included. Such set of actions are referred to as a terminal set. The LTSA reports this violation by showing a trace of actions to the terminal set and the terminal set itself.

```
Trace to property violation in SFY:
 trader1.equityServer1.receivetraderupdate
 equityServer1.receivetraderupdate
 equityServer1.receivetraderupdate_reply
 trader1.equityServer1.receiveInvocationReply
 equityServer1.notifier1.receiveequitydata
 notifier1.receiveequitydata
 notifier1.trader2.receiveserverupdates
```

**Fig. 17.** LTSA Safety Violation Trace

## 9  Relating Results

A key requirement of this research is to enable designers to reason about distributed object designs entirely using the UML notation. To attain this goal, we translate the traces of actions generated due to safety and liveness property violations into UML Sequence Diagrams. Sequence Diagrams offer a comprehensive and intuitive manner of showing a designer counter-examples of how their properties can be potentially violated.

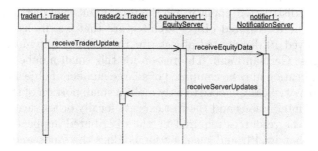

**Fig. 18.** Violation of Safety Property depicted in Fig. 8

Fig. 18 shows the sequence diagram generated for the safety property violation shown in Fig. 17. The sequence diagram shows how the application design allows a potential execution where by the instance **notifier1** could send updates to the **trader2** object, thus violating the safety property.

We envisage the process of design verification to be iterative. So at this stage the user should make any required modifications, to make their design rid of the potential problem and repeat the verification on the new modified design model.

## 10  Evaluation

In order to analyse the effectiveness of the suggested minimisation methods we have carried out an evaluation using the equity trading scenario introduced in

Section 2. The experiment is based on the configuration shown in Fig. 6 and carried out on a x86 architecture machine with dual 1.7GHz Xeon processors and 1GB of memory. The variant was the number of `Trader` instances executing in parallel along with the instances, `notifier1` and `equityServer1`. The main point of interest was the size of the state space gained by using the different approaches.

Fig. 19 shows the results of the evaluation. Not shown in the chart is the size of the maximum state space which ranged from $2^{31}$-$2^{71}$ for the set of traders shown on the x-axis. The line on the left hand side in the chart plots the state space gained by using the Compositional Reachability Analysis (CRA) [1] of the LTSA model checker without applying any minimisation. The line on the right hand side shows the performance of our minimisation technique. The CRA line is discontinued for all values above 7 traders since the model checker runs out of memory after generating 5300000 states. Whilst both techniques exhibit exponential growth, our minimisation approach has a lower growth factor and supports the validation of larger systems. In this case our minimisation approach was able to almost double the performance of the CRA method. Moreover our early evaluation was carried out on a relatively modest machine. We envisage designers to operate the MUDV tool on a stronger machine, thus yielding even better results.

When interpreting absolute state space size, the reader should bear in mind that in realistic distributed applications the total number of distributed objects is fairly low. The distributed object architecture that we discussed in [4], for example, deployed 10 distributed objects for the trading system integration of the sixth largest German bank. The reason for this small number of objects is that while application may be composed of a large number of objects and components, developers typically choose to only make a small portion of them available for distributed interactions and the rest execute locally or are deactivated. This is to minimise the resources required by the distributed application which include network bandwidth and memory for holding the stubs and skeletons of distributed objects.

## 11  MUDV Tool

Our "Modelchecking UML Design Verifier (MUDV)" is the tool that we have built in order to apply and evaluate our approach. The core task of the MUDV tool is to generate process algebra specification from input annotated UML models. An overview architecture of the tool is shown in Fig. 20. Designers use off-the-shelf UML CASE tools to create their system design. Most of these tools now support export into the Object Management Group's XML Metadata Interchange [27] (XMI) format. XMI is a standard for encoding UML models in XML. The wide support of XMI in UML CASE tools and the intuitive methods of information extraction from XML documents makes it a suitable input notation for the MUDV.

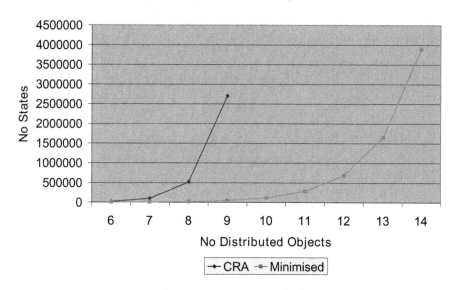

**Fig. 19.** State Space Size Comparison

The MUDV tool generates the process algebra specification of the input design model. We then use the Labelled Transition System Analyser (LTSA), a model checker for FSP, to verify the conformance of all possible execution traces with the provided properties. This architecture gives designers the flexibility of using any UML design application with XMI support as well as decoupling it from the model checking tool. This allows us to create mappings to different formal specifications and integrate them into the overall architecture seamlessly.

Fig. 21 shows the design of the MUDV tool. The main feature of this design is the use of the Visitor pattern [7], which accommodates the seamless integration of new formal specification mappings. The three UML diagram types that we use in our approach are represented by the three classes which realise the general MUDVElement interface. All classes of type MUDVElement support the method accept which takes as input-parameter a reference to an instance of the general type Visitor. Instances of this type hold the functionality for producing specific types of formal specification. Once a MUDVElement has been passed a Visitor instance, via the MUDVTool class, it invokes the appropriate method for it to be analysed and mapped to a specification. This design makes the MUDV tool flexible and with low cohesion between its components. We have implemented the plug-in for the generation of FSP specifications and are currently creating a SPIN [13] plug-in to demonstrate the general applicability of our approach.

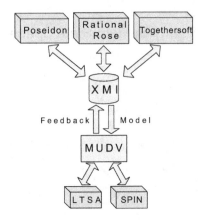

**Fig. 20.** MUDV Architecture

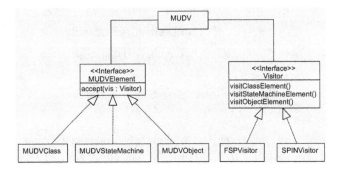

**Fig. 21.** MUDV Core Design

## 12    Related Work

The notion of accelerating the development life-cycle of software methodologies through automation is an appealing idea with a long history. This originally started with the introduction of Computer Aided Software Engineering(CASE) tools in the 80s. The OMG's Model Driven Architecture [6] is the most recent attempt at standardising the automation of deployment design and substantial implementation tasks.

The work done in [18] is similar to our approach in that a formal specification is generated from UML design models. One of the assumptions made, however, is that each instance of the modelled class runs in a separate process. This is not the case for object middleware as many server objects can run in the same process. In [15] automatic deadlock free synthesis of COM/DCOM architecture connectors is achieved from the dynamic behaviour specification of the components, but no general safety or liveness properties are enforced. The work of the same authors reported in [14] is related in that the authors also translate UML designs into SPIN models. The most important difference is that we explicitly use stereotypes to express the synchronisation and threading policies and that we aim to hide the complexity of using a model checker completely.

In [30], FSP specifications are generated from an extended version of Message Sequence Charts (MSC) for the synthesis of system behaviour models. Whilst scenario-based specification is a suitable method for checking and communicating the key scenarios of a system it cannot be applied to detailed design models for the purposes of thorough validation and verification. The large number of key scenarios in a typical industrial case are too large to make this a scalable solution for design verification.

The pUML [5] research attempts to give formal semantics of UML diagrams using the Z notation, allowing them to verify UML models. The approach taken in the Hydra project [21] is provide a mapping from the UML metamodel to formal language metamodels. This mapping leads to a set of rules which govern the automation of a particular formal specification. This mapping does not cover the whole of the UML diagrams set, specifically UML stereotypes which is the basis of conveying middleware related information in our approach.

# 13   Summary and Conclusion

It is our belief that the advances in distributed object and component technologies need to be complemented by new software engineering methods and tools to guide developers in increasingly complex situations [3]. The work presented in this paper focuses on automatically verifying the non-deterministic synchronisation behaviour of object middleware applications, caused by the interaction between distributed objects executing in parallel.

This paper reports on a number of new contributions. By extending the semantics of UML state diagrams and the introduction of new stereotypes, we provide designers with the ability to express safety and liveness properties in the UML notation. Formal specifications of the properties are automatically generated and composed with the process algebra specification of the system. Feedback on any property violations is done via UML sequence diagrams, maintaining transparency of the heavy formal specification to designers. Traditional property specification techniques, such as those using temporal logic, offer a more expressive power than our approach. However, this comes at a cost of being user-unfriendly and difficult to master, which we have often found to be a stumbling block for the industrial adoption of these techniques. Taking into consideration the fact that this research is aimed at supporting general industrial practitioners with little or no experience of formal techniques, we feel that our approach maintains a suitable balance in this trade off.

Our second contribution is the integration of models for the deployment of distributed components and their interconnection via the use of UML object diagrams. This enables designers to experiment with and verify different run-time configurations of a distributed object system without any modification required to other models. The analysis of an application at an instance level is further reflected in the generated process algebra and the feedback sequence diagrams. Furthermore, by solely modelling object interactions where indicated in an object diagram we reduce the complexity, and thus the state space, of the formal model, leading to more efficient model checking.

We also presented and evaluated the methods we employ to tackle the state explosion problem. By exploiting domain specific (object middleware) knowledge of the nature of the applications being modelled, we build further minimisation methods on top of what is typically offered by model checkers, with the goal of reducing a model's state space. Only actions that correspond to remote object interactions, making up the synchronisation behaviour of an application, are model checked. By modelling the entity responsible for receiving and delivering requests in a distributed system we also gain incremental minimisation.

Even though the minimisation techniques we presented above greatly improve the usability of our approach and facilitate verification of medium-sized industrial models, we are aware that they do not yet scale up to large scale distributed systems with several hundred distributed objects. In order to achieve this scalability, we need to take advantage of the fact that these objects are often isolated from each other and partitioned into federations of distributed objects. Fortunately, the federations of objects that do interact with each other are rarely larger than the ones that we can model check. We can then analyse these federations in isolation from each other and in that way achieve the scalability required in practice.

We are currently developing a new semantic mapping of UML models into Promela specifications, the input notation for the SPIN model checker. This will demonstrate the general applicability of our approach to various formal semantics as well as benefiting from the advantages of the SPIN model checker, such as support for timeouts, assertions and optional compact searches as opposed to an exhaustive one. We plan to further evaluate our approach by carrying out a case-study obtained from our industrial collaborators.

The techniques that we have outlined in this paper are providing feedback on *qualitative* properties of distributed object design. We have started investigating reasoning techniques for *quantitative* properties, such as scalability, performance and reliability of distributed object and component designs. It would be highly desirable to avoid costly risk mitigation iterations during a development process and address the question of whether an architecture scales and performs efficiently and reliably by analytic means. The performance modelling literature includes a large body of work on *stochastic process algebras*, which use distribution functions with which transitions are executed [12, 9, 8]. It seems natural to extend the research that we presented here to performance, scalability and reliability properties of UML models that can then be expressed and analysed with stochastic process algebras.

In [24, 25], we have described xlinkit, a consistency checker that can be used to validate the static consistency of software engineering documents represented in XML. That research is largely complementary to the techniques for establishing behavioural consistency that we have presented in this paper. A combination of the two approaches would enable us to statically validate the correctness of the various relationships between the different diagrams, such as that for each object in an object diagram, there is a class in a class diagram whose name is identical to the type of the object and would therefore enhance the usability of our our model checker. We therefore plan to address this integration in the immediate future.

# References

[1] S.-C. Cheung and J. Kramer. Checking Safety Properties Using Compositional Reachability Analysis. *ACM Transactions on Software Engineering and Methodology*, 8(1):49–7, 1999.

[2] W. Emmerich. *Engineering Distributed Objects*. John Wiley & Sons, April 2000.

[3] W. Emmerich. Distributed Component Technologies and their Software Engineering Implications. In *Proc. of the 24$^{th}$ Int. Conf. on Software Engineering, Orlando, Florida*. ACM Press, 2002. To appear.

[4] W. Emmerich, E. Ellmer, and H. Fieglein. TIGRA – An Architectural Style for Enterprise Application Integration. In *Proc. of the 23$^{rd}$ Int. Conf. on Software Engineering, Toronto, Canada*, pages 567–576. IEEE Computer Society Press, 2001.

[5] A. Evans, R. France, K. Lano, and B. Rumpe. The UML as a Formal Modeling Notation. In Pierre-Alain Muller and Jean Bézivin, editors, *Proc. of the International Conference on the Unified Modeling Language (UML): Beyond the Notation*, volume 1618 of *Lecture Notes in Computer Science*, pages 336–348. Springer-Verlag, 1998.

[6] D. Frankel. *Model Driven Architecture – Applying MDA to Enterprise Computing*. OMG Press. Wiley, 2003.

[7] Erich Gamma, Richard Helm, Ralph Johnson, and John Vlissides. *Design Patterns: Elements of Reusable Object-Oriented Software*. Addison Wesley, Massachusetts, 1994.

[8] S. Gilmore, J. Hillston, and M. Ribaudo. An efficient algorithm for aggregating PEPA models. *IEEE Transactions on Software Engineering*, 27(5):449–464, 2001.

[9] N. Götz, U. Herzog, and M. Rettelbach. The Integration of Functional Specification and Performance Analysis using Stochastic Process Algebras. In *Proc. of the 16$^{th}$ Int. Symposium on Computer Performance Modelling, Measurement and Evaluation (PERFORMANCE 93)*, volume 729, pages 121–146. Springer, 1993.

[10] D. Harel. Statecharts: A Visual Formalism for Complex Systems. *Science of Computer Programming*, 8(3):231–274, 1987.

[11] David Harel, Orna Kupferman, and Moshe Y. Vardi. On the complexity of verifying concurrent transition systems. In *International Conference on Concurrency Theory*, pages 258–272, 1997.

[12] J. A. Hillston. *A Compositional Approach to Performance Modelling*. PhD thesis, Dept. of Computer Science, University of Edinburgh, UK, 1994.

[13] Gerard J. Holzmann. The Model Checker SPIN. *IEEE Transactions on Software Engineering*, 23(5):279–295, 1997.

[14] P. Inverardi, H. Muccini, and P. Pelliccione. Automated Check of Architectural Models Consistency using SPIN. In *Proc. of the 16$^{th}$ Automated Software Engineering Conference, Coronado Island, CA*, pages 346–349. IEEE Computer Society Press, 2001.

[15] P. Inverardi and S. Scriboni. Connector Synthesis for Deadlock-Free Component Based Architectures. In *Proc. of the 16$^{th}$ Automated Software Engineering Conference, Coronado Island, CA*, pages 174–181. IEEE Computer Society Press, 2001.

[16] N. Kaveh. Model Checking Distributed Objects. In W. Emmerich and S. Tai, editors, *Proc. of the 2$^{nd}$ Int. Workshop on Distributed Objects, Davis, Cal, Nov. 2000*, volume 1999 of *Lecture Notes in Computer Science*, pages 116–128. Springer, 2001.

[17] N. Kaveh and W. Emmerich. Deadlock Detection in Distributed Object Systems. In V. Gruhn, editor, *Joint Proc. of the 8$^{th}$ European Software Engineering Conference and the 9$^{th}$ ACM SIGSOFT Symposium on the Foundations of Software Engineering*, pages 44–51. ACM Press, 2001.

[18] J. Lilius and I. Paltor. A Tool for verifying UML models. In *Proc. of the 14$^{th}$ Int. Conference on Automated Software Engineering, Cocoa Beach, Florida*, pages 255–258. IEEE Computer Society Press, 1999.

[19] J. Magee, N. Dulay, S. Eisenbach, and J. Kramer. Specifying Distributed Software Architectures. In W. Schafer and P. Botella, editors, *Proc. 5th European Software Engineering Conf. (ESEC 95)*, volume 989, pages 137–153, Sitges, Spain, 1995. Springer-Verlag, Berlin.

[20] J. Magee and J. Kramer. *Concurrency: Models and Programs – From Finite State Models to Java Programs*. John Wiley, 1999.

[21] W. E. McUmber and B. H. C. Cheung. A General Framework for Formalizing UML with Formal Languages. In *Proc. of the 23$^{rd}$ Int. Conf. on Software Engineering, Toronto, Canada*, pages 433–442. IEEE Computer Society Press, 2001.

[22] R. Monson-Haefel. *Enterprise Javabeans*. O'Reilly UK, 1999.

[23] G. Naumovich and L. A. Clarke. Classifying Properties: An Alternative to the Safety-Liveness Classification. Technical Report UM-CS-2000-012, Dept. of Computer Science, University of Massachusetts in Amherst, 2000.

[24] C. Nentwich, L. Capra, W. Emmerich, and A. Finkelstein. xlinkit: A Consistency Checking and Smart Link Generation Service. *ACM Transactions on Internet Technology*, 2002. To appear.

[25] C. Nentwich, W. Emmerich, and A. Finkelstein. Static Consistency Checking for Distributed Specifications. In *Proc. of the 16$^{th}$ Automated Software Engineering Conference, Coronado Island, CA*, pages 115–124. IEEE Computer Society, 2001.

[26] Object Management Group. *The Common Object Request Broker: Architecture and Specification Revision 2.3*. 492 Old Connecticut Path, Framingham, MA 01701, USA, December 1998.

[27] Object Management Group. *XML Meta Data Interchange (XMI) – Proposal to the OMG OA&DTF RFP 3: Stream-based Model Interchange Format (SMIF)*. 492 Old Connecticut Path, Framingham, MA 01701, USA, October 1998.

[28] A. Pnueli. The Temporal Logic of Programs. In *Proc. 18th IEEE Symp. Foundations of Computer Science*, pages 46–57, Providence, R.I., 1977.

[29] J. Rumbaugh, I. Jacobson, and G. Booch. *The Unified Modeling Language Reference Manual*. Addison Wesley, 1999.

[30] Sebastian Uchitel and Jeff Kramer. A Workbench for Synthesising Behaviour Models from Scenarios. In *Proc. of the 23$^{rd}$ Int. Conf. on Software Engineering, Toronto, Canada*, pages 188–197. ACM Press, 2001.

# Software Architecture for Correct Components Assembly

Paola Inverardi and Massimo Tivoli

University of L'Aquila
Dip. Informatica
fax: +390862433057
via Vetoio 1, 67100 L'Aquila
{inverard, tivoli}@di.univaq.it

**Abstract.** Correct automatic assembly in software components is an important issue in CBSE (Commercial-Off-The-Shelf). Building a system from reusable software components or from COTS (*Commercial-Off-The-Shelf*) components introduces a set of problems. One of the main problems in components assembly is related to the ability to properly manage the dynamic interactions of the components. Component assembling can result in architectural mismatches when trying to integrate components with incompatible interaction behavior like deadlock and other software anomalies. This problem represents a new challenge for system developers. The issue is not only in specifying and analyzing a set of properties rather in being able to enforce them out of a set of already implemented (local) behaviors. Our answer to this problem is a software architecture based approach in which the software architecture imposed on the assembly allows for detection and recovery of COTS integration anomalies. Starting from the specification of the system to be assembled and of its properties we develop a framework which automatically derives the glue code for the set of components in order to obtain a properties-satisfying system (i.e. the failure-free version of the system).

## 1  Introduction

Nowadays there is the need to built high quality software systems in short time. This moves developers toward reuse-based development methodologies. CBSE (*Component Based Software Engineering*) is a process focussed on the software systems design and developing by assembling reusable software components. Clemens (1995) describes the CBSE process as follows: *the CBSE is changing the methods to develop huge-size software systems. It adopts the philosophy "Buy! No Build!" followed by Fred Brooks et al. The CBSE moves the attention of the software developers to the software systems assembly (i.e. component assembly). The implementation has been replaced from the integration.*

Thus in CBSE the integration is the real challenge. Building a system from a set of COTS(*Commercial-Off-The-Shelf*) [26] components introduces a set of

M. Bernardo and P. Inverardi (Eds.): SFM 2003, LNCS 2804, pp. 92–121, 2003.
© Springer-Verlag Berlin Heidelberg 2003

problems. Many of these problems arise because of the nature of COTS components. They are truly black-box and developers have no method of looking inside the box. This limit is coupled with an insufficient behavioral specification of the component which does not allow to understand the component interaction behavior in a multi-component system. Component assembling can result in architectural mismatches [9] when trying to integrate components with incompatible interaction behavior like deadlock and other software anomalies. Thus if we want to assure that a component based system validates specified dynamic properties, we must take into account the component interaction behavior. In this context, the notion of software architecture assumes a key role since it represents the reference skeleton used to compose components and let them interact. In the software architecture domain, the interaction among the components is represented by the notion of software connector [2, 10].

Our approach to the assembly problem is to compose systems by assuming a well defined architectural style [15, 14] in such a way that it is possible to detect and to fix software anomalies. Moreover we assume that a specification of the desired assembled system is available and that a precise definition of the properties to satisfy exists. With these assumptions we are able to develop a framework that automatically derives the assembly code for a set of components so that, if possible, a properties-satisfying system is obtained (i.e. the failure-free version of the system). The assembly code implements an explicit software connector which mediates all interactions among the system components as a new component to be inserted in the composed system. The connector can then be analyzed and modified in such a way that the behavioral (i.e. functional) properties of the composed system are satisfied. Depending on the kind of property, the analysis of the connector is enough to obtain a property satisfying version of the system. Otherwise, the property is due to some component internal behavior and cannot be fixed without directly operating on the component code. In a component based setting in which we are assuming black-boxes components, this is the best we can expect to do. We assume that components behavior is only partially and indirectly specified by using bMSC (*basic Message Sequence Charts*) and HMSC (*High level MSC*) specifications [1] of the desired assembled system and we address behavioral properties of the assembly code together with different recovery strategies. The behavioral properties we deal with are the deadlock freeness property [15, 14] and generic coordination policies of the components interaction behavior [16].

The paper is organized as follows. Section 2 introduces background notions and theoretical foundations in order to understand our approach. Section 3 formalizes the method concerning the behavioral failures-free connectors synthesis which is also applied to an explanatory example. Section 4 describes a realistic application example of our approach. Section 5 presents related works and Section 6 discusses future work and concludes.

## 2   Background

In this section we provide the background needed to understand the approach formalized in Section 3.

### 2.1   The Reference Architectural Style

The architectural style we use, called *Connector Based Architecture* (CBA), is derived from C2 architectural style [22] and consists of components and connectors which define a notion of top and bottom. The top (bottom) of a component may be connected to the bottom (top) of a single connector. There is no bound on the number of components that may be attached to a single connector. Components can only communicate via connectors. It is disallowed the direct connection between connectors. Each component is connected to the connector through a synchronous communication channel. Components communicate synchronously by passing two type of messages: notifications and requests. A notification is sent downward, while a request is sent upward. Requests are service or data demands, while notifications are reply to requests, and they announce state changes or return data. Both components and connectors have a top-domain and a bottom-domain. A top-domain of a component or of a connector is the set of requests sent upward and of received notifications. A bottom-domain of a component or of a connector is the set of received requests received and of notifications sent downward. Connectors are responsible for the routing of messages and they exhibit a strictly sequential input-output behavior[1]. CBA is a generic layered style. Since it is always possible to decompose a $n$-layered CBA system in $n$ single-layered CBA systems (see the right side of Figure 1), in the following of this paper we will only deal with single layered systems. This decomposition is done by considering for each intermediate component (i.e. a component of an intermediate layer) two behavioral views: i) the component's behavior with respect to the messages exchanged on the component's top-domain and ii) the component's behavior with respect to the messages exchanged on the component's bottom-domain [15]. This decomposition is possible because each layer of a multi-layered CBA system is independent from the other ones. Thus to cope with multi-layered systems we apply the formalized approach for each single-layered sub-system.

In Figure 1 we show an instance of the CBA style made of two components and one connector.

### 2.2   CCS

For our purpose we need to summarize the most relevant definitions regarding CCS (*Calculus of Communicating Systems*), we refer to [23] for more details.

---

[1] Each input action is strictly followed by the corresponding output action.

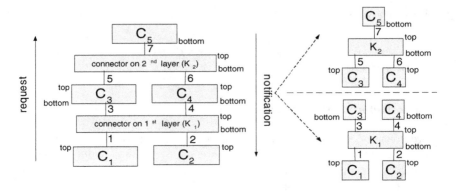

**Fig. 1.** An instance of the 2-layered CBA style and its decomposition

The CCS syntax is the following:

$$p ::= \mu.p \mid nil \mid p + p \mid p|p \mid p \backslash A \mid x \mid p[f]$$

Terms generated by $p$ (*Terms*) are called *process terms* (called also *processes* or *terms*); $x$ ranges over a set $\{X, Y, ..\}$, of process variables. A process variable is defined by a process definition $x \overset{def}{=} p$, ($p$ is called the expansion of $x$). As usual, there is a finite set of visible actions $Vis = \{a, \overline{a}, b, \overline{b}, ...\}$ over which $\alpha$ ranges, while $\mu, \nu$ range over $Act = Vis \cup \{\tau\}$, where $\tau$ denotes the so-called *internal action*. We denote by $\overline{\alpha}$ the action complement: if $\alpha = a$, then $\overline{\alpha} = \overline{a}$, while if $\alpha = \overline{a}$, then $\overline{\alpha} = a$. By $nil$ we denote the empty process. The operators to build process terms are prefixing ($\mu.p$), summation ($p + p$), parallel composition ($p|p$), restriction ($p \backslash A$) and relabelling ($p[f]$), where $A \subseteq Vis$ and $f : Vis \to Vis$.

An operational semantics $OP$ is a set of inference rules defining a relation $D \subseteq Terms \times Act \times Terms$. The relation is the least relation satisfying the rules. If $(p, \mu, q) \in D$, we write $p \overset{\mu}{\to}_{OP} q$. The rules defining the semantics of CCS [23], from now on referred to as $SOS$, are here recalled:

$$Act \quad \frac{}{\alpha.P \overset{\alpha}{\to} P} \qquad Synch \quad \frac{P \overset{\alpha}{\to} P', Q \overset{\overline{\alpha}}{\to} Q'}{P|Q \overset{\tau}{\to} P'|Q'}$$

$$Sum \quad \frac{P \overset{\alpha}{\to} P'}{P + Q \overset{\alpha}{\to} P'} \qquad Rel \quad \frac{P \overset{\alpha}{\to} P'}{P[f] \overset{f(\alpha)}{\to} P'[f]}$$

$$Comp \quad \frac{P \overset{\alpha}{\to} P'}{P|Q \overset{\alpha}{\to} P'|Q} \qquad Res \quad \frac{P \overset{\alpha}{\to} P', \alpha \notin L \cup \overline{L}}{P \backslash L \overset{\alpha}{\to} P' \backslash L}$$

$$Con \quad \frac{P \overset{\alpha}{\to} P', A \overset{def}{=} P}{A \overset{\alpha}{\to} P'}$$

The rules *Sum* and *Comp* have a symmetric version which is omitted.

A *labelled transition system (LTS)* (or simply *transition system*) $TS$ is a quadruple $(S, T, D, s_0)$, where $S$ is a set of states, $T$ is a set of transition labels, $s_0 \in S$ is the initial state, and $D \subseteq S \times T \times S$. A transition system is finite if $D$ is finite.

A finite computation of a transition system is a sequence $\mu_1 \mu_2 .. \mu_n$ of labels such that:
$$s_0 \xrightarrow{\mu_1}_{OP} .. \xrightarrow{\mu_n}_{OP} s_n.$$

Given a term $p$ (and a set of process variable definitions), and an operational semantics $OP$, $OP(p)$ is the transition system $(Terms, Act, D, p)$, where $D$ is the relation defined by $OP$. For example, $SOS(p)$ is the transition system defined by the SOS semantics for the term $p$. CCS can be used to define a wide class of systems, that ranges from Turing machines to finite systems [27]; therefore, in general, CCS terms cannot be represented as finite state systems. For our purposes we will in the following assume that all the systems we will deal with are finite state. In general a correspondence between CCS terms and LTSs can be always defined. A CCS term may be encoded in LTS as follows:

- LTS states are CCS terms;
- transitions given by $\rightarrow_{OP}$, i. e. by operational semantics;
- the LTS start state is the one corresponding to the encoded CCS term;

  and any finite-state LTS can be encoded in CCS as follows:

- associate a process $S_i$ to each LTS state $s_i$;
- in declaration of $S_i$, sum (summation operator $+$) together terms of form $\alpha.S_j$ for each transition $s_i \xrightarrow{\alpha} s_j$ in LTS;
- the CCS term is the one corresponding to the encoded LTS start state.

## 2.3   Configuration Formalization

In order to describe components and system behaviors we use the CCS [23] notation. For the purpose of this paper this is a fair assumption. Actually our framework allows to automatically derive these CCS descriptions from the HMSC and bMSC specifications [1] of the system [29, 25]. These kinds of specifications are common in practice thus CCS can merely be regarded as an internal to the framework specification language. In Section 4 we show a complete treatment of a case study starting from a HMSC and bMSC specification of the system. Since HMSC and bMSC specifications model finite-state behaviors of a system we will use finite-state CCS. To our purposes we need to formalize two different ways to compose a system. The first one is called *Connector Free Architecture* (CFA) and is defined as *a set of components directly connected in a synchronous way* (i.e. without a connector). The second one is called *Connector Based Architecture* (CBA) and is defined as *a set of components directly connected in a synchronous way to one or more connectors*:

**Definition 1 (Connector Free Architecture (CFA)).**
$CFA \equiv (C_1 \mid C_2 \mid ... \mid C_n)\backslash\bigcup_{i=1}^{n} Act_i$ *where for all* $i = 1,..,n,$ $Act_i$ *is the actions set of the CCS process* $C_i$.

**Definition 2 (Connector Based Architecture (CBA)).**
$CBA \equiv (C_1[f_1] \mid C_2[f_2] \mid ... \mid C_n[f_n] \mid K)\backslash\bigcup_{i=1}^{n} Act_i[f_i]$ *where for all* $i = 1,..,n,$ $Act_i$ *is the actions set of the CCS process* $C_i$ *and* $f_i$ *is a relabelling functions such that* $f_i(\alpha) = \alpha_i$ *for all* $\alpha \in Act_i$ *and* $K$ *is the CSS process representing the connector.*

$\alpha$ in a CFA denotes a visible action (i.e. an input action or an output action). $\alpha_i$ in the corresponding CBA denotes the same visible action performed on the communication channel $i$. The channel $i$ connects the component has performed $\alpha_i$ with the connector. In Figure 2 we show an example of a CFA system and of the corresponding CBA system. The double circled states represent initial states.

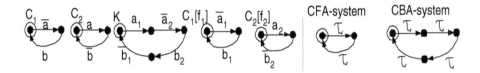

**Fig. 2.** CFA and corresponding CBA

In Figure 3, we show a graphic representation of the CFA and CBA systems showed in Figure 2.

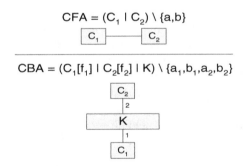

**Fig. 3.** A graphic representation of the CFA and CBA systems of Figure 2

## 3   Approach Description

The problem we want to treat can be informally phrased as follows: *given a CFA system T for a set of black-box interacting components and a set of coordination properties P automatically derive the corresponding CBA system V which satisfies every property in P.*

We are assuming that a specification of the system to be assembled is provided in terms of bMSCs and HMSCs. Referring to Definition 1, we also assume that for each component a description of its behavior as finite-state CCS term (i.e. LTS *Labelled Transitions System*) has been automatically derived from the bMSCs and HMSCs specification [29, 25]. Moreover we assume that a specification of the coordination properties to be checked exists. In the following, by means of a working example, we discuss our method proceeding in three steps as illustrated in Figure 4.

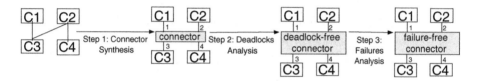

**Fig. 4.** 3 step method

The first step builds a connector following the CBA style constraints. The second step performs the deadlocks detection and recovery process. Finally, the third step performs the check of the specified coordination properties against the deadlock-free connector model and then synthesizes a properties-satisfying connector model.

Note that although in principle we could carry on the second and third step together, for the sake of clarity we decided to keep them separate. Actually, the current framework implementation follows this schema.

### 3.1   First Step: Connector Synthesis

The first step of our method (see Figure 4) starts with a CFA system and produces the equivalent CBA system. It is worthwhile noticing that this can always be done [15]. As we will see in Section 3.2 the two systems behave equivalently, under a suitable notion of equivalence. We proceed as follows:

i) By taking into account the bMSCs and the HMSCs specification of the composed system and the CFA architectural style, we first derive the CCS specification for each component and then for each finite-state CCS component specification (in the CFA system) we derive the corresponding AC-Graph. AC-Graphs model components behavior in terms of interactions with the external environment. The external environment for a component $C_i$ is represented by the parallel composition of the components $C_j, j \neq i$. The term *actual* emphasizes the difference between component behavior and the intended, or assumed, behavior of the environment. AC graphs model components in an intuitive way. Each node represents a state of the component and the root node represents its initial state. Each arc represents the possible transition into a new state where the transition label is the action performed by the component. AC-Graph carry on information on both labels and states:

**Definition 3 (AC-Graph).** *Let $\langle S_i, L_i, \rightarrow_i, s_i \rangle$ be a labelled transition system of a component $C_i$. The corresponding Actual Behavior (AC) Graph $AC_i$ is a tuple of the form*
$\langle N_{AC_i}, LN_{AC_i}, A_{AC_i}, LA_{AC_i}, s_i \rangle$ *where $N_{AC_i} = S_i$ is a set of nodes, $LN_{AC_i}$ is a set of state labels, $LA_{AC_i}$ is a set of arc labels with $\tau$ ( $LA_{AC_i} = L_i \bigcup \tau$), $A_{AC_i} \subseteq N_{AC_i} \times LA_{AC_i} \times N_{AC_i}$ is a set of arcs and $s_i$ is the root node.*

- *We shall write $g \xrightarrow{l} h$, if there is an arc $(g, l, h) \in A_{AC_i}$. We shall also write $g \rightarrow h$ meaning that $g \xrightarrow{l} h$ for some $l \in LA_{AC_i}$.*
- *If $t = l_1 \cdots l_n \in LA^*_{AC_i}$, then we write $g \xrightarrow{t}{}^* h$, if $g \xrightarrow{l_1} \cdots \xrightarrow{l_n} h$. We shall also write $g \longrightarrow^* h$, meaning that $g \xrightarrow{t}{}^* h$ for some $t \in LA^*_{AC_i}$.*
- *We shall write $g \xRightarrow{l} h$, if $g \xrightarrow{t}{}^* h$ for some $t \in \tau^*.l.\tau^*$.*

In Figure 5 we show the AC-Graphs of the CFA system of our working example.

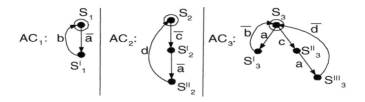

**Fig. 5.** AC-Graphs of the example

ii) By taking into account the deadlock freeness property and the CFA architectural style, we derive from AC-Graph the requirements on its environment that guarantee deadlock freedom. Referring to Definition 1, we recall that the environment of a component $C_i$ is represented by the set of components $C_j$ ($j \neq i$) in parallel. A component will not block if its environment can always provide the actions it requires for changing state. This is represented as AS-Graphs (Figure 6):

**Definition 4 (AS-Graph).** *Let* $(N_{AC_i}, LN_{AC_i}, A_{AC_i}, LA_{AC_i}, s_i)$ *be the AC-Graph* $AC_i$ *of a component* $C_i$, *then the corresponding ASsumption (AS) Graph* $AS_i$ *is* $(N_{AS_i}, LN_{AS_i}, A_{AS_i}, LA_{AS_i}, s_i)$ *where* $N_{AS_i} = N_{AC_i}$, $LN_{AS_i} = LN_{AC_i}$, $LA_{AS_i} = LA_{AC_i}$ *and*
$$A_{AS} = \{(\nu, \bar{a}, \nu') \mid (\nu, a, \nu') \in A_{AC}\} \bigcup \{(\nu, b, \nu') \mid (\nu, \bar{b}, \nu') \in A_{AC}\}.$$

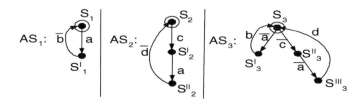

**Fig. 6.** AS-Graphs of the example

Analogously to AC-Graphs we have one graph for each component. The only difference from AC-graphs is in the arcs labels, which are symmetric since they model the environment as each component expects it.

iii) Now if we consider Definition 2 (i.e. by taking into account CBA architectural style), the environment of a component can only be represented by connectors. Thus we can refine the definition of AS-Graph in a new graph, the EX-Graph, that represents the behavior that the component expects from the connector (Figure 7). We know that the connector performs strictly sequential input-output operations only, thus if it receives an input from a component it will then output the received input message to the destination component. Analogously, if the connector outputs a message, this means that immediately before it inputs that message. Intuitively, for each transition labelled with a visible action $\alpha$ ($\bar{\alpha}$) in the AS graph, in the corresponding EX graph there are two strictly sequential transition labelled $\alpha_i$ and $\overline{\alpha_?}$ ($\alpha_?$ and $\overline{\alpha_i}$), respectively. Let $C_i$ the component for which we are deriving from the AS-Graph the corresponding EX-Graph; referring to CBA in Section 2.3, action $\alpha_i$ ($\overline{\alpha_i}$) denotes an input (output) action $\alpha$ towards the connector on the communication channel that connects $C_i$ to the connector (i. e. the communication channel $i$). Action $\alpha_?$ ($\overline{\alpha_?}$) denote an input (output) action $\alpha$ towards the connector on a communication channel that connects the connector to a component different than $C_i$; thus this communication channel is unknown for $C_i$ (we denotes this unknown channel by using the question mark):

**Definition 5 (EX-Graph).** *Let* $(N_{AS_i}, LN_{AS_i}, A_{AS_i}, LA_{AS_i}, s_i)$ *be the AS-Graph* $AS_i$ *of a component* $C_i$; *we define the connector EXpected (EX) Graph* $EX_i$ *from the component* $C_i$ *the graph* $(N_{EX_i}, LN_{EX_i}, A_{EX_i}, LA_{EX_i}, s_i)$, *where:*

- $N_{EX_i} = N_{AS_i}$ and $LN_{EX_i} = LN_{AS_i}$
- $A_{EX_i}$ and $LA_{EX_i}$ are empty
- $\forall\ (\mu,\ \alpha,\ \mu') \in A_{AS_i}$, with $\alpha \neq \tau$
  - *Create a new node $\mu_{new}$ with a new unique label, add the node to $N_{EX_i}$ and the unique label to $LN_{EX_i}$*
  - *if $(\mu,\ \alpha,\ \mu')$ is such that $\alpha$ is an input action (i.e. $\alpha = a$, for some a )*
    * *add the labels $a_i$ and $\overline{a}_?$ to $LA_{EX_i}$*
    * *add $(\mu,\ a_i,\ \mu_{new})$ and $(\mu_{new},\ \overline{a}_?,\ \mu')$ to $A_{EX_i}$*
  - *if $(\mu,\ \alpha,\ \mu')$ is such that $\alpha$ is an output action (i.e. $\alpha = \overline{a}$, for some a )*
    * *add the labels $\overline{a}_i$ and $a_?$ to $LA_{EX_i}$*
    * *add $(\mu,\ a_?,\ \mu_{new})$ and $(\mu_{new},\ \overline{a}_i,\ \mu')$ to $A_{EX_i}$*
- $\forall\ (\mu,\ \tau,\ \mu') \in A_{AS_i}$ add $\tau$ to $LA_{EX_i}$ and $(\mu,\ \tau,\ \mu')$ to $A_{EX_i}$

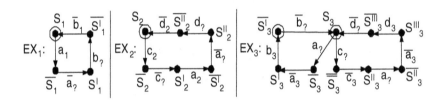

**Fig. 7.** EX-Graphs of the example

iv) Each EX-Graph represents a partial view of the connector behavior. It is partial since it only reflects the expectations of a single component. We derive the connector global behavior through an EX-Graphs unification algorithm. We refer to [13, 15] for a formal definition of the EX-Graphs unification algorithm. Informally this unification algorithm is based on syntactic unification. For each step the unification procedure attempts to match actions on known communication channels (i.e. terms) in a EX-Graph with actions on unknown communication channels (i.e. variables) in another EX-Graph. Each match represents a new transition (in the connector graph) from the current node to the next new (i.e. not yet considered) adjacent node. Then the algorithm proceeds in the unification procedure from each adjacent node. It is worthwhile noticing that in a generic step it could be possible to not find matches representing new transitions from the current node. In this case we obtain a stop node (i.e. a node without outgoing arcs) in the connector graph. In Figure 8 we show the effect of the first step of the above unification procedure on the EX-Graphs of our working example.

In Figure 9 we show the connector graph $K$ for the example illustrated in this section. The $i - th$ generated node of the connector graph is annotated as $K_i$ and its label is reported in the figure. The resulting CBA system is built as defined in Definition 2.

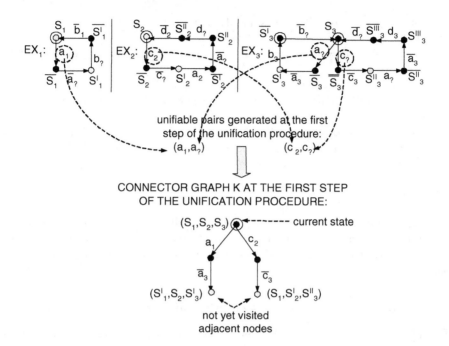

CONNECTOR GRAPH K AT THE FIRST STEP
OF THE UNIFICATION PROCEDURE:

**Fig. 8.** An example of execution of the first step of the unification procedure

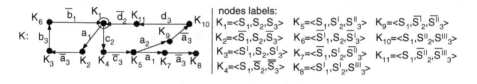

**Fig. 9.** Connector graph $K$ of the example

## 3.2  Correctness and Completeness of the Approach

In [15] we have proved that the CBA-system obtained by the connector synthesis process is equivalent to the corresponding CFA-system. To do this we have proved the following proposition:

**Proposition 1.** *Let $T$ be a CFA-system, and let $V$ be the corresponding CBA-system; then $T$ can be CB-simulated from $V$.*

Where we define the notion of CB-Simulation as follows:

**Definition 6 (CB-Simulation).** *Let $S$ and $T$ be two systems and $s$ and $t$ two generic states of the systems;*

– *a relation $\leq_{CB}$ is called* CB-simulation *if $s \leq_{CB} t$ then:*
  - *the label of s is equal to the label of t;*
  - *if $s \rightarrow s'$ then there exists $n > 0$, $t_0, ..., t_n$ such that $t = t_0$ and for all $i < n$ :*
    *$t_i \rightarrow t_{i+1}$, $s' \leq_{CB} t_n$.*
– *A state t CB-simulates a state s ($s \leq_{CB} t$) if it exists a relation of CB-simulation between s and t*
– *A path $\sigma$ CB-simulates a path $\rho$, ($\rho \leq_{CB} \sigma$), if $\rho$ can be partitioned as $\rho_1 \rho_2...$ and $\sigma$ can be partitioned as $\sigma_1 \sigma_2...$ in such a way that, for all j, the sequences $\rho_j$ and $\sigma_j$ are not empty and $\rho_j \leq_{CB} \sigma_j$*

In other words we have proved the correctness of the synthesis by proving that the CFA-system can be simulated by the synthesized CBA-system under a suitable notion of *"state based"*[2] equivalence called CB-Simulation. The starting point of CB-Simulation is the stuttering equivalence [24]. In [15], we have also proved that the connector does not introduce in the system any new logic (completeness of the synthesis).

## 3.3 Second Step: Deadlocks Analysis and Recovery

The second step concerns the deadlock freeness analysis, which is performed on the CBA system. Depending on the deadlock type we can operate on the connector in order to obtain a deadlock-free equivalent system. We distinguish between: i) deadlocks due to wrong coordination among components and ii) deadlocks due to wrong components assumptions.

The former are deadlocks due to a bad coordination of components interactions, while the latter are due to components incorrect internal behaviors (e.g. buffer size). It is worthwhile recalling we are dealing with black-box components, whose only known behavior concerns the interactions with the others components into the system. This means that we can only operate on the components interaction behavior and we cannot operate on the components internal behavior. Thus we can only deal with wrong coordination deadlocks. In a black-box setting this is the best we can expect to do in terms of deadlocks prevention. In terms of deadlocks detection we could detect not only wrong coordination deadlocks but also wrong components assumption deadlocks [15]. To do this we need a more complete specification than the bMSCs and HMSCs specification. Actually we need to know not only the observable components interactions but also the hidden interactions of a component. An hidden interaction represents the situation in which the component changes (in an autonomous way) its internal state because of some internal event (e.g. buffer overflow). An hidden interaction is represented on the component's AC-Graph through a $\tau$ transition. Refer to [15] for a detailed description of the detection process of wrong components assumptions deadlocks.

---

[2] By definition, both CFA and CBA systems exhibit only $\tau$ transitions.

We can formally define wrong coordination deadlocks as follows:

**Definition 7 (Wrong coordination deadlock).** *Let $K$ be the connector graph synthesized by the unification of EX-Graphs $EX_1, .., EX_n$ of the CFA-system components $C_1, .., C_n$ respectively. We define a wrong coordination deadlock of $K$ as a stop node of $K$ (i.e. a node without outgoing arcs).*

If a wrong coordination deadlock is possible, then this results in a precise connector behavior that is detectable by observing the connector graph. To fix this problem it is enough to prune all the finite branches of the connector transition graph. The pruned connector preserves all the correct (with respect to deadlock freeness) behaviors of CFA-system (Proposition 2). Refer to [15] for a proof of Proposition 2. In Figure 10 we show the wrong coordination deadlock-free connector graph.

**Proposition 2.** *Let $T$ be a CFA-system, let $V_{df}$ be the corresponding CBA-system based on wrong coordination deadlock-free connector and let $\Pi_T^{inf}$ be $T$ without the finite paths; then $\Pi_T^{inf}$ can be CB-Simulated from $V_{df}$.*

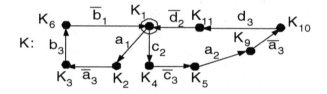

**Fig. 10.** Deadlock-free connector graph of the example

## 3.4   Third Step: Behavioral Failures Analysis and Recovery

In this section we formalize the third step of the method of Figure 4. This step concerns properties enforcing on the connector graph.

### General Behavioral Properties Specification:

The behavioral properties we want to enforce are related to behaviors of the CFA system that concern coordination policies of the interaction behavior of the components in the CFA system. The CFA behaviors that do not comply to the specified properties represent behavioral failures. A behavior of the CFA system is given in terms of sequences of actions performed by components in the CFA system. In specifying properties we have to distinguish an action $\alpha$ performed by a component $C_i$ with the same action $\alpha$ performed by a component $C_j$ $(i \neq j)$. Thus, referring to Definition 1, the behavioral properties (i.e.

coordination properties) can only be specified in terms of visible actions of the components $C_1[f_1], C_2[f_2], .., C_n[f_n]$ where for each $i = 1, .., n$, $f_i$ is a relabelling function such that $f_i(\alpha) = \alpha_i$ for all $\alpha \in Act_i$ and $Act_i$ is the actions set for $C_i$. By referring to the usual model checking approach [7] we specify every property through a temporal logic formalism. We choose $LTL$ [7] (*Linerar-time Temporal Logic*) as specification language. We define $AP = \{\gamma \ : \ \gamma = l_i \ \vee \ \gamma = \bar{l}_i \ with \ l \in LA_{AC_i}, l \neq \tau, i = 1, .., n\}$ as the set of atomic proposition on which we define the LTL formulas corresponding to the coordination policies.

## LTL Syntax:

Referring to [7], we give the standard syntax for the LTL. Given a set of atomic propositions $AP$, a LTL formula is either:

- if $p \in AP$, then $p$ is a LTL formula;
- if $f$ and $g$ are LTL formulas, then:
  - $!f$ (logical not),
  - $f \vee g$ (logical or),
  - $f \wedge g$ (logical and),
  - $f \longrightarrow g$ (logical implication $\equiv !f \vee g$),
  - $\mathbf{X}f$ ("next time" temporal operator),
  - $\mathbf{F}f$ ("eventually" or "in the future" temporal operator),
  - $\mathbf{G}f$ ("always" or "globally" temporal operator),
  - $f\mathbf{U}g$ ("until" temporal operator),
  - and $f\mathbf{R}g$ ("release" temporal operator) are LTL formulas.

## LTL Semantics:

Referring to [7], we give the standard semantics for the LTL. We define the semantics of LTL with respect to a Kripke structure. Recall that a Kripke structure $M$ is a quadruple $(S, R, S_0, L)$, where $S$ is the set of states; $R \subseteq S \times S$ is the total transition relation; $L : S \to 2^{AP}$ is a function that labels each state with a set of atomic proposition true in that state; and $S_0 \subseteq S$ is the set of initial states. A *path* in $M$ is an infinite sequence of states, $\pi = s_0, s_1, ..$ such that for every $i \geq 0$ $(s_i, s_{i+1}) \in R$ and $s_0 \in S_0$. We use $\pi^i$ to denote the *suffix* of $\pi$ starting at $s_i$.

If $f$ is a LTL formula the notion $M, \pi^i \models f$ means that $f$ holds along every path starting from the state $s_i$ of the path $\pi$ in the Kripke structure $M$. The relation $\models$ is defined inductively as follows (assuming that $f$ and $g$ are LTL formulas):

- for all $f \in AP$, $M, \pi^i \models f$ iff $f \in L(s_i)$;
- $M, \pi^i \models !f$ iff not $M, \pi^i \models f$;
- $M, \pi^i \models f \vee g$ iff $M, \pi^i \models f$ or $M, \pi^i \models g$;

- $M, \pi^i \models f \wedge g$ iff $M, \pi^i \models f$ and $M, \pi^i \models g$;
- $M, \pi^i \models f \longrightarrow g$ iff not $M, \pi^i \models f$ or $M, \pi^i \models g$;
- $M, \pi^i \models \mathbf{X}f$ iff $M, \pi^{i+1} \models f$;
- $M, \pi^i \models \mathbf{F}f$ iff there exists a $k \geq i$ such that $M, \pi^k \models f$;
- $M, \pi^i \models \mathbf{G}f$ iff for all $k \geq i$, $M, \pi^k \models f$;
- $M, \pi^i \models f\mathbf{U}g$ iff there exists a $k \geq i$ such that $M, \pi^k \models g$ and for all $i \leq j < k$, $M, \pi^j \models f$;
- $M, \pi^i \models f\mathbf{R}g$ iff for all $k \geq i$, if for every $j < k$, not $M, \pi^j \models f$ then $M, \pi^k \models g$.

### Enforcing a Behavioral Property:

The semantics of a LTL formula is defined with respect to a model represented by a Kripke structure. We consider as Kripke structure corresponding to the connector graph $K$ a connector model $KS_K$ that represents the Kripke structure of $K$. $KS_K$ is defined as follows:

**Definition 8 (Kripke structure of a connector graph $K$).** Let $(N, LN, LA, A, k_1)$ be the connector graph $K$. We define the Kripke Structure of $K$, the Kripke structure $KS_K = (V, T, \{k_1\}, LV)$ where $V = N$, $T = A$, $LV = 2^{LA}$ with $LV(k_1) = \{\alpha_i : LA((\overline{k}, k_1)) = \alpha_i, (\overline{k}, k_1) \in A\}$. For each $v \in V$ then $LV(v)$ is interpreted as the set of atomic propositions true in state $v$.

In Figure 11, we show the Kripke structure of $K$. The node with an incoming little-arrow is the initial state (i.e. $k_1$).

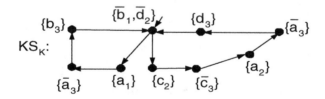

**Fig. 11.** Kripke structure of $K$

In Section 3.4 we have described how we can specify a property in terms of desired CFA behaviors. We have also said that all the undesired behaviors represent CFA failures. Analogously to deadlocks analysis, we can solve behavioral failures of the CFA system that are identifiable in the corresponding CBA system with precise behaviors of the synthesized connector. A connector behavior is simply an execution path into the connector graph. An execution path is a sequence of state's transition labels. It is worthwhile noticing that the behavioral properties (i.e. coordination properties) that we specify for the CFA system are corresponding to behavioral properties of the connector in the CBA system. In fact every action $\gamma = \alpha_i \in AP$ can be seen as the action $\bar{\alpha}$ (into the connector graph) performed on the communication channel that connects $C_i$ to the connector. This is true for construction (see Section 3.1). Thus let $P$ be a behavioral property specification (i.e. LTL formula) for the CFA system, we can translate $P$ in another behavioral property: $P_{cba}$. $P_{cba}$ is automatically obtained by applying the CCS complement operator to the atomic propositions in $P$. $P_{cba}$ is the property specification for the CBA system corresponding to $P$. Then we translate $P_{cba}$ in the corresponding Büchi Automaton [7] $B_{P_{cba}}$:

**Definition 9 (Büchi Automaton).** *A Büchi Automaton B is a 5-tuple*
$< S, A, \triangle, q_0, F >$, *where S is a finite set of states, A is a set of actions,* $\triangle \subseteq S \times A \times S$ *is a set of transitions , $q_0 \in S$ is the initial state, and $F \subseteq S$ is a set of accepting states. An execution of B on an infinite word $w = a_0 a_1 ...$ over A is an infinite sequence $\sigma = q_0 q_1 ...$ of elements of S, where $(q_i, a_i, q_{i+1}) \in \triangle, \forall i \geq 0$. An execution of B is accepting if it contains some accepting state of B an infinite number of times. B accepts a word w if there exists an accepting execution of B on w.*

Referring to our example we consider the following behavioral property: $P = F((\bar{a}_1 \wedge X(!\bar{a}_1 U \bar{a}_2)) \vee (\bar{a}_2 \wedge X(!\bar{a}_2 U \bar{a}_1)))$. This property specifies all CFA system behaviors that guarantee the evolution of all components in the system. It specifies that the components $C_1$ and $C_2$ can perform the action $a$ by necessarily using an alternating coordination policy. In other words it means that if the component $C_1$ performs an action $a$ then $C_1$ cannot perform $a$ again if $C_2$ has not performed $a$ and viceversa. The connector to be synthesized will avoid starvation by satisfying this property. In Figure 12 we show $B_{P_{cba}}$. We recall that $P_{cba} = F((a_1 \wedge X(!a_1 U a_2)) \vee (a_2 \wedge X(!a_2 U a_1)))$; $p_0$ and $p_2$ are the initial and accepting state respectively.

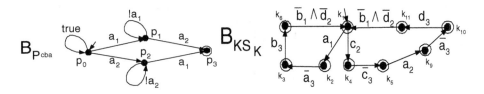

**Fig. 12.** Büchi Automata $B_{P_{cba}}$ and $B_{KS_K}$ of $P_{cba}$ and $KS_K$ respectively

Given a Büchi Automaton $A$, $L(A)$ is the *language* consisting of all words accepted by $A$. Moreover to a Kripke structure $T$ corresponds a Büchi Automaton $B_T$ [7]. We can derive $B_{KS_K}$ as the Büchi Automaton corresponding to $KS_K$ (see Figure 12). The double-circled states are accepting states.

Given $B_{KS_K} = (N, \Delta, \{s\}, N)$ and $B_P = (S, \Gamma, \{v\}, F)$ the method performs the following enforcing procedure in order to synthesize a deadlock-free connector graph that satisfies the property $P$:

1. build the automaton that accepts $L(B_{KS_K}) \cap L(B_{P_{cba}})$; this automaton is defined as $B_{intersection}^{K,P} = (S \times N, \Delta', \{< v, s >\}, F \times N)$ where $(< r_i, q_j > , a, < r_m, q_n >) \in \Delta'$ if and only if $(r_i, a, r_m) \in \Gamma$ and $(q_j, a, q_n) \in \Delta$;
2. if $B_{intersection}^{K,P_{cba}}$ is not empty return $B_{intersection}^{K,P_{cba}}$ as the Büchi Automaton corresponding to the $P$-satisfying execution paths of $K$.

In Figure 13, we show $B_{intersection}^{K,P_{cba}}$.

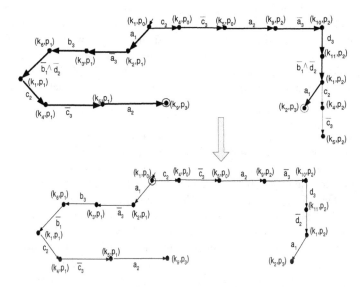

**Fig. 13.** $B_{intersection}^{K,P_{cba}}$ and deadlock-free property-satisfying connector graph of the explanatory example

Finally our method derives from $B_{intersection}^{K,P_{cba}}$ the corresponding connector graph. This graph is constructed by considering the execution paths of $B_{intersection}^{K,P_{cba}}$ that are only *accepting* (see the path made of bold arrows in Figure 13); we define an *accepting execution path* of $B_{intersection}^{K,P_{cba}}$ as follows:

**Definition 10 (Accepting execution path of $B_{intersection}^{K,P_{cba}}$).** Let $B_{intersection}^{K,P_{cba}} = (S \times N, \Delta', \{< v, s >\}, F \times N)$ be the automaton that accepts $L(B_{KS_K}) \cap L(B_{P_{cba}})$. We define an accepting execution path of $B_{intersection}^{K,P_{cba}}$ a sequence of states $\gamma = s_1, s_2, .., s_n$ such that $\forall\ i = 1, .., n\ :\ s_i \in\ S \times N$; for $1 \leq\ i \leq\ n - 1,\ (s_i, s_{i+1}) \in\ \Delta'$ and $(s_n, s_1) \in\ \Delta'$ or $(s_n, s_1) \notin\ \Delta'$; and $\exists\ k = 1, .., n\ :\ k \in\ F \times N$.

It is worthwhile noticing that (depending on the property) an accepting execution path of $B_{intersection}^{K,P_{cba}}$ could be also cyclic (for example if we consider a property using the *always* temporal operator). In this case (in order to build the property-satisfying connector graph) we do not consider the cyclic execution paths without accepting states (refer to [13] for an example in which we find cyclic accepting execution paths in $B_{intersection}^{K,P_{cba}}$).

In Figure 13, we show the deadlock-free property-satisfying connector graph for our explanatory example. Depending on the property, this graph could contain finite paths (i.e. paths terminating with a stop node). Note that at this stage the stop nodes representing accepting states. In fact we have obtained the deadlock-free property-satisfying connector graph by considering only the accepting execution paths of $B_{intersection}^{K,P_{cba}}$, thus stop nodes represent connector states satisfying the property. Once the connector has reached an accepting stop node it will return to its initial state waiting for a new request from an its client. Returning to the initial state is not explicitly represented in the deadlock-free property-satisfying connector graph but it will be implicitly considered in the automatic derivation of the code implementing the deadlock-free property-satisfying connector.

By visiting this graph and by exploiting the information stored in its states and transitions we can automatically derive the code that implements the P-satisfying deadlock-free connector (i.e. the coordinator component) analogously to what done for deadlock-free connectors [14]. The implementation refers to Microsoft COM (*Component Object Model*) components and uses C++ wiht ATL (*Active Template Library*) as programming environment. A single-layered CFA system can be considered a client-server COM system. Into the CFA of our example we have two COM clients components ($C_1$ and $C_2$) and one COM server component ($C_3$). $C_3$ exports to its clients an interface $IC3$ declaring two methods: input actions $a$ and $c$ on $AC_3$ (see Figure 5). All the other actions ($\overline{b}$ and $\overline{d}$ on $AC_3$) are responses to the requests of $a$ and $c$. The connector component $K$ implements the COM interface $IC3$ of the component $C_3$ by defining a COM class $K$ and by implementing a wrapping mechanism in order to wrap the requests that $C_1$ and $C_2$ perform on component $C_3$ (actions $\overline{a}$ and $\overline{c}$ on $AC_1$ and $AC_2$ of Figure 5). In the following we show fragments of the IDL (*Interface Definition Language*) definition for $K$, of the $K$ COM library and of the $K$ COM class respectively. *c3Obj* is an instance of the inner COM server corresponding to $C_3$ and encapsulated into connector component $K$.

```
import ic3.idl; ... library K_Lib {
   ...
   coclass K {
      [default] interface IC3;
   }
}
```

...

```
class K : public IC3 {
    // stores the current state of the connector
    private static int sLbl;

    // stores the current state of the
    // property automaton
    private static int pState;

    // stores the number of clients
    private static int clientsCounter = 0;

    // channel's number of a client
    private int chId;

    // COM smart pointer; is a reference to
    // the C3 server object
    private static C3* c3Obj;

    ...

    // the constructor
    K() {
        sLbl = 1;
        pState = 0;
        clientsCounter++;
        chId = clientsCounter;
        c3Obj = new C3();
        ...
    }

    // implemented methods
    ...
}
```

In the following we show the deadlock-free property-satisfying code implementing the methods *a* and *c* of the connector component $K$. Even if the property $P$ of our example considers a coordination policy only for action $a$, we have
to coordinate also the requests of $c$ in order to satisfy $P$. Actually, as we can
see in Figure 13, the deadlock-free property-satisfying connector has execution
paths in which transitions labelled with $c$ there exist.

```
HRESULT a(/* params list of a */) {
    if(sLbl == 1) {
        if((chId == 1) && (pState == 0)) {
            return c3Obj->a(/* params list of a */);
            pState = 1; sLbl = 1; //it goes on the state preceding the next
                                  //request of a method from a client
        }
```

```
        else if((chId == 1) && (pState == 2)) {
            return c3Obj->a(/* params list of a */);
            pState = 0; sLbl = 1; //since it has found an accepting stop node,
                                  //it returns to its initial state
        }
    }
    else if(sLbl == 5) {
        if((chId == 2) && (pState == 1)) {
            return c3Obj->a(/* params list of a */);
            pState = 0; sLbl = 1; //since it has found an accepting stop node,
                                  //it returns to its initial state
        }
        else if((chId == 2) && (pState == 0)) {
            return c3Obj->a(/* params list of a */);
            pState = 2; sLbl = 1; //it goes on the state preceding the next
                                  //request of a method from a client
        }
    }

    return E_HANDLE;
}

HRESULT c(/* params list of c */) {
    if(sLbl == 1) {
        if((chId == 2) && (pState == 1)) {
            return c3Obj->a(/* params list of a */);
            pState = 1; sLbl = 5; //it goes on the state preceding the next
                                  //request of a method from a client
        }
        else if((chId == 2) && (pState == 0)) {
            return c3Obj->a(/* params list of a */);
            pState = 0; sLbl = 5; //it goes on the state preceding the next
                                  //request of a method from a client
        }
    }

    return E_HANDLE;
}
```

## 3.5   Correctness of the Approach

The following proposition states the correctness of the property enforcing procedure. For the complete proof, please refer to [18]. We prove that the CBA-system based on the property-satisfying deadlock-free connector preserves all the property-satisfying behaviors of the corresponding deadlock-free CFA-system.

**Proposition 3.** *Let $T$ be a CFA-system, let $V_P$ be the corresponding CBA-system based on a $P$-satisfying deadlock-free connector and let $\Pi_T^P$ be $T$ without the finite paths then $\Pi_T^P$ can be CB-Simulated from $V_P$ except for the execution* paths $\rho$ of $\Pi_T^P$ that are also execution paths of the automaton $B_{!P}$ (! is the logical not).

## 4  An Application Example

In this section we present a real-scale application example of the approach formalized in Section 3. We use our approach to build from a set of suitable COTS components a collaborative writing (CW) system [20, 19, 8, 21]. Refer to [17, 16] for a detailed description of the CW system and of the complete application of the approach to it. In this paper we just reuse a sub-system of the CW system described in [17, 16]. We apply our approach to this sub-system in order to derive an assembly satisfying a property different than the property enforced for the whole system in [17, 16].

Based on a detailed analysis [17] of many CW systems [20, 19, 8, 21] we can identify the COTS computational components that provide the main features of a CW system. These four types of COTS components are showed in Figure 14.

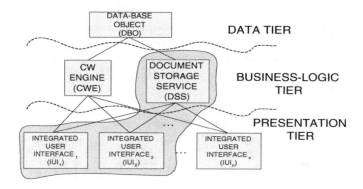

**Fig. 14.** Architecture of the CW system

Our CW system is a three-tier application. According to our approach, it is composed through coordinators components automatically synthesized in order to satisfy a specified coordination policy. In the following, we briefly describe our CW system and apply our approach to a sub-system of it (namely the grey area in Figure 14).

In order to build our CW system we have identified the following four COTS components. 1) **DBO**: This component is a data-base. The data-base stores all group awareness information useful to support a group activity. 2) **CWE**: This is a CW engine; it provides all services useful to perform a group activity in the CW context. It is an handler of all group awareness information stored in

*DBO* and of the typical CW activities [17]. 3) **DSS**: A document is a set of document's partitions. This component is an abstraction of the physical container of the shared documents that are logically partitioned according to their structure. In an asynchronous working mode we use version-controlled documents. In a synchronous working mode it is shared among the users and we have to use pessimistic concurrency control. Referring to the version-controlled hierarchical documents [21], a local copy of a document is an alternative and the globally shared document is the last document's version. When a user wants to work in asynchronous mode, *DSS* expects that all the other users work in asynchronous mode too. In this way *DSS* can maintain a consistent version of the globally shared document and it evolves in a new consistent version only after the merging of all users alternatives. 4) **IUI**: This component is an integrated environment of tools for editing, navigation, display of awareness communication among the group members and import and export of data from external applications. It is composed of a CW user interface supporting all CW operations, editors for many data types, communication tools such as e-mail and chat.

Let us suppose that the designer of the composed CW system provides a behavioral specification in terms of bMSCs and HMSCs see Figures 15 and 16. The continued lines in the bMSCs are method calls; the hatched lines are the corresponding responses. In our example we consider only two instances of $IUI_i$: $IUI_1$ and $IUI_2$. Moreover we provide the system's behavioral specification only for the part of the CW system identified in the grey area of Figure14. This sub-system is composed by the components $IUI_1$, $IUI_2$ and *DSS*.

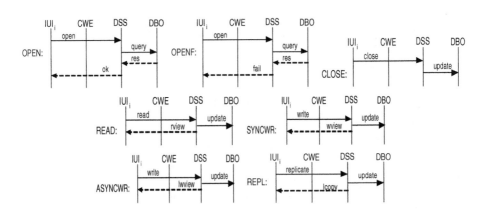

**Fig. 15.** bMSCs of OPEN, OPENF, CLOSE, READ, SYNCWR, ASYNCWR and REPL scenarios

In Figure 15 we show the bMSCs representing the 'open work session', the 'close work session', the 'data displaying', the 'data synchronous updating', the 'data asynchronous updating' and the 'data replication for asynchronous writing' scenarios. $DSS$ is a server for the two clients $IUI_1$ and $IUI_2$. It exports an interface $IDSS$ declaring five methods (**open**, **close**, **read**, **write** and **replicate**) whose behavior is described in the above five scenarios.

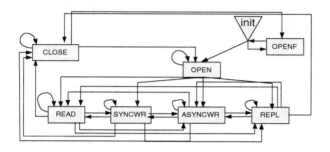

**Fig. 16.** HMSC of the CW sub-system

In Figure 16 the HMSC specification for the composed CW sub-system is reported in. Let us suppose that the designer of the CW system wants that the composed system satisfies a particular coordination policy. The policy is specified in form of the following behavioral LTL property:
$P = F(\overline{write_1} \wedge X(!\overline{write_1}U\overline{write_2}))$. $P$ specifies that when the client $IUI_1$ wants to update the document it necessarily has to use an alternating coordination policy with $IUI_2$. Once $IUI_1$ has performed a **write** request it cannot perform it again before $IUI_2$ has not performed a **write** request. From the HMSC and bMSCs specification we can automatically derive the AC-Graphs for each component in our CW sub-system (see Figure 17).

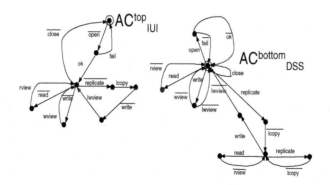

**Fig. 17.** AC-Graphs of components $IUI_1$, $IUI_2$ and $DSS$

According to Section 3, from the AC-Graphs of $IUI_1$, $IUI_2$ and $DSS$ we derive the corresponding AS-Graphs and then we derive the corresponding EX-Graphs (see Figure 18).

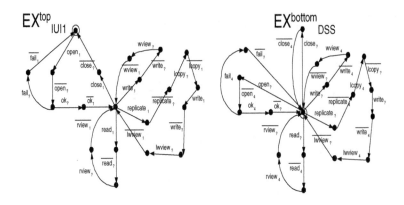

**Fig. 18.** EX-Graphs of components $IUI_1$, $IUI_2$ and $DSS$

Referring to Figure 18, the EX-Graph of $IUI_2$ is different from the EX-Graph of $IUI_1$ only in the identifier of the channel specified in known actions labels (2 instead of 1). We derive the connector global behavior through the EX-Graphs unification algorithm described in Section 3.1. In this paper, for the sake of presentation, we only show a sub-graph of the connector global behavior graph (see Figure 19) and we reduce the analysis of the whole connector to the sub-graph $K_{1.1}$ of the connector global behavior graph. Refer to [17] for a complete visualization of the connector graph.

The sub-connector $K_{1.1}$ has two deadlocks represented by two finite branches. These deadlocks are related to the consistency maintenance in an asynchronous writing scenario. We recall that in order to maintain a consistent version of the shared document, the $DSS$ expects that all users work in asynchronous mode every time another user chooses to work in asynchronous mode. The third-party components $IUI_1$ and $IUI_2$ do not respect this $DSS$ assumption. Thus the composed system has concurrency conflicts. This puts in evidence a typical problem in COTS components assembling. In order to synthesize the deadlock-free version of $K_{1.1}$ we simply prune the two finite branches. The deadlock-free $K_{1.1}$ forces $IUI_1$ and $IUI_2$ to respect the $DSS$ assumption. According to our approach, once obtained the deadlock-free version of the connector our framework performs the coordination policy enforcing step (see Section 3.4).
In Figure 20 we have shown the $P$-satisfying and deadlock-free connector model for $K_{1.1}$.

As said in Section 3.4, this behavioral model is enough to derive the deadlock-free property-satisfying connector code that implements the connector methods

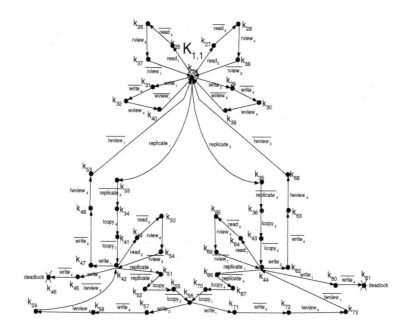

**Fig. 19.** Sub-graph $K_{1.1}$ of the global connector graph

related to the LTL property specification. The only methods relating to property $P$ are the methods **write** and **replicate** (see Figure 20). For all the others methods (i.e. **open, close** and **read**) the connector is a simple delegator since property $P$ has not influence on them. In the following we show the deadlock-free property-satisfying code implementing the method **write** of the connector component $K_{1.1}$. We refer to [17], for the complete implementation of $K_{1.1}$. The implementation refers to Microsoft COM (*Component Object Model*) components and uses C++ wiht ATL (*Active Template Library*) as programming environment. The method **write** of the inner *DSS* object gets a parameter of type **S_DA**. **S_DA** is a document alternative *"struct"*. It contains information about the document update to be realized.

```
HRESULT write(S_DA da) {
   if(sLbl == 24) {
      if((chId == 1) && (pState == 0)) {
         return dssObj->write(da);
         pState = 1; sLbl = 24;
      }
      else if((chId == 2) && (pState == 1)) {
         return dssObj->write(da);
         pState = 0; sLbl = 24;
      }
   }
}
```

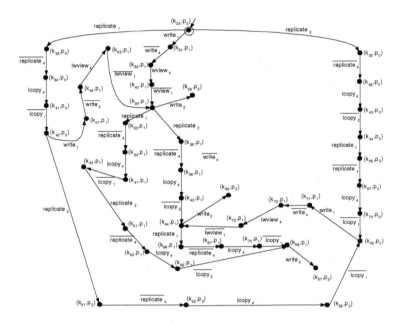

**Fig. 20.** $P$-satisfying connector model for $K_{1.1}$

```
else if(sLbl == 56) {
   if((chId == 1) && (pState == 0)) {
      return dssObj->write(da);
      pState = 1; sLbl = 44;
   }
   else if((chId == 2) && (pState == 1)) {
      return dssObj->write(da);
      pState = 0; sLbl = 42;
   }
}
else if(sLbl == 42) {
   if((chId == 1) && (pState == 0)) {
      return dssObj->write(da);
      pState = 1; sLbl = 24;
   }
}
else if(sLbl == 44) {
   if((chId == 2) && (pState == 1)) {
      return dssObj->write(da);
      pState = 0; sLbl = 24;
   }
}

   return E_HANDLE;
}
```

This code is automatically synthesized by visiting the sub-automaton of Figure 20 and by exploiting the information stored in its states and transitions labels. The connector component $K_{1.1}$ is an aggregated server component that encapsulates an instance of the inner $DSS$ component.

## 5  Related Works

The architectural approach to correct and automatic connector synthesis presented in this paper is related to a large number of other problems that have been considered by researchers over the past two decades. For the sake of brevity we mention below only the works closest to our approach. The most strictly related approaches are in the *"scheduler synthesis"* research area. In the discrete event domain they appear as *"supervisory control"* problem [3, 4, 28]. In very general terms, these works can be seen as an instance of a problem similar to the problem treated in our approach. However the application domain of these approaches is sensibly different from the software component domain. Dealing with software components introduces a number of problematic dimensions to the original synthesis problem: i) the computational complexity and the state-space explosion and ii) in general the approach is not compositional. The first problem can be avoided by using a logical encoding of the system specification in order to use a more efficient data structure (i. e. BDD (Binary Decision Diagram)) to perform the supervisor synthesis; however the second problem cannot be avoided and only under particular conditions it is possible to synthesize the global complete supervisor by composing modular supervisors. While the state-space explosion is a problem also present in our approach, on the other side we have proved in [15] that our approach is compositional to some extents. It means that if we build the connector for a given set of components and later we add a new component in the resulting system we can extend the already available connector and we must not perform again the entire synthesis process.

Other works that are related to our approach, appear in the *model checking of software components* context in which CRA (*Compositional Reachability Analysis*) techniques are largely used [12, 11]. Also these works can be seen as an instance of the general problem formulated in Section 3. They provide an optimistic approach to software components model checking. These approaches suffer the state-space explosion problem too. However this problem is raised only in the worst case that may not be the case often in practice. In these approaches the assumptions that represent the *weakest* environment in which the components satisfy the specified properties are automatically synthesized. However the synthesized environment does not provide a model for the properties satisfying glue code. The synthesized environment may be rather used for runtime monitoring or for components retrieval.

Recently promising formal techniques for the compositional analysis of component based design have been developed [5, 6]. The key of these works is the modular-based reasoning that provides a support for the modular checking of behavioral properties. The goal of these works is quite different from our in fact they are related only to software components interfaces compatibility check. Thus they provide only a check on component-based design level.

# 6   Conclusion and Future Work

In this paper we have described a connector-based architectural approach to component assembly. Our approach focusses on detection and recovery of the assembly concurrency conflicts and on enforcing of coordination policies on the interaction behavior of the components constituting the system to be assembled.

A key role is played by the software architecture structure since it allows all the interactions among components to be explicitly routed through a synthesized connector. By imposing this software architecture structure on the composed system we isolate the components interaction behavior in a new component (i.e. the synthesized connector) to be inserted into the composed system. By acting on the connector we have two effects: i) the components interaction behavior can satisfies the properties specified for the composed system and ii) the global system becomes flexible with respect to specified coordination policies.

Our approach requires to have a bMSC and HMSC specification of the system to be assembled. Since these kinds of specifications are common practice in real-scale contexts, this is an acceptable assumption. Moreover we assumed to have a LTL specification of the coordination policies to be enforced.

The complexity of the synthesis and analysis algorithm is exponential either in space and time. This value of complexity is obtained by considering the unification process complexity and the size of the data structure used to build the connector graph. At present we are studying better data structures for the connector model in order to reduce their size. By referring to the automata based model checking [7], we are also working to perform on the fly analysis during the connector model building process. Other possible limits of the approach are: i) we completely centralize the connector logic and we provide a strategy for the connector source code derivation step that derives a centralized implementation of the connector component. We do not think this is a real limit because even if we centralize the connector logic we can actually think of deriving a distributed implementation of the connector component; ii) we assume that an HMSC and bMSC specification for the system to be assembled is provided. Although this is reasonable to be expected, it is interesting to investigate testing and inspection techniques to directly derive from a COTS (black-box) component some kind (possibly partial) behavioral specification; iii) we assume also an LTL specification for the coordination policy to be enforced. It is interesting to find a more user-friendly coordination policy specification; for example by extending the HMSC and bMSC notations to express more complex system's components interaction behaviors.

# Acknowledgements

This work has been partially supported by Progetto MIUR SAHARA and by Progetto MURST CNR-SP4.

# References

[1] Itu telecommunication standardisation sector, itu-t reccomendation z.120. message sequence charts. (msc'96). Geneva 1996.

[2] R. Allen and D. Garlan. A formal basis for architectural connection. *ACM Transactions On Software Engineering and Methodology, Vol. 6, No. 3, pp. 213-249*, 6(3):213–249, July 1997.

[3] S. Balemi, G. J. Hoffmann, P. Gyugyi, H. Wong-Toi, and G. F. Franklin. Supervisory control of a rapid thermal multiprocessor. *IEEE Transactions on Automatic Control*, 38(7):1040–1059, July 1993.

[4] B. A. Brandin and W. M. Wonham. Supervisory control of timed discrete-event systems. *IEEE Transactions on Automatic Control*, 39(2), February 1994.

[5] L. de Alfaro and T. Heinzinger. Interface automata. In *ACM Proc. of the joint 8th ESEC and 9th FSE, ACM Press*, Sep 2001.

[6] L. de Alfaro and T. Heinzinger. Interface theories for component-based design. In *In Proc. of EMSOFT'01: Embedded Software, LNCS 2211, pp. 148-165. Springer-Verlang*, 2001.

[7] O. G. Edmund M. Clarke, Jr. and D. A. Peled. *Model Checking*. The MIT Press, Cambridge, Massachusetts, London, England, 2001.

[8] C. A. Ellis and S. J. Gibbs. Concurrency control in groupware systems. In *Proceedings of the 1989 ACM SIGMOD international conference on Management of data*, pages 399–407, 1989.

[9] D. Garlan, R. Allen, and J. Ockerbloom. Architectural mismatch: Why reuse is so hard. *IEEE Software, 12(6), November*, 1995.

[10] D. Garlan and D. E. Perry. *Introduction to the Special Issue on Software Architecture, Vol. 21. Num. 4. pp. 269-274*, April 1995.

[11] D. Giannakopoulou, J. Kramer, and S. Cheung. Behaviour analysis of distributed systems using the tracta approach. *Journal of Automated Software Engineering, special issue on Automated Analysis of Software*, 6(1):7–35, January 1999.

[12] D. Giannakopoulou, C. S. Pasareanu, and H. Barringer. Assumption generation for software component verification. *Proc. 17th IEEE Int. Conf. Automated Software Engineering 2002*, September 2002.

[13] P. Inverardi and M. Tivoli. Failure-free connector synthesis for correct components assembly. *Specification and Verification of Component-Based Systems (SAVCBS'03) - Workshop at ESEC/FSE 2003. September 1-2, 2003. Helsinki, Finland.*

[14] P. Inverardi and M. Tivoli. Automatic synthesis of deadlock free connectors for com/dcom applications. In *ACM Proceedings of the joint 8th ESEC and 9th FSE, ACM Press*, Vienna, Sep 2001.

[15] P. Inverardi and M. Tivoli. Connectors synthesis for failures-free component based architectures. *Technical Report, University of L'Aquila, Department of Computer Science, http://sahara.di.univaq.it/tech.php?id_tech=7 or http://www.di.univaq.it/~tivoli/ffsynthesis.pdf*, ITALY, January 2003.

[16] P. Inverardi, M. Tivoli, and A. Bucchiarone. Automatic synthesis of coordinators of cots group-ware applications: an example. In *International Workshop on Distributed and Mobile Collaboration (DMC 2003)*. *To be published by the IEEE Computer Society Press in the post-proceedings of the 12th IEEE International Workshops on Enabling Technologies: Infrastructure for Collaborative Enterprises (WETICE 2003)*, 9-11 June, Linz, Austria 2003.

[17] P. Inverardi, M. Tivoli, and A. Bucchiarone. Coordinators synthesis for cots group-ware systems: an example. *Technical Report, University of L'Aquila, Department of Computer Science, http://www.di.univaq.it/tivoli/cscw_techrep.pdf*, ITALY, March 2003.

[18] P. Inverardi, M. Tivoli, and A. Bucchiarone. Failures-free connector synthesis for correct components assembly. *Technical Report, University of L'Aquila, Department of Computer Science, http://www.di.univaq.it/tivoli/ffs_techrep.pdf*, ITALY, March 2003.

[19] M. Koch. Design issues and model for a distributed multi-user editor. *Computer Supported Cooperative Work, International Journal*, 5(1), 1996.

[20] M. Koch and J. Kock. Using component technology for group editors - the iris group editor environment. In *In Proc. Workshop on Object Oriented Groupware Platforms*, pages 44–49, Sep 1997.

[21] B. G. Lee, K. H. Chang, and N. H. Narayanan. A model for semi-(a)synchronous collaborative editing. In *Proceedings of the Third European Conference on Computer Supported Cooperative Work, ECSCW 93*, pages 219–231, September 1993.

[22] N. Medvidovic, P. Oreizy, and R. N. Taylor. Reuse of off-the-shelf components in c2-style architectures. In *In Proceedings of the 1997 Symposium on Software Reusability and Proceedings of the 1997 International Conference on Software Engineering*, May 1997.

[23] R. Milner. *Communication and Concurrency*. Prentice Hall, New York, 1989.

[24] R. D. Nicola and F. Vaandrager. Three logics for branching bisimulation. *Journal of the ACM*, 42(2):458–487, 1995.

[25] P.Inverardi and M.Tivoli. Automatic failures-free connector synthesis: An example. *Technical Report, published on the Monterey 2002 Workshop Proceedings: Radical Innovations of Software and Systems Engineering in the Future, Universita' Ca' Foscari di Venezia, Dip. di Informatica, Technical Report CS-2002-10*, September 2002.

[26] C. Szyperski. *Component Software. Beyond Object Oriented Programming*. Addison Wesley, Harlow, England, 1998.

[27] D. Taubner. Finite representations of ccs and tcsp programs by automata and petri nets. *LNCS 369*, 1989.

[28] E. Tronci. Automatic synthesis of controllers from formal specifications. *Proc. of 2nd IEEE Int. Conf. on Formal Engineering Methods*, December 1998.

[29] S. Uchitel, J. Kramer, and J. Magee. Detecting implied scenarios in message sequence chart specifications. In *ACM Proceedings of the joint 8th ESEC and 9th FSE*, Vienna, Sep 2001.

# Formal Methods in Testing Software Architectures

Antonia Bertolino[1], Paola Inverardi[2], and Henry Muccini[2]

[1] Istituto di Scienza e Tecnologie dell'Informazione "A. Faedo" (ISTI-CNR),
Area della Ricerca CNR di Pisa,
56100 Pisa, Italy
antonia.bertolino@isti.cnr.it
[2] Dipartimento di Informatica, Universitá dell'Aquila,
Via Vetoio 1,
67100 L'Aquila, Italy
[muccini,inverard]@di.univaq.it

**Abstract.** SAs provide a high-level model of large, complex systems using suitable abstractions of the system components and their interactions. SA dynamic descriptions can be usefully employed in testing and analysis. We describe here an approach for SA-based conformance testing: architectural tests are selected from a Labelled Transition System (LTS) representing the SA behavior and are then refined into concrete tests to be executed on the implemented system. To identify the test sequences, we derive abstract views of the LTS, called the ALTSs, to focus on relevant classes of architectural behaviors and hide away uninteresting interactions. The SA description of a Collaborative Writing system is used as an example of application. We also briefly discuss the relation of our approach with some recent research in exploiting the standard UML notation as an Architectural Description Language, and in conformance testing of reactive systems.

## 1 Introduction

Software testing consists of the dynamic verification of a program's behavior, performed by observing its execution on a selected set of test cases [5]. Depending on the strategy adopted for test selection, and on the notation and technologies employed in development, testing can take myriads of forms.

Traditionally, software testing was mostly a manual, error-prone and expensive process, whose importance in achieving quality was underestimated. Recently, however, more emphasis is given to this phase, and more rigorous and automated approaches are sought. In particular, as opposed to ad-hoc derivation of test cases based on the tester's intuition, the highly greater value of systematic derivation of test cases from a model of the system (model-based testing) is now generally recognized.

Conformance testing checks that an implementation fulfills its specifications, and a suite of black-box tests is executed in an attempt to "capture" all and only

M. Bernardo and P. Inverardi (Eds.): SFM 2003, LNCS 2804, pp. 122–147, 2003.
© Springer-Verlag Berlin Heidelberg 2003

the relevant behaviors. The usage of formal methods in software development was initially advocated in the specification and design stages, to allow for the formal verification of system properties, and for supporting formal refinement along the subsequent development steps. However, as several recent studies suggest (e.g., [18,43,44,28]), formal methods can be also advantageously employed in conformance testing, allowing for the systematic and automated synthesis of test cases from a system's formal model.

For large, complex systems, the testing task is usually organized into stages, i.e., it is partitioned into a phased process, addressing at each step the testing of increasingly larger subsystems. The aim is to keep complexity under control and to eventually reach the final stage of system testing with all the composing subsystems extensively tested. At each stage, the strategies that can be used for tests selection are closely related with the object under test (e.g., its abstraction level, the modelling notation, etc.).

With the emergence of Software Architecture (SA) as an autonomous discipline to describe and analyze large, complex systems, several authors have advocated the use of the architectural models also to drive testing, and in particular to select relevant behaviors of interactions between system components, based on the early SA specification.

The topic of architectural testing has thus recently raised some interest, and some contributions have been proposed. In [40], the authors define six architectural-based testing criteria, adapting specification-based approaches; in [7], the authors analyze the advantages in using SA-level testing for reuse of tests and to test extra-functional properties. In [22] Harrold presents approaches for using software architecture for effective regression testing, and in [23], she also discusses the use of software architecture for testing. In [41], the authors present an architecture-based integration testing approach that takes into consideration architecture testability, simulation, and slicing. However, to the best of our knowledge, our approach is the only comprehensive attempt to tackle the whole cycle of SA-based testing [38,8,9]. It spans the whole spectrum from test derivation down to test execution, and relies on empirical hands-on experience on real-world case studies.

Our approach is based on the specification of SA dynamics, which is used to identify useful schemes of interactions between system components, and to select test classes corresponding to relevant architectural behaviors. The goal is to provide a test manager with a systematic method to extract suitable test classes for the higher levels of testing and to refine them into concrete tests at the code level.

The approach relies on a formal description of the SA. In particular, we refer to a Labeled Transition System (LTS), modelling the SA dynamics. In general, an LTS provides a global, monolithic description of the set of all possible behaviors of the system; a path on the LTS can be taken as a test sequence. The problem is that the LTS describes a vast amount of information flattened into a graph. Trying to enforce any coverage criteria on the LTS would be out of question. We need means for tackling the state-space large scale problem, and for selecting a manageable number of test sequences.

In our approach, we provide the software architect with a key to decipher the LTS by building an Abstract LTS (ALTS), that represents a suitable abstraction of the LTS. ALTSs offer specific views of the SA dynamics by concentrating on relevant features and abstracting away from uninteresting ones. Intuitively, deriving an adequate set of test classes entails deriving a set of paths that appropriately cover the ALTS.

Then the architectural tests must be refined into code-level tests in order to be executed. To this end, we have followed a stepwise, manual methodology, to deal with the lack of a formal relation between the SA description and the code.

The technical underpinnings of our SA-based approach are in line with recent research in conformance testing of reactive systems, that also uses an LTS for modelling the behavior semantics of a formally described system [43,44,28]. In the paper we will discuss the relation between these two research areas.

The approach we describe here relies on an input description of the SA components into the FSP language [21,34]. However, a large interest comes from industry for using the standard UML as the Architectural Description Language (ADL). With a rigorous use of UML state diagrams and of appropriate stereotypes and tags this is a potential useful generalization of our approach. We only briefly outline how this will be done in future research.

The paper is structured as follows: in the next section we introduce some basic concepts of software testing, focusing more extensively on model-based testing from LTS. In Section 3 we overview issues in SA-based testing. Our approach is then presented in Section 4: we describe the Test Selection stage (in Subsection 4.1), and the Test Execution stage (in Subsection 4.2). An example of application of the approach to a case study is illustrated in Section 5, and details on the tools used are provided in Section 6. We finally discuss in Section 7 the relation of our approach with some recent research in exploiting the standard UML notation as an ADL (Subsection 7.1), and in conformance testing of reactive systems (Subsection 7.2). Conclusions and future plans are drawn in Section 8.

## 2    Software Testing

Software testing refers to the dynamic verification of a system's behavior based on the observation of a selected set of controlled executions, or test cases [5].

### 2.1    Basic Concepts

Testing is a crucial part of the software life cycle, and recent trends evidence the importance of this activity along the whole development process. The testing activities have to start at the requirement specification-level and have to be propagated down to the code-level, all along the various subsequent refinement steps. As discussed in [6], testing involves several demanding tasks: the ability to launch the selected tests (in a controlled host environment, or worse in the tight target environment of an embedded system); deciding whether the test outcome is acceptable or not (which is referred to as the *test oracle* problem); if not, evaluating the impact of the failure and finding its direct cause (the fault), and the indirect one (Root Cause Analysis); judging whether the test campaign is sufficient, which in turn would require having at hand measures of the effectiveness of the tests: one by one, each of these tasks presents tough challenges for the tester.

However, the problem that has received the highest attention in the literature is by far test-case selection: in brief, how to identify a suite of test cases that is effective in demonstrating that the software behaves as intended, or, otherwise, in evidencing the existing malfunctions. Clearly, a good test suite is in fact the crucial starting point to a successful testing session.

In contrast with the conventional practice of handcrafted ad-hoc test cases, or of random input generation, many methods for systematic test selection have been proposed in the past decades [5]. No method is superior to the others, thus several methods should be used in combination throughout the lifecycle, with focus shifting, as development proceeds, on differing aspects of software behavior, and also on differing projections of the system.

The term *model-based testing* refers to test case derivation from a model representing the software behavior. Indeed, testing is always against an expected behavior: the difference being essentially whether such a model is explicit (which is clearly better!), or implicit, i.e., in the mind of the testers. In particular, when there exists a specification of the system to be tested in some formal language, this can be used as the reference model both for test-case selection and as an oracle. This allows for rigorous mathematical analysis, and automated processing.

Testing an implementation against its (formal) specifications is also known as *conformance testing*, which, looking at the big picture of test strategies, belongs to the *black box* class, because we do not consider the internals of a system, but only its input/output behavior.

After the test cases are derived from the specifications, two major problems remain to be solved: traceability and test execution.

- *Traceability* concerns "relating the abstract values of the specification to the concrete values of the implementation" [18]. In fact, the synthesized test cases describe sequences of actions that have an interpretation at the abstract level of the specification. To be able to execute these tests on the code, we need to refine the test cases into more concrete sequences, that have a meaningful interpretation in terms of the actual system I/O interface.
- *Test execution* entails forcing the Implementation Under Test (IUT) to execute the specific sequence of events that has been selected. A problem arises with concurrent programs which, starting from the same input, may exercise different sequences of interactions (among several concurrent processes) and produce different results. This problem has already been analyzed in the literature, and deterministic- and nondeterministic-testing approaches have been proposed. In *nondeterministic testing*, the approach is to repeat the

launching of a program run under some specified input conditions several times until the desired test sequence is observed (or a maximum number of iterations is reached). In contrast, the *deterministic testing* approach (proposed by Carver and Tai [14]) forces a program to execute a specified test sequence by instrumenting it with synchronization constructs that deterministically reproduce the desired sequence.

## 2.2   Testing from Labeled Transition Systems

While formal testing includes several research directions, we restrict here to test derivation from *Labelled Transition Systems*, for which a quite mature theory of conformance testing now exists. We recall the definition of an LTS:

**Definition 1.** A Labeled Transition System (LTS) is a quintuple $(\mathcal{S}, \mathcal{L}, S_0, \mathcal{S_F}, \mathcal{T})$, where $\mathcal{S}$ is the set of states, $\mathcal{L}$ is the set of distinguished labels (actions) denoting the LTS alphabet, $S_0 \in \mathcal{S}$ is the initial state, $\mathcal{S_F} \subseteq \mathcal{S}$ is the set of final states, and $\mathcal{T} = \{ \xrightarrow{l} \subseteq \mathcal{S} \times \mathcal{S} \mid l \in \mathcal{L} \}$ is the transition relation labeled with elements of $\mathcal{L}$.

This theory has been originated by Tretmans [43,44], rooting on earlier results on equivalence testing of transition systems [17]. It addresses the conformance testing of reactive systems (i.e., systems which behave by reacting to the environment stimuli). The following of this section refers to work from [43,44,28], to which we send for further information.

The aim of a formal testing framework is to define a *conformance relation* between the implementation $I$ and the (formal) specification $S$. Such a relation precisely establishes when $I$ is a correct implementation of $S$. However, to do this, we need to reason on the naturally informal implementations as if they were formal objects [46]. The prerequisite to this is the *test hypothesis*: this consists into assuming that $I$ can be modeled by a formal object $MOD$ (even though it is not required that this model $MOD$ is known a priori), such that all the observations that we can take (of the black boxes) of $I$ and of $MOD$ along the executions of all defined test cases cannot be distinguished. In such a way, we can formally define an "implementation relation" ($imp$) that correlates $S$ with $MOD$: then, we conclude that $I$ conforms to $S$ iff $MOD$ is $imp$-correct with respect to $S$.

When a test is executed, what we observe are the outputs provided by the implementation. Translated in practical terms, the test hypothesis is what allows a tester to assume that the output observed for one test case can be taken as a representative for (infinite) many other possible executions. The set of all executed test cases forms an *observational framework*.

In Tretmans' approach, both the specification $S$ and the model $MOD$ of the implementation $I$ are expressed using Input/Output Transition Systems (IOTSs), an extension of the classical LTS model, in which the set of actions are partitioned into the Input actions and the Output actions. This partition is useful for testing purposes, to allow the tester to distinguish between the *controllable* events and the *observable* events, respectively. Also the possible absence of Outputs is modelled, using the special action *quiescence*, labelled by $\delta$ (and observed in practice by means of timers). Moreover, it is assumed that all inputs are enabled in any state.

The implementation relation *imp* used is of the form **ioco**, that is a relation holding when $MOD$ can never produce an output (included $\delta$) which could not have been produced by $S$ after the same sequence of actions, or *trace* [46].

Having established formally a conformance relation, formal techniques can now be used to automatically derive from the IOTS of the specifications an ideal test suite $T$, i.e., a set of tests by which for any implementation its **ioco**-correctness can be established. This ideal test suite is called *complete*, and holds the properties of *soundness*: conformant implementations are never rejected, and *exhaustiveness*: all non conformant implementations are rejected. The latter property however would require infinite test suites in almost all practical cases, therefore a selection of a finite test suite is made, by which only soundness is preserved, while exhaustiveness is lost.

The selection can be made randomly, as currently implemented in the TorX tool [42]. Alternatively, the tester can use his/her knowledge of the implementation under test and of the context to guide the selection; this second approach is implemented in the TGV tool [28] and is formalized through the notion of a *test purpose* [28,46]. Informally, test purposes describe the behaviors to be tested. More formally, they are themselves modelled by I/O automata, plus two distinct sets of trap states called Accept and Refuse.

Both TorX and TGV have been experimented on several case studies, some of industrial size, and are now quite mature. Although their use clearly requires some expertise in formal methods, which is not obviously yielded in standard test laboratories, they demonstrate that formal testing can and should be pursued, to get more effective test suites.

## 3 Software Architecture and Testing

SA represents the most promising approach to tackle the problem of scaling up in software engineering, because, through suitable abstractions, it provides the way to make large applications manageable. Nowadays, SA descriptions are commonly integrated into the software development process, e.g. [24,4].

However, SA production and management are, in general, quite expensive tasks. Therefore the effort is worthwhile if the SA artifacts are extensively used for multiple purposes. Typical use of SA is as a high-level design blueprint of the system to be used during system development and later on for maintenance and reuse. In particular, the importance of the role of SA in testing and analysis is evident.

As witnessed in this book, SA formal dynamic descriptions are used for many different kinds of analysis. We are here interested in SA primarily as a means for driving the testing of large, complex systems. Our concern is on exploiting the information described at the SA level to drive the testing of the implementation. What we discuss in Section 4 is how formal SA descriptions (and the obtained models) can be used for testing purposes. In other words, we assume the SA description is correct and we are investigating approaches to specification-based integration and system testing, whereby the reference model used to generate the test cases is the SA description.

In general, deriving a functional test plan means to identify those classes of behavior that are relevant for testing purposes. A functional equivalence class collects all those system executions that, although different in details, carry on the same informative contents for functional verification. I.e., the tester's expectation/hope is that any test execution among those belonging to a class would be equally likely to expose possible non conformities to the specification.

These high level tests are finally passed to the software tester, who has to i) derive code level tests corresponding to the specified architectural test sequences, and ii) actually run the tests and observe if the current implementation conforms to its architectural model. We say that *the implementation does not conform to the specification if some interactions described at the architectural level would not be allowed in the implementation.*

However, despite the high-level of abstraction, the SA can be still *too complex* to be described and managed, especially in industrial contexts. A strategic tool to manage the description of real systems is the use of views, by which different aspects of the system can be handled separately. Several slightly different types of views are defined in different approaches, e.g., [24,30,27], and different notations, generally graphical, have been introduced for views representation. Also, approaches have been proposed to check views consistency.

## 4     An Approach to SA-based Testing

The goal of our approach is to use the SA for code testing. As the starting point for this approach, we assume that the software architect, by looking at the SA dynamics from different viewpoints, defines various observation functions, in brief *obs*-functions, over the SA model. Each *obs*-function highlights a specific perspective of interest for a test session; in line with what we said above, it identifies a specific SA view. In fact, by applying an *obs*-function to the LTS, an Abstract LTS (ALTS) is automatically generated, which is a reduced LTS showing only interesting behaviors according to the selected view. This graph offers a much more manageable model than the original LTS. The software architect can thus choose on it a set of important patterns of behaviors (paths over the ALTS) to be tested. Finally, these high-level tests are passed to the software tester, who runs the tests and observes whether the current implementation "conforms" to its architectural model. We also refer informally to an *obs*-function as a "testing criterion".

Summarizing, our approach to SA-based testing consists of four logical steps:

- Step 1: Definition of an *obs*-function relative to a selected test concern;
- Step 2: Derivation, from the SA LTS, of the Abstract LTS (ALTS) corresponding to the defined *obs*-function;

- Step 3: Selection of a set of test classes over the derived ALTS;
- Step 4: Execution of the selected tests on the source code.

These four steps altogether cover both stages of testing: the *selection stage*, in which some criterion is applied to select a suitable set of test cases, and the *execution stage*, in which the selected tests are executed against the implementation.

The first stage is covered by Steps 1 to 3: they form a rigorous method to extract architectural tests from an architectural specification, which has been first presented in [8]. The first stage is where application of formal methods mostly helps. Step 4 covers the second stage: it deals with the execution of these tests at the code level, and has been discussed in [9]. As far as the fourth step is concerned, we cannot always rely on a strictly formal refinement process from SA to code. We use a less formal approach which comes out of our experience in dealing with a real-world case study [9].

In the following of this section we provide a brief description of our approach. A detailed description can be found in [38].

## 4.1   Test Selection Stage

From the SA specification of the system under analysis, we derive an LTS which models the SA dynamics. Such LTS can be automatically generated from formal ADLs [25,2,21,33] or drawn using existing formalisms (e.g., UML state diagrams or Harel's statecharts).

LTS node and arc labels represent, respectively, states and transitions relevant in the context of SA dynamics. A path $p$ on an LTS, where $p = S_0 \xrightarrow{l_1} S_1 \xrightarrow{l_2} S_2 \xrightarrow{l_3} \ldots \xrightarrow{l_n} S_n$, is a *complete path* if $S_0$ is the initial state and $S_n$ is a final state. Hereafter, for the sake of brevity, an LTS path will also be denoted by its sequence of labels (e.g., $p = l_1.l_2. \ldots .l_n$). In the following, we use the terms LTS "labels" and "actions" interchangeably.

In principle, the LTS can directly be used as the reference model for deriving the test scenarios. The problem is that this graph provides a global, monolithic description; it is a vast amount of information flattened into a graph. Extracting from this global model the observations of system behavior that are relevant for validation is a difficult task.

This is a problem that always arises in formal testing: with the exception of very small routines, we need ways for exploring the LTS and deriving representative behaviors that constitute the test suite.

The basic idea of our SA-based test approach is to allow for the formal derivation (from the LTS) of reference models for testing, each representing a relevant pattern of behavior which we want to focus attention on. In other words, our approach provides software architects with a key to decipher the LTS.

As we have discussed earlier in Section 3, a common practice in the analysis of complex systems is to derive from the global SA model a set of simplified models that provide different system views. We do this here by partitioning the LTS actions $\mathcal{L}$ into two groups: relevant interactions $\mathcal{R}$ (i.e., those we want to observe by testing) and non-relevant interactions $\mathcal{NR}$ (i.e., those we are not interested in at this time), so that $\mathcal{L} = \mathcal{R} \cup \mathcal{NR}$ and $\mathcal{R} \cap \mathcal{NR} = \emptyset$. Formally, we define an *obs*-function that maps the relevant LTS labels to a specified interpretation domain $\mathcal{D}$, whereas any other (non-relevant) one is mapped to a distinct element $\tau$. The *obs*-function may also be considered as a *hiding* operator that makes a set of actions invisible to its environment and may *relabel* the others in an interpretation domain $\mathcal{D}$. The relabeling may help emphasize the semantic meaning of observable actions. More precisely:

$obs : \mathcal{L} \longrightarrow \mathcal{L}'$, so that

$obs(r \in \mathcal{R}) = \mathrm{d} \in \mathcal{D}$, $obs(n \in \mathcal{NR}) = \tau$, and $\mathcal{L}' = \mathcal{D} \cup \tau$.

We can also extend the *obs*-function definition to LTS paths so that if $p = l_1.l_2. \dots .l_n$, $obs(p) = \mathrm{obs}(l_1.l_2. \dots .l_n) = obs(l_1).obs(l_2). \dots .obs(l_n)$.

We then use the *obs*-function as a means to derive a smaller automaton from the LTS which still expresses all high-level behaviors we want to test, but hides away any other irrelevant behavior. The automaton is called an *Abstract LTS* (ALTS).

The ALTS is obtained from the LTS via two transformations: i) by relabeling each transition in LTS according to the *obs*-function, and ii) by minimizing the resulting automaton with respect to a selected equivalence relation. The relabeled automaton is called the ObsLTS, and the minimized one is the ALTS.

For minimization, we analyzed trace- and bisimulation-based equivalences, both familiar from the theory of concurrency [36]. If one wants to reduce as much as possible the number of $\tau$ transitions and corresponding nodes, then a *trace* equivalence can be considered. In fact, this equivalence abstracts from $\tau$-labeled transitions and for any computational paths concentrates only on transitions that are different from $\tau$. A *bisimulation*-based equivalence is more suited when one wants to observe how the system evolves step-by-step, even along $\tau$-moves (preserving the LTS branching structure).

Figure 1 gives an example of the ALTS construction: the original LTS is analyzed, identifying the observation of interest (Figure 1.a); the abstraction is applied over this LTS with respect to the selected *obs*-function (Figure 1.b); and finally the trace equivalence minimization function is applied. The resulting ALTS is shown in Figure 1.c. Figure 1.d, in contrast, presents a bisimulation-based minimization. It can be seen that the latter gives more information on the original LTS structure.

Taking into consideration that i) the aim of ALTS is to provide a more compact and analyzable graph, and that ii) the ALTS automaton is built to highlight only interesting behaviors, the trace equivalence is more suitable for our purposes.

In [39] we prove that the ALTS generation process is *correct* and *complete*, that is, each ALTS path comes from a LTS path (ALTS does not introduce new paths) and each LTS path can be mapped onto an ALTS path (ALTS does not lose information).

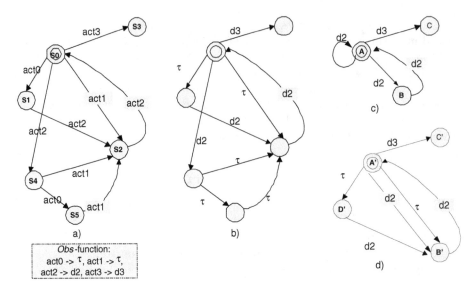

**Fig. 1.** a) LTS; b) ObsLTS; c) trace-based ALTS; d) bisimulation-based ALTS

The ALTS derivation is completely automated: we customized the existing FC2Tools [19], taking advantage of the functions "fc2explicit" and "fc2weak." The tools supporting our approach are described in Section 6.

Once the ALTS associated with a SA testing criterion via an *obs*-function has been derived, the task of deriving an adequate set of tests according to the selected test criterion is converted into the task of deriving a set of complete paths appropriately covering the ALTS.

Given the relatively small dimensions of an ALTS, a tester might consider to apply extensive coverage criteria on it. However, ALTS paths clearly specify architectural behaviors at a higher abstraction level than the original LTS because they are based on an *obs*-function applied over the LTS. Thus, one ALTS complete path can correspond to many possible LTS paths. Therefore, less thorough coverage criteria seem more practical.

We apply here the well known McCabe's [47] test technique since it is a good compromise between arc and path coverage in the case of ALTS coverage; in fact, any base set of paths covers all edges and nodes in the graph (i.e., this coverage subsumes branch and statement coverage testing).

When considering what to take as the specification of an "architectural test" we are left with two options. The first option, which is the one we take in this paper, is to consider an ALTS complete path as the test specification. In this case, the test is specified at a more abstract level and the tester instinctively focuses the testing on a restricted set of interactions (those in the ALTS alphabet). A second option is to identify those LTS paths of which the selected ALTS path is an abstraction. Because LTS paths are more detailed than ALTS paths, in this case the tester would have more information about how to perform the tests, but also stricter requirements; that is, the tester doesn't have as much freedom in choosing the code-level tests. In practice, it might actually be more difficult to test the conformance of source code to the test specification.

In either case (ALTS or LTS path), an architectural test is essentially a *sequence of system actions that are meaningful at the SA level.* They can be represented by UML-like sequence diagrams in which each box represents a SA component, while arrows represent actions performed by the components, i.e., the (A)LTS labels. The difference in the two options is the level of abstraction at which the sequence is described.

To derive from an ALTS path one or more corresponding LTS paths, we have developed an algorithm, described in [39]. The idea is that after an ALTS-based set of paths has been chosen, we can find out what the selected observation function is hiding; that is, we can identify those LTS paths corresponding to the selected ALTS path. This step could also be automated by adapting the Test Generation and Verification (TGV) tool [20], inside the Caesar/Aldebaran [13] toolset (see also Section 7.2).

In this process, we may find many LTS paths corresponding to an abstract path. The strategy we applied for reducing the number of LTS paths is a *transition rules coverage criterion*: for each ALTS path, we want to derive enough LTS paths to cover as many transition rules as possible, in a sense trying to consider all possible system behaviors corresponding to an abstract test sequence.

## 4.2   Test Execution Stage

In this section we will try to understand how a tester can use the architectural paths to actually test whether the source code conforms to the architectural description.

Of course, the two problems of traceability and test execution, introduced in Section 2.1, remain. Note that the traceability problem is here even exacerbated by the distance between the code and the SA-level of abstraction, which is necessarily high. Several researchers have recognized the importance and difficulty of this problem [48,41], but no one has yet found a general solution.

In our analysis, we identify different factors characterizing the mapping between the two levels: the development process, the relationships among architectural components and the source code, and the SA-level of abstraction.

If a well-formalized architecture-based development process is in place, SA specifications can be used to formally drive the generation of low-level design and code, and thus the correspondence is maintained throughout the process. For instance, some ADLs (such as C2ADL [11] and xADL [16]) provide development support for implementing software architectures in Java and C++ [12]. Explicit mapping rules drive the source-code implementation of architectural components, connectors, and messages via objects. However, such a process cannot generally be assumed, and would severely restrict the software developer's choices. Moreover, rigorous formal approaches to relate architectural elements and code are not yet current practice in SA-based processes, as illustrated for instance in [4,27].

In our experience, due to real-world constraints, SA specifications and low-level design have been intermixed without any formal mapping. While this is certainly not an ideal process, it is a realistic and plausible approach. In general, the problem is to provide a way to identify a sequence of low-level operations implementing a high-level behavior.

We first analyzed the system implementation to understand how architectural actions (e.g., high-level functionalities) are implemented in the code by sequences of partially ordered code level operations.[3]

Assuming for instance that the SA is implemented in Java, we map actions into sequences of method calls. If each action is implemented, at the low level, by a sequence of methods calls, it would be useful to understand how sequences of these actions (i.e., an architectural test) are implemented by the source code.

Two alternatives may be taken into account: i) each action is implemented by a sequence of operations, and they run sequentially; or ii) the actions can run concurrently. In the former case, a sequence of architectural actions is implemented by the sequential execution of the respective low-level sequence diagrams. In the latter case, the operations may interleave with each other. Note that in this context, "$act_i$ before $act_j$" (where $act_k$ is a generic action) does not mean that all the operations implementing $act_i$ must run before all the operations implementing $act_j$. It means that some operations that identify the action termination must be executed following a given order, whereas the others may be run in any order.

We finally run the code and evaluate the execution traces with respect to the expected ones to analyze the source code conformance with respect to the architectural behavior. To execute the desired test sequence, one can use either a deterministic or a nondeterministic approach (see Section 2.1).

In summary, the approach we devised can be conceptually decomposed into four substeps:

1. the SA path to be tested is represented as an ordered sequence of events. For instance, UML [45] stereotyped Sequence diagrams [24] can be used to represent these scenarios, where each box represents an SA component, while arrows represent actions performed by the components;

2. for each action in the SA path, the tester identifies the code level sequence (again, for instance, specified as UML Sequence Diagrams) implementing its behavior. These sequence diagrams represent how one action of the SA path is implemented in the code;

3. given the SA path to be tested, the tester combines the code level sequence diagrams corresponding to each action. The global sequence diagram so obtained represents a source code scenario implementing the SA path. The technical details of this step are discussed in [9];

4. the tester runs the code to check whether the sequence diagram generated in substep 3 is correctly implemented by the system. Since the system runs

---

[3] Note that more than one implementation sequence, might correspond to one LTS action. In such cases, to test the architectural action, all of them should be considered.

several concurrent processes, in general it is very difficult to trace system behavior. In fact, multiple executions of a concurrent program with the same input may exercise different sequences of interactions and may produce different results. A pragmatic approach here is to apply nondeterministic testing for some attempts; if the expected sequence of events is not observed, then a deterministic approach [14] could be applied to force the desired behavior.

Implementing each of the above substeps, in practice, involves several difficult problems, as we discussed in [9].

## 5   An Application Example

Collaborative writing (CW) is one discipline of the multi-disciplinary research area known as Computer Supported Cooperative Working (CSCW). Collaborative writing is defined in [32] as: "the process in which authors with different expertise and responsibilities interact during the invention and revision of a common document". A CW system involves two or more people (geographically distributed) working together to produce a common document. CW systems are often categorized according to the time/location matrix in two major groups. First, there are systems supporting *synchronous* editing. This group of CW system provides changes to the cooperative team partners (i.e. authors and co-authors) in real time. The second group is related to *asynchronous* writing tools. To better support all the CW stages, in literature have been proposed also *semi-synchronous* CW systems supporting the integration of asynchronous and synchronous styles of work. Since semi-synchronous CW systems seem to be the best solution for the complete support of all the activities related to the CW we focus on such systems.

The actors of a CW system are authors, co-authors and the manager. The *manager* divides the work of writing between groups of users (authors and co-authors). She will provide document templates, links and whatever may be of help to the realization of the document. *Authors* can be required to write a specific portion of a book/paper. They have to observe the document formats proposed by the manager and they can delegate one of more *co-authors* to produce portions of the document. The realization of such a document foresees a certain cooperation, and information exchange, between the manager and authors, between the authors and co-authors and among the authors themselves. A list of requirements a CW has to implement is described in [26].

From an architectural viewpoint, a CW system operates in a heterogeneous hardware environment where authors can edit, change and exchange documents, which are stored in a shared database. The CW software architecture we use in this paper is borrowed from [26]. This CW system is a three-tier application composed by the following four components:

- an Integrated User Interface (IUI): it is an integrated environment of tools for editing, navigation, display of awareness communication among the group members and import and export of data from external applications;

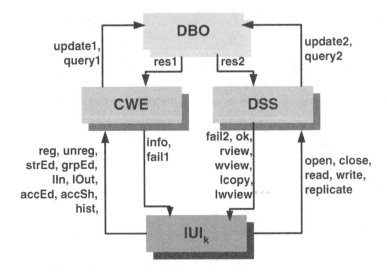

**Fig. 2.** A Software Architecture description of a CW system

- a CW Engine (CWE): it provides all services useful to perform a group activity in the CW context. It handles a list of CW activities, such as, user registration and deregistration, user login and logout, users group definition and editing;
- a Document Storage Service (DSS): it is an abstraction of the physical container of the shared documents that are logically partitioned according to their structure. In an asynchronous working mode we use version-controlled documents. In a synchronous working mode it is shared among the users and we have to use pessimistic concurrency control;
- a Database Object (DBO): it stores all group awareness information useful to support a group activity.

Figure 2 shows the CW SA. It depicts the different components, the architecture topology and the list of services each component provides and/or requires. The meaning of each service is explained in [26]. The notation $IUI_k$ means that many instances of the IUI component can be present at the same time. The behavior of each component (in terms of services required and provided) has been specified using the Finite State Process (FSP2) [21] process algebra. Each component behavior is described by an LTS which is automatically generated by the Labeled Transition System Analyzer (LTSA) tool [31].

By running the LTSA tool on the CW FSP specification (assuming that two IUIs are working concurrently), we obtain a (minimized) LTS composed of 47 states with 76 transitions (assuming only one IUI is connected). On this we apply the method for test selection described in Section 4. A list of interesting observations we could make on this global LTS includes:

1. Interaction between a subset of the architecture components;
2. Scenario-based testing (given a selected interaction scenario, we want to test a subgraph implementing only such scenario);
3. Input/Output for a selected component only.

In the following of this section, we propose samples of the first two observations listed above.

Related to the first observation (interaction between components), we focus on the following testing criterion: "all those behaviors involving the interactions from IUI to CWE". This criterion needs to be formally expressed by an *obs*-function. In this case, $D$ will contain all and only the actions (i.e., elements of the LTS alphabet) that specifically involve the communication among the selected components. Such actions are "reg", "unreg", "strEd", "grpEd", "lin", "lout", "accEd", "accSh", and "hist". Figure 3 shows the obs-function defined for the given criterion, called IUI-to-CWE obs.

---

**D = {reg, unreg, strEd, grpEd, lin, lout, accEd, accSh, hist}**

**obs (reg) = Register**
**obs (unreg) = Unregister**
**obs (strEd) = Structure Editing**
**obs (grpEd) = Group Editing**
**obs (lin) = Login**
**obs (lout) = Logout**
**obs (accEd) = Access to Documents**
**obs (accSh) = Access Information**
**obs (hist) = History**

**For any other $T_i$, obs $(T_i)$ = tau**

---

**Fig. 3.** Obs-function for the IUI-to-CWE testing criterion

Given the IUI-to-CWE criterion, and by applying reduction and minimization algorithms, we have derived the ALTS depicted in Figure 4 (label S0 identifies the initial state, that in this example also coincides with the only final one). This ALTS represents in a concise, graphical way how the IUI requires services to the CWE component.

Following the McCabe's path coverage criterion [47], we can select on this graph $NP = m - n + 1$ independent paths, where "m" identifies the ALTS arcs and "n" the ALTS nodes. NP is "precisely the minimum number of paths that can, in (linear) combination, generate all possible paths through the module" [47]. Applying this metric to the IUI-to-CWE criterion, we can get 8 independent paths as listed below:

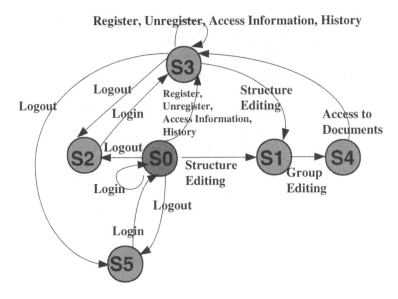

**Fig. 4.** ALTS for the IUI-to-CWE testing criterion

Path1: $S_0 \xrightarrow{StructureEditing} S_1 \xrightarrow{GroupEditing} S_4 \xrightarrow{AccesstoDocuments} S_3 \xrightarrow{Logout} S_5 \xrightarrow{Login} S_0$

Path2: $S_0 \xrightarrow{StructureEditing} S_1 \xrightarrow{GroupEditing} S_4 \xrightarrow{AccesstoDocuments} S_3 \xrightarrow{StructureEditing} S_1 \xrightarrow{GroupEditing} S_4 \xrightarrow{AccesstoDocuments} S_3 \xrightarrow{Logout} S_5 \xrightarrow{Login} S_0$

Path3: $S_0 \xrightarrow{StructureEditing} S_1 \xrightarrow{GroupEditing} S_4 \xrightarrow{AccesstoDocuments} S_3 \xrightarrow{Logout} S_2 \xrightarrow{Login} S_3 \xrightarrow{Logout} S_5 \xrightarrow{Login} S_0$

Path4: $S_0 \xrightarrow{Login} S_0$

Path5: $S_0 \xrightarrow{Logout} S_5 \xrightarrow{Login} S_0$

Path6: $S_0 \xrightarrow{AccessInformation} S_3 \xrightarrow{StructureEditing} S_1 \xrightarrow{GroupEditing} S_4 \xrightarrow{AccesstoDocuments} S_3 \xrightarrow{Logout} S_5 \xrightarrow{Login} S_0$

Path7: $S_0 \xrightarrow{Logout} S_2 \xrightarrow{Login} S_3 \xrightarrow{Logout} S_5 \xrightarrow{Login} S_0$

Path8: $S_0 \xrightarrow{Logout} S_2 \xrightarrow{Login} S_3 \xrightarrow{Unregister} S_3 \xrightarrow{StructureEditing} S_1 \xrightarrow{GroupEditing} S_4 \xrightarrow{AccesstoDocuments} S_3 \xrightarrow{Logout} S_2 \xrightarrow{Login} S_3 \xrightarrow{Logout} S_5 \xrightarrow{Login} S_0$

Some of these paths are particularly interesting for testing purposes. For example, Paths 1 to 3 show how the IUI component can initially edit the document structure, edit information on other authors, access the document, and eventually logout from the system. Path6 considers the case where an author initially checks how other authors are modifying the paper, then, starts accessing the paper and finally logouts.

Related to the second observation (the scenario-based one), we define the following testing criterion: "the OPEN scenario, i.e., all the operations related to the execution of the open action". This criterion is called OpenScenario_Obs and is formally expressed by the *obs*-function in Figure 5: "pre" is a path of actions performed before "open", "postOpen" is a path of actions performed after "open", while "postZ" is a path of actions performed after "z", which generically denotes an alternative path to Open.

> **obs(pre.open.postOpen) = pre.open.postOpen**
> **obs(pre.z.postZ) = pre.tau, with z different from open**

**Fig. 5.** Obs-function for the OpenScenarios-Obs testing criterion

Figure 6 shows the ALTS for the OpenScenario-Obs. Label S0 identifies the initial state, that is also a final state. There is another final state, that is labelled as S4.

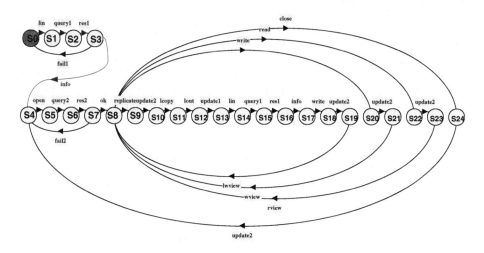

**Fig. 6.** ALTS for the OpenScenarios-Obs testing criterion

A list of ALTS test paths, derived according to McCabe's technique, is the following:

Path1: $S_0 \xrightarrow{lin} S_1 \xrightarrow{query1} S_2 \xrightarrow{res1} S_3 \xrightarrow{fail1} S_0$

Path2: $S_0 \xrightarrow{lin} S_1 \xrightarrow{query1} S_2 \xrightarrow{res1} S_3 \xrightarrow{info} S_4 \xrightarrow{open} S_5 \xrightarrow{query2} S_6 \xrightarrow{res2} S_7 \xrightarrow{fail2} S_4$

Path3: $S_0 \xrightarrow{lin} S_1 \xrightarrow{query1} S_2 \xrightarrow{res1} S_3 \xrightarrow{info} S_4 \xrightarrow{open} S_5 \xrightarrow{query2} S_6 \xrightarrow{res2} S_7 \xrightarrow{ok} S_8 \xrightarrow{close}$
$S_{24} \xrightarrow{update2} S_4$

Path4: $S_0 \xrightarrow{lin} S_1 \xrightarrow{query1} S_2 \xrightarrow{res1} S_3 \xrightarrow{info} S_4 \xrightarrow{open} S_5 \xrightarrow{query2} S_6 \xrightarrow{res2} S_7 \xrightarrow{ok} S_8 \xrightarrow{write}$
$S_{20} \xrightarrow{update2} S_{21} \xrightarrow{wview} S_8 \xrightarrow{close} S_{24} \xrightarrow{update2} S_4$

Path5: $S_0 \xrightarrow{lin} S_1 \xrightarrow{query1} S_2 \xrightarrow{res1} S_3 \xrightarrow{info} S_4 \xrightarrow{open} S_5 \xrightarrow{query2} S_6 \xrightarrow{res2} S_7 \xrightarrow{ok} S_8 \xrightarrow{read}$
$S_{22} \xrightarrow{update2} S_{23} \xrightarrow{rview} S_8 \xrightarrow{close} S_{24} \xrightarrow{update2} S_4$

Path6: $S_0 \xrightarrow{lin} S_1 \xrightarrow{query1} S_2 \xrightarrow{res1} S_3 \xrightarrow{info} S_4 \xrightarrow{open} S_5 \xrightarrow{query2} S_6 \xrightarrow{res2} S_7 \xrightarrow{ok}$
$S_8 \xrightarrow{replicate} S_9 \xrightarrow{update2} S_{10} \xrightarrow{lcopy} S_{11} \xrightarrow{lout} S_{12} \xrightarrow{update1} S_{13} \xrightarrow{lin} S_{14} \xrightarrow{query1} S_{15} \xrightarrow{res1}$
$S_{16} \xrightarrow{info} S_{17} \xrightarrow{write} S_{18} \xrightarrow{update2} S_{19} \xrightarrow{lwview} S_8 \xrightarrow{close} S_{24} \xrightarrow{update2} S_4$

Path1 shows how the precondition for the execution of the "open" action may fail. Path2 shows that the open action may fail. Paths 3 to 6 describe the sequences of actions that may happen when an open is successfully performed.

## 6    Approach Automation

In our approach, we used several tools to implement the different steps. Initially, an architectural language is used to specify our software architecture. An LTS model of the SA dynamics is then automatically generated from this specification, and abstraction and minimization are applied over the LTS to build an Abstract LTS. Finally, we instrument the source code to analyze the CW behavior with respect to the architectural tests. Figure 7 summarizes the framework we use:

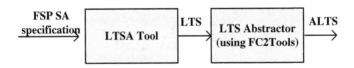

**Fig. 7.** The framework

1. The **Finite State Process (FSP)** [21,34] process algebra is used to specify software component behaviors.
2. The **LTSA tool** [31] takes an FSP SA specification and gives the corresponding LTS as a result.

3. The **LTS Abstractor** builds abstracted views of the LTS (based on the previously discussed theory). It has been implemented by using the existing FC2Tools [19].

The FSP language provides a concise way of describing LTSs; each FSP expression can be mapped onto a finite LTS and vice versa. The FSP specification is based on the definition of processes, whose behavior is modeled by LTSs; each process instance implements an architectural component; several processes can be combined (with a parallel composition operator) to describe the interaction between different processes. An FSP specification comprises a declarative section defining variables and ranges, a section defining the process initial state, and a section describing the other reachable states. Semantically, an FSP process waits for an action (e.g., for receiving messages), performs actions (e.g., for sending messages) and changes its state. The LTS alphabet is composed of the exchanged messages.

Figure 8 shows a portion of the FSP specification for the CW system. For those not familiar with FSP, Figure 8.a specifies the behavior of the IUI component. The prefixes "in_" and "out_" identify which are IUI's inputs and outputs, respectively. Figure 8.b is used to put the various processes in parallel, specifying how the LTSs cooperate. This specifies how the CW system behaves, that is, how the IUI, DBO, CWE, DSS and DBO processes have to be put in parallel to describe the whole system behavior.

Each FSP process can be described by an LTS model that contains all the states a process may reach and all the transitions it may perform. The LTSA tool supports the FSP language by automatically generating the LTSs of each FSP process. The tool provides graphical and textual visualization of the resulting LTSs, allows for evaluating process properties (i.e., safety, deadlock, reachability), supports specification animation to facilitate interactive exploration of system behavior and can be used to put different processes in parallel. This last feature allows us to obtain a global LTS model of the system.

The observation of the LTS via an abstraction mechanism has been implemented by using the FC2Tool. In particular, we took advantage of a function called "fc2explicit" provided by the tool for comparing two ".FC2" graphs. The first graph is the one we want to abstract (the architectural LTS), and the second one (in the following, *Obs*-graph) is a graph we generate once the observation is specified.

By running the "fc2explicit -abstract LTS.fc2 Obsgraph.fc2 > ALTS-nm.fc2" command, we can compare the two graphs and generate a non-minimized ALTS. The "fc2explicit -<opt> ALTS-nm.fc2 > ALTS.fc2" command generates the minimized graph, i.e., the ALTS.

# 7    Putting the Approach in the Global Picture

We have described so far an original approach for the derivation of SA-based conformance test cases. Our aim is to integrate this approach in industrial practice.

```
/** IUI Component */                                                          a)

IUI = (out_lin -> STEP1),
STEP1 = (in_info -> STEP2|in_fail1 -> IUI),
STEP2 = (out_lout -> IUI| out_reg -> in_info -> STEP2|out_unreg -> in_info -> STEP2|out_accSh -> in_info -> STEP2|out_hist ->
in_info -> STEP2| out_strEd -> out_grpEd -> out_accEd -> in_info -> STEP2 | out_open -> (in_fail2 -> STEP2|in_ok -> STEP3)),
STEP3 = (out_close -> STEP2 | out_read -> in_rview -> STEP3| out_write -> in_wview -> STEP3|
out_replicate -> in_lcopy -> out_lout -> out_lin -> in_info -> out_write -> in_lwview -> STEP3).
```

```
/** CW    */                                                                 b)

||CW = (IUI||DBO||CWE||DSS)/
{out_lin/in_lin,
out_info/in_info,
out_fail1/in_fail1,
out_fail2/in_fail2,
out_lout/in_lout,
out_reg/in_reg,
out_unreg/in_unreg,
out_strEd/in_strEd,
out_grpEd/in_grpEd,
out_accEd/in_accEd,
out_accSh/in_accSh,
out_hist/in_hist,
out_open/in_open,
out_close/in_close,
out_read/in_read,
out_write/in_write,
out_replicate/in_replicate,
out_ok/in_ok,
out_rview/in_rview,
out_wview/in_wview,
out_lcopy/in_lcopy,
out_update1/in_update1,
out_query1/in_query1,
out_res1/in_res1,
out_update2/in_update2,
out_query2/in_query2,
out_res2/in_res2,
out_lwview/in_lwview}.
```

**Fig. 8.** CW FSP Specification

This requires that the approach is enhanced in two dimensions: standardizing the input modelling notation, i.e., the SA description; and, increasing the degree of automation, that can be done efficiently by exploiting existing tools.

### 7.1   Standardizing SA Description

SA stakeholders in academia and in industry understand SAs in different ways, use them with different goals and unfortunately, specify them with different formalisms. Researchers have proposed formal ADLs in order to make automatic analysis and validation possible. Practitioners use more informal notations, sometimes, just simple box-and-line notations.

As a way to provide a standard notation to describe SAs, the Unified Modeling Language (UML) [45] is more and more used. UML has now gained a wide acceptance as the de-facto standard for object oriented modeling. Although its original purpose was for detailed design, its extension mechanisms (i.e., the possibility to extend the UML semantics associated to modeling elements) make it potentially applicable in contexts outside the object-oriented world (e.g., [15,29]). Moreover, its multi-view modeling approach [30] allows to use different diagrams to describe different system perspectives.

In the last few years, various approaches to incorporate architectural descriptions in the UML framework have been proposed. In [35], the authors discuss two different approaches, adhering to the requirement that the resulting notation still complies to *standard* UML.

In the first approach, UML is used "as is", i.e., the existing UML notation is used to represent SAs. One relevant drawback of this approach is that specific SA concepts (for example, connectors and rules) do not have direct counterparts in UML. Moreover, UML imposes structural and compositional constraints which do not apply to SA descriptions and viceversa.

The second approach, instead, constrains the UML meta model using UML built-in mechanisms. It has been used to formalize architectures in C2, Rapide and Wright [11,33,2]. However, application of this approach showed that the use of the formal Object Constraint Language (OCL), in order to extend the UML standard notation, strongly limits the use of UML tools to support architectural models. Moreover, the ambiguity still existing in the UML semantics, makes it difficult to model some architectural concepts.

This research direction can also be relevant for testing purposes, because UML-based testing is a very active research area (e.g., [3,1,10]). For testing, we need to express besides the structure also the behavior of the architecture under analysis. As already said, behavioral modelling is in fact the key instrument in SA conformance testing. For instance in [35], state diagrams have been used to specify behavioral information.

Indeed, the use of a UML compliant model for SAs would allow us to export results from the UML-based testing area to the SA domain.

Several methods and tools for UML-based testing have been proposed. None of these however focuses explicitly on testing of the SA. An ongoing European project for automated generation of test cases from a UML model [4] is AGEDIS [1]. Interestingly, the system model it takes in input is essentially composed of class diagrams, for describing the system components, and state diagrams, for describing the behavior of components, plus stereotypes and tagged values. This coincides exactly with the basic set of diagrams identified in the second approach of [35]. Therefore, it is possible that a tool such as AGEDIS could be adapted to SA-based testing. However, even though the notation and underlying techniques are the same, conceptual differences exist and should be investigated by experimentation.

---

[4] More precisely, a subset of UML, called the AML, for Agedis Modelling Language, has been formally defined.

## 7.2   Importing Automation from Existing Tools

If we rethink our approach in terms of the existing and now well-settled theory of conformance testing from formal specifications (as summarized in Section 2.2), it is evident that from a technical point-of-view several commonalities exist.

Indeed, the methodology and tools used are basically the same. The behavior semantics of the system is expressed in both cases by LTSs, possibly with some extensions (in Tretmans' testing theory IOTSs, including input and output labelling of events). On the LTS model, formal methods need to be applied for restricting the analysis to relevant classes of behavior, because an exhaustive coverage of the LTS is not feasible. More precisely, we need a technique for reducing the possible sequences of transitions to a limited number of test sequences. In our approach we have used an observation function on the LTS which finally (after renaming and reductions) gives back an ALTS. On the ALTS we can then more easily identify a set of test sequences, but as we have shown these are very abstract and far from the concrete level at which these tests have to be eventually executed. In contrast, in TGV, the identification of relevant test sequences is made by specifying a test purpose. Given a test purpose, a set of paths on the LTS is derived which satisfies the test purpose and corresponds to a set of test sequences, defined over the LTS.

Roughly, a test purpose would correspond in our approach to a path on the ALTS. Intuitively, then, we could in principle reformulate our approach within the context of TGV (by translating the *obs*-function in terms of guidelines for deriving a test purpose), with the advantage of being able to use a well developed and mature set of tools [13]. Actually, the above cited AGEDIS project [1] incorporates the TGV algorithms.

However, the intermediate step of the ALTS is not explicitly supported in TGV, and we believe that it introduces a useful and intuitive means for reasoning at the complex architectural level by separately considering differing classes of behavior. ALTSs offer specific views of the SA dynamics by concentrating on relevant features and abstracting away from less interesting features. ALTS is a graphical tool we provide that allows the software architect to more easily identify those behavioral patterns that are meaningful for validation purposes.

Conceptually, there are significant differences between our approach and existing ones:

i) The SA description tries to capture SA-relevant behaviors alone, while abstracting away other system functions. Thus, our tests specifically belong to the integration testing stages and certainly do not aim to test the system as completely as possible, as in traditional specification-based test approaches.

ii) The abstraction level of the reference model and its relative "distance" from the implementation under test varies much in the two contexts. In SA-based testing, this distance is *purposely* very high, whereas in existing approaches to specification-based testing, this is often thought as being low. In other words, a high abstraction level is a basic assumption of our approach, whereas traditional approaches require a close distance between the reference model and the implementation.

## 8   Conclusions and Future Perspectives

As testified by the collection of papers in this book, SA can play an important role throughout the software life cycle. However, while the literature is rich in approaches for design and analysis based on SA, relatively little has been proposed so far for SA-based testing. Our research investigates how the SA concepts, methods, and tools can be usefully exploited in the conformance testing of a large distributed system against its high-level specifications.

Our approach to SA-based testing essentially consists of deriving a set of architectural test sequences by covering abstracted views of the LTS description of the SA behavior. We have here illustrated it on the CW case study.

Our experience in using the approach on some real-world case studies revealed that practical difficulties can hinder its direct application in industry. Deriving suites of architectural test cases according to some notion of coverage may be relatively easy, with the support of adequate tools. What can be more complicated is to subsequently establish a relationship that maps these high-level test sequences on concrete, executable test cases. The problem arises especially in absence of a rigorous, formalized refinement process from the SA specification down to the source-code, as it is still common industrial practice. In our view, the only means to investigate such a tough problem is through empirical, hands-on investigation.

On the other hand, we might not even have a global architectural model at our disposal. This can happen for several reasons: i) architectural components may be described through complex models, in terms of states and transitions and putting these models together may give rise to a state explosion problem. ii) The architectural models may be incomplete, which means that some component behaviors are unknown or components are not completely specified. These may be very common situations in industrial contexts. We thus are investigating the possibility of generating abstract observations and test sequences directly from partial architectural models.

As discussed in the paper, future developments of the approach will encompass on one side the possibility of using the standard UML notation for modelling the SA behavior. This can be useful in two respects: for pushing the industrial usage of rigorous SA-based testing methods, and for exploiting the rich repository of UML-based test techniques. On the other side, we are also investigating the relation between our approach and the framework of conformance testing of distributed reactive systems, already implemented in the TorX and TGV tools, and under development in the AGEDIS tool.

Finally, empirical investigations on more case studies, possibly developed by using different development processes and programming paradigms, are necessary to further generalize and refine the approach.

## Acknowledgments

We would like to acknowledge the Italian MURST/MIUR national projects SALADIN and SAHARA, which partially supported this work. We are indebted to

Antonio Bucchiarone, who provided the CW case study, and to Thierry Jeron for his constructive help in applying the TGV tool on the CW.

# References

1. The AGEDIS Project: Automated Generation and Execution of Test Suites for Distributed Component-based Software. On-line at http://www.agedis.de
2. Allen, R., Garlan, D.: A Formal Basis for Architectural Connection. *ACM Trans. on Software Engineering and Methodology*, Vol. 6, N. 3, pp. 213-249, July 1997.
3. Basanieri, F., Bertolino, A., Marchetti, E.: The Cow_Suite Approach to Planning and Deriving Test Suites in UML Projects. In Proc. 5th Int. Conf. UML 2002, Dresden, Germany. LNCS 2460 (2002), pp. 383-397.
4. Bass, L., Clements, P., Kazman, R.: Software Architecture in Practice. *SEI Series in Software Engineering*, Addison-Wesley, 1998.
5. Bertolino, A.: Knowledge Area Description of Software Testing. In *SWEBOK*, Joint IEEE-ACM Software Engineering Coordinating Committee. On-line at: <http://www.swebok.org>.
6. Bertolino, A.: Software Testing Research and Practice. Invited presentation at ASM 2003, Taormina, Italy. LNCS 2589 (2003), pp. 1-21.
7. Bertolino, A., Inverardi, P.: Architecture-based software testing. In *Proc. ISAW96*, October 1996.
8. Bertolino, A., Corradini, F., Inverardi, P., Muccini, H.: Deriving Test Plans from Architectural Descriptions. In *ACM Proc. Int. Conf. on Software Engineering* (ICSE2000), pp. 220-229, June 2000.
9. Bertolino, A., Inverardi, P., Muccini, H.: An Explorative Journey from Architectural Tests Definition downto Code Tets Execution. In *IEEE Proc. Int. Conf. on Software Engineering* (ICSE2001), pp. 211-220, May 2001.
10. Briand, L., Labiche, Y.: A UML-Based Approach to System Testing. Software and System Modeling 1(1), 2002, pp. 10-42.
11. The C2 style and ADL. Project web page on-line at: <http://www.isr.uci.edu/architecture/c2.html>.
12. The C2 Framework. On-line at: <http://www.isr.uci.edu/architecture/software.html>.
13. Caesar/Aldebaran Tool (CADP). On-line at: <http://inrialpes.fr/vasy/cadp>.
14. Carver, R. H., Tai, K.-C.: Use of Sequencing Constraints for Specification-Based Testing of Concurrent Programs. *IEEE Trans. on Software Engineering*, Vol. 24, N. 6, pp. 471-490, June 1998.
15. Conallen, J.: Building Web Applications with UML. The Addison-Wesley Object Technology Series.
16. Dashofy, E. M., van der Hoek, A., Taylor, R. N.: An Infrastructure for the Rapid Development of XML-Based Architecture Description Languages. In Proc. of the 24th Int. Conf. on Software Engineering, 2002.
17. De Nicola, R., Hennessy, M.: Testing Equivalences for Processes. Theoretical Computer Science, 34: 83-133, (1984).
18. Dick, J., Faivre, A.: Automating the Generation and Sequencing of Test Cases from Model-Based Specifications. In J.C.P. Woodcock and P.G. Larsen (Eds.), *FME'93: Industrial-Strenght Formal Methods*, pp. 268-284. *LNCS 670*, Springer Verlag, 1993.
19. FC2Tools. On-line at: <http://www-sop.inria.fr/meije/verification/quick-guide.html>.

20. Fernandez, J.-C., Jard, C., Jeron, T., Nedelka, L., Viho, C.: An Experiment in Automatic Generation of Test Suites for Protocols with Verification Technology. Special Issue of *Science of Computer Programming*, Vol. 29, pp. 123-146, 1997.
21. Finite State Process (FSP). On-line at: <http://www.dse.doc/ic.ac.uk/~jnm/book/ ltsa/Appendix-A.html>.
22. Harrold, M. J.: Architecture-Based Regression Testing of Evolving Systems. In *Proc. Int. Workshop on the ROle of Software Architecture in TEsting and Analysis* (ROSATEA), CNR-NSF, pp. 73-77, July 1998.
23. Harrold, M. J.: Testing: A Roadmap. In A. Finkelstein (Ed.), *ACM ICSE 2000, The Future of Software Engineering*, pp. 61-72, 2000.
24. Hofmeister, C., Nord, R. L., Soni, D.: *Applied Software Architecture*. Addison Wesley, 1999.
25. Inverardi, P., Wolf, A. L.: Formal Specifications and Analysis of Software Architectures Using the Chemical Abstract Machine Model. *IEEE Trans. on Software Engineering*, Vol. 21, N. 4, pp. 100-114, April 1995.
26. Inverardi, P., Tivoli, M., Bucchiarone, A.:    Coordinators synthesis for COTS group-ware systems: an example.   In Proc. Int. Workshop on Distributed and Mobile Collaboration, 2003 (DMC 2003).   Extended version as technical Report, University of LAquila, Department of Computer Science, http://www.di.univaq.it/tivoli/cscw_techrep.pdf, March 2003.
27. Jacobson, I., Booch, G., Rumbaugh, J.: *The Unified Software Development Process.* Addison Wesley, Object Technology Series, 1999.
28. Jard, C., Jéron, T.: TGV: Theory, Principles and Algorithms. Proc. Conf. IDPT 2002. Pasadena (USA), (2002).
29. Jrjens, J.: UMLsec: Extending UML for Secure Systems Development. Proc. UML 2002, Dresden, Sept. 30 - Oct. 4, 2002, LNCS.
30. Kruchten, P.: Architectural Blueprints - The "4+1" View Model of Software Architecture. IEEE Software, 12(6) November 1995, pp. 42-50.
31. Labelled Transition System Analyzer (LTSA). On-line at: <http://www-dse.doc.ic.ac.uk/~jnm/book/>.
32. Lay, M., Karis, M.: Collaborative writing in industry: Investigations in theory and practice. Baywood Publishing Company, Amityville, 1991.
33. Luckham, D. C., Kenney, J. J., Augustin, L. M., Vera, J., Bryan, D., Mann, W.: Specification and Analysis of System Architecture Using Rapide. *IEEE Trans. on Software Engineering*, Special Issue on Software Architecture, Vol. 21, N. 4, pp. 336-355, April 1995.
34. Magee, J., Kramer, J.: *Concurrency: State Models & Java Programs*. Wiley, April 1999.
35. Medvidovic, N., Rosenblum, D. S., Redmiles, D. F., Robbins, J. E.: Modeling software architectures in the Unified Modeling Language. ACM Transactions on Software Engineering and Methodology (TOSEM), Vol. 11 , Issue 1, Jan. 2002.
36. Milner, R.: *Communication on Concurrences*. International Series on Computer Science. Prentice Hall International, 1989.
37. Muccini, H.: Software Architecture for Testing, Coordination Models and Views Model Checking.   PhD thesis, University of L'Aquila, year 2002.   On-line at: <http://www.HenryMuccini.com/publications.htm>.
38. Muccini, H., Bertolino, A., Inverardi, P.: Using Software Architecture for Code Testing Submitted for publication.
39. Muccini, H., Bertolino, A., Inverardi, P.: Using Software Architecture for Code Testing. Long version of [38]. On-line at http://www.HenryMuccini.com/publications.htm

40. Richardson, D. J., Wolf, A. L.: Software testing at the architectural level. *ISAW-2* in Joint Proc. of the *ACM SIGSOFT '96* Workshops, pp. 68-71, 1996.
41. Richardson, D. J., Stafford, J., Wolf, A. L.: A Formal Approach to Architecture-based Software Testing. Technical Report, University of California, Irvine, 1998.
42. TorX Test Tool Information.
    http://fmt.cs.utwente.nl/tools/torx/introduction.html
43. Tretmans, J.: Test Generation with Inputs, Outputs and Repetitive Quiescence. Software–Concepts and Tools, 17(3):103-120, 1996.
44. Tretmans, J.: Testing Concurrent Systems: A Formal Approach. Proc. of CON-CUR'99, LNCS 1664 (1999), pp. 46–65.
45. UML. Object Management Group: OMG  Unified Modeling Language (UML), V1.4, 2001. http://www.omg.org
46. de Vries, R. G., Tretmans, J.: Towards Formal Test Purposes. Proc. FATES'01, Aalborg, Denmark (2001).
47. Watson, A. H., McCabe, T. J.: *Structured Testing: A Testing Methodology Using the Cyclomatic Complexity Metric.* NIST Special Publication 500-235, August 1996.
48. Young, M.: Testing Complex Architectural Conformance Relations. In *Proc. Int. Workshop on the ROle of Software Architecture in TEsting and Analysis* (ROSATEA), CNR-NSF, pp. 42-45, July 1998.

# Architecture Based Evolution of Software Systems

Luis Filipe Andrade[1] and José Luiz Fiadeiro[2]

[1]ATX Software S.A., Alameda António Sérgio 7 – 1 C,
2795-023 Linda-a-Velha, Portugal
landrade@atxsoftware.com

[2]Department of Computer Science, University of Leicester
University Road, Leicester LE1 7RH, UK
jose@fiadeiro.org

**Abstract.** Although architectural concepts and techniques have been considered mainly as a means of controlling the complexity of developing software, we argue, and demonstrate, that they can play a vital role in supporting current needs for systems that can evolve and adapt, in run-time, to changes that occur in the application or business domain in which they operate.

## 1 Introduction

Our contribution is motivated by the growing need that companies and organisations have for software systems that can react and adapt, in a flexible and timely way, to changes occurring in the application domain, the technologies that support their deployment, or the more general business infrastructure in which they operate. In other words, whereas the pressure on the Software Engineering community used to be for coming up with methods and techniques that address the complexity of *constructing* software systems, a new challenge is there for controlling the complexity of the *evolution* of such systems. After a brief overview of the context in which these challenges have been arising, we identify the shortcomings of current methods and techniques to address them, and suggest that current work on Software Architectures has a very important contribution to make. Our own contribution, the "three Cs", is then expanded in the rest of the paper.

### 1.1 All Change!

Over the last few years, we have witnessed a significant shift in the way organisations are structured and operate by becoming "information-based". This shift is having tremendous implications in society and the economy in general, with consequent levels of pressure on all those engaged in the software industry. As, more and more, business is based on, or directly operated through, organisations' information systems, people in the software areas are required to work out "miracles" in keeping up with the ever changing expectations of the commercial and strategy management areas.

M. Bernardo and P. Inverardi (Eds.): SFM 2003, LNCS 2804, pp. 148–181, 2003.
© Springer-Verlag Berlin Heidelberg 2003

Indeed, information systems are now at the core of the competitive edge of every organisation, and all traditional business thrusts such as *differentiation, cost, innovation, growth, alliances* and *time* have a direct impact on the way systems have to be conceived, developed and maintained [18]. Systems must now provide *different* services by making *innovative* use of technological advances (Internet, wireless technology, and so on) and, at the same time, be easily *integrated* with other systems in order to support business *alliances*. In the rules of the "new" or "now"-Economy, this is supposed to happen in "real-time", or "just-in-time", and, as usual, at low cost!

In other words, *agility* is, now, the prime feature required of any information system. As a consequence, software teams are struggling to compete with speeding business and technology evolution, making the ability to *change* systems a more important goal than the ability to build them *ab initio*. Quoting directly from [14], "... the ability to change is now more important than the ability to create [e-commerce] systems in the first place. Change becomes a first-class design goal and requires business and technology architecture whose components can be added, modified, replaced and reconfigured".

All this means that the "complexity" of software has definitely shifted from *construction* to *evolution*, and that methods and technologies are required that address this new level of complexity and adaptability. We believe that, similarly to what happened with software construction, complexity in evolution is, first of all, a problem of level of abstraction. That is to say, we need to find the abstractions that allow us to expose the "structure" of the problem. Because evolution, as characterised above, is driven by the business domain – be it either as a consequence of changes in the business rules or a merger of enterprises that share some part of the market – it seems to make sense to look for software structures that reflect the structure of the domain itself.

To meet this goal, there are two important aspects that need to be accounted for. On the one hand, we need *modelling* approaches that direct us to the identification of components that relate directly to business entities, and to component interconnections that reflect the business rules according to which the business entities interoperate. On the other hand, we need to provide implementation solutions that are *compositional* with respect to the structures offered by the modelling primitives. By compositionality we mean the ability for the structure obtained at the modelling level to be reflected directly at the implementation level so that changes operated at the level of the business model do not require a global reconfiguration of the system but, rather, only local changes that can be performed at run-time, without interruption of the other services being offered by the system.

## 1.2    No Change with OO

In order to address these new levels of complexity, organisations are looking for answers mainly in the context of object-oriented (OO) development techniques (usually based on the UML [9]), component-based (CB) frameworks [42], design patterns [15] and, most recently, aspect-oriented programming [10]. However, although these techniques have proved useful in taming the complexity of software *construction*, they cannot cope, on their own, with the levels of agility required for *evolution*.

Object-oriented techniques such as inheritance and clientship are too "static" and "white box" when it comes to change. The use of inheritance requires us to know, understand, and modify the internals of objects. In many circumstances, this may not be acceptable (e.g. for economic or security reasons) or even possible (in the case of third-party, closed components, e.g. legacy systems). On the other hand, because interactions in object-oriented approaches are based on *identities* [20], in the sense that, through clientship, objects interact by invoking specific methods of specific objects (instances) to get something specific done, the resulting systems are too rigid to support the identified levels of agility [40]. Any change on the collaborations that an object maintains with other objects needs to be performed at the level of the code that implements that object and, possibly, of the objects with which the new collaborations are established. See [3] for an expanded explanation around an example.

Naturally, object-oriented technology does not prevent more flexible modes of interconnections to be *implemented*. Design mechanisms that make use of event publishing/subscription through brokers and other well-known patterns [15] have already found their way into commercially available products that support implicit invocation [36] instead of feature calling (explicit invocation). However, solutions based on the use of design patterns or, for that matter, Aspect-Oriented Programming, are not at the level of abstraction in which the need for change arises and needs to be managed. Being mechanisms that operate at the design level, there is a wide gap that separates them from the business modelling levels at which change is better perceived and managed. This conceptual gap is not easily bridged, and the process that leads from the business requirements to the identification and instantiation of the relevant design patterns is not easily documented or made otherwise explicit in a way that facilitates changes to be operated. Once instantiated, design patterns code up interactions in ways that, typically, requires evolution to be intrusive because they were not conceived to be evolvable; as a consequence, most of the times, the pattern will dissolve as the system evolves. Therefore, we need semantic primitives through which interconnections can be externalised, modelled explicitly, and evolved directly as representations of business rules.

## 1.3   Architectures for Change

Our own experience in developing applications in one of the most volatile business areas, banking, has shown that the changes that are most often required on a system do not concern the basic computations performed by its components but the way they interact. Indeed, we often forget that the global behaviour of a system emerges both from the local computations that are performed by its components *and* the way they are interconnected. The functionalities that make a system useful cannot be achieved by its components in isolation but only through the collaborations that are established between them. Hence, in very dynamic areas, the most frequent changes are likely to occur not at the level of the core entities of the domain (say, the notion of a bank account) but of the business rules or the protocols that determine how these core entities interact (say, how customers interact with their accounts). Hence, there is an important role to be played by methodological concepts and supporting technology that promote interactions as first-class entities, leading to systems that are "exoskeletal" in the sense that they exhibit their configuration structure explicitly [26].

This is why we believe "Software Architectures" have an important contribution to make: architectural concepts and techniques, as described in [8,38,41], promote a gross decomposition of systems into *components* that perform basic computations and *connectors* that ensure that they interact in ways that make required global system properties to emerge. Such an externalisation of the interconnections should allow for systems to be reconfigured, in a compositional, non-intrusive way, by acting directly on the entities that capture the interactions between components, leading to an evolution process that follows the architecture of the system.

The scope of Software Architectures intersects several other research areas in Software Engineering and Programming Languages. For instance, the crucial separation between "Computation" – the way basic functionalities of system services are ensured – and "Coordination" – the mechanisms through which components interact – has been the core subject of the community that gathers around "Coordination Languages and Models" [16]. Mechanisms through which systems can be dynamically reconfigured have been developed in the area of "Configurable Distributed Systems" [25]. In this paper, we provide an overview of an approach to system evolution that brings together all these different streams of research and has been tested in several application domains [4,23,24]. In section 2, we further motivate and outline the basic principles of the approach. In section 3, we address the way business rules can be modelled through semantic primitives that, basically, amount to architectural connectors. In section 4, we focus on supporting evolution through programmed and reactive dynamic reconfiguration. In section 5, we address the way the approach can be automated and supported by tools. Finally, in section 6, we conclude with comparisons with other work and an outlook of current and planned developments.

## 2    The Three Cs of Architectures

The architectural approach that we will be describing is based on the crucial separation between "three Cs": Computation, Coordination, and Configuration. This separation needs to be supported at two different levels. On the one hand, through semantic primitives that address the "business architecture", i.e. the means that need to be provided for modelling business entities (Computation), the business rules that determine how the entities can interact (Coordination), and the business contexts through which specific rules can be superposed, at run-time, to specific entities (Configuration). On the other hand, the architectural properties of the deployment infrastructures that can carry this distinction to the design and implementation layers, and support the levels of agility identified in the previous section. We start by discussing the latter. An overview of the semantic primitives is then given as a motivation for the subsequent sections, which explain them in detail.

## 2.1   The CCC System Architecture

As already mentioned, the rationale for the methodology and technologies that we have been building is in the *strict* separation between three aspects of the development and deployment of any software system: the *computations* performed locally in its components, the *coordination* mechanisms through which global properties can emerge from those computations, and the *configuration* operations that ensure that the system will evolve according to given constraints such as organisational policies, legislation, and other. Such layering should be strict in order to allow for changes to be performed at each layer without interfering with the levels below.

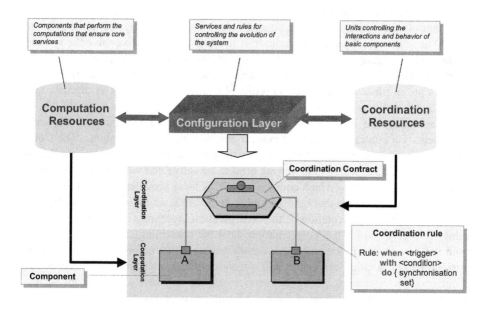

The Computation Layer should contain the components that perform the computations that ensure the basic services provided within the system. Each component has two interfaces: a functional interface that includes the operations that allow one to query and change the encapsulated component state; and a configuration interface that provides the component's constructors and destructors, and any other operations that are necessary to the correct management of dynamic reconfiguration. One such operation is querying whether the component is in a "stable" state in which the component may be deleted or its "connections" to other components can be changed; another example is an operation that can temporarily block the component's execution while a reconfiguration that involves it is processed. The reason for separate interfaces is to be able to constrain the access that the various parts of the architecture have to each other and, hence, achieve a cleaner separation of concerns. In the case of the coordination layer, we require that no component should be able to invoke another component's configuration operations: components should not create other components because that is a change to the currently existing configuration and, as such, should be explicitly managed by the configuration layer.

The Coordination Layer defines the way computational components are interconnected for the system to behave, as a whole, according to set requirements. In the terminology of Software Architecture, this layer is populated by the *connectors* that regulate the interactions between the components of the layer below. We call such connectors *coordination contracts* or, for simplicity, *contracts*. We also require each contract to provide a functional and a configuration interface; each constructor in the configuration interface must include as arguments the components that the connector instance to be created will coordinate. We impose two restrictions: a contract may not use the configuration interface of any contract or component; and a contract may not use another contract's functional interface. The rationale for the first condition is again that configuration operations should only be performed by the configuration layer. The reason for the second condition is to make it possible to evolve the system through (un)plugging of individual contracts between components, which is only possible if there are no dependencies among contracts. The coordination effects that contracts put in place are described in terms of trigger-reaction rules as discussed in section 3.

At each state, the interconnections put in place among the population of basic components via contracts define the current configuration of the system. The Configuration Layer is responsible for managing the current configuration, i.e., for determining, at each state, which components need to be active and what interconnections need to be in place among which components. This layer provides a set of high-level reconfiguration operations that enforce global invariants over the system's configuration. The actual implementation of the configuration layer may follow the technical architecture given in [34]: a configuration database containing updated information about the current configuration, a consistency manager that enforces a "stable" state in which reconfiguration can occur, and a reconfiguration manager that executes the reconfiguration operations, using the services of the database and the consistency manager. The implementation of the reconfiguration operations makes use not only of the configuration interfaces provided by the components and contracts, but also of the functional interfaces because some changes to the configuration may depend on the current state of components and contracts, and may trigger state modifications to restore application-wide consistency.

Systems whose design architecture supports this separation of concerns through a strict layering can be evolved in a compositional way. Changes that do not require different computational properties can be brought about either by reconfiguring the way components interact, or adding new connectors that regulate the way existing components operate, instead of performing changes in the components themselves. This can be achieved by superposing, dynamically, new coordination and configuration mechanisms on the components that capture the basic business entities. If the interactions were coded in the components themselves, such changes, if at all possible thanks to the availability of the source code, besides requiring the corresponding objects to be reprogrammed, with possible implications on the class hierarchy, would probably have side effects on all the other objects that use their services, and so on, triggering a whole cascade of changes that would be difficult to control.

On the other hand, the need for an explicit configuration layer, with its own primitives and methodology, is justified by the need to control the evolution of the configuration of the system according to the business policies of the organisation or, more generally, to reflect constraints on the configurations that are admissible (configuration invariants). This layer is also responsible for the degree of self-adaptation that the system can exhibit. Reconfiguration operations should be able to be programmed at this level that enable the system to react to changes perceived in its environment by putting in place new components or new contracts. In this way, the system should be able to adapt itself to take profit of new operating conditions, or reconfigure itself to take corrective action, and so on.

According to the nature of the platform in which the system is running, this strict layering may be more or less directly enforced. For instance, we have already argued that traditional object-oriented and component-based development infrastructures do not support this layering from first-principles, which motivates the need for new semantic modelling primitives as discussed below. However, this does not mean that they cannot accommodate such an architecture: design techniques such as reflection or aspect-oriented programming, or the use of design patterns, can be employed to provide the support that is necessary from the middleware. In fact, we have shown how the separation between computation and coordination can be enforced in Java through the use of well known design patterns, leading to what we called the "Coordination Development Environment" or CDE [5,17,27], which we will discuss in section 5.

The design patterns that we use in the CDE provide what we can call a "micro-architecture" that enforces the externalisation of interactions, thus separating coordination from computation. It does so at the cost of introducing an additional layer of adaptation that intercepts direct communication through feature calling (clientship) and, basically, enforces an event-based approach. In this respect, platforms that rely on event-based or publish-subscribe interaction represent a real advantage over object-based ones: they support directly the modelling primitives that we will be discussing in the paper.

## 2.2   The CCC Business Architecture

The separation of coordination from computation has been advocated for a long time in the Coordination Languages community [16], and the separation of all three concerns is central to Software Architecture, which has put forward the distinction between components, connectors and architectures [38]. The Configurable Distributed Systems community [29], in particular the Configuration Programming approach [25], also gives first-class status to configuration. However, these approaches do not provide a satisfying way to model the three concerns in a way that supports evolution. Coordination languages do not make the configuration explicit or have a very low-level coordination mechanism (e.g. tuple spaces); architecture description languages do not handle evolution from first principles or do it in a deficient way; configuration programming is not at the business modelling level.

For instance, the reconfiguration operations that we provide through *coordination contexts* correspond more to what in other works is called a reconfiguration script [11] than the basic commands provided by some ADLs to create and remove components, connectors, and bindings between them [30]. Coordination contexts also make explicit which invariants the configuration has to keep during evolution. It is natural to express these invariants in a declarative language with primitive predicates to query the current configuration (e.g., whether a contract of a given type connects some given components). Such languages have been proposed in Distributed Systems (e.g., Gerel-SL [11]) and Software Architecture approaches (e.g., Armani [35]). However, all these approaches *program* the reconfiguration operations, i.e. they provide an operational specification of the changes. Our position, as expanded in section 4, is that, at the modelling level, those operations should also be specified in a declarative way, using the same language as for invariants, by stating properties of the configuration before and after the change. In other words, the semantics of each reconfiguration operation provided in this layer is given by its pre- and post-conditions.

On the other hand, it is true that modelling languages like the UML [9] already provide techniques that come close to our intended level of abstraction. For instance, "use cases" come close to coordination contexts: they describe the possible ways in which the system can be given access and used. However, they do not end up being explicitly represented in the (application) architecture: they are just a means of identifying classes and collaborations. More precisely, they are not captured through formal entities through which run-time configuration management can be explicitly supported. The same applies to the externalisation of interactions. Although the advantage of making relationships first-class citizens in conceptual modelling has been recognised by many authors (e.g. [22]), which led to the ISO General Relationship Model (ISO/IEC 10165-7), things are not as clean when it comes to supporting a strict separation of concerns.

For instance, one could argue that mechanisms like association classes provide a way of making explicit how objects interact, but the typical implementation of associations through attributes is still "identity"-based and does not really externalise the interaction: it remains coded in the objects that participate in the association. The best way of implementing an interaction through an association class would seem to be for a new operation to be declared for the association that can act as a mediator, putting in place a form of implicit invocation [36]. However, on the one hand, the fact that a mediator is used for coordinating the interaction between two given objects does not prevent direct relationships from being established that may side step it and violate the business rule that the association is meant to capture. On the other hand, the solution is still intrusive in the sense that the calls to the mediator must be explicitly programmed in the implementation of the classes involved in the association.

Moreover, the use of mediators is not incremental in the sense that the addition of new business rules cannot be achieved by simply introducing new association classes and mediators. The other classes in the system need to be made aware that new association classes have become available so that the right mediators are used for establishing the required interactions. That is, the burden of deciding which mediator to interact with is put again on the side of clients. Moreover, different rules may interact with each other thus requiring an additional level of coordination among the mediators themselves to be programmed. This leads to models that are not as abstract as they ought to be due to the need to make explicit (even program) the relationships that may exist between the original classes and the mediators, and among the different mediators themselves. In summary, we end up facing the problems that, in the introduction, we identified for the use of design patterns in general.

The primitive – *coordination law* – that we have developed for modelling this kind of contractual relationship between components circumvents these problems by abandoning the "identity"-based mechanism on which the object-oriented paradigm relies for interactions, and adopting instead a mechanism of superposition that allows for collaborations to be modelled outside the components as connectors (coordination contracts) that can be applied, at run-time, to coordinate their behaviour. From a methodological point of view, this alternative approach encourages developers to identify dependencies between components in terms of *services* rather than identities. From the implementation point of view, superposition of coordination contracts has the advantage of being non-intrusive on the implementation of the components. That is, it does not require the code that implements the components to be changed or adapted, precisely because there is no information on the interactions that is coded inside the components. As a result, systems can evolve through the addition, deletion or substitution of coordination contracts without requiring any change in the way the core entities have been deployed.

This is the approach that we are going to present in the rest of the paper. We start by presenting the primitives that support the separation between computation and coordination and the modelling of business rules as architectural connectors – coordination laws and interfaces. We then discuss the primitives – coordination contexts – that we provide for configuring and controlling the evolutionary process.

## 3     Modelling Interactions

The semantic primitive that we provide for externalising interactions – coordination contract – makes available the expressive power of a *connector* in the terminology of software architectures. It consists of a prescription of certain coordination effects (the *glue* of the connector in the sense of [1]) that can be superposed on a collection of partners (system components) when the occurrence of one of the contract *triggers* is detected in the system. Contracts establish interactions at the instance level when superposed on a running system as the result of the instantiation of a *coordination law*. These capture connector types as in Architecture Description Languages. In the description of a coordination law, the nature of the partners over which the law can be instantiated are identified as *coordination interfaces* (the *roles* of the connector type in the sense of [1]). These act as types that can be instantiated with components of the system when a contract that instantiates the law needs to be activated on a particular configuration of the running system.

### 3.1    Laws and Interfaces for Coordination

We are going to illustrate our approach with a very simple example from banking. As a core concept of banking, we assume that an account offers three basic services – `balance():money`, `credit(n:money)`, and `debit(n:money)`. The methodology that we are building around the CCC-approach suggests that, in order to model specific business activities that involve bank accounts, we should superpose whatever coordination mechanisms are required to model business rules as external entities, rather than specialise the class with new, "hard-wired" features each time a new business rule, or changes to existing business rules, come into play.

For instance, restrictions on debits should not be "hard-wired" as pre-conditions on the basic method that performs the debit but, rather, as contracts that coordinate specific interactions that involve the method. As a business activity, a withdrawal by a given customer is an operation that involves both an account and a customer, regardless of the way that the customer is represented in the system, i.e. of whether it is a software component in the information system, an interface object that captures an external agent of the system, etc. Hence, we model customers through a coordination interface that is agnostic with respect to any specific form of representation and allows for such representations to evolve as new decisions are made during the lifetime of the system. In terms of our example, we assume that customer interfaces include `owns(a:account):Boolean`, and `withdrawal(n:money,a:account)`.

```
coordination interface customer-withdrawal
import types  money, account;
services      owns(a:account):Boolean
events        withdrawal(n:money; a:account)
end interface
```

The difference between *services* and *events* is quite simple: *services* identify operations that instances of the interface need to provide for the contract to operate according to the law; *events* identify situations produced during system execution that are required to be detected as triggers for the contract to react and activate a *coordination rule* as discussed below. For the proposed coordination mechanism, we are required to detect as triggers events that consist of customers performing withdrawals, and be provided with services that query about the account ownership relation.

In the traditional, object-oriented way, typical events are feature calls. In fact, in an object-oriented setting, a withdrawal would normally be modelled as a direct call to the debit operation of the corresponding account. That is to say, as part of the design of the system, `withdrawal(n,a)` establishes a call `a.debit(n)`. As argued in [3,40], this form of direct invocation leads to systems in which components are too tightly coupled, making any change on the interactions to be intrusive on the code that implements the components. The alternative that we propose through coordination contracts consists in providing an explicit representation of the interaction outside the components that can be superposed on them when needed without their knowledge.

The coordination interface that corresponds to the other partner of this business rule is as follows:

```
coordination interface account-debit
import types  money;
```

```
services      balance():money;
              debit(a:money)  post balance() = old balance()-a
end interface
```

The inclusion of properties in an interface, e.g. the pre and post-conditions on debits, is meant to provide means for requirements to be specified on the components that can be bound to the interface and become under the coordination of the law. In this example, we are stating minimal properties on the functional behaviour of the services included in the interface, namely that debits interact with observations of the balance as expected.

Given these two coordination interfaces, we can specify the law that models standard withdrawals as follows:

```
coordination law standard-withdrawal
partners a:account-debit; c:customer-withdrawal
rules        when  c.withdrawal(n,a)
             with  a.balance() • n & c.owns(a)
             do    a.debit(n);
end law
```

Besides identifying the coordination interfaces, a coordination law specifies the rules that apply to the partners over which it is instantiated in order to coordinate their interaction. Such coordination rules are of the form:

```
when  condition
with  condition
do    set of operations
```

Each coordination rule identifies, under the "when" clause, a trigger to which the contracts that instantiate the law will react – a request by the customer for a withdrawal in the case at hand. The trigger can be just an event observed directly over one of the partners or a more complex condition built from one or more events. Under the "with" clause, we include conditions (guards) that should be observed for the reaction to be performed. If any of the conditions fails, the reaction is not performed and the occurrence of the trigger fails. Failure is handled through whatever mechanisms are provided by the language used for deployment.

The reaction to be performed to occurrences of the trigger is identified under the "do" clause as a set of operations – a debit for the amount and on the account identified in the trigger. This set may include services provided by one or more of the partners as well as operations that are proper to the law itself (as illustrated in section 3.2). The whole interaction is handled as a single transaction, i.e. it consists of an atomic event in the sense that the trigger reports a success only if all the operations identified in the reaction execute successfully and the conditions identified under the "with" clause are satisfied. Therefore, every coordination rule specified in a law identifies a point of "rendez-vous" in which the partners are brought together to synchronise their lives.

As we have just mentioned, in execution terms, the rendez-vous is an indivisible, atomic action. This paradigm of "joint actions" is present in a number of approaches to parallel program design (e.g. [6]), as well as in recent languages for information system modelling like MERODE [39]. When instantiated over a running configuration, each partner participates in the rendez-vous according to the services declared in the corresponding interface, but unaware of the type of coordination to which it is being subjected. Notice that the execution of the services is performed locally by the components that hold them and, as such, may be subject to further local constraints. Hence, the whole reaction may fail even if the "with"-clause is satisfied because some of the operations involved may not execute successfully.

The "with"-clause plays a fundamental role in the externalisation of business rules in the sense that it allows for the effects of operations (the computations that they perform) to be handled locally, and the conditions under which they are performed to be controlled, totally or partially, at the level of coordination contracts. Deciding what is part of an entity and what pertains to a business rule is not an easy matter and requires a good expertise on the business domain itself. For instance, market evolution has shown that the circumstances under which a withdrawal can be accepted keeps changing as competition dictates banks to come up with new ways for customers to interact with their accounts. Therefore, it should not be too difficult to come to the conclusion that the precondition on debits derives more from the specification of a business requirement than an intrinsic constraint on the functionality of a basic business entity like account. Hence, it seems best to shift the precondition to the law so that the contract that regulates how a given costumer interacts with a given account can be replaced without interfering with the code that implements the debit. For instance, a customer may get an upgraded service by subscribing to a VIP-package:

```
coordination law VIP-withdrawal
partners     a:account-debit; c:customer-withdrawal
operations   credit():money
rules        when  c.withdrawal(n,a)
             with  a.balance()+credit()• n & c.owns(a)
             do    a.debit(n);
end law
```

As illustrated in this example, it is possible to declare features that are local to the law itself. For instance, in the case of VIP-withdrawals, it makes sense to assign the credit-limit that is negotiated between the customer and the bank to the law itself rather than the customer or the account. This is because we may want to be able to assign different credit limits to the same customer but for different accounts, or for the same account but for different owners.

One could argue for a separate partner of the law to be defined for credit but, being a feature that is local to the law, it should not be externalised. Indeed, although every contract (instance of the law) has an associated component for implementing these local features, this component should not be public. For instance, a law does not define a public class and its instances are not considered as ordinary components of the system.

This is one of the reasons why association classes, as available in the UML, are not expressive enough to model the coordination mechanisms of contracts. Although coordination laws allow for interactions to be made explicit in conceptual models, they should not be accessed in the same way as the classes that model the core business entities. Contracts do not provide services: they coordinate the services made available by the core entities. Another shortcoming of association classes, and the use of mediators as discussed in the previous section, is that they do not enforce the synchronisation and atomicity requirements of the proposed coordination mechanisms.

We need to stress the fact that coordination interfaces are defined so as to state *requirements* placed by laws on the entities that can be subjected to its rules and not as a declaration of features or properties that entities offer to be coordinated. This means that coordination interfaces should restrict themselves to what is essential for the definition of given laws and hence, in the extreme, can be local to the laws themselves. However, for the sake of reusability and simplification of the binding process, it is useful to externalise coordination interfaces from the laws in the context of which they are defined, and establish a hierarchy between them that is consistent with the compliance relationship in the sense that a component that complies with a given interface also complies with any ancestor of that interface or, that any binder of the component for that interface will also serve as a binder for any ancestor. Hence, in a sense, coordination interfaces fulfil the role of representations of abstract business entities in the sense that the hierarchy of interfaces will, ultimately, provide a taxonomy of all the business uses that are made of entities in the application domain.

Given this, we insist that, as a methodological principle, the definition of coordination interfaces should be driven by the modelling of the business rules as coordination laws and not by the modelling of the entities of the business domain as it is usual in object-oriented and other traditional "product"-oriented approaches. In this sense, it makes no sense to define a coordination interface for accounts in general but, instead, and in the extreme, as many interfaces as the business rules that apply to accounts require (something that is evolutionary in nature because it is as impossible to predict how an information system will evolve as for how the business of an organisation will grow). Ultimately, these will identify all the usages that the specific business makes of the notion of account in a "service-oriented" perspective. As the business rules evolve, new coordination interfaces are defined and placed in the hierarchy. In a product-oriented notion of interface, each such change in the business rules would require a change in the account interface, which is against the spirit of "agility-enhancer" that our method is supposed to deliver.

We should also stress the fact that a binding/compliance mechanism needs to be established for each target development environment. Each time a technological change is introduced that makes it necessary for an application to be redeployed, the binding mechanism will be likely to have to change accordingly and, hence, the compliance relations will need to be re-established or the corresponding binders redefined. Again, some degree of automatic synthesis would be welcome but, at least, computational support should be provided for the redefinition of the binders.

## 3.2     Business Rules as Coordination Laws

The discussion so far has focused on the binding of coordination interfaces to given components of the system that we want to interconnect in order for some global property of the system to emerge from their collaboration. However, coordination interfaces can also act as useful abstractions for either events or services that lie outside the system, or global phenomena that cannot be necessarily localised in specific components. In the case of events, this allows for the definition of reactions that the system should be able to perform to triggers that are either global (e.g. a deadline) or are detected outside the system. In the case of reactions, this allows us to identify services that should be procured externally. This is particularly useful for B2B operations and the modelling of Web-services, the paradigms into which e-business is evolving. What is important is that a uniform notation and semantics is maintained for all cases in order not to compromise changes in the boundaries of the system.

For instance, one could define a law for handling transfers that arrive at a bank from outside by relying on the following interfaces:

```
coordination interface account-credit
import types  money;
services      balance():money;
              credit(a:money)  post balance() =
                            old balance()+a
end interface

coordination interface external-transfer
import types  money, account, transfer-id;
events            transfer(n:money;a:account;t:transfer-id)
end interface
```

When defining the corresponding law

```
coordination law external-transfer-handler
partners     a:account-credit; external-transfer
operations   ackn(t:transfer-id)
rules        when  transfer(n,a,t)
             with  a.exists
             do    n•1000:a.credit(n-100)
                     & n<1000:a.credit(90%n)
                     & ackn(t)
end law
```

we do not provide any formal parameter of type external-transfer because it is not intended to be bound to any specific component of the system. Notice that the synchronisation set is now more complex than in the previous examples: an acknowledgment is sent and a commission is charged – 100 units if the transfer is above 1000 or a 10% commission for amounts below 1000.

The examples that we have just seen illustrate situations in which a coordination law is defined to model the interaction that is required between certain components of the business domain to ensure some functionality. There are other situations in which coordination laws are defined in order just to *monitor* the behaviour of given components. For instance, assume that new legislation is passed that requires credits over a certain amount to be reported to the central bank – e.g. as a means of detecting money laundering. Rather than revise the implementation of credits to take care of this new requirement, it is better to superpose a contract over every account to perform the required monitoring activity:

```
coordination interface account-credit-event
import types  money;
events            credit(a:money)
end interface
```

```
coordination law report-big-credits
partners    a:account-credit-event
operations  big():money;
            report(n:money);
            set-big(n:money) post big()=n
rules       when a.credit(n) & n•big()
            do  report(n);
end law
```

Notice that the interface `account-credit` that we defined for the laws on withdrawals did not include debits as events but as services. Hence, we cannot reuse it for this law.

Contracts can also be used for superposing *regulators* over certain components of the system. As an example, consider the situation in which the bank decides to penalise customers who fail to keep a given minimum average balance by charging a monthly commission. This situation can be modelled through the superposition of a contract over every bank account through the following interface:

```
coordination interface average-balance
import types money
services    average():money;
            debit(n:money)
end interface
```

The corresponding law is:

```
coordination law commission-on-low-balance
partners    a:average-balance
operations  minimum():money; charge():money
rules       when end-of-month
            do  minimum>a.average():a.debit(charge())
end law
```

We are assuming that `end-of-month` is a global trigger that the system detects through some calendar mechanism that we take for granted. Otherwise, we could define a global interface as illustrated for the external transfers.

We are now going to illustrate a more complex use of coordination laws. It refers to a banking product that involves two accounts, typically a checking account and a savings account, transferring money from one to the other in order to keep the balance of one of them – the checking account – between a given minimum and a given maximum. On subscription of this package, the contract is superposed over the two accounts through the following interface:

```
coordination interface account-debit&credit
type-id     account
events      balance():Money;
services    debit(a:Money);
            credit(a:Money);
            balance():Money;

properties  balance() after credit(a) is balance()+a
            balance() after debit(a) is balance()-a
end interface
```

Notice that `balance` is now included as an event as well. This means that components that are partner instances are required to make available state changes on the current balance as observable triggers.

The proposed law is:

```
coordination law flexible-package
partners      c,s:account-debit&credit
operations    minimum,maximum:money
rules         when  c.balance()<minimum
              do    s.debit(min(s.balance(),maximum-c.balance())
                      & c.credit(min(s.balance(),maximum-c.balance()))
              when  c.balance()>maximum
              do    c.debit(c.balance()-maximum)
                      & s.credit(c.balance()-maximum)
end law
```

The "do" clauses in the coordination rules are now more complex in the sense that the reactions to be performed on occurrence of the triggers involves more than one operation: they both define sets of actions that we call the *synchronisation sets* associated with the rules. As already mentioned, the reactions are executed as transactions, which means that the synchronisation sets are executed atomically. In what concerns the language in which the reactions are defined, the primitives supported by the transaction manager of the target implementation environment should be allowed. However, at higher levels of modelling, we normally use a more abstract notation for defining the synchronisation set as above.


## 4     Configuring and Evolving Interactions

The purpose of coordination laws, as discussed in the previous section, is to provide a level of representation for business rules that is, basically, application-independent. This is because we want to make available a level of business modelling that is invariant with respect to evolution taking place in the "technological axis" and that may lead to changes on the way applications are deployed. It is clear that changes at this level should not induce changes on the business model but only on the way the model is being reified in terms of the specific applications that are being (re)deployed.

In this section, we are concerned with the mechanisms through which laws can be instantiated over running systems and the primitives through which the evolution of the configuration of the system can be controlled so as to ensure global policies of an organisation.


### 4.1     Configuring Interactions

Coordination laws model the collaborations that need to be put in place among components to ensure that the global properties that are required of the system in any given state can emerge from the interactions and the computations that are being performed locally within the components that are present in the configuration of the system, at that same state. In broad terms, a configuration of a system consists of a collection of components that deploy core entities of the business domain and a collection of instances of laws that coordinate the interactions between them. Such instances – called (coordination) *contracts* – are components that execute the coordination rules of the law by reacting to the triggers, evaluating the guards and executing the synchronisation sets.

An example of a configuration in the banking domain that we have been discussing is given below in terms of a diagrammatic notation that should be self-explaining (rectangles represent components and scrolls represent contracts): two customers, mary and john, are joint owners of account aaa/bbb; mary uses a VIP-withdrawal package with credit 3000 and john a standard-withdrawal package; mary is the owner of a second account ccc/ddd with a standard-withdrawal contract and is monitored for credits above 10000.

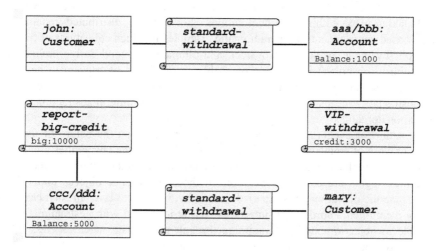

For the reader who is familiar with our previous publications on "coordination contracts", coordination laws may appear to be a mere syntactic variation. A more careful analysis will show that there are fundamental generalisations whose aim is to provide mechanisms for addressing a more abstract level of "shearing" (to use an "architectural" metaphor). In previous publications, starting with [2], we defined coordination contracts having in mind their use in the context of object-oriented modelling, e.g. through the UML. Hence, in the description of a contract (type), the partners to which contract instances can be applied were identified as object classes of the system and additional rules on the population of these classes. Typically, such classes will be already present or will end up in the class diagram defined for the application.

The need for application-independent level of business modelling led us to generalise this characterisation of the business entities (subjects) to which the business rule applies. This generalisation was made, on the one hand, to remove the bias towards object-oriented approaches and, on the other hand, the direct connection to the class diagram of the application. For this purpose, in coordination laws, subjects are identified in terms of a number of *coordination interfaces* – an abstraction of the notion of *role* of architectural connectors similar to the one formalised in [1]. The use of these laws in a specific application requires *interface instantiation mechanisms* through which one can determine, for any component of the application and interface of a coordination law, whether the component *complies* with the interface in the sense that it can be used as a subject or, better still, if and how it can be adapted to comply and become a subject of the law through that interface. Ideally, this process of instantiation should be automated, leading to the synthesis of the necessary adaptor. A very simple example, but probably the case that is likely to be most frequent in the immediate future use of the concept, is the one in which coordination interfaces correspond to notions like Java-class interfaces and the instantiation mechanism is the one that Java provides through the "implements" relationship between interfaces and classes.

The degree of dynamic reconfigurability that can be achieved through coordination interfaces and laws depends directly on the ability of the execution environment to make available, as recognisable triggers, interactions between entities as well as events taking place within individual entities. For instance, distributed systems and object-based environments are paradigmatic examples in which collections of triggers are explicitly made available. However, and ultimately, a good design architecture (e.g. publish/subscriber) is a means of enabling collections of triggers to be made available in environments that do not support directly any notion of interaction. Compositionality means that triggers can be mapped to meaningful abstractions of the application domain.

The nature of events and services can vary depending on the nature of the language, or class of languages, in which the entities to which the law applies are, or are likely to be, implemented. In an object-oriented environment, typical events that constitute triggers are calls for operations/methods of instance objects, and typical services are the operations that are made public by the object class. In such cases, as already mentioned, coordination interfaces can be identified with abstractions made available in object-oriented programming through mechanisms such as class interfaces in Java, pure virtual classes in C++, and abstract classes in Eiffel. Another class of events that we have found useful as triggers is the observation of changes taking place in the system. For such changes to be detected, components must make available methods through which the required observations can be made (something that the mechanism of interface instantiation must check), and a detection mechanism must be made available in the implementation platform to enable such changes to be effectively monitored (something that is not universally provided).

What is important to stress is that, throughout the paper, we do not address object-based development specifically. Instead, we have aimed for more general notions to which the coordination technologies that we are developing apply. Hence, the notion of component that we assume is the more general one that has been popularised in [42] by which we mean "a unit of composition with contractually specified interfaces and explicit context dependencies only".

A coordination interface is, therefore, something more generic than an object instance type. It represents the signature of services and events that a component (software module) has to offer to be "compliant" with that interface, i.e. for that interface to be able to be instantiated by that component. This means that we cannot assume that any given interface is going to be instantiated necessarily, or always, by an object class. In the cases in which this does happen, the interface can be seen as an abbreviation of the use of the type associated with that class. These remarks should not be taken lightly because they can, and should, have a profound impact in the methods and languages that we use for developing systems. For instance, by assuming that we are not dealing necessarily with object instances implies that we cannot use instance operations during the specification of interfaces, something far too radically distant from for what any object-oriented language can offer.

When a coordination interface is instantiated with a specific component as part of the activation of a law over a given configuration of the system, the features declared in that interface must be formally related with what the component makes available through its own interface. Again, this process of instantiation will depend on the nature of the deployment of the component itself. For instance, as already mentioned, programming languages such as Java provide mechanisms for interfaces to be implemented through object classes. Ideally, the component definition language should support the distinction between *event* (to be used for triggers) and *services* (to be used for reactions), but this is not necessary. We decided to separate concerns in coordination interfaces as much as possible as a means of setting the direction in which we think Interface Definition Languages could evolve, but this separation does not need to be enforced for our techniques to be applicable. Hence, for instance, typical notions of interface in which components declare which methods are public can be used: events can be detected as calls to the public methods of the component and services can be effected through the invocation of these methods by the contract.

This separation between the coordination interface and the components themselves is, indeed, an essential mechanism for being able to interconnect heterogeneous components and, hence, not to compromise the ability of the system to evolve by upgrading its basic components or integrating third-party components. Furthermore, it enforces the required degree of "business centricity" in the sense that a coordination law, as a direct representation of a business rule, should apply, through contracts that enforce that law, to whatever components embody the business entities involved in the rule. In other words, the coordination interfaces that constitute the subject roles of the law act as abstract descriptions of the business entities that can become involved in instantiations of any contract that enforces the law.

## 4.2  Evolving Interactions

The use of coordination contracts for representing business rules leads to an approach to the evolution process that is based on reconfiguration techniques as known from Configurable Distributed Systems [25,29]. At each moment of the life of the system, its configuration can be identified with the collection of components that have been created (but not destroyed) interconnected through the contracts that will have been superposed among them. As part of the evolution process, new components may be added, existing components may be removed, new contracts may be superposed, existing contracts can be removed or replaced, and so on. All these operations rewrite the configuration, producing a new configuration for the system. The new configuration will dictate how the system will behave from then on, computationally speaking, through the revised set of components and interactions among them. On the other hand, as a result of the computations performed by the components, or the interactions that are maintained with the environment, the global state of the system changes, which may require a reconfiguration to adapt it to the new circumstances.

Having mechanisms for evolving systems is not the same as prescribing when and how these mechanisms should be applied. Evolution is a process that needs to be subject to rules that aim at enforcing given policies of organisations over the way they wish or are required, e.g. through legislation, to see their businesses conducted. For this purpose, we provide a modelling primitive – coordination contexts – through which the reconfiguration capabilities of the system can be automated, both in terms of ad-hoc services that can be invoked by authorised users, and programmed reconfigurations that allow systems to react to well identified triggers and, hence, adapt themselves to changes brought about on their state or configuration.

For instance, in the banking domain that we have been using as an example, a coordination context normally exists for each customer. The purpose of this context is to manage the relationships that the customer may hold with its various accounts according to the packages that the bank offers. Such contexts are made available to bank managers each time the customer goes to a branch, or to the customer itself through the Internet or ATMs.

The syntax that we are developing for contexts can be illustrated as follows:

```
coordination context customer(c:customer)
workspace
    component types  account, customer
    contract types standard-withdrawal, VIP-withdrawal,
                          pensioner-package, home-owner-package
constants min-VIP: money
attributes  avg-balance = …
services
    subscribe_VIP(a:account,V:money):
            pre:   c.owns(a) & avg-balance•min-VIP &
                   not exists home-owner-package(c,a)
            post:  exists' VIP-withdrawal(c,a) &
                          VIP-withdrawal(c,a)'.credit=V
    subscribe_home(a:account):
            pre:   not exists pensioner-package(c)
            post:  c.owns(a)' & exists' home-owner-package(c,a)
    subscribe_pensioner:
            pre:   not exists pensioner-package(c) &
                          not exists home-owner-package(c,a)
            post:  exists' pensioner-package(c)
    rules
    VIP-to-std:
            when exists VIP-withdrawal(c,a) & avg-balance<min-VIP
            post not exists' VIP-withdrawal(c,a) &
                          exists' standard-withdrawal(c,a)
    end context
```

Besides the laws that we introduced in the previous sections for managing withdrawals, we have added the names of a few other ones just to make the example more "interesting". These account for other financial packages such as those concerned with retirement pensions and credit for home-purchase. We leave their specification to the reader as an exercise!

Each instance of a coordination context is "anchored" to a component or set of components. In the example, the anchor is a customer instance, referred to as $c$ in the definition of the context (type). Under "workspace" we identify the component and contract types (laws) that are made available for evolving the way the anchor interacts with the rest of the system.

Configuration services correspond to operations for ad-hoc reconfiguration, i.e. they are performed on demand from users of the system. Notice that we include in this category operations that, in traditional OO modelling, are assigned to classes like object creation. The rationale is that, by interfering with the population of the system, such operations address the evolution of its configuration and, hence, their use should be regulated in the scope of a coordination context. Configuration services involve both components and contracts. In the example above, besides the creation of new accounts, three other services are provided for each of the contracts that models a financial package that can be offered to the customer. These services have pre-conditions through which business policies are enforced. For instance, VIP-withdrawals are not available on accounts that support a home-owner package; pensioners are not allowed to subscribe home-owner packages.

Configuration rules correspond to different ways of programmed reconfiguration, i.e. to the ability of the system to reconfigure itself in reaction to external events or internal state changes. In the example above, a VIP-package is replaced by a standard one when the average balance of the customer falls below the minimum value set up for being a VIP. Typically, the programmed configuration rules capture more dynamic properties that require specific actions to be taken in reaction to certain state changes, for instance to restore consistency with respect to policies like the ones that regulate VIP-status for customers.

Notice the use of a post-condition in the configuration rule instead of a specific (trans)action to be performed as a reaction. Together with the use of pre/post-conditions in the definition of services, this allows us to separate context interfaces from their implementations, which adds to flexibility by allowing the choice of the actual reconfiguration operations to depend on "lower level" issues like the physical distribution topology. The pre/post-conditions capture business policies that should be elicited during analysis, like eligibility conditions as illustrated in the example, or dependencies that regulate the subscription of different business products, as well as legislation that becomes applicable, etc. When writing post-conditions, we use primed expressions to denote the value that they take in the state that is obtained by executing the service or rule.

Contexts should not be treated as "normal" components in the sense that they are not used in configurations to add new functionalities to the system. That is, they are not defined in order to contribute to the functional properties that the system can exhibit but only to manage the way the system is allowed to evolve.

Each context provides a set of business services that, taken together, form a "profile" of business activity. Such services are implemented using the configuration layer (to query and change the current configuration) and the functional operations provided by components and contracts. Since the environment can only access and manipulate the system through the provided contexts, i.e., the bottom three layers are not visible to outside the system, contexts set constraints on the nature of the operations that can be performed. These constraints add to whatever policies, rules, and invariants have been declared for the configuration, contracts, and components, and should reflect properties that are specific to a business context. For example, the withdrawal service in the ATM context has a fixed limit on the amount that can be withdrawn, irrespective of the balance in the customer account. This constraint will be added to whatever business rules are in effect for withdrawals performed by that customer, because the service will call directly the debit operation on the account, which in turn will trigger whatever contracts are in effect.

Indeed, although the example above does not illustrate it, contexts can also make available operations that act on the states of the components through the methods that these offer through their public interfaces. Different contexts may even make use of different implementations for the same operations, for instance reflecting the fact that access to the system may be provided through different channels. For instance, the withdrawal service is typically offered in a coordination context that models access over the counter at the local branch, but not if the access is via the Internet, whereas the amount that can be requested will be limited for accesses via an ATM.

Contexts can be used to model actors as in use cases [9], i.e., the mechanisms through which "users" (regardless of whether they are human, physical, software, etc) have access to the system, except that, now, such users can interfere with the configuration of the system, not just with its state. Each context has a local state that consists of the projection of the global system configuration to the components and coordination contracts declared in the context. This projection defines a "subsystem". However, the notion of "subsystem" cannot be identified with that of context as a modelling primitive: a context defines a subsystem implicitly but the same or overlapping subsystems may be associated with other contexts. Furthermore, contexts can define subsystems at different levels of abstraction,

From a methodological point of view, contexts become necessary, and come into play, during the transition from a business model to a conceptual/logical model of the intended software system. This should be the first time in the process that a boundary starts to be drawn between the information system and the business environment, leading to the need for deciding on the interface in which it will be managed.

Concerning the relationship between coordination contexts and business policies, for simplicity, we take policies to be cast as properties of system configuration that are required to be invariants of the evolution process. The language that we use for representing business invariants is a first order language over the observable attributes of components (methods that return values) extended with a predicate **exists** that indicates whether a given component or contract instance is part of the current configuration, i.e. of the subsystem defined by the context. Examples of business policies expressed in this language are "**forall** a:account, **not** (**exists** VIP(c,a) **and exists** home-owner(c,a))" and "**forall** a:account, **not** (**exists** home-owner(c,a) **and exists** pensioner(c))". Both these properties can be proved to be invariants for the coordination context that we defined above. Once a property is proved to be an invariant of every coordination context defined for the application, it will be an invariant for the whole system, meaning that it will emerge as a property of every configuration that can be reached during the evolution of the system.

# 5    Tool Support

There are two important aspects to discuss as far as automation and tool support for the proposed architectural approach is concerned. On the one hand, the nature of an environment in which development can be supported. On the other hand, specific techniques that support the coordination-based approach over platforms that do not offer first-class primitives for implementing coordination rules.

## 5.1    Architecture of an Environment for Coordination

Using an architectural-based approach for software development requires new activities to be integrated in the process. An environment that supports the CCC-approach should have a tool dedicated to the coordination layer development and, at the same time, providing support for run-time reconfiguration. Such a tool may be autonomous or integrated with the rest of the environment by one of the several integration techniques currently available. In this section, we describe the main characteristics of an environment that we have been developing – the CDE (Coordination Development Environment) – as a proof of concept and prototype for testing the viability of a larger and more comprehensive coordination-based support to software development.

The main functionality of the CDE is to allow the definition of contract types (laws) and provide the necessary deployment of the final pieces of the system. It is assumed that the components to be coordinated are somehow available, developed in another part of the environment, or given by the developer. The CDE should provide facilities not only for the development/testing of coordination, but also run-time facilities for the management of contracts such as manual creation/deletion of contracts between objects, configuration of policies for automatic creation of contracts and priorities among others. The logical architectural components of the CDE, namely the Editor, the Repository, the Builder and the Animator, that support the previous activities, are shown below.

At the development level, the CDE provides the following functionalities:

- *Registration*: components are registered to the tool as candidates for coordination.
- *Edition*: Contract types (laws) are defined connecting some registered components. Coordination rules and constraints are defined on those contracts.
- *Deployment*: the code necessary to implement the coordinated components and the contract semantics in the final system is produced by *generating* the necessary parts according to a contract micro-architecture we have developed (see section 5.2). This micro-architecture is based on the Proxy and Chain of Responsibility design patterns and handles the superposition of the coordination contracts over existing components in a way that is transparent to the component and contract designer. The micro-architecture allows coordination contracts to be directly implemented using OO languages, fulfilling the following very important required properties:

- components are not aware of the presence of contracts and, therefore, any number of contracts can be added/removed without having to modify the components,
- contracts can be added/deleted in a "plug and play" mode, even at run time,
- even existing components can be easily adapted to accept contracts without making any modifications elsewhere in the application, thus allowing for easier reengineering/evolving of existing applications.

- *Animation*: facilities are provided allowing testing/prototyping of contract semantics. This layer provides a simple way of creating a system configuration and triggering operations on application objects, observe their state, and the dynamics associated with the existence of contracts at work.

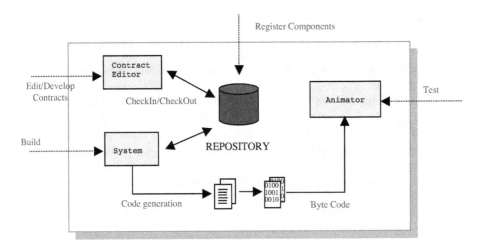

The architectural concepts described herein may be applied to different levels during system development depending on several factors, such as the characteristics of the components, the way components are built, the development phase where the coordination concept is going to be used, among others. One of the main motivations in the development of the modelling primitives discussed in the previous sections was to provide coordination as a top-level abstraction in development, right from the modelling phases. By using these concepts, one can provide a clear separation between computational concerns and the communication aspects, leading to flexible and clear models. Current modelling techniques that are used in industry, even state-of-the-art such as UML, do not provide any similar concept. Therefore, to be more effective in a working environment, a tool providing coordination facilities may be integrated with existing UML modelling tools. However, developers may choose to work with the contract coordination concept at a more detailed design/implementation level, where coordination aspects do not appear as modelling artefacts but, rather, as implementation constructs that provide more flexibility in terms of evolution. These two contexts of use can be summarised as follows:

- *Model Coordination:* Coordination is used at the Analysis or Design phases. Components are model classes (e.g. UML classes). Coordination contracts make a Coordination Model on top of the Analysis/Design Model. The deployment activity must take into account the way final coded components are obtained from model components and provide the necessary integration.

- *Construction Coordination:* Coordination is used in the construction phase. Components are the final coded components of the basic building blocks of the system. Coordination contracts are defined directly over implementation classes. It is suitable to be applied on the evolution of an existing system. The first version of CDE we have already developed works in such a context with Java as the target deployment language and animation capabilities based on sequence diagrams.

It should be clear, however, that the type of components under potential coordination may define the context and capabilities in which the CDE is used. Furthermore, the specific language and technical environment may impose constraints on the coordination features that can be used because techniques to achieve the implementation of its semantics may not be available. For instance, if Java is the target deployment language, synchronisation sets (the actions of all the coordinations active) may not be fully transactional in the sense that there is no rollback associated, when a failure or exception occurs. This is due to the semantics of the underlying language (Java). In other words, it should be clear that the output is strongly dependent on several other environmental conditions.

Therefore, in order to effectively use coordination technology in the development process, two main aspects must be clearly defined first: where to use it, and what are the building blocks that can be put under coordination. On the other hand, the real effectiveness of coordination laws as a semantic primitive for conceptual modelling depends on the availability of support tools such as CDE, which provide automatic code generation from higher-level specifications. Such tools hide the implementation complexity of coordination, allowing the developer just to handle the law itself. But, even in the absence of such tools, we feel that coordination laws provide a useful abstraction mechanism to be used in conceptual modelling because they direct developers to the identification and promotion of interactions as first-class citizens, a precondition for taming the complexity of system construction and evolution.

## 5.2     A Micro-Architecture for Coordination

As already explained in previous sections, a contract (instance of a law) works as an active agent that coordinates a number of partners (components that instantiate the coordination interfaces of the law). In this section, we are concerned with the way these coordination mechanisms can be implemented in general and the specific way in which they are handled in the CDE.

When defining an implementation, we need to have in mind that, as motivated in the introduction, we should be able to superpose a contract to given objects in a system and coordinate their behaviour as intended *without having to modify the way these objects are implemented.* This degree of flexibility is absolutely necessary when the implementation of these objects is not available or cannot be modified, as in legacy systems. It is also a distinguishing factor of contracts when compared with existing mechanisms for modelling object interaction, and one that makes contracts particularly suited in business domains where the ability to support the definition and dynamic application of new forms of coordination is a significant market advantage.

Different standards for component-based software development have emerged in the last few years. However, none of these standards provide a convenient and abstract way of supporting coordination as a first-class mechanism. Because of this, we propose our solution as a micro-architecture that exploits some widely available properties of object-oriented programming languages such as polymorphism and subtyping, and is based on other well known design patterns, namely the Broker, and the Proxy or Surrogate [15].

It is important to stress that what we are proposing is just a possible solution for implementing contracts, a concrete evidence that the concept can be made effective in our working environments. Other patterns may well be used and other mechanisms may very well prove to be more useful for capturing the required coordination effects in specific development platforms. For instance, the use of reflection is an alternative that looks promising enough to be explored.

More specifically, our aim in the paper is not to promote the use of the specific patterns that we are going to show: these patterns have existed for a long time, and other patterns exist that fulfil the same purpose. Our contribution is in the modelling primitives that we are proposing for supporting the externalisation of interactions as first-class citizens in conceptual models. The patterns are not the instrument that will assist conceptual modelling: coordination laws are.

The proposed micro-architecture is depicted below in terms of two main structures. One of them, what we have called the *component pattern*, consists of the features that have to be provided for each component so that it can become coordinated by a contract. In a nutshell, these features support the externalisation of the interface of each component as formalised in [13]. They provide a specific interface *(Interface)*, as an abstract class, for every component. This interface is linked to the real program *(RealSubject)* through a dynamically reconfigurable proxy reference. The classes that participate in the component pattern can be summarised as follows:

*Interface* – an abstract class that defines the common interface of services provided by *ImplemProxy* and *Subject.*

*Subject* – a broker (concrete class) maintaining a reference that lets the subject delegate received requests to *ImplemProxy* using the polymorphic entity proxy. At run-time, it may point to a *RealSubject* if no contract is involved, or point to a *PartnerConnector* that links the real subject to the contracts that coordinate its behaviour.

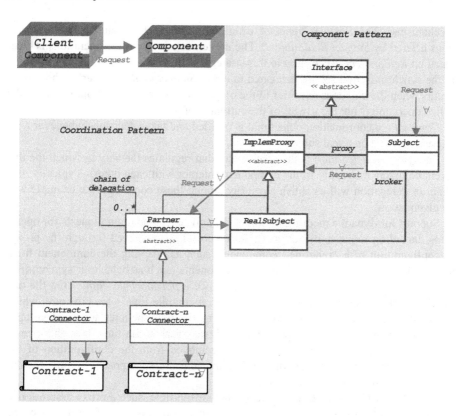

*ImplemProxy* – an abstract class that defines the common interface of *RealSubject* and *PartnerConnector*. The interface is inherited form *Interface* to guarantee that all these classes offer the same interface as *Subject* (the broker) with which real subject clients have to interact. It is also extended with a new operation that can be redefined in *RealSubject* and *PartnerConnector* to monitor state changes in the partner represented by *RealSubject*. The implementation of this operation in *PartnerConnector* delegates to each contract the execution of the synchronisation sets that are triggered by conditions on the monitored state.

*RealSubject* – the concrete domain class with the business logic that defines the real object that the broker represents. The concrete implementation of provided services is in this class.

The second structure in the micro-architecture concerns the mechanisms that coordinate the given component as achieved through the contracts that are in place for that component. The classes involved in this pattern are as follows.

*PartnerConnector* – maintains the connection between the real object (*RealSubject*) and the contracts in place for it. Adding or removing contracts to coordinate that real object does not require the creation of a new instance of this class but only of a new association with the new contract and an instantiation link with the existing instance of *PartnerConnector*. This means that there is only one instance of this class associated with one instance of *RealSubject*. A chain of delegation, also depicted in the diagram, controls the way the different contracts superpose their own coordination mechanisms. The *PartnerConnector* offers an interface that includes all the operations offered by *Subject/RealSubject*. The implementation of these operations is delegated on *RealSubject*. According to this strategy, calls to this pattern that are included in the synchronisation set are delegated to either *Subject* or *RealSubject*. The former occurs when the call does not refer to the operations under coordination, i.e. when the called operation is not the trigger of the current coordination.

*Contract* – a coordination object that is notified and takes decisions whenever a request is invoked on a real subject.

The *chain of delegation* is the mechanism that regulates the way in which the different contracts that apply to the component interact with each other. Typically, this chain of delegation will establish a priority among these contracts. An example will be given below.

Support for dynamic reconfiguration of the code executed upon requests for operations, including requests by *self* as in active objects, is achieved through the proxy. Reconfiguration of a predefined component (such as adapting the component for a specific use) or coordination of various components (such as behaviour synchronisation) is achieved by making the proxy reference a *polymorphic entity*. On the one hand, this proxy is provided with a *static type* at compile-time – the type with which this entity is declared (*ImplemProxy*) – that complies with the interface of the component. On the other hand, the type of its values may vary at run-time through *Partner-Connector* as connectors are superposed or removed from the configuration of the system. These types, the ones that can be dynamically superposed, become the entity's *dynamic type* (dynamic binding).

The notion of dynamic binding means that, at run-time, such a proxy assumes different values of different types. However, when a request is made for services of the component, it is the dynamic binding mechanism of the underlying object-oriented language (e.g. C++, Java) that makes the choice of the operation implementation to execute (*RealSubject* or *PartnerConnector*) based on the type to which the proxy belongs.

In order to explain, in more detail, how coordination is handled by the proposed pattern, consider a specific example: two accounts – a checking account and a savings account – under the coordination of a Flexible Package, such that the savings account is also subject to a VIP-package. The figure below depicts the chain of actions among the concrete classes involved in the pattern that are triggered by a withdrawal request received by the checking account.

The request is handled by the broker of the target of the request (the checking account) and, through the proxy, is delegated on the FlexiblePackage connector. This connector handles the request as specified in the previous section: it transfers funds from the other partner – the savings account – if the current balance of the checking account is not enough to satisfy the request. If such a transfer is necessary, the withdrawal from the savings account falls under the coordination of the VIP-connector. The diagram depicts a situation in which the chain of delegation controlling the contracts on the savings account gives priority to the flexible package connector, which then delegates on the VIP connector because the withdrawal action on the savings account is not under the coordination of the flexible package. The final withdrawal, the effective one, is performed on the real savings account after having been cleared by the VIP-connector. All this is done atomically. In particular, if the VIP-connector refuses the request for a withdrawal from the savings account, the original withdrawal sent to the checking account is also refused and any alterations made in the mean-while on the state of the objects involved are undone.

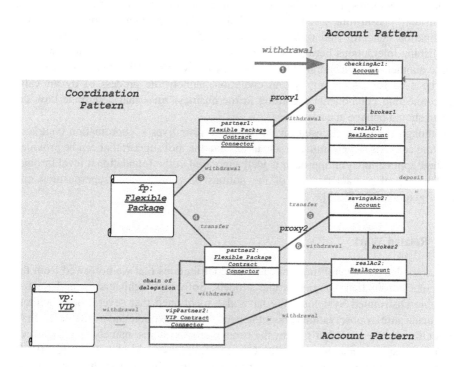

Notice that, as explained above, there is only one instance of *PartnerConnector* connected to the proxy. It is important to notice that before the partner connector gives rights to the real object implementation to execute a request, it intercepts the request and gives right to the contract to decide if the request is valid and perform other actions. This interception allows us to impose other contractual obligations on the interaction between the caller and the callee. On the other hand, it allows the contract to perform other actions before or after the real object executes the request. On the other hand, if there are no contracts coordinating a real subject, the only over-head imposed by the pattern is an extra call from the broker to the real object. We believe that this is a small price to pay for the added flexibility that the pattern brings to system evolution as a whole.

## 6     Concluding Remarks

In this paper, we presented a set of techniques that, in our opinion and from our ex-perience, can supplement the shortcomings of object-oriented approaches in endowing systems with the levels of agility required for operating in "internet-time" and support the next generation of the e-world – Web Services, B2B, P2P...

Basically, we argued that the move from an "identity" to a "service"-oriented approach, replacing the tight coupling that explicit feature calling – the basic mechanism of OO-computation – imposes on systems in favour of interconnections that can be established "just-in-time", can be supported by clearly separating computation and coordination concerns and relying on the superposition of external connectors for establishing interactions between components that are otherwise completely unaware of one another. Reconfiguration techniques as known from Distributed Systems can then be used for addressing system evolution, namely the process of dynamically interconnecting components according to the business rules that determine how the system should behave at each time.

Although the paper focused on the semantic primitives – coordination contracts, laws and contexts – their intuitive semantics, and the tool support that can be provided for their application, our approach is well supported at the foundational level through a mathematical characterisation of the notions of coordination, superposition and reconfiguration [e.g.13,43].

## 6.1   Related Work

We acknowledged several times already the contributions that we borrowed from the areas of Coordination Languages and Models, Software Architectures, and Reconfigurable Distributed Systems. We have also mentioned that several other authors have made similar observations about the need to make explicit and available, as first-class citizens, the rules that govern the behaviour of systems, namely in [22], which became the subject matter of the ISO General Relationship Model (ISO/IEC 10165-7). The semantic primitives that we proposed in the paper are in the spirit of this work but add to it the evolutionary aspects that they inherit from the architectural approaches, and the concurrency and synchronisation aspects that they inherit from Distributed System Design. A recent evolution of this approach that we intend to investigate in relationship to ours is the treatment of roles (and templates) in RM-ODP [21].

Another notion of contract can also be found in [7] that emerged in the context of the action-systems approach to parallel program design [6]. Like in our approach, it promotes the separation between the specification of what actors can do in a system and how they need to be coordinated so that the computations required of the system are indeed part of the global behaviour. However, the architectural and evolutionary dimensions are not explored as such.

Concrete extensions to the UML in order to provide automated support for evolution are proposed in [31] through "evolution contracts". The idea behind evolution contracts is that incremental modification and evolution of software artifacts is made explicit by means of a formal contract between the provider and the modifier of the artifact. The purpose of the evolution contract is to make evolution more disciplined. The coordination contracts that we presented can also extend the UML but at the level of the semantic primitives that can be used for modelling, facilitating evolution, not managing it. For managing evolution, we provide explicit primitives at the configuration layer as already discussed.

Besides these related notions of contract, it is important to mention the work of N.Minsky and his colleagues who, for quite some time, have been developing what they call Law-Governed Systems/Architectures/Interactions (e.g. [33]). However, the emphasis is put more on the architectural aspects of system design (e.g. as enforcing a token-ring architecture throughout evolution) whereas we tend to focus more on policies and other properties that relate to the business level. This is a rather simplistic and reductionist comparison because, on the one hand, we have also explored our coordination technologies for design and technical architectures and, on the other hand, Minsky's work seems to be applicable to the earlier levels of development as well. Hence, the truth is that more research is necessary to investigate how the two approaches actually relate and can benefit from the experience that both groups have developed in applying them.

## 6.2    Future Perspectives

The methodology and language that supports the definition of policies (e.g. as invariants) and contexts is still very much in its infancy but quickly progressing, mainly through the application of the approach to a number of case studies [e.g.4,23,24]. Even at this early stage, it is clear that coordination contexts provide an effective means of defining the way in which the evolution process can be controlled and the enforcement of business policies automated. We are now extending tool-support [5,17] and logical analysis [12] to this particular activity. Part of this effort is being planned as a collaboration initiative with Leonor Barroca at the Open University and Kevin Lano at King's College London.

Work is progressing in several other fronts, including the extension of the architectural approach to distribution and mobility in the IST project 2001-32747 (AGILE – Architectures for Mobility) in which ATX Software and the University of Leicester are partners together with IEI/CNR and the Universities of Florence, Lisbon, Munich, Pisa and Warsaw. Preliminary results can be found in [4,28]. Applications to data-intensive systems are also being planned as part of a research collaboration with the CERN. The integration of the method, semantic modelling primitives, and support tools with OMG activities around the UML is being planned in collaboration with a team of researchers coordinated by A.Moreira at the New University of Lisbon.

# Acknowledgements

The material included in this paper is the result of a research effort that, over several years, has involved many people, both in industry and academia. We are deeply grateful to the following people in particular, for their continued contribution and dedication to this project: J.Gouveia, G.Koutsoukos, A.Lopes, and M.Wermelinger,

# References

1. R.Allen and D.Garlan, "A Formal Basis for Architectural Connectors", *ACM TOSEM,* 6(3), 1997, 213-249.
2. L.F.Andrade and J.L.Fiadeiro, "Interconnecting Objects via Contracts", in R.France and B.Rumpe (eds), *UML'99 – Beyond the Standard,* LNCS 1723, Springer Verlag 1999, 566-583.
3. L.F.Andrade and J.L.Fiadeiro, "Service-Oriented Business and System Specification: Beyond Object-orientation", in H.Kilov and K.Baclwaski (eds), *Practical Foundations of Business and System Specifications,* Kluwer Academic Publishers 2003, 1-23.
4. L.F.Andrade, J.L.Fiadeiro, A.Lopes and M.Wermelinger, "Architectural Techniques for Evolving Control Systems", in *Formal Methods for Railway Operation and Control Systems,* G.Tarnai & E.Schnieder (eds), L'Harmattan Press, 2003
5. L.F.Andrade, J.Gouveia, G.Koutsoukos and J.L.Fiadeiro, "Coordination Contracts, Evolution and Tools", *Journal on Software Maintenance and Evolution: Research and Practice* 14(5), 2002, 353-369.
6. R.Back and R.Kurki-Suonio, "Distributed Cooperation with Action Systems", *ACM TOPLAS* 10(4), 1988, 513-554.
7. RJ.Back, L.Petre and I.Paltor, "Analysing UML Use Cases as Contracts", in *UML'99 – Beyond the Standard,* R.France and B.Rumpe (eds), LNCS 1723, Springer Verlag 1999, 518-533.
8. L.Bass, P.Clements and R.Kasman, *Software Architecture in Practice,* Addison Wesley 1998.
9. G.Booch, J.Rumbaugh and I.Jacobson, *The Unified Modeling Language User Guide,* Addison-Wesley 1998.
10. T.Elrad, R.Filman and A.Bader (Guest editors). Special Issue on Aspect Oriented Programming. *Communications of the ACM.* October 2001; 44(10)
11. M.Endler and J.Wei, "Programming Generic Dynamic Reconfigurations for Distributed Applications", in *Proc. 1st Intl. Workshop on Configurable Distributed Systems,* 1992, 68-79.
12. J.L.Fiadeiro, N.Martí-Oliet, T.Maibaum, J.Meseguer and I. Pita, "Towards a Verification Logic for Rewriting Logic", in *Recent Trends in Algebraic Development Techniques,* D.Bert and C.Choppy (eds), LNCS 1827, pp. 438-458, Springer-Verlag 2000
13. J.L.Fiadeiro, A.Lopes and M.Wermelinger, "A Mathematical Semantics for Architectural Connectors", in *Generic Programming,* R.Backhouse and J.Gibbons (eds), LNCS, Springer-Verlag, in print.
14. P.Finger, "Componend-Based Frameworks for E-Commerce", Communications of the ACM 43(10), 2000, 61-66.
15. E.Gamma, R.Helm, R.Johnson and J.Vlissides, *Design Patterns: Elements of Reusable Object Oriented Software,* Addison-Wesley 1995
16. D.Gelernter and N.Carriero, "Coordination Languages and their Significance", *Communications ACM* 35(2), 1992, 97-107.
17. J.Gouveia, G.Koutsoukos, L.Andrade and J.Fiadeiro, "Tool Support for Coordination-Based Software Evolution", in *Technology of Object-Oriented Languages and Systems – TOOLS 38,* W.Pree (ed), IEEE Press 2001, 184-196.
18. P.Herzum and O.Sims, *Business Component Factory,* Wiley 2000.
19. J.Hopkins, "Component Primer", *Communications of the ACM* 43(10), 2000, 27-30.

20. W.Kent, "Participants and Performers: A Basis for Classifying Object Models", in *Proc. OOPSLA 1993 Workshop on Specification of Behavioral Semantics in Object-Oriented Information Modeling*, 1993
21. H.Kilov, *Business Models*, Prentice-Hall 2002.
22. H.Kilov and J.Ross, *Information Modeling: an Object-oriented Approach*, Prentice-Hall 1994.
23. G.Koutsoukos, J.Gouveia, L.Andrade and J.L.Fiadeiro, "Managing Evolution in Telecommunications Systems", in *New Developments on Distributed Applications and Interoperable Systems*, K.Zielinski, K.Geihs and A. Laurentowski (eds), Kluwer Academic Publishers 2001; 133-139.
24. G.Koutsoukos, T.Kotridis, L.Andrade, J.L.Fiadeiro, J.Gouveia and M.Wermelinger, "Coordination technologies for business strategy support: a case study in stock-trading", in R.Corchuelo, A,Ruiz and M.Toro (eds), *Advances in Business Solutions*, Catedral Publicaciones 2002, 45-56.
25. J.Kramer, "Configuration Programming – A Framework for the Development of Distributable Systems", in *Proceedings CompEuro'90*, IEEE Computer Society Press 1990; 374-384.
26. J.Kramer, "Exoskeletal Software", in *Proc. 16th ICSE*, 1994, 366.
27. K.Lano, J.Fiadeiro and L.Andrade, *Software Design in Java 2*, Palgrave-Macmillan, 2002.
28. A.Lopes, J.Fiadeiro and M.Wermelinger, "Architectural Primitives for Distribution and Mobility", *SIGSOFT 2002/FSE-10*, ACM Press 2002, 41-50.
29. J.Magee and J.Kramer, "Dynamic Structure in Software Architectures", in *4th Symp. on Foundations of Software Engineering*, ACM Press 1996, 3-14.
30. N.Medvidovic and R.Taylor, "A Classification and Comparison Framework for Software Architecture Description Languages", *IEEE Trans. on Software Eng.*, 26(1), Jan. 2000, 70-93.
31. T.Mens and T.D'Hondt, "Automating Support for Software Evolution in UML", in *Automated Software Engineering Journal 7*, Kluwer Academic Publishers, 2000, 39-59.
32. B.Meyer, "Applying Design by Contract", in *IEEE Computer* (25)10, 1992, 40-51.
33. N.Minsky and V.Ungureanu, "Law-Governed Interaction: A Coordination & Control Mechanism for Heterogeneous Distributed Systems" in *ACM TOSEM* 9(3), 2000, 273-305.
34. K.Moazami-Goudarzi, *Consistency Preserving Dynamic Reconfiguration of Distributed Systems*, PhD Thesis, Imperial College London, 1999.
35. R.Monroe, *Capturing Software Architecture Design Expertise with Armani*, Tech. Rep. CMU-CS-98-163, School of Computer Science, Carnegie Mellon University, Oct. 1998.
36. D.Notkin, D.Garlan, W.Griswold and K.Sullivan, "Adding Implicit Invocation to Languages: Three Approaches", in *Object Technologies for Advanced Software*, S.Nishio and A.Yonezawa (editors), LNCS 742, Springer-Verlag 1993, 489-510.
37. P.Oreizy, N.Medvidovic and R.Taylor, "Architecture-based Runtime Software Evolution", in *Proc. ICSE'98*, IEEE Computer Science Press 1998
38. D.Perry and A.Wolf, "Foundations for the Study of Software Architectures", *ACM SIGSOFT Software Engineering Notes* 17(4), 1992, 40-52.
39. M.Snoeck, G.Dedene, M.Verhels and A-M.Depuydt, *Object-oriented Enterprise Modelling with MERODE*, Leuvense Universitaire Press, 1999.
40. M.Shaw, "Procedure Calls are the Assembly Language of Software Interconnection: Connectors Deserve First-Class Status", in D.A. Lamb (Ed.), *Studies of Software Design*, LNCS 1078, Springer-Verlag 1996.
41. M.Shaw and D.Garlan, *Software Architecture: Perspectives on an Emerging Discipline*, Prentice-Hall 1996.

42. C.Szyperski, *Component Software: Beyond Object-Oriented Programming*, Addison Wesley 1998.
43. M.Wermelinger, A.Lopes and J.L.Fiadeiro, "A Graph Based Architectural (Re)configuration Language", in *ESEC/FSE'01*, V.Gruhn (ed), ACM Press 2001, 21-32.

# Software Architecture for Mobile Computing

Amy L. Murphy[1], Gian Pietro Picco[2], and Gruia-Catalin Roman[3]

[1] University of Rochester, Rochester NY 14607, USA,
murphy@cs.rochester.edu,
http://www.cs.rochester.edu/u/murphy
[2] Politecnico di Milano, Milan, Italy,
picco@elet.polimi.it
http://www.elet.polimi.it/~picco
[3] Washington University, St. Louis MO 63130, USA,
roman@cse.wustl.edu
http://www.cse.wustl.edu/~roman

**Abstract.** One form of software architecture is a framework for systems that serve the needs of a specific domain. These frameworks must contain sufficient detail to not lose the interesting aspects of the environment, yet they must not expose so many details as to be overwhelming and force the developer to lose the big picture. As the environments we develop for become more complex, it becomes more necessary to compose these frameworks in order to manage the complexity. Mobility is precisely one such environment that is emerging as computing components shrink in size and become more portable. As these components change location in space, their connectivity to other components changes and thus their access to data changes. Some programs needs to be able to respond to this change in connectivity. Others are able to abstract it away, simply perceiving changes in connectivity as changes in data availability. In this paper, we overview a solution to managing the complexity of applications for the the mobile environment in the context of a middleware. First, we present a meta-model, or a framework for generating middleware for mobile environments. Second, we show how this meta-model has been instantiated in the LIME middleware and how it has been used to develop several mobile applications.

## 1 Introduction

Mobility entails the study of systems in which components change location, in a voluntary or involuntary manner, and move across a space that may be defined to be either logical or physical. By definition, systems of mobile components are distributed systems, and while distributed computing has been carefully studied for decades, mobility poses new challenges that have not previously been addressed.

The development of compact computing devices such as notebook computers and personal digital assistants allow people to carry computational power with them as they change their physical location in space. The number of such components is steadily increasing. One goal, referred to as ubiquitous computing [21], is

M. Bernardo and P. Inverardi (Eds.): SFM 2003, LNCS 2804, pp. 182–206, 2003.
© Springer-Verlag Berlin Heidelberg 2003

for these devices to become seamlessly integrated into the environment until we are no longer explicitly aware of their presence, much the way that the electric motor exists in the world today. Part of enabling this vision is coordinating the actions of these devices, most likely through wireless mediums such as radio or infrared.

Logical mobility, or the movement of code and state through a fixed infrastructure of servers, is emerging as a powerful design abstraction for distributed systems. The pervasiveness of the Java programming language and its portability have led to a wealth of mobile agent systems. Demonstration purpose applications built on top of these systems range from logical agents managing physical objects in a kitchen [11] to agents managing the placement of a video conferencing server to minimize bandwidth consumption [1].

Developing applications in the mobile environment is a difficult task. Many existing applications restrict themselves to addressing a specific aspect of mobility in a highly specialized environment, such as disconnected operation in the Coda filesystem [8] or using agents to perform remote queries on a database as in the Oracle Agent System [13]. Development of these systems requires highly specialized knowledge of low level networking as well as details of the application domain.

Our goal is to enable the development of diverse classes of applications by providing flexible abstractions that can be applied in a variety of settings. Our success in this area comes from an integrated research approach that involves analyzing the needs of mobile applications, formulating models to describe the key concepts of our approaches, specifying formally these models, implementing the abstractions, and returning to the development of applications to evaluate our results.

Our work focuses on mobile ad hoc networks where no infrastructure exists to support communication among physically mobile hosts. Instead, hosts communicate directly with one another and the distance between hosts determines connectivity. A system is typically composed of multiple groups of hosts with connectivity available within the group but no communication from one group to another. Changes in connectivity and corresponding changes in available resources make this a challenging environment for application design.

Our strategy for development in this arena is the design for new high-level coordination abstractions, generically referred to as *global virtual data structures*. The abstraction presented to the application programmer is simply a local data structure whose content changes according to connectivity. Conceptually each component stores a piece of a global data structure, when components are within communication range these pieces are transiently shared and accessible to other components. Interaction with the data structure occurs exclusively by executing operations on the local data structure, however, transient sharing enables transparent interaction with other mobile components.

One of the features of this approach is its ability to facilitate the development of applications that never explicitly access remote data. We term this *context-transparent interaction*, where the data is part of the current context in which a mobile component finds itself. The distribution and changes to the data structure are hidden from the application programmer by the abstraction itself. Alternately, *context-aware interaction* can easily be provided as an extension to the basic model by explicitly introducing the notion of location.

We have successfully applied this strategy in the development of LIME, Linda In a Mobile Environment, which provides the simple mobile coordination abstraction through transiently shared Linda tuple spaces, enabling application programmers to clearly separate the concerns of computation from the communication among hosts. The implementation of LIME in the form of middleware presents the same interface and semantics as the model, simplifying the implementation process. Mobile application developers utilizing the LIME concepts need not concern themselves with any of the low level details of communication or changing connections, as all of these are handled within the implementation of the middleware.

Work with the LIME system has shown it to be a clean conceptual tool for introducing programmers to the concepts of mobility. Several applications have been built on top of the middleware, demonstrating its usefulness in a variety of mobility scenarios.

In this paper, Section 2 provides an introduction to the concept of global virtual data structures, Section 3 describes the instantiation of this concept in the LIME coordination model, Section 4 steps through an application that sits on top of LIME, and Section 5 concludes with future directions for this work.

## 2    Global Virtual Data Structures

Physical mobility through space can be categorized into base station mobility and ad hoc mobility. Base station mobility is similar to the cellular telephone system, where mobile components (i.e., mobile telephones) communicate with one another and with the fixed network by always communicating first with a base station (i.e., cellular tower). Ad hoc mobility distinguishes itself from base station mobility by completely removing the fixed infrastructure, leaving only direct communication among hosts. In a mobile ad hoc network, the distance between components determines connectivity. As components move, the system is continuously reshaped into multiple partitions, with connectivity available within each partition but not across partitions.

Freeing mobile users from a fixed infrastructure makes the ad hoc network model ideal for many scenarios such as systems of small components with limited resources to spend on communication, situations in which the infrastructure has been destroyed such as following a natural disaster, and for settings in which establishing an infrastructure is impossible as in a battlefield environment or economically impractical as in a short duration meeting or conference.

The application needs in these scenarios can be classified broadly by how they interact with their changing environment, or *context*. The context of a mobile unit consists of two primary components: system configuration and data. System configuration context describes the knowledge about which mobile units are connected and possibly also about topology information concerning physical location in space or logical connectivity. This knowledge is limited to the current partition of the network in which the mobile unit finds itself. We refer to this as the current transient group. Because communication cannot extend beyond the group, knowledge of configuration beyond the boundaries of the group is not possible. Data context refers to the more passive data elements and resources that are carried by the mobile components.

This view of context fosters two distinct programming styles: *context aware programming* and *context transparent programming*. Context aware applications are those that access both the system configuration context and the data context explicitly. For example, a context aware application may store a piece of new data on a specific mobile host, or retrieve a piece of data from a named mobile host. All operations must be carried out within the current connectivity context, but this style is distinguished by the needs of the application to be aware of the current context. In contrast, context transparent applications can be developed without explicit knowledge of the current context. Data access is performed on the data in the current context without regard to where it is located. Such applications do not need to be aware of the details of the configuration changes, but simply aware that they are occurring and that these changes affect the available resources. Many applications require a combination of both context aware and context transparent programming.

Our goal is to enable the rapid and dependable development of both styles of application programs for the mobile ad hoc environment. Fundamentally our approach is to design abstractions tailored to the ad hoc environment that hide many of the unnecessary details, but give the programmer sufficient power to tailor the abstraction to their specific needs. This involves providing both context aware and context transparent operations within the same abstraction. At the same time, implementations of these abstractions must be responsive to the technical challenges of the environment.

Our approach to abstractions to simplify the programming task comes from a study of coordination models for distributed computing that separate the computation, or the task-specific programming, from the communication, or the interaction among processes. Distributed coordination models also consider the need to take local decisions while still conceptualizing the effect of these actions on the global scale. Thus, our driving design strategy can be summarized by the desire to coordinate mobile ad hoc applications by thinking globally but acting locally.

## 2.1   The GVDS Model

One common coordination mechanism in distributed systems is shared memory, or more structured shared data structures. Through this, the complexity of large systems is managed by accessing a single, global data structure. An implementation may be distributed, but the user is not aware of this. The concept of shared memory is appealing in the mobile environment, which is itself a distributed

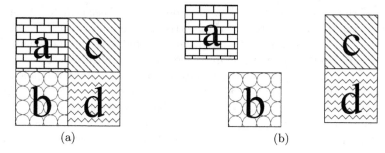

(a)                                                    (b)

**Fig. 1.** Transforming a matrix into a global virtual data structure by distributing it among mobile units.

system, however disconnections and the resulting inaccessibility of data make a direct application of shared memory to mobile systems impossible.

By applying our design strategy to shared memory data structures the global data structure emerges as the concept we wish to conceive of globally, but connectivity does not allow this. The first step toward a mobility-viable global data structure is to make explicit the distribution of data across the mobile components, or mobile hosts. For example, Figure 1(a) shows how a large matrix can be evenly divided among four hosts. While all mobile components are within communication range, the entire structure remains accessible to all processes.

When mobile components move and connectivity changes, the available portions of the data change to reflect only reachable data. In Figure 1(b) mobile components $a$ and $b$ are each isolated from all other components, restricting access only to their local partitions of the matrix. However, components $c$ and $d$ remain connected to one another and have access to the combination of $c$'s and $d$'s data.

The global matrix data structure of Figure 1(a) can be visualized at any time from outside the system by ignoring connectivity constraints and combining the data from all mobile components. This is, however, only a *virtual* data structure because it cannot be created in reality. Despite this it remains a powerful concept to the programmer to view how local changes affect the entire system.

We have discussed how connectivity limits the availability of data, but we must also consider how the operations that access the data structure change in response to this accessibility constraint. Some operations must clearly be restricted if full connectivity is not available. In the matrix example, computations such as matrix inversion require the entire matrix and must be restricted. Many operations, however, require no changes and can simply be evaluated over the current projection of the global virtual data structure. These operations play an important role in implementing context-transparent applications as they do not require the programmer to be aware of the details of the environment, but are simply aware that it is changing. Finally some operations can be extended to explicitly address the distribution of data over the hosts. Consider an alternate division of the matrix example that distributes data based on some aspect of the data other than its location in the matrix. In this case, it may be meaningful to query the part of the distributed data located at a specific agent. These operations are likely to play a role in context-aware applications.

For any global virtual data structure to be successful, its development cycle must include not only the model definition, but also formal specification and implementation. The informal model presents the underlying data structure, how it changes with respect to connectivity, what the primitives are, and how they are affected and extended. Most importantly, the informal model also describes the abstraction provided to the programmer and a way of thinking to effectively develop applications on top of the model. Next, formal semantics force clear definitions of all model concepts and how they are affected by mobility before beginning an implementation. The formal specification also enables user applications to be formally specified and reasoned about, lending dependability to the resulting system. Finally, the data structures must be implemented and applications built. One mechanism to deliver the data structures is via a middleware that sits between the application and the operating system, providing the abstractions defined by the model and formal specification.

The key to development from these three key perspectives is to allow each step to inform the others in an iterative fashion. By considering the needs of the applications, the primitives of the model can be defined and extended to meet the demands of the application programmer. A formal specification can reveal key parts in the model where restrictions must be made to keep the operations computable in the presence of disconnections. The formal specification also informs the implementation, showing where the complexity is involved in the interactions of concurrent programs. A proper implementation must adhere to the formal specification. The process of implementing may reveal atomicity assumptions of the model that are either impossible or impractical to implement. This can lead to an expansion of the model to include more elements of the environment, or to a weakening of the model constructs to make them more practical. Complementary changes must also be made to the formal specification.

## 2.2   Instantiating a GVDS

Many standard distributed data structures have the potential to be converted into global virtual data structures. For each structure, the fundamental issues to address as part of the evaluation and development processes are similar: Does the data structure match the basic needs of the underlying application? Is there a natural and useful partitioning of the data structure across units in a mobile ad hoc network? How is the data structure perceived by the individual units as changes in connectivity occur?

A tree, as in Figure 2, could be partitioned among units with the nodes where a cut occurs being replicated. A global naming convention would allow communicating units to determine the relation between the tree fragments they carry and make content and structural changes (e.g., swapping subtrees) as long as no disconnected units are affected. In principle, certain operations (e.g., adding a

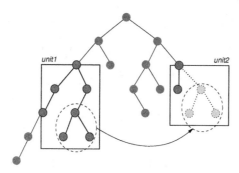

**Fig. 2.** A hierarchical data structure where units in range agree to transfer a subtree that is under their jurisdiction even though parts of the global structure remain hidden. Moving a subtree distributes data to a different location to satisfy changing access patterns.

leaf node) could be issued at any time with their evaluation being delayed until such time that the affected units are within range. Attempts to access nodes on disconnected units may result in blocking the respective agent. The generalization to a directed graph is straightforward and can overcome the problems caused by the possible loss of one of the units.

Other data structures may be devised to meet the needs of highly specialized applications. For instance, resource-limited units searching a physical space may appear logically as ants crawling on a fixed network of passageways (Figure 2.2). Each unit's knowledge of the surrounding geography is enhanced by the knowledge of all the other units within range. As the density of units decreases, each unit must maintain more and more information. Finally, at a point when the unit's memory is full, information needs to be dropped, e.g., only the main passageways are kept. In an application involving the construction of distributed predictive models of the changes taking place in a physical environment it is conceivable to have the units tied together by a complex structure that combines information about space and time. Each unit may be exploring and collecting data in the present while simulating the future in order to build a predictive model. As units meet they may exchange information about the present but also about various points in the future since some units may be further ahead than others in their simulation.

In the field of parallel programming, tuple space communication à la Linda provides a good example of how coordination can simplify the programming task. Tuple space coordination facilitates temporal and spatial decoupling among parallel programs. By limiting the power of the tuple space access primitives, efficient implementation is achieved as well. The programmer is presented with the appearance of a persistent global data structure that can be readily understood and operated on: a set of tuples accessed by content. Applying the concept of global virtual data structures to Linda yields a model that distributes the global

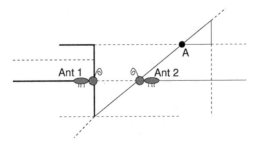

**Fig. 3.** Ant 1 learns from Ant 2 about landmark $A$ when, by virtue of being in range, the locally built maps are merged. Solid lines denote paths explored by Ants 1 and 2, and dashed lines denote unexplored regions. After sharing, each ant has the same knowledge of the global structure.

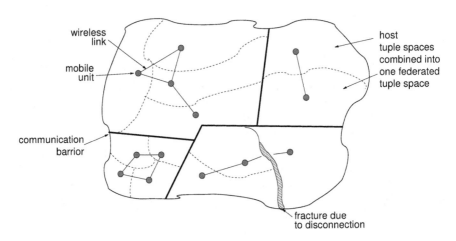

**Fig. 4.** Creating the illusion of a globally shared tuple space.

tuple space among the mobile units and limits access to the confines of each mobile ad hoc network. For a programmer, mobility is perceived simply as an independently evolving host tuple space, i.e., a continuously changing context. When the mobile components are co-located, the tuple spaces are transiently shared and all tuple space accesses, including pattern matching for reading and removing data, are done on the now shared data space (see Figure 4). Additional primitives with extensions for location are straightforward to access specific tuple spaces, however the presence of the specified tuple space is dependent on connectivity. This data structure has been explored in detail and has resulted in the LIME model, Linda in a Mobile Environment. The details of LIME are presented in the next section.

# 3   LIME, a GVDS

The LIME model [15, 12] is the first full instantiation of the GVDS concept, and as such, it provides a proof of concept of the idea itself. LIME borrows and adapts the communication model made popular by Linda [4] to provide a coordination abstraction for the mobile environment. After presenting a concise Linda primer, the remainder of this section discusses how the core concepts of Linda are reshaped in the LIME model and embodied in the programming interface of the corresponding middleware implementation.

## 3.1   Linda in a Nutshell

In Linda, processes communicate through a shared *tuple space* that acts as a repository of elementary data structures, or *tuples*. A tuple space is a multiset of tuples that can be accessed concurrently by several processes. Each tuple is a sequence of typed fields, such as ⟨"foo", 9, 27.5⟩, and contains the information being communicated.

Tuples are added to a tuple space by performing an **out**($t$) operation, and can be removed by executing **in**($p$). Tuples are anonymous, thus their selection takes place through pattern matching on the tuple content. The argument $p$ is often called a *template* or *pattern*, and its fields contain either *actuals* or *formals*. Actuals are values; the fields of the previous tuple are all actuals, while the last two fields of ⟨"foo", ?integer, ?float⟩ are formals. Formals act like "wild cards", and are matched against actuals when selecting a tuple from the tuple space. For instance, the template above matches the tuple defined earlier. If multiple tuples match a template, the one returned by **in** is selected non-deterministically. Tuples can also be read from the tuple space using the non-destructive **rd**($p$) operation. Both **in** and **rd** are blocking, i.e., if no matching tuple is available in the tuple space the process performing the operation is suspended until a matching tuple becomes available. A typical extension to this synchronous model is the provision of a pair of asynchronous primitives **inp** and **rdp**, called *probes*, that allow non-blocking access to the tuple space[4]. Moreover, some variants of Linda (e.g., [19]) provide also *bulk operations*, which can be used to retrieve all matching tuples in one step. In LIME we provide a similar functionality through the **ing** and **rdg** operations, whose execution is asynchronous like in the case of probes[5].

## 3.2   The LIME Model

Linda characteristics resonate with the mobile setting. In particular, communication in Linda is decoupled in *time* and *space*, i.e., senders and receivers do not

---

[4] Additionally, Linda implementations often include an **eval** operation that provides dynamic process creation and enables deferred evaluation of tuple fields. For the purposes of this work, however, we do not consider this operation further.

[5] Hereafter we often do not mention this pair of operations, since they are useful in practice but do not add significant complexity either to the model or to the implementation.

need to be available at the same time, and mutual knowledge of their identity or location is not necessary for data exchange. This form of decoupling is of paramount importance in a mobile setting, where the parties involved in communication change dynamically due to their migration or connectivity patterns. Moreover, the notion of tuple space provides a straightforward and intuitive abstraction for representing the computational context perceived by the communicating processes. On the other hand, decoupling is achieved thanks to the properties of the Linda tuple space, namely its global accessibility to all the processes, and its persistence—properties that are clearly hard if not impossible to maintain in a mobile environment. Finally, these properties make Linda tuple spaces amenable to providing the basis for the GVDS meta-model.

**The Core Idea: Transparent Context Maintenance** In Linda, the data accessible through the tuple space represents the data *context* available during process interaction. In the model underlying LIME, the shift from a fixed context to a dynamically changing one is accomplished by breaking up the Linda tuple space into many tuple spaces, each permanently associated to a mobile unit, and by introducing rules for transient sharing of these individual tuple spaces based on connectivity.

The individual tuple space permanently and exclusively attached to a mobile unit is referred to as the *interface tuple space* (ITS) because it provides the only access to the data context for that mobile unit. Each ITS contains the tuples the mobile unit is willing to make available to other units, and access to this data structure uses standard Linda operations, whose semantics remain basically unaffected. These tuples represent the only context accessible to a mobile unit when it is alone.

When multiple mobile units are able to communicate, either directly or transitively, we say these units form a LIME *group*. We can restrict the notion of group membership beyond simple communication, but for the purposes of this paper, we consider only connectivity. Conceptually, the contents of the ITSs of all group members are merged, or transiently shared, to form a single, large context that is accessed by each unit through its own ITS. The sharing itself is transparent to each mobile unit, however as the members of the group change, the content of the tuple space each member perceives through operations on the ITS changes in a transparent way.

The joining of a group by a mobile unit, and the subsequent merging of its local context with the group context is referred to as *engagement*, and is performed as a single, atomic operation. A mobile unit leaving a group triggers *disengagement*, that is, the atomic removal of the tuples representing its local context from the remaining group context. In general, whole groups can merge, and a group can split into several groups due to changes in connectivity.

In LIME, agents may have multiple ITSs distinguished by a name since this is recognized [2] as a useful abstraction to separate related application data. The sharing rule in the case of multiple tuple spaces relies on tuple space names: only identically-named tuple spaces are transiently shared among the members of a

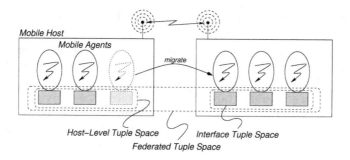

**Fig. 5.** Transiently shared tuple spaces encompass physical and logical mobility.

group. Thus, for instance, when an agent $a$ owning a single tuple space named $X$ joins a group constituted by an agent $b$ that owns two tuple spaces named $X$ and $Y$, only $X$ becomes shared between the two agents. Tuple space $Y$ remains accessible only to $b$, and potentially to other agents owning $Y$ that may join the group later on.

Transient sharing of the ITS constitutes a very powerful abstraction, as it provides a mobile unit with the illusion of a local tuple space that contains all the tuples coming from all the units belonging to the group, without any need to know the members explicitly. The notion of transiently shared tuple space is a natural adaptation of the Linda tuple space to a mobile environment. When physical mobility is involved, and especially in the radical setting defined by mobile ad hoc networking, there is no stable place to store a persistent tuple space. Connections among machines come and go and the tuple space must be partitioned in some way. Analogously, in the scenario of logical mobility, maintaining locality of tuples with respect to the agent they belong to may be complicated. LIME enforces an a priori partitioning of the tuple space in subspaces that get transiently shared according to precise rules, providing a tuple space abstraction that depends on connectivity.

**Encompassing Physical and Logical Mobility** In LIME, mobile hosts are connected when a communication link is available. Availability may depend on a variety of factors, including quality of service, security considerations, or connection cost; all of which can be represented in LIME, although in this paper we limit ourselves to availability determined by the presence of a functioning link. Mobile agents are connected when they are co-located on the same host, or they reside on hosts that are connected. Changes in connectivity among hosts depend only on changes in the physical communication links. Connectivity among mobile agents may depend also on arrival and departure of agents, with creation and termination of mobile agents being regarded as a special case of connection and disconnection, respectively. Figure 5 depicts the model adopted by LIME. Mobile agents are the only active components; mobile hosts are mainly roaming containers that provide connectivity and execution support for agents. In other words, mobile agents are the only components that carry a "concrete" tuple space with them.

The transiently shared ITSs belonging to multiple agents co-located on a host define a *host-level tuple space*. The concept of transient sharing can also be applied to the host-level tuple spaces of connected hosts, forming a *federated tuple space*. When a federated tuple space is established, a query on the ITS of an agent returns a tuple that may belong to the tuple space carried by that agent, to a tuple space belonging to a co-located agent, or to a tuple space associated with an agent residing on some remote, connected host.

In this model, physical and logical mobility are separated in two different tiers of abstraction. Nevertheless, many applications do not need both forms of mobility, and straightforward adaptations of the model are possible. For instance, applications that do not exploit mobile agents but run on a mobile host can employ one or more stationary agents, i.e., programs that do not contain migration operations. In this case, the design of the application can be modeled in terms of mobile hosts whose ITS is a fixed host-level tuple space. Applications that do not exploit physical mobility—and do not need a federated tuple space spanning different hosts—can exploit only the host-level tuple space as a local communication mechanism among co-located agents.

Nevertheless, it is interesting to note how mobility is not dealt with directly in LIME, i.e., there are no constructs for triggering the mobility of agents or hosts. Instead, the effect of migration is made indirectly manifest to the model and middleware only through the changes observed in the connectivity among components. This choice, that sets the nature of mobility aside, keeps our model as general as possible and, at the same time, enables different instantiations of the model based on different notions of connectivity.

**Controlling Context Awareness** Thus far, LIME appears to foster a style of coordination that reduces the details of distribution and mobility to content changes in what is perceived as a local tuple space. This view is very powerful, and has the potential for greatly simplifying application design in many scenarios by relieving the designer from the chore of maintaining explicitly a view of the context consistent with changes in the configuration of the system. On the other hand, this view may hide too much in domains where the designer needs more fine-grained control over the portion of the context that needs to be accessed. For instance, the application may require control over the agent responsible for holding a given tuple, something that cannot be specified only in terms of the global context. Also, performance and efficiency considerations may come into play, as in the case where application information would enable access aimed at a specific host-level tuple space, thus avoiding the greater overhead of a query spanning the whole federated tuple space. Such fine-grained control over the context perceived by the mobile unit is provided in LIME by extending the Linda operations with tuple location parameters that operate on user-defined projections of the transiently shared tuple space. Further, all tuples are implicitly augmented with two fields, representing the tuple's *current* and *destination* *location*. The current location identifies the single agent responsible for holding the tuple when all agents are disconnected, and the destination location indicates the agent with whom the tuple should eventually reside.

The **out**[$\lambda$] operation extends **out** with a location parameter representing the identifier of the agent responsible for holding the tuple. The semantics of **out**[$\lambda$]($t$) involve two steps. The first step is equivalent to a conventional **out**($t$), the tuple $t$ is inserted in the ITS of the agent calling the operation, say $\omega$. At this point the tuple $t$ has a current location $\omega$, and a destination location $\lambda$. If the agent $\lambda$ is currently connected, the tuple $t$ is moved to the destination location in the same atomic step. On the other hand, if $\lambda$ is currently disconnected the tuple remains at the current location, the tuple space of $\omega$. This *"misplaced"* tuple, if not withdrawn[6], will remain misplaced unless $\lambda$ becomes connected. In the latter case, the tuple will migrate to the tuple space associated with $\lambda$ as part of the engagement. By using **out**[$\lambda$], the caller can specify that the tuple is supposed to be placed within the ITS of agent $\lambda$. This way, the default policy of keeping the tuple in the caller's context until it is withdrawn can be overridden, and more elaborate schemes for transient communication can be developed.

Variants of the **in** and **rd** operations that allow location parameters are allowed as well. These operations, of the form **in**[$\omega, \lambda$]($p$) and **rd**[$\omega, \lambda$]($p$), enable the programmer to refer to a projection of the current context defined by the value of the location parameters, as illustrated in Table 1. The current location parameter enables the restriction of scope from the entire federated tuple space (no value specified) to the tuple space associated to a given host or even a given agent. The destination location is used to identify misplaced tuples.

| Current location | Destination location | Defined projection |
|---|---|---|
| unspecified | unspecified | Entire federated tuple space |
| unspecified | $\lambda$ | Tuples in the federated tuple space and destined to $\lambda$ |
| $\omega$ | unspecified | Tuples in $\omega$'s tuple space |
| $\Omega$ | unspecified | Tuples in $\Omega$'s host-level tuple space, i.e., belonging to any agent at $\Omega$ |
| $\omega$ | $\lambda$ | Tuples in $\omega$'s tuple space and destined to $\lambda$ |
| $\Omega$ | $\lambda$ | Tuples in $\Omega$'s host-level tuple space and destined to $\lambda$ |

**Table 1.** Accessing different portions of the federated tuple space by using location parameters. In the table, $\omega$ and $\lambda$ are agent identifiers, while $\Omega$ is a host identifier.

---

[6] Note how specifying a destination location $\lambda$ implies neither guaranteed delivery nor ownership of the tuple $t$ to $\lambda$. Linda rules for non-deterministic selection of tuples are still in place; thus, it might be the case that some other agent may withdraw $t$ from the tuple space before $\lambda$, even after $t$ reached $\lambda$'s ITS.

**Reacting to Changes in Context** In the fluid scenario we target, the set of available data, hosts, and agents change rapidly according to the reconfiguration induced by mobility. Reacting to changes constitutes a significant fraction of an application's activities. At first glance, the Linda model would seem sufficient to provide some degree of reactivity by representing relevant events as tuples, and by using the **in** operation to execute the corresponding reaction as soon as the event tuple appears in the tuple space. Nevertheless, in practice this solution has a number of drawbacks. For instance, programming becomes cumbersome, since the burden of implementing a reactive behavior is placed on the programmer rather than the system. Moreover, enabling an asynchronous reaction would require the execution of **in** in a separate thread of control, hence degrading performance. Therefore, LIME explicitly extends the basic Linda tuple space with the notion of *reaction*. A reaction $\mathcal{R}(s, p)$ is defined by a code fragment $s$ that specifies the actions to be executed when a tuple matching the pattern $p$ is found in the tuple space. The semantics of reactions are based on the Mobile UNITY reactive statements [10]. Informally, a reaction can *fire* if a tuple matching pattern $p$ exists in the tuple space. After every regular tuple space operation, a reaction is selected non-deterministically and, if it is enabled, the statements in $s$ are executed in a single, atomic step. This selection and execution continues until no reactions are enabled, at which point normal processing resumes. Blocking operations are not allowed in $s$, as they may prevent the execution of $s$ from terminating.

LIME reactions can be explicitly registered and deregistered on a tuple space, and hence do not necessarily exist throughout the life of the system. Moreover, a notion of *mode* is provided to control the extent to which a reaction is allowed to execute. A reaction registered with mode ONCE is allowed to fire only one time, i.e., after its execution it becomes automatically deregistered, and hence removed from the reactive program. Instead, a reaction registered with mode ONCEPERTUPLE is allowed to fire an arbitrary number of times, but never twice for the same tuple. Finally, reactions can be annotated with location parameters, with the same meaning discussed earlier for **in** and **rd**. Hence, the full form of a LIME reaction is $\mathcal{R}[\omega, \lambda](s, p, m)$, where $m$ is the mode.

Reactions provide the programmer with very powerful constructs. They enable the specification of the appropriate actions that need to take place in response to a *state* change and allow their execution in a single atomic step. In particular, it is worth noting how this model is much more powerful than many event-based ones [18], including those exploited by tuple space middleware such as TSpaces [6] and JavaSpaces [7], that are typically stateless and provide no guarantee about the atomicity of event reactions.

Nevertheless, this expressive power comes at a price. In particular, when multiple hosts are present, the content of the federated tuple space depends on the content of the tuple spaces belonging to physically distributed, remote agents. Thus, maintaining the requirements of atomicity and serialization imposed by reactive statements requires a distributed transaction encompassing several hosts for every tuple space operation on any ITS—very often, an impractical solution.

For specific applications and scenarios, e.g., those involving a very limited number of nodes, these kind of reactions, referred to as *strong reactions*, would still be reasonable and therefore they remain part of the model. For practical performance reasons, however, our implementation currently limits the use of strong reactions by restricting the current location field to be a host or agent, and by enabling a reaction to fire only when the matching tuple appears on the same host as the agent that registered the reaction. As a consequence, a mobile agent can register a reaction for a host different from the one where it is residing, but such a reaction remains disabled until the agent migrates to the specified host. These constraints effectively force the *detection* of a tuple matching $p$ and the corresponding *execution* of the code fragment $s$ to take place (atomically) on a single host, and hence does not require a distributed transaction.

To strike a compromise between the expressive power of reactions and the practical implementation concerns, we introduce a new reactive construct that allows some form of reactivity spanning the whole federated tuple space but with weaker semantics. The processing of a *weak reaction* proceeds as in the case of a strong reaction, but detection and execution do not happen atomically: instead, execution is guaranteed to take place only eventually, after a matching tuple is detected. The execution of $s$ takes place on the host of the agent that registered the reaction.

**Exposing System Configuration** It is interesting to note that the extension of Linda operations with location parameters, as well as the other operations discussed thus far, foster a model that hides completely the details of the system (re)configuration that generated those changes. For instance, if the probe $inp[\omega, \lambda](p)$ fails, this simply means that no tuple matching $p$ is available in the projection of the federated tuple space defined by the location parameters $[\omega, \lambda]$. It cannot be directly inferred whether the failure is due to the fact that agent $\omega$ does not have a matching tuple, or simply agent $\omega$ is currently not part of the group.

Without awareness of the system configuration, only a partial context awareness can be accomplished, where applications are aware of changes in the portion of context concerned with application data. Although this perspective is often enough for many mobile applications, in many others the portion of context more closely related to the system configuration plays a key role. For instance, a typical problem is to react to departure of a mobile unit, or to determine the set of units currently belonging to a LIME group. Interestingly, LIME provides this form of awareness of the system configuration by using the same abstractions discussed thus far: through a transiently shared tuple space conventionally named LimeSystem to which all agents are permanently bound. The tuples in this tuple space contain information about the mobile units present in the group and their relationship, e.g., which tuple spaces they are sharing or, for mobile agents, which host they reside on. Insertion and withdrawal of tuples in LimeSystem is a prerogative of the run-time support. Nevertheless, applications can read tuples and register reactions to respond to changes in the configuration of the system.

```
public class LimeTupleSpace {
  public LimeTupleSpace(String name);
  public String getName();
  public boolean isOwner();
  public boolean isShared();
  public boolean setShared(boolean isShared);
  public static boolean setShared(LimeTupleSpace[] lts, boolean isShared);
  public void out(ITuple tuple);
  public ITuple in(ITuple template);
  public ITuple rd(ITuple template);
  public void out(AgentLocation destination, ITuple tuple);
  public ITuple in(Location current, AgentLocation destination, ITuple template);
  public ITuple inp(Location current, AgentLocation destination, ITuple template);
  public ITuple[] ing(Location current, AgentLocation destination, ITuple template);
  public ITuple rd(Location current, AgentLocation destination, ITuple template);
  public ITuple rdp(Location current, AgentLocation destination, ITuple template);
  public ITuple[] rdg(Location current, AgentLocation destination, ITuple template);
  public RegisteredReaction[] addStrongReaction(LocalizedReaction[] reactions);
  public RegisteredReaction[] addWeakReaction(Reaction[] reactions);
  public void removeReaction(RegisteredReaction[] reactions);
  public boolean isRegisteredReaction(RegisteredReaction reaction);
  public RegisteredReaction[] getRegisteredReactions();
}
```

**Fig. 6.** The class LimeTupleSpace, representing a transiently shared tuple space.

Together, the LimeSystem tuple space and the other application-defined transiently shared tuple spaces enable the definition of a fully context aware style of computing.

### 3.3  Programming with LIME

We complete the presentation of the LIME model by concisely illustrating the application programming interface provided in the current implementation[7] of LIME.

The class LimeTupleSpace, whose public interface is shown[8] in Figure 6, embodies the concept of a transiently shared tuple space. In the current implementation, agents are single-threaded and only the thread of the agent that creates the tuple space is allowed to perform operations on the LimeTupleSpace object; accesses by other threads fail by returning an exception. This represents the constraint that the ITS must be permanently and exclusively attached to the corresponding mobile agent. The name of the tuple space is specified as a parameter of the constructor.

Agents may also have *private* tuple spaces, i.e., not subject to sharing and not appearing in the LimeSystem tuple space. A private LimeTupleSpace can be used as a stepping stone to a shared data space, allowing the agent to populate it with data prior to making it publicly accessible, or it can be useful as a primitive data structure for local data storage. All tuple spaces are initially created private, and sharing must be explicitly enabled by calling the instance method

---

[7] The LIME Web site [20] contains extensive documentation and programming examples.

[8] Exceptions are not shown for the sake of readability.

setShared. The method accepts a boolean parameter specifying whether the transition is from private to shared (true) or vice versa (false). Calling this method effectively triggers engagement or disengagement of the corresponding tuple space. The sharing properties can also be changed in a single atomic step for multiple tuple spaces owned by the same agent by using the static version of setShared (see Figure 6). Engagement or disengagement of an entire host, instead, can be triggered explicitly by the programmer by using the methods engage and disengage, provided by the LimeServer class, not shown here. Otherwise, they are implicitly called by the run-time support according to connectivity. The LimeServer class is essentially an interface towards the run-time support, and exports additional system-related features, e.g., loading of an agent into a local or remote run-time support, setting of properties, and so on. In particular, it also allows the programmer to define whether transient sharing is constrained to a host-level tuple space, or whether it spans the whole federated tuple space.

LimeTupleSpace contains the Linda operations needed to access the tuple space, as well as the operation variants annotated with location parameters. The only requirement for tuple objects is to implement the interface ITuple, which is defined in a separate package providing access to a lightweight tuple space implementation. As for location parameters, LIME provides two classes, AgentLocation and HostLocation, which extend the common superclass Location, enabling the definition of globally unique location identifiers for hosts and agents. Objects of these classes are used to specify different scopes for LIME operations, as described earlier. For instance, a probe inp(cur,dest,t) may be restricted to the tuple space of a single agent if cur is of type AgentLocation, or it may refer the whole host-level tuple space, if cur is of type HostLocation. The constant Location.UNSPECIFIED is used to allow any location parameter to match. Thus, for instance, in(cur,Location.UNSPECIFIED,t) returns a tuple contained in the tuple space of cur, regardless of its final destination, including also misplaced tuples. Note how typing rules allow the proper constraint of the current and destination location according to the rules of the LIME model. For instance, the destination parameter is always an AgentLocation object, as agents are the only carriers of "concrete" tuple spaces in LIME. In the current implementation of LIME, probes are always restricted to a local subset of the federated tuple space, as defined by the location parameters. An unconstrained definition, as the one provided for in and rd, would involve a distributed transaction in order to preserve the semantics of the probe across the federated tuple space.

All the operations retain the same semantics on a private tuple space as on a shared tuple space, except for blocking operations. Since the private tuple space is exclusively associated to one agent, the execution of a blocking operation when no matching tuple is present would suspend the agent forever, effectively waiting for a tuple that no other agent can possibly insert. Hence, blocking operations always generate a run-time exception when invoked on a private tuple space.

```
public abstract class Reaction {
  public final static short ONCE;
  public final static short ONCEPERTUPLE;
  public ITuple getTemplate();
  public ReactionListener getListener();
  public short getMode();
  public Location getCurrentLocation();
  public AgentLocation getDestinationLocation();
}
public class UbiquitousReaction extends Reaction {
  public UbiquitousReaction(ITuple template, ReactionListener listener, short mode);
}
public class LocalizedReaction extends Reaction {
  public LocalizedReaction(Location current, AgentLocation destination,
                           ITuple template,ReactionListener listener, short mode);
}
public class RegisteredReaction extends Reaction {
  public String getTupleSpaceName();
  public AgentID getSubscriber();
  public boolean isWeakReaction();
}
public class ReactionEvent extends java.util.EventObject {
  public ITuple getEventTuple();
  public RegisteredReaction getReaction();
  public AgentID getSourceAgent();
}
public interface ReactionListener extends java.util.EventListener {
  public void reactsTo(ReactionEvent e);
}
```

**Fig. 7.** The classes Reaction, RegisteredReaction, ReactionEvent, and the interface ReactionListener, required for the definition of reactions on the tuple space.

The remainder of the interface of LimeTupleSpace is devoted to managing reactions; other relevant classes for this task are shown in Figure 7. Reactions can either be of type LocalizedReaction, where the current and destination location restrict the scope of the operation, or UbiquitousReaction, that specifies the whole federated tuple space as a target for matching. The type of a reaction is used to enforce the proper constraints on the registration through type checking. These two classes share the abstract class Reaction as a common ancestor, which defines a number of accessors for the properties established for the reaction at creation time. Creation of a reaction is performed by specifying the template that needs to be matched in the tuple space, a ReactionListener object that specifies the actions taken when the reaction fires, and a mode. The ReactionListener interface requires the implementation of a single method reactsTo that is invoked by the run-time support when the reaction actually fires. This method has access to the information about the reaction carried by the ReactionEvent object passed as a parameter to the method. The reaction mode can be either of the constants ONCE or ONCEPERTUPLE, defined in Reaction. Reactions are added to the ITS by calling either addStrongReaction or addWeakReaction, depending on the desired semantics. As we discussed earlier, in the current implementation strong reactions are confined to a single host, and hence only a LocalizedReaction can be passed to the first method. Registration of a reaction returns an object RegisteredReaction, that can be used to deregister a reaction with the method `removeReaction`, and provides additional information about the registration process. The decoupling between the reaction used for the registration and the `RegisteredReaction` object returned allows for registration of the same reaction on different ITSs and for the same reaction to be registered with strong and, subsequently, with weak semantics.

# 4    Application Development

LIME has been used in the development of a variety of mobile applications. In this section, we focus on applications dealing with physical mobility of hosts and first present a high level description of several different applications built on top of LIME, then we go into detail of another application that shows how physical hosts can perform collaborative tasks in the presence of disconnection.

## 4.1    Three Brief Examples

The first two applications presented here are not stand-alone applications, but instead add an additional layer of abstraction on top of LIME to support the development of mobile applications. The third is a mobile game that exploits the system configuration information available through LIME to react to changes in connectivity.

Because mobility of hosts defines a working environment in which the accessible components is constantly in flux, applications that must avail themselves of services need a mechanism to discover those services in a dynamic manner. A group from Washington University built a Jini-like service discovery mechanism as an application layer on top of LIME [5]. This project uses the tuple space for sharing service advertisements and performing pattern-based service discovery. This extends the client-server model of service discovery for the mobile ad hoc environment by coupling the services available for discovery with the services available in the network, and maintaining this connection even as connectivity changes.

In another project at Politecnico di Milano, the LIME tuple space is used to support code mobility by storing Java class bytecode [14]. The class loading mechanism is extended to resolve class names by searching the federated tuple space, instead of a well-known, centralized code repository. This mechanism enables the code on demand paradigm for code mobility in the mobile ad hoc environment, where connections to specific code servers are not always available.

The third application exploits the context aware features of LIME. It is a spatial game we refer to as REDROVER, in which individuals equipped with small mobile devices form teams and interact in a physical environment augmented with virtual elements. This forces the participants to rely to a great extent on information provided by the mobile units and not solely on what is visible to the naked eye. The display to the players is dominated by a *radar-like* image with an icon of the player in the middle, and icons indicating the current locations of the other connected players. Up-to-date location information is maintained by each player periodically inserting a tuple into their local tuple space indicating their current location. All other players register a reaction for these location tuples, and are notified when a player moves. When a player disconnects, their icon is changed to indicate their temporary unavailability. This functionality is attained with a single reaction registered on the LimeSystem tuple space whose listener changes the icon of the disconnected player. REDROVER also exploits the ability to create multiple tuple spaces for a single application. Location updates are fed to a common tuple space that is shared by all player, but REDROVER uses separate team-only tuple spaces to share private information, such as the location of a flag when playing "capture the flag".

## 4.2    Extended Example: Accessing Shared Data

ROAMINGJIGSAW, is a multi-player jigsaw assembly game. A group of players cooperate in a disconnected fashion on the solution of the jigsaw puzzle. They can construct assemblies independently (e.g., while disconnected), and share intermediate results or acquire pieces from each other when connected. Play begins with one player loading the puzzle pieces into a shared workspace that is visualized by the user as a *puzzle tray*. The workspace is shared among all connected users, therefore the puzzle trays of all users show the same set of puzzle pieces at this point.

Players can select pieces in the puzzle tray by clicking on them. The visual effect is that the piece outline is highlighted on all users' displays with the color of the selecting player. Selection has deeper consequences. In fact, although all the puzzle pieces are displayed on the tray, a player can make assemblies using only the pieces that she has selected, and that are currently displayed with her color. A player can select pieces or assemblies that are currently selected by another player, provided that the target player is connected.

Disconnection of a player does not have an immediate effect on the puzzle tray of the others. Nevertheless, pieces that have been selected by the departing player can no longer be selected by the others—and vice versa. Hence, the disconnected player can now construct assemblies by using only the pieces outlined with her color. Nevertheless, the pieces of all players remain visible. The assemblies made by each player during disconnection become visible to the others when connectivity among the players is restored. At this point, the view provided by the user interfaces is reconciled with the changes made during disconnection, and the selection of a piece belonging to a connected player is again possible. Figure 8 shows the appearance of the puzzle tray during disconnection and after reconnection.

From the description, it is evident that ROAMINGJIGSAW embodies a pattern of interaction where the shared workspace displayed by the user interface of each player provides an accurate image of the state of all connected players, but only a weakly consistent image of the global state of the system. For instance, a user's display contains only the last known information about each puzzle piece in the tray. If two pieces have been assembled by a disconnected player, this change is not visible to others. However, this still allows the players to work towards

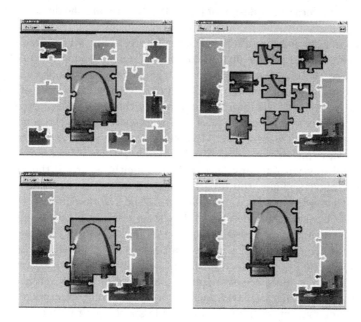

**Fig. 8.** RoamingJigsaw. The top two images show the puzzle trays of the black and white players while they are disconnected and able to assemble only their selected pieces. The bottom two images show the black and white puzzle trays after the players re-engage and see the assemblies that occurred during disconnection.

achieving the global goal, i.e., the solution of the puzzle, through incremental updates of their local state.

RoamingJigsaw is a simple game that nonetheless exhibits the characteristics of a general class of applications in which data sharing is the key element. Hence, the design strategy we exploited in RoamingJigsaw may be adapted easily to handle updates in the data being shared by real applications. One example could be provided by collaborative work applications involving mobile users, where our mechanism could be used to deal with changes in sections of a document, or with paper submissions and reviews to be evaluated by a program committee.

*Design and Implementation.* In our design of RoamingJigsaw, we chose to represent pieces and assemblies as tuples, and the shared workspace as a tuple space. When a player selects a piece, the corresponding tuple is withdrawn and subsequently reinserted in the tuple space, with the field indicating the current "owner" automatically changed by Lime. Similarly, when a player builds an assembly out of several pieces, a new tuple is written containing information about the assembled pieces; the tuples associated with the latter are removed from the tuple space.

The critical issues in the design of ROAMINGJIGSAW are the detection of piece selection and assembly, the reconciliation of the puzzle tray taking place on re-connection, and the joining of a new player. Interestingly, all of these rely upon a single weak reaction of type `UbiquitousReaction` and mode ONCEPERTUPLE. Registration of the reaction is specified so that its template looks for any new tuple corresponding to a puzzle piece, while its listener takes care of updating the puzzle tray by using the information found in the tuple, thus correctly main-taining the weakly consistent view of the workspace. Since the reaction type sets its scope to the whole federated tuple space, the application receives up-dates about new pieces regardless of where and why they have been inserted, and hence notably without any need to be explicitly aware of the arrival and departure of players. Thus, the programming effort can be rightfully spent on handling data changes, rather than monitoring the system configuration.

Although the processing described thus far operates on the federated tuple space, fine-grained control over the location of tuples is critical in dealing with disconnections. To ensure that a player can access her selected pieces during a disconnection period, piece selection should actually transfer the corresponding tuple into the local tuple space of the player's application. Moreover, according to what we discussed earlier, a player must be prevented from selecting a piece that is currently not present in the federated tuple space. For this reason, selection is performed by the application agent by issuing an **inp** operation on the tuple space of the player last known to have the piece. If the piece is returned, it is reinserted in the local tuple space of the new owner, thus leading to a successful selection. Otherwise, if no tuple is returned it means that the piece is unavailable for selection, and a message is displayed to the user.

*Design Process.* The LIME version of ROAMINGJIGSAW was developed as a port of a previous version written on top of the TSpaces middleware [6]. In this version, all puzzle pieces were held at the tuple space server and players issued remote operations. Porting the application to the mobile environment and LIME involved only minor changes to the application, including the introduction of puzzle piece ownership and the conversion of TSpaces clients to LIME agents.

Interestingly, the coordination necessary to handle the inaccessibility of tu-ples due to disconnection was already addressed in the original application. In the original, when two pieces are assembled, two independent **inp** operations are performed to remove the separate pieces, following by a single **out** to insert the joined piece. If one of the original two pieces is not present (i.e., the **inp** returns `null`), the non-mobile application assumes that some other player is attempting to assemble the same piece simultaneously, and therefore the player backs-off, allowing the other player to continue. If the conflict occurs on the second piece removed, then the first removed piece must be reinserted. The same problem occurs in the mobile version, and similar corrective action is required. Also in the mobile version, a similar issue arises when a player tries to select a piece to become the owner. This operation involves an **inp** that may fail either because another player is trying to select the same piece or because the piece is not acces-sible due to disconnection. The significance of this is that the programmer of the mobile version had already encountered complex coordination issues during the development of the server version, and the mobile issues were much the same.

Finally, in converting from TSpaces to LIME, the event mechanisms were changed. TSpaces uses events that fire in response to an operation on the tuple space. Therefore, in order to update a player's puzzle tray, an event was registered on the insertion (i.e., **out**) of a tuple. In LIME, reactions are registered on the state of the tuple space. By replacing the original TSpaces event with a LIME ONCEPERTUPLE reaction, we achieved the same functionality, and simultaneously were able to update the player puzzle trays to reflect changes that occurred during disconnection.

## 5   Conclusions and Future Directions

Mobility is emerging as an important area for computing research, posing many challenges that must be overcome in a society that is increasingly placing demands on computing technology. Our research into methods for designing middleware for mobile computing, specifically the instantiation of the global virtual data structures concept in LIME has demonstrated the benefit of providing high level abstractions to application developers, easing the software development process and ultimately resulting in reliable applications built on top of a stable platform.

Future work remains to be done in adapting other data structures to the GVDS concept, although some work has already proceeded in this direction. For example, the XMIDDLE [9] system developed at University College of London presents the user with a tree data structure based on XML data. When connectivity becomes available, trees belonging to different users can be composed, based on the node tags. After disconnection, operations on replicated data are still allowed, and their effect is reconciled when connectivity is restored. Also PEERWARE [3], a project at Politecnico di Milano, exploits a tree data structure, albeit in a rather different way. In PEERWARE, each host is associated with a tree of document containers. When connectivity is available, the trees are shared among hosts, meaning that the document pool available for searching under a given tree node includes the union of the documents at that node on all connected hosts. We are also working on a parallel project to formalize the GVDS concept, identifying the core concepts, making it more accessible to other researchers, and clarifying the process of instantiating the model.

LIME itself is a promising middleware that has taken on a life of its own outside the GVDS model. While the version LIME described here has already been shown to be useful for a variety of applications, and is general enough to provide a foundation for additional mobile ad hoc services, the model itself makes strong guarantees about connectivity that are not always possible in the mobile ad hoc environment. For example, even by incorporating the notion of *safe distance* [17] as part of the engagement and disengagement protocols, it is still possible for a host to disconnect without prior warning. Work is continuing on LIME to weaken the model to both handle unannounced disconnection and to remove the transactional nature of engagement. We expect this weakening to result in an implementation which is widely applicable, but for which guarantees are difficult to formally describe and even to achieve. We have also begun to explore the issues of security in tuple space based mobile ad hoc environments [16] by allowing applications to protect selected tuple spaces and even individual tuples through the use of passwords. The same passwords are also used to encrypt communication among hosts when exchanging messages related to sharing specific tuples spaces.

Finally, LIME, in addition to demonstrating the practical use of coordination technology in mobile computing, opens a new area of research involving the application of state-based coordination models and middleware to context-aware computing. The complex mobile environment becomes manageable with the abstractions provided by the middleware, the software development process is simplified, and the resulting applications are more reliable.

*Availability.* LIME continues to be developed as an open source project, available under GNU's LGPL license. Source code and development notes are available at `lime.sourceforge.net`.

# References

[1] M. Baldi and G.P. Picco. Evaluating the Tradeoffs of Mobile Code Design Paradigms in Network Management Applications. In *Proc. of the 20<sup>th</sup> Int. Conf. on Software Engineering*, 1998.

[2] N. Carriero, D. Gelernter, and L. Zuck. Bauhaus-Linda. In *Workshop on Languages and Models for Coordination, European Conference on Object Oriented Programming*, 1994.

[3] G. Cugola and G.P. Picco. PEERWARE: Core middleware support for peer-to-peer and mobile systems. Technical report, Politecnico di Milano, Italy, 2001. Available at `www.elet.polimi.it/upload/picco`.

[4] D. Gelernter. Generative Communication in Linda. *ACM Computing Surveys*, 7(1):80–112, Jan. 1985.

[5] R. Handorean and G.-C. Roman. Service provision in ad hoc networks. In F. Arbab and C. Talcott, editors, *Proceedings of the 5<sup>th</sup> International Conference on Coordination Models and Languages*, LNCS 2315, pages 207–219, York, UK, April 2002. Springer.

[6] IBM. TSpaces Web page. `http://www.almaden.ibm.com/cs/TSpaces`.

[7] JavaSpaces. The JavaSpaces Specification web page. `http://www.sun.com/jini/specs/js-spec.html`.

[8] J.J. Kistler and M. Satyanarayanan. Disconnected Operation in the Coda File System. *ACM Trans. on Computer Systems*, 10(1):3–25, 1992.

[9] C. Mascolo, L. Capra, S. Zachariadis, and W. Emmerich. XMIDDLE: A data-sharing middleware for mobile computing. *Kluwer Personal and Wireless Communications Journal*, 21(1), April 2002.

[10] P.J. McCann and G.-C. Roman. Compositional Programming Abstractions for Mobile Computing. *IEEE Trans. on Software Engineering*, 24(2):97–110, 1998.

[11] N. Minar, M. Gray, O. Roup, R. Krikorian, and P. Maes. Hive: Distributed Agents for Networking Things. In *Proc. of the 1ˢᵗ Int. Symp. on Agent Systems and Applications and 3ʳᵈ Int. Symp. on Mobile Agents (ASA/MA '99)*, pages 118–129, Palm Springs, CA, USA, October 1999. IEEE Computer Society.

[12] A.L. Murphy, G.P. Picco, and G.-C. Roman. LIME: A Middleware for Physical and Logical Mobility. In F. Golshani, P. Dasgupta, and W. Zhao, editors, *Proc. of the 21ˢᵗ Int. Conf. on Distributed Computing Systems (ICDCS-21)*, pages 524–533, May 2001.

[13] Oracle. Oracle 8*i* Lite web page. http://www.oracle.com/, 1999.

[14] G.P. Picco and M.L. Buschini. Exploiting transiently shared tuple spaces for location transparent code mobility. In F. Arbab and C. Talcott, editors, *Proc. of the 5ᵗʰ Int. Conf. on Coordination Models and Languages*, LNCS 2315, pages 258–273, York, UK, April 2002. Springer.

[15] G.P. Picco, A.L. Murphy, and G.-C. Roman. LIME: Linda Meets Mobility. In D. Garlan, editor, *Proc. of the 21ˢᵗ Int. Conf. on Software Engineering*, pages 368–377, May 1999.

[16] G.-C. Roman and R. Handorean. Secure Sharing of Tuple Spaces in Ad Hoc Settings. Technical Report WUCS-02-31, Dept. of Computer Science and Engineering, Washington Univ. in St. Louis, MO, USA, 2003.

[17] G.-C. Roman, Q. Huang, and A. Hazemi. Consistent group membership in ad hoc networks. In *Proceedings of the 23ʳᵈ Int. Conf. on Software Engineering*, pages 381–388, Toronto, Canada, May 2001.

[18] D.S. Rosenblum and A.L. Wolf. A Design Framework for Internet-Scale Event Observation and Notification. In *Proc. of the 6ᵗʰ European Software Engineering Conf. held jointly with the 5ᵗʰ ACM SIGSOFT Symp. on the Foundations of Software Engineering (ESEC/FSE97)*, number 1301 in LNCS, Zurich (Switzerland), September 1997. Springer.

[19] A. Rowstron. WCL: A coordination language for geographically distributed agents. *World Wide Web Journal*, 1(3):167–179, 1998.

[20] Lime Team. LIME Web page. lime.sourceforge.net.

[21] M. Weiser. The computer for the 21st century. *Scientific American*, 265(3):94–104, 1991.

# Performance Evaluation
# at the Software Architecture Level

Simonetta Balsamo[1], Marco Bernardo[2], and Marta Simeoni[1]

[1] Università "Ca' Foscari" di Venezia
Dipartimento di Informatica
Via Torino 155, 30172 Mestre, Italy
{balsamo, simeoni}@dsi.unive.it
[2] Università di Urbino "Carlo Bo"
Istituto di Scienze e Tecnologie dell'Informazione
Piazza della Repubblica 13, 61029 Urbino, Italy
bernardo@sti.uniurb.it

**Abstract.** When tackling the construction of a software system, at the software architecture design level there are two main issues related to the system performance. First, the designer may need to choose among several alternative software architectures for the system, with the choice being driven especially by performance considerations. Second, for a specific software architecture of the system, the designer may want to understand whether its performance can be improved and, if so, it would be desirable for the designer to have some diagnostic information that guide the modification of the software architecture itself. In this paper we show how these two issues can be addressed in practice by employing a methodology relying on the combined use of Æmilia — an architectural description language based on stochastic process algebra — and queueing networks — structured performance models equipped with fast solution algorithms — which allows for a quick prediction, improvement, and comparison of the performance of different software architectures for a given system. The methodology is illustrated through a case study in which a sequential architecture, a pipeline architecture, and a concurrent architecture for a compiler system are compared on the basis of typical average performance indices.

## 1 Introduction

Software architecture (SA) is an emerging discipline within software engineering, aiming at describing the structure and the behavior of the software systems at a high level of abstraction [43,46]. A SA represents the structure and the behavior of a software system in an early stage of the development cycle, the phase in which basic design choices of components and interactions among components are made and clearly influence the subsequent development and deployment phases. Appropriate languages and tools are required to give precise descriptions of SAs and to support the efficient analysis of their properties in a way that

M. Bernardo and P. Inverardi (Eds.): SFM 2003, LNCS 2804, pp. 207–258, 2003.
© Springer-Verlag Berlin Heidelberg 2003

provides component-oriented diagnostic information in case of malfunctioning detection.

A crucial issue in the software development cycle is that of integrating the analysis of nonfunctional system properties since the early stages, where performance is one of the most influential factors that drive the design choices. To this purpose, in the formal method research field several description and analysis techniques have been proposed in the past twenty years, like stochastic Petri nets (SPN; see, e.g., [39,1]) and stochastic process algebras (SPA; see, e.g., [29,31,30,14]). On the side of the system performance evaluation research field, various models and methods have been proposed for the quantitative evaluation of hardware and sofware systems, which were traditionally based mostly on queueing networks (QN; see, e.g., [34,35,37,33,42,50,8]). However, only more recently some research has been truly focused on the integration of specific performance models in the software development cycle (see, e.g., [47,52,3]).

In this paper, which is a full and revised version of [7] that builds on material in [16,3], we propose a methodology to evaluate the performance of SAs, which combines formalisms and techniques developed in the two different communities in a way that can be integrated in the software development cycle. More precisely, the methodology is based on both SPA modeling and QN analysis and is realized through a transformation of SPA specifications into QN models.

On the modeling side, we choose SPAs because they are compositional languages permitting the description of functional and performance aspects, which can be enhanced to act as fully fledged architectural description languages (ADL) that elucidate the architectural notions of component and interaction and support the detection of architectural mismatches arising when assembling several components together. The specific ADL that we consider is Æmilia [16], which is based on the stochastic process algebra EMPA$_{gr}$ [14]. Æmilia is illustrated in Sect. 2.

On the analysis side, we choose QNs for several reasons. First, QNs are structured performance models, therefore they should support the possibility of keeping track of the correspondence between their constituent service centers and the components of the architectural specifications. Second, typical performance measures can be computed both at the level of the overall QNs and at the level of their constituent service centers. Such global and local performance indicators can then be interpreted back at the level of the overall architectural specifications and at the level of their constituent components, respectively, so that useful diagnostic information can be obtained in the case of poor global performance. Third, QNs are equipped with efficient solution techniques that do not require the construction of the underlying state space, so that scalability with respect to the number of components in the architectural specifications should be achieved. Fourth, the solution of the QNs can be expressed symbolically in the case of simple open topologies, and can be approximated through an asymptotic bound analysis. This feature is useful in the early stages of the software development cycle, since the actual values of the system parameters, as well as its complete behavior, may be unknown. The basic concepts and results about QNs are recalled in Sect. 3.

The translation of Æmilia specifications into QN models is not straightforward, because the two formalisms are quite different from each other. On the one hand, Æmilia is a component-oriented language for handling both functional and performance characteristics, in which all the details must be expressed in an action-based way. On the other hand, QNs result in a queue-oriented graphical notation for performance modeling purposes only, in which some details — notably the queueing disciplines — are described in natural language. In addition to that, the components of the Æmilia specifications cannot be mapped to QN service centers, but on finer parts that we call QN basic elements. As a consequence, the translation can be applied only to a (reasonably wide) class of Æmilia specifications that satisfy certain syntax restrictions, which ensure that each component in such specifications is a QN basic element, i.e. an arrival process, a buffer, a fork process, a join process, or a service process. The translation, whose complexity is linear in the number of components declared in the Æmilia specifications, leads to the generation of open, closed or mixed QN models with phase-type interarrival and service time distributions, queueing disciplines with noninterruptable service, fork and join nodes for handling parallelism and synchronization, and arbitrary topologies. Depending on the type of QN model, various solution algorithms, either exact or approximate, can be applied to efficiently evaluate some average performance indices that are eventually interpreted back at the Æmilia specification level. The translation is defined in Sect. 4.

Based on the above translation of Æmilia specifications into QN models, we develop a practical multi-phase methodology to quickly predict, improve, and compare the performance of different architectures for the same software system. In the proposed methodology, the first step is to model with Æmilia all the architectural alternatives devised by a designer for the same system. Such Æmilia specifications may then need to be manipulated in such a way that they satisfy the syntax restrictions that make it possible to derive QN models out of them. Once the QN models for the architectural alternatives are obtained by applying the above translation, they are in turn manipulated so that some typical average performance measures can efficiently be computed in several scenarios of interest. The previous approximations, both at the Æmilia level and at the QN level, are justified at the architectural level of abstraction by the fact that we are more interested in rapidly getting an indication about the performance of the architectural alternatives, rather than in their precise evaluation. On the basis of the computed average performance measures, the designer gets a feedback that can be used to guide the modification of the Æmilia specifications of some architectural alternatives in order to ameliorate their performance. Once the predict-improve cycle is terminated, the architectural alternatives are compared on the basis of the values of the average performance measures obtained in the considered scenarios, in order to single out the best one. Because of the approximations that might have been performed in the previous phases, and the fact that the considered average performance measures are not necessarily related to the performance requirements of the system under study, the exact Æmilia specification of the selected architectural design is finally checked against the specific performance requirements. The methodology is presented in Sect. 5.

The application of the methodology and the translation of Æmilia specifications into QN models are clarified in Sect. 6 by means of a case study in which three different architectures — a sequential one, a pipeline one, and a concurrent one — for a compiler system are compared in different scenarios on the basis of average performance indices like the mean number of programs compiled per unit of time, the mean fraction of time during which the compiler is being used, the mean number of programs in the compiler system, and the mean compilation time.

Finally, in Sect. 7 we report some concluding remarks about future perspectives.

## 2    Æmilia: A SPA-based ADL

In this section we present the main ingredients of Æmilia [16], a performance-oriented ADL. Æmilia is the result of the integration of two earlier formalisms: PADL [15,17,18,2] and EMPA$_{gr}$ [14]. The former is a process-algebra-based ADL, which is equipped with some architectural checks for the detection of deadlock-related architectural mismatches within families of software systems called architectural types. The latter is an expressive SPA, which allows for both the functional verification and the performance evaluation of concurrent and distributed systems. Below we recall through a running example how PADL and EMPA$_{gr}$ have been combined together in order to give rise to the syntax, the semantics, and the analysis support for Æmilia.

### 2.1    Textual and Graphical Notation

A description in Æmilia represents an architectural type. An architectural type is an intermediate abstraction between a single SA and an architectural style [46], which results in a family of software systems sharing certain constraints on the component observable behavior as well as on the architectural topology [15,17,18].

As shown in Table 1, the description of an architectural type starts with the name of the architectural type and its formal parameters, which can represent variables as well as exponential rates, priorities, and weights for EMPA$_{gr}$ actions. Each architectural type is defined as a function of its architectural element types (AETs) and its architectural topology. An AET, whose description starts with its name and its formal parameters, is defined as a function of its behavior, specified either as a list of sequential EMPA$_{gr}$ defining equations or through an invocation of a previously defined architectural type, and its interactions, specified as a set of EMPA$_{gr}$ action types occurring in the behavior that act as interfaces for the AET.

| | |
|---|---|
| ARCHI_TYPE | ⟨name and formal parameters⟩ |
|   ARCHI_ELEM_TYPES | ⟨architectural element types:  behaviors and interactions⟩ |
| | |
|   ARCHI_TOPOLOGY | |
|     ARCHI_ELEM_INSTANCES | ⟨architectural element instances⟩ |
|     ARCHI_INTERACTIONS | ⟨architectural interactions⟩ |
|     ARCHI_ATTACHMENTS | ⟨architectural attachments⟩ |
| END | |

**Table 1.** Structure of an Æmilia textual description

A sequential $\text{EMPA}_{\text{gr}}$ defining equation specifies a possibly recursive behavior in the following way:

$$behavior\_id(formal\_parameter\_list; local\_variable\_list) = sequential\_term$$

where a sequential $\text{EMPA}_{\text{gr}}$ term is written according to the following syntax:

$$
\begin{aligned}
sequential\_term ::= &\ \mathtt{stop} \\
| &\ <action\_type, action\_rate> . sequential\_term\_1 \\
| &\ \mathtt{choice}\,\{\, sequential\_term\_2\_list\,\} \\
sequential\_term\_1 ::= &\ sequential\_term \\
| &\ behavior\_id(actual\_parameter\_list) \\
sequential\_term\_2 ::= &\ sequential\_term \\
| &\ \mathtt{cond}(boolean\_guard) \rightarrow sequential\_term
\end{aligned}
$$

Every behavior is given an identifier, a possibly empty list of comma-separated formal parameters, and a possibly empty list of comma-separated local variables. The admitted data types for parameters and variables are boolean, integer, bounded integer interval, real, list, array, and record. The sequential term $\mathtt{stop}$ cannot execute any action. The sequential term $<action\_type, action\_rate>$ . $sequential\_term\_1$ can execute an action having a certain type and a certain rate and then behaves as specified by $sequential\_term\_1$, which can be in turn a sequential term or a behavior invocation with a possibly empty list of comma-separated actual parameters. The action type can be a simple identifier (unstructured action), an identifier followed by the symbol "?" and a list of comma-separated variables enclosed in parentheses (input action), or an identifier followed by the symbol "!" and a list of comma-separated expressions enclosed in parentheses (output action). The action rate can be the identifier or the numeric value for the rate of an exponential distribution (exponentially timed action), the keyword $\mathtt{inf}$ followed by the identifiers or the numeric values of a priority level and a weight enclosed in parentheses (immediate action), or the symbol "∗" followed by the identifiers or the numeric values of a priority level and a weight enclosed in parentheses (passive action). Finally, the sequential term $\mathtt{choice}\,\{\, sequential\_term\_2\_list\,\}$ expresses a choice among at least two comma-separated alternatives, each of which may be subject to a boolean guard. If all the alternatives with a true guard start with an exponentially timed action, then the race policy applies: each involved action is selected with a probability proportional to its rate. If some of the alternatives with a true guard start with an immediate action, then such immediate actions take precedence over the exponentially timed ones and the generative preselection policy applies: each involved immediate action with the highest priority level is selected with a probability proportional to its weight. If some of the alternatives with a true guard start with a passive action, then the reactive preselection policy applies to them: for every action type, each involved passive action of that type with the highest priority level is selected with a probability proportional to its weight (the choice among passive actions of different types is nondeterministic).

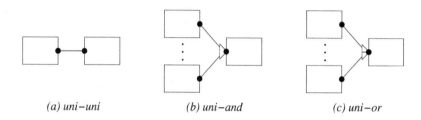

(a) uni−uni          (b) uni−and          (c) uni−or

**Fig. 1.** Legal attachments

The architectural topology is specified through the declaration of a set of architectural element instances (AEIs) representing the system components, a set of architectural (as opposed to local) interactions given by some interactions of the AEIs that act as interfaces for the whole architectural type, and a set of directed architectural attachments among the interactions of the AEIs. Alternatively, the architectural topology can be specified through the Æmilia graphical notation inspired by flow graphs [38], in which the boxes denote the AEIs, the black circles denote the local interactions, the white squares denote the architectural interactions, and the directed edges denote the attachments.

Every interaction is declared to be an input interaction or an output interaction and every attachment must go from an output interaction to an input interaction of two different AEIs. In addition, every interaction is declared to be a uni-interaction, an and-interaction, or an or-interaction. As shown in Fig. 1, the only legal attachments are those between two uni-interactions, an and-interaction and a uni-interaction, and an or-interaction and a uni-interaction. An and-interaction and an or-interaction can be attached to several uni-interactions. In the case of execution of an and-interaction, it synchronizes with all the uni-interactions attached to it. In the case of execution of an or-interaction, instead, it synchronizes with only one of the uni-interactions attached to it. An AEI can have different types of interactions (input/output, uni/and/or, local/architectural). Every local interaction must be involved in at least one attachment, while every architectural interaction must not be involved in any attachment. No isolated groups of AEIs are admitted in the architectural topology. On the performance side, we have two additional requirements. For the sake of modeling consistency, all the occurrences of an action type in the behavior of an AET must have the same kind of rate (exponential, or infinite with the same priority level, or passive with the same priority level). In order to comply with the generative-reactive synchronization discipline of EMPA$_{gr}$, which establishes that two nonpassive actions cannot synchronize, every set of attached interactions must contain at most one interaction whose associated rate is exponential or infinite.

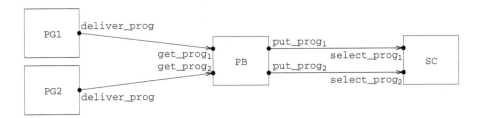

**Fig. 2.** Graphical description of SeqCompSys

As an example, we show in Table 2 an Æmilia textual description for an architectural type representing a compiler system. The compiler we consider is a sequential monolithic compiler that carries out all the phases (lexical analysis, parsing, type checking, code optimization, and code generation), with each phase introducing an exponentially distributed delay. For the sake of performance evaluation, the description of the compiler system comprises a generator of programs to be compiled, where the program interarrival times are assumed to follow an exponential distribution, as well as un unbounded buffer in which such programs wait before being compiled one at a time. We suppose that there are two different classes of programs: those whose code must be optimized and those whose code must not. As can be noted, the description of the architectural type SeqCompSys is parametrized with respect to the arrival rates of the two classes of programs $(\lambda_1, \lambda_2)$ and the service rates of the five compilation phases $(\mu_1, \mu_p, \mu_c, \mu_o, \mu_g)$. The omitted values for the priority levels and the weights of the infinite and passive rates in the specification are taken to be 1. The same sequential compiler system is depicted in Fig. 2 through the Æmilia graphical notation.

## 2.2   Formal Semantics and Analysis Support

The semantics of an Æmilia specification is given by translation into EMPA$_{gr}$. This translation is carried out in two steps. In the first step, the semantics of each AEI is defined to be the behavior of the corresponding AET — in which the formal rates, priority levels, and weights are replaced by the corresponding actual ones — projected onto its interactions. Such a projected behavior is obtained from the list of sequential EMPA$_{gr}$ defining equations representing the behavior of the AET by applying a hiding operator on all the actions that are not interactions. In this way, we abstract from all the internal details of the

```
ARCHI_TYPE               SeqCompSys(rate λ₁, λ₂, μ₁, μₚ, μc, μₒ, μg)
  ARCHI_ELEM_TYPES

    ELEM_TYPE            ProgGenT(rate λ)
      BEHAVIOR          ProgGen(void; void) =
                          <generate_prog, λ>.<deliver_prog, inf>.ProgGen()
      INPUT_INTERACTIONS
      OUTPUT_INTERACTIONS UNI deliver_prog

    ELEM_TYPE           ProgBufferT(integer h₁, h₂)
      BEHAVIOR          ProgBuffer(integer h₁, h₂; void) =
                          choice
                          {
                            <get_prog₁, *>.ProgBuffer(h₁ + 1, h₂),
                            <get_prog₂, *>.ProgBuffer(h₁, h₂ + 1),
                            cond(h₁ > 0) -> <put_prog₁, *>.ProgBuffer(h₁ − 1, h₂),
                            cond(h₂ > 0) -> <put_prog₂, *>.ProgBuffer(h₁, h₂ − 1)
                          }
      INPUT_INTERACTIONS  UNI get_prog₁; get_prog₂
      OUTPUT_INTERACTIONS UNI put_prog₁; put_prog₂

    ELEM_TYPE           SeqCompT(rate μ₁, μₚ, μc, μₒ, μg)
      BEHAVIOR          SeqComp(void; void) =
                          choice
                          {
                            <select_prog₁, inf>.<recognize_tokens, μ₁>.
                              <parse_phrases, μₚ>.<check_phrases, μc>.
                              <optimize_code, μₒ>.<generate_code, μg>.SeqComp(),
                            <select_prog₂, inf>.<recognize_tokens, μ₁>.
                              <parse_phrases, μₚ>.<check_phrases, μc>.
                              <generate_code, μg>.SeqComp()
                          }
      INPUT_INTERACTIONS  UNI select_prog₁; select_prog₂
      OUTPUT_INTERACTIONS
  ARCHI_TOPOLOGY

    ARCHI_ELEM_INSTANCES  PG₁ : ProgGenT(λ₁);
                          PG₂ : ProgGenT(λ₂);
                          PB : ProgBufferT(0, 0);
                          SC : SeqCompT(μ₁, μₚ, μc, μₒ, μg)
    ARCHI_INTERACTIONS

    ARCHI_ATTACHMENTS   FROM PG₁.deliver_prog TO PB.get_prog₁;
                        FROM PG₂.deliver_prog TO PB.get_prog₂;
                        FROM PB.put_prog₁ TO SC.select_prog₁;
                        FROM PB.put_prog₂ TO SC.select_prog₂
END
```

**Table 2.** Textual description of SeqCompSys

behavior of the AEI. In addition, the projected behavior must reflect the fact that an or-interaction can result in several distinct synchronizations. Therefore, every or-interaction is rewritten as a choice among as many indexed instances of uni-interactions as there are attachments involving the or-interaction. Recalled that in $\text{EMPA}_{gr}$ the hiding operator is denoted by the symbol "/", for our compiler system example we have:

$$[\![PG_1]\!] = ProgGen_1 \, / \, \{generate\_prog\}$$
$$[\![PG_2]\!] = ProgGen_2 \, / \, \{generate\_prog\}$$
$$[\![PB]\!] = ProgBuffer(0,0)$$
$$[\![SC]\!] = SeqComp \, / \, \{recognize\_tokens, parse\_phrases, check\_phrases,$$
$$optimize\_code, generate\_code\}$$

where $ProgGen_1$ (resp. $ProgGen_2$) is obtained from $ProgGen$ by replacing each occurrence of $\lambda$ with $\lambda_1$ (resp. $\lambda_2$).

In the second step, the semantics of an architectural type is obtained by composing in parallel the semantics of its AEIs according to the specified attachments, after relabeling to the same fresh action type all the interactions attached to each other. This relabeling is required by the synchronization mechanism of $\text{EMPA}_{gr}$, which establishes that only actions with the same type can synchronize. Recalled that in $\text{EMPA}_{gr}$ the relabeling operator is denoted by the symbols "[" and "]" and that the left-associative parallel composition operator is denoted by the symbol "$\|_S$" where $S$ is the set of action types on which the synchronization is enforced, for our compiler system example we have:

$$[\![SeqCompSys]\!] = [\![PG_1]\!][deliver\_prog \mapsto a_1] \, \|_\emptyset$$
$$[\![PG_2]\!][deliver\_prog \mapsto a_2] \, \|_{\{a_1,a_2\}}$$
$$[\![PB]\!][get\_program_1 \mapsto a_1, get\_program_2 \mapsto a_2,$$
$$put\_program_1 \mapsto b_1, put\_program_2 \mapsto b_2] \, \|_{\{b_1,b_2\}}$$
$$[\![SC]\!][select\_prog_1 \mapsto b_1, select\_prog_2 \mapsto b_2]$$

Given the translation above, Æmilia inherits the semantic models of $\text{EMPA}_{gr}$. More precisely, the semantics of an Æmilia specification is a state-transition graph called the integrated semantic model, whose states are represented by $\text{EMPA}_{gr}$ terms and whose transitions are labeled with $\text{EMPA}_{gr}$ actions together with the related guards arising from the use of the choice operator. This graph is finite state and finitely branching unless variables taking values from infinite domains are used (like in the buffer of the compiler system example), in which case a symbolic representation of the state space is employed in accordance with [13]. After pruning the lower priority transitions from the integrated semantic model, it is possible to derive a functional semantic model, by removing the action rates from the transitions, and a performance semantic model, by removing the action types from the transitions. The performance semantic model, which is defined only if the integrated semantic model has neither passive transitions nor transitions with a guard different from true, is a continuous-time or a discrete-time Markov chain [48] depending on whether the integrated semantic model has exponentially timed transitions or not.

On the analysis side, Æmilia inherits from $\text{EMPA}_{gr}$ standard techniques to assess functional properties as well as performance measures. Among such techniques we mention model checking [23], equivalence checking [24], Markovian analysis [48] based on rewards [32] as described in [14], and discrete event simulation [51], all of which are available in the Æmilia-based software tool TwoTowers 3.0 [12]. In addition to these capabilities, Æmilia comes equipped with some specific checks for the detection of architectural mismatches — and the provision of related diagnostic information — that may arise when assembling the components together. The first group of checks ensures that deadlock freedom is preserved when building a system from deadlock-free components [15,2]. The second group of checks makes sure that assembling components with partially specified performance details (i.e., with passive actions occurring in their behaviors) results in a system with fully specified performance aspects [16]. Finally, the third group of checks comes into play in case of hierarchical modeling, i.e. whenever the description of a component behavior contains an architectural type invocation. Such checks guarantee that the actual parameters of an invocation of an architectural type conform to the formal parameters of the definition of the architectural type, in the sense that the actual components have the same observable behavior as the corresponding formal components [15] and that the actual topology is a legal extension of the formal topology [17,18].

## 3   Queueing Networks

QN models have been widely applied as system performance models to represent and analyze resource sharing systems [34,35,37,33,42,50,8]. In essence, a QN model is a collection of interacting service centers, representing system resources, and a set of customers, representing the users sharing the resources. The customers' competition for the resource service corresponds to queueing into the service centers. The popularity of QN models for system performance evaluation is due to their relatively high accuracy in performance results and their efficiency in model analysis and evaluation. In this section we briefly recall the basic notions and properties of QN models. In particular, we shall focus on the class of product form QNs, which admit fast solution techniques.

### 3.1   Queueing Systems

As depicted in Fig. 3($a$), the simplest case of QN is the one in which there is a single service center together with a source of arrivals, which is referred to as a queueing system (QS). Every QS is completely described by the customer interarrival time distribution, the customer service time distribution, the number of independent servers, the queue capacity, the customer population size, and the queueing discipline. The first five parameters are summarized by using the Kendall's notation $A/B/m/c/p$, with A and B ranging over a set of probability distributions — 'M' for memoryless distributions, 'D' for deterministic values, 'PH' for phase-type distributions, and 'G' for general distributions — and $m$, $c$, and $p$ being natural numbers. If $c$ and $p$ are unspecified, they are assumed to be $\infty$, i.e. to describe an unlimited queue capacity and an unlimited population.

Every customer needing a certain service arrives at the QS, waits in the queue for a while, is served by one of the servers, and finally leaves the QS.

The queueing discipline is an algorithm that determines the order in which the customers in the queue are served. Such a scheduling algorithm may depend on the order in which the customers arrive at the QS, the priorities assigned to the customers, or the amounts of service already provided to the customers. Here are some commonly adopted queueing disciplines:

- First come first served (FCFS): the customers are served in the order of their arrival.
- Last come first served (LCFS): the customers are served in the reverse order of their arrival.
- Service in random order (SIRO): the next customer to be served is chosen probabilistically, with equal probabilities assigned to all the waiting customers.
- Nonpreemptive priority (NP): the customers are assigned fixed priorities; the waiting customer with the highest priority is served first; if several waiting customers have the same highest priority, they are served in the order of their arrival; once begun, a service cannot be interrupted by the arrival of a higher priority customer.
- Preemptive priority (PP): same as NP, but each arriving higher priority customer interrupts the current service, if any, and begins to be served; a customer whose service was interrupted resumes service at the point of interruption when there are no higher priority customers to be served.
- Last come first served preemptive resume (LCFS-PR): same as LCFS, but each arriving customer interrupts the current service, if any, and begins to be served; the interrupted service of a customer is resumed when all the customers that arrived later than that customer have departed.
- Round robin (RR): each customer is given continuous service for a maximum interval of time called a quantum; if the customer's service demand is not satisfied during the quantum, the customer reenters the queue and waits to receive an additional quantum, repeating this process until its service demand is satisfied; the waiting customers are served in the order in which they last entered the queue.
- Processor sharing (PS): all the waiting customers receive service simultaneously with equal shares of the service rate.
- Infinite server (IS): no queueing takes place as each arriving customer always find an available server.

If the queueing discipline is omitted in the QS notation, it is assumed to be FCFS.

The QS behavior can be analyzed either during a given time interval (transient analysis) or by assuming that it reaches a stationary condition (steady-state analysis). The analysis of the QS is based on the definition of an underlying continuous-time Markov chain. The QS steady-state analysis usually evaluates a set of four average performance indices after computing the queue length distribution, i.e. the distribution of the number of customers in the QS. The four

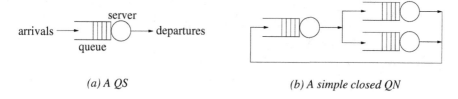

(a) A QS                                        (b) A simple closed QN

**Fig. 3.** QN graphical representation

average performance indices are the throughput (mean number of customers leaving the system per unit of time), the utilization (average fraction of time during which the servers are used), the mean number of customers in the QS, and the mean response time experienced by the customers visiting the QS.

For instance, let us consider the simplest case of QS M/M/1 with arrival rate $\lambda$ and service rate $\mu$ [34]. Although the stochastic process underlying the QS M/M/1 is an infinite-state continuous-time Markov chain, where each state represents the number of customers in the system, the particular structure of this Markov chain allows us to easily derive that the distribution of the number $N_1$ of customers in the system — on the basis of which the four average measures above are defined — is geometrical with parameter given by the traffic intensity $\rho_1 = \lambda/\mu$. The steady-state analysis of this QS requires that the stability condition $\rho_1 < 1$ holds, i.e., that the customer arrival rate is less than the service rate. In this case we can easily derive the four average perfomance indices as follows:

- The throughput is given by the probability that there is at least one customer in the system multiplied by the service rate, i.e. $\overline{X}_1 = \Pr\{N_1 > 0\} \cdot \mu = \rho_1 \cdot \mu = \lambda$.
- The utilization is given by the probability that there is at least one customer in the system, i.e. $\overline{U}_1 = \Pr\{N_1 > 0\} = \rho_1$.
- The mean number of customers in the system is the expected value of the geometrical distribution describing the number of customers in the system, i.e. $\overline{N}_1 = \rho_1/(1 - \rho_1)$.
- The mean response time is obtained from Little's law as the ratio of the mean number of customers in the system to the arrival rate, i.e. $\overline{R}_1 = \overline{N}_1/\lambda = 1/[\mu \cdot (1 - \rho_1)]$.

It can be shown that all the queueing disciplines with noninterruptable, nonprioritized service — like FCFS, LCFS, and SIRO — together with PS — which is a good approximation of RR — and LCFS-PR are equivalent with respect to the four average performance measures above for a QS M/M/1.

In the more general case of a QS M/M/m with arrival rate $\lambda$, which has $m$ identical servers that operate independently and in parallel each with service rate $\mu$, the traffic intensity is defined by $\rho_m = \lambda/(m \cdot \mu)$ and, under the stability condition $\rho_m < 1$, the four average performance indices are given by:

$$\overline{X}_m = \sum_{i=1}^{m-1} i \cdot \mu \cdot \Pr\{N_m = i\} + \sum_{i=m}^{\infty} m \cdot \mu \cdot \Pr\{N_m = i\} = \lambda$$

$$\overline{U}_m = 1 - \Pr\{N_m = 0\}$$

$$\overline{N}_m = m \cdot \rho_m + \frac{\Pr\{N_m=0\} \cdot \rho_m \cdot (m \cdot \rho_m)^m}{m! \cdot (1-\rho_m)^2}$$

$$\overline{R}_m = \frac{1}{\mu} \cdot \left(1 + \frac{\Pr\{N_m=0\} \cdot \rho_m \cdot (m \cdot \rho_m)^{m-1}}{m! \cdot (1-\rho_m)^2}\right)$$

where:

$$\Pr\{N_m = 0\} = \left(\sum_{i=0}^{m-1} \frac{(m \cdot \rho_m)^i}{i!} + \frac{(m \cdot \rho_m)^m}{m! \cdot (1 - \rho_m)}\right)^{-1}$$

## 3.2   Networks of Queueing Systems

A QN is composed of a set of interconnected service centers. When describing a QN, which can be represented — as shown in Fig. 3(b) — through a directed graph whose nodes are the service centers and whose edges represent the behavior of the customers' service requests, it is necessary to specify for each service center the service time distribution, the number of servers, the queue capacity, the queueing discipline, and the routing probabilities for the customers leaving the service center. A QN can be open or closed, depending on whether external arrivals and departures are allowed or not, or mixed. In an open QN, a customer that completes service at a service center immediately enters another service center, reenters the same service center, or departs from the network. In a closed QN, instead, a fixed number of customers circulate indefinitely among the service centers.

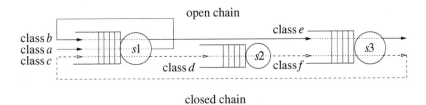

**Fig. 4.** A mixed network with three service centers, an open chain with classes $a, b, e$, and a closed chain with classes $c, d, f$.

Different types of customers in the QN model can be used to represent different behaviors. This in fact allows various types of external arrival process, different service demands, and different types of network routing to be modeled. A chain gathers the customers of the same type. A chain consists then of a set of classes that represent different phases of processing in the system for a given type of customers. Classes are partitioned within the service centers and each customer in a chain moves between the classes. A chain can be used to represent a customer routing behavior dependent on the past history. For example, two classes of the same chain in a service center can represent the customer requirement of two successive services. Each chain can be open or closed depending on whether external arrivals and departures are allowed or not. Multiclass or multichain networks can be open or closed if all the chains are open or closed, respectively. A mixed network has both open and closed chains. Fig. 4 shows an example of a multiclass network with two chains and six classes. The open chain describes the routing behavior of the type 1 customers: two successive visits to the service center $s1$ followed by a visit to service center $s3$. Chain 2 is closed and there is a constant number of type 2 customers circulating between service centers $s1$, $s2$, and $s3$.

Evaluating a QN model means obtaining a quantitative description of its behavior by computing a set of figures of merit, such as the four average performance indices considered for a single QS. The analysis of a QN model provides information both on the local and on the global performance, i.e. the performance of each service center and the overall system performance. A QN can be analyzed by defining and solving the underlying stochastic process, which under general assumptions is a countinous-time Markov chain. Unfortunately, its solution can often become unfeasible since its state space size grows exponentially with the number of components of the QN model. However, some efficient solution algorithms can be defined for the special subclass of product form QNs, which we briefly introduce in the next section. Such algorithms provide a powerful tool for performance analysis based on QNs.

### 3.3   Product Form QNs

Product form QNs (see [6] for a complete survey) avoids the state space explosion problem because they can be solved compositionally. Given that the state of a QN is a tuple consisting of the number of customers in the various service centers, the probability of a product form QN state is simply obtained as the product of the probabilities of its constituent service center states, up to a normalizing constant in the case of closed QNs. An important characterization of product form QNs is given by the BCMP theorem [10], which defines the BCMP class of product form open, closed and mixed QNs with multiple classes of customers, Poisson arrivals (i.e. exponentially distributed interarrival times) with rates possibly depending on the total population of the QN or on the population of a chain, and arbitrary Markovian routing. According to the BCMP theorem, each multiclass service center can have one combination of the following queueing disciplines and service time distributions:

- FCFS with exponentially distributed service times, with the same rate for all the classes of customers;
- PS, LCFS-PR, or IS with phase-type distributed service times, possibly different for the various classes of customers.

In the second case, only the expected values of the phase-type service time distributions affect the QN solution in terms of the four average performance indices, so when computing such indices the phase-type distributions can be replaced with exponential distributions having the same expected values.

In the case of an open product form QN, the four average performance measures can easily be obtained at the global level and at the local level from the analysis of the constituent service centers, when considered as isolated QSs with Poisson arrivals, by exploiting the two groups of formulas at the end of Sect. 3.1. The arrival rates are derived by solving the linear system of the traffic equations defined by the routing probabilities among the service centers. The same average indices can be obtained at the global level and at the local level for a closed or mixed product form QN by applying one of the following algorithms: the convolution algorithm [19], the mean-value analysis algorithm (MVA) [44], the local balance algorithm for normalizing constants (LBANC) [20], and the recursion-by-chain algorithm (RECAL) [25]. These algorithms also provide the basis for most approximate analytical methods that need to be applied whenever the QN model under consideration does not belong to the class of product form QNs (see, e.g., [36]).

An important property of product form QNs is exact aggregation, which allows replacing a subnetwork with a single service center, in such a way that the new aggregated QN has the same behavior in terms of the four average performance indices. Thus, exact aggregation can be used to represent and evaluate a system at different levels of abstraction. Moreover, exact aggregation for product form QNs provides a basis for approximate solution methods of more general QNs that are not product form (see, e.g., [36]).

Various extensions of the class of BCMP product form QNs have been derived. They include QNs with other queueing disciplines, QNs with state dependent routing, some special cases of QNs with finite capacity queues, subnetwork popolation constraints, and blocking, and QNs with batch arrivals and batch services. Another extension of QNs networks with product form is the class of G-networks [28], which comprise both positive and negative customers.

## 3.4   QN Extensions

Extensions of classical QN models, named extended QN (EQN) models, have been introduced in order to represent several interesting features of real systems, such as synchronization and concurrency constraints, finite capacity queues, memory constraints, and simultaneous resource possession.

In particular, concurrency and synchronization among tasks are represented in an EQN model by fork and join nodes. A fork node starts the parallel execution on distinct service centers of the different tasks in which a customer's request can be split, while a join node represents a synchronization point for the termination of all such tasks. A few cases of QNs with forks and joins have been solved with exact and approximate analytical techniques (see, e.g., [40,4,9]).

QNs with finite capacity queues and blocking have been introduced as more realistic models of systems with finite resources and population constraints. When a customer arrives at a finite capacity queue that is full, the customer cannot enter the queue and it is blocked. Various blocking mechanisms can be

defined — like blocking after or before service and repetitive service — that
specify the behavior of the customers blocked in the network. Except for a few
cases that admit product form solutions, QNs with blocking are solved through
approximate techniques (see, e.g., [42,8]).

Another extension of the QN model is given by the layered queueing network
(LQN) model, which allows client-server communication patterns to be modeled
in concurrent and/or distributed software systems. LQN models can be solved
by analytic approximation methods based on standard methods for EQNs with
simultaneous resource possession and MVA (see, e.g., [45,52,27]).

The exact and approximate analytical methods for solving EQNs require that
a set of assumptions and constraints are satisfied. Should this not be the case,
EQN models can be analyzed via simulation, at the cost of higher development
and computational times to obtain accurate results.

Examples of performance evaluation tools based on QNs and their extensions
are RESQ [21], QNAP2 [49], HIT [11], and LQNS [26].

## 4   Translating Æmilia Specifications into QN Models

In this section we provide a translation that maps an Æmilia specification into
a QN model to be used to predict and improve the performance of the described
SA. As mentioned in Sect. 1, there are several good reasons for resorting to
QN models at the SA level of design, instead of the flat state-transition graphs
used as semantic models for Æmilia. First, QNs are structured performance
models whose constituent service centers can be put in correspondence with
groups of AEIs of the Æmilia specifications. Second, typical average performance
measures can be computed at the level of the overall QNs and interpreted at the
level of the groups of AEIs of the Æmilia specifications corresponding to their
constituent service centers, thus providing a useful feedback. Third, QNs do not
suffer from the state space explosion problem, as they are equipped with efficient
solution techniques that avoid the construction of the state space. Finally, QNs
can sometimes be solved symbolically, without having to instantiate the values
of the corresponding parameters in the Æmilia specifications.

To carry out the translation, first of all we observe that the two formalisms
that we are considering are quite different from each other. On the one hand,
Æmilia is a component-oriented language for handling both functional and performance characteristics, in which all the details must be expressed in an action-
based way. On the other hand, QNs result in a queue-oriented graphical notation
for performance modeling purposes only, in which some details — notably the
queueing disciplines — are described in natural language. As a consequence,
there will be Æmilia specifications that cannot be converted into QN models,
either because they do not follow a queue-oriented pattern, or because it is hard
to understand — by looking at their process algebraic defining equations — the
queueing disciplines that they encode. Therefore, we shall impose some general
syntax restrictions that single out a reasonably wide class of Æmilia specifications for which a QN model may be derived.

Within the class of Æmilia specifications that obey the general syntax restrictions, given a specification we try to map each of its constituent AEIs into a part of a QN model. In principle, it would seem to be natural to map each AEI into a QS PH/PH/$m/c/p$. However, this is not always possible because the AEIs are usually finer than the QSs. As a consequence, we identify five classes of QN basic elements — which we call arrival processes, buffers, fork processes, join processes, and service processes, respectively, and graphically represent through an extension of the traditional notation used for QNs — and we impose some further specific syntax restrictions to single out those AEIs that fall into one of the five classes. For each Æmilia specification obeying both the general and the specific syntax restrictions, the translation is accomplished by first mapping each of its constituent AEIs into the corresponding QN basic element and then composing the previously obtained QN basic elements according to the attachments declared in the Æmilia specification. The translation will be illustrated by means of the sequential compiler system example introduced in Sect. 2.

## 4.1   General Syntax Restrictions: Benefits and Limitations

The general syntax restrictions helps identifying the Æmilia specifications for which it is possible to derive an open, closed or mixed QN model comprising arrival processes, buffers, fork processes, join processes, and service processes. The general restrictions are mainly based on the observation that an AEI describes a sequential software component, which thus runs on a single computational resource.

The first general restriction is that every AEI of an Æmilia specification must be an arrival process, a buffer, a fork process, a join process, or a service process, and must be properly connected to the other AEIs in order to obtain a well-formed QN. This is achieved through specific syntax restrictions depending on the particular QN basic element, which will be introduced in the next sections.

The second general restriction aims at easing the identification of those AETs that represent arrival or service processes, which are built around exponentially timed actions describing the relevant delays. The second general restriction establishes that the interactions of an Æmilia specification cannot be exponentially timed, i.e. they must be immediate or passive.

The third general restriction aims at avoiding the unnatural application of the race policy to several distinct activities within the same (sequential) AEI, thus causing the various arrival and service processes to be modeled separately with different AEIs. The third general restriction establishes that, within the behavior of the AETs of an Æmilia specification, no exponentially timed action can be alternative to another exponentially timed action.

The fourth general restriction aims at allowing interarrival and service times to be characterized through precisely defined phase-type distributions. The fourth general restriction establishes that, within the behavior of the AETs of an Æmilia specification, no exponentially timed action can be alternative to an immediate or passive action, no immediate action can be alternative to a passive action, and no interaction can be alternative to a local action.

The last three general restrictions, as well as the specific restrictions illustrated in the next sections that implement the first general restriction, can automatically be checked at the syntax level, without constructing the underlying state space of the entire Æmilia specification. They preserve much of the modeling power that Æmilia inherits from EMPA$_{gr}$, without hampering the description of typical situations like parallel executions, synchronization constraints, probabilistic/prioritized choices, and activities whose duration is or can be approximated with a phase-type distribution. It is straightforward to verify that SeqCompSys defined in Table 2 satisfies the last three general restrictions.

The four general restrictions, together with the specific syntax restrictions accompanying the first general one, introduce two main limitations. First, due to the fourth general restriction, the Æmilia specifications modeling preemption cannot be dealt with, as it is not possible to express the fact that the service of a customer of a certain class is interrupted by the arrival of a customer of another class having higher service priority. Second, as we shall see when presenting the specific syntax restrictions for the buffers, we only address queueing disciplines with noninterruptable service for a fixed number of servers, like FCFS, LCFS, SIRO, and NP, thus excluding those policies in which the service of a customer can be interrupted (PP, LCFS-PR) or divided into several rounds (RR, PS), as well as those policies in which no queueing takes place as every incoming customer always finds an available server (IS).

## 4.2   Modeling Phase-Type Distributions

Since the interarrival times and the service times are allowed to follow phase-type distributions, before proceeding with the translation it is worth recalling how the phase-type distributions can be modeled in a language like Æmilia, where only exponentially distributed delays can directly be specified. A continuous phase-type distribution [41] describes the time to absorption in a finite-state continuous-time Markov chain having exactly one absorbing state. Well known examples of phase-type distributions are the exponential distribution, the hypoexponential distribution, the hyperexponential distribution, and combinations thereof, which are characterized in terms of time to absorption in a finite-state continuous-time Markov chain with one absorbing state as depicted in Fig. 5, where the numbers labeling the states describe the initial state probability functions.

Observed that an absorbing state can be modeled by term stop, the three phase-type distributions above can easily be modeled through a suitable interplay of exponentially timed actions and immediate actions as follows. An exponential distribution with rate $\lambda$ can be modeled through the following equation:

$$\mathtt{Exp}_\lambda(\mathtt{void};\mathtt{void}) = <\mathtt{phase}, \lambda>.\mathtt{stop}$$

An $n$-stage hypoexponential distribution with rates $\lambda_1, \ldots, \lambda_n$ can be modeled through the following equation:

$$\mathtt{Hypoexp}_{\lambda_1,\ldots,\lambda_m}(\mathtt{void};\mathtt{void}) = <\mathtt{phase}, \lambda_1>.\ldots.<\mathtt{phase}, \lambda_n>.\mathtt{stop}$$

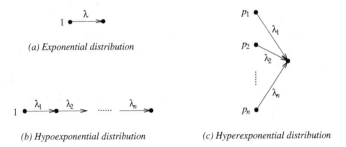

(a) Exponential distribution

(b) Hypoexponential distribution                    (c) Hyperexponential distribution

**Fig. 5.** Typical phase-type distributions

An $n$-stage hyperexponential distribution with rates $\lambda_1, \ldots, \lambda_n$ and branching probabilities $p_1, \ldots, p_n$ can be modeled through the following equation:

$$\mathtt{Hyperexp}_{\lambda_1,\ldots,\lambda_n,p_1,\ldots,p_n}(\mathtt{void};\mathtt{void}) =$$

```
        choice
        {
            <branch, inf(1, p₁)>.<phase, λ₁>.stop,
            ⋮
            <branch, inf(1, pₙ)>.<phase, λₙ>.stop
        }
```

In the arrival processes and in the service processes with phase-type distributed delays, the occurrences of `stop` will be replaced by suitable invocations of the behaviors that must take place after the delays have elapsed.

### 4.3   Arrival Processes

An arrival process is a generator of arrivals of customers of a certain class, whose interarrival times follow a phase-type distribution. As depicted in Fig. 6, we distinguish between two different kinds of arrival processes depending on whether the related customer population is unbounded or finite.

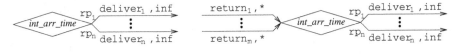

(a) Arrival process for unbounded population          (b) Arrival process for single customer of finite population

**Fig. 6.** Graphical representation of the arrival processes

In the case of an unbounded customer population, the customer interarrival time distribution refers to the whole population, so there is no need to explicitly model the return of a customer after its service termination. As an example, the behavior of an AEI, which acts as an arrival process for an unbounded population of customers whose interarrival time is exponentially distributed with rate $\lambda$, where each customer has a set of n different forks or service centers as destinations chosen according to the intraclass routing probabilities $rp_1, \ldots, rp_n$, must be equivalent [3] to the following one:

```
UnboundedPopArrProc(void; void) =
    <generate, λ>.UnboundedPopArrProc'()
UnboundedPopArrProc'(void; void) =
    choice
    {
        <choose₁, inf(1, rp₁)>.<deliver₁, inf>.UnboundedPopArrProc(),
        ⋮
        <chooseₙ, inf(1, rpₙ)>.<deliverₙ, inf>.UnboundedPopArrProc()
    }
```

with $deliver_1, \ldots, deliver_n$ being output interactions attached to input interactions of buffers (not related to join processes), fork processes with no buffer, or service processes with no buffer. The specific syntax restriction requires that, in order for an AEI to be classified as an arrival process for an unbounded population of customers, its behavior and interactions must be equivalent to the previous ones, with: the exponentially timed action possibly replaced by a term describing a more general phase-type distribution where UnboundedPopArrProc'() is substituted for each occurrence of stop; the destination choice actions omitted if there is only one possible destination; the delivery actions possibly having specific priority levels and specific weights if the related destinations are service processes with no buffer.

If the customer population is finite, instead, then the customer interarrival time distribution for the whole population varies proportionally to the number of customers that are not requesting any service, hence the return of a customer after its service termination must explicitly be modeled. In this case, the customers are represented separately through independent instances of the same AET with the same individual interarrival time distribution, in order to easily achieve the global interarrival time distribution scaling. For instance, the behavior of an AEI, which acts as an arrival process for a single customer belonging to a finite population of customers whose individual interarrival time is exponentially distributed with rate $\lambda$, where the customer has a set of n different forks or service centers as destinations chosen according to the intraclass routing probabilities $rp_1, \ldots, rp_n$ and can return from m distinct joins or service processes, must be equivalent to the following one:

---

[3] In our framework, equivalence can formally be checked on the basis of the notion of strong extended Markovian bisimulation [14].

```
SingleCustArrProc(void; void) =
    <generate, λ>.SingleCustArrProc'()
SingleCustArrProc'(void; void) =
    choice
    {
        <choose₁, inf(1, rp₁)>.<deliver₁, inf>.SingleCustArrProc''(),

        ⋮

        <chooseₙ, inf(1, rpₙ)>.<deliverₙ, inf>.SingleCustArrProc''()
    }
SingleCustArrProc''(void; void) =
    choice
    {
        <return₁, *>.SingleCustArrProc(),

        ⋮

        <returnₘ, *>.SingleCustArrProc()
    }
```

with: $deliver_1, \ldots, deliver_n$ being output interactions attached to input or-interactions of buffers (not related to join processes), fork processes with no buffer, or service processes with no buffer; $return_1, \ldots, return_m$ being input interactions attached to output or-interactions of join processes or service processes. The specific syntax restriction requires that, in order for an AEI to be classified as an arrival process for a single customer belonging to a finite population of customers, its behavior and interactions must be equivalent to the previous ones, with the remaining constraints similar to those for the arrival processes for unbounded populations. In addition, all the AEIs modeling the customers of the same finite population must be instances of the same AET characterized by the same individual interarrival time distribution and must be attached to the same input or-interactions of buffers (not related to join processes), fork processes with no buffer, or service processes with no buffer as well as to the same output or-interactions of join processes or service processes.

To conclude, for the sequential compiler system of Sect. 2 we observe that $PG_1$ and $PG_2$ are arrival processes for unbounded populations of customers of two different classes, each having a single destination.

## 4.4   Buffers

A buffer is a repository of customers of different classes that are waiting to be served. As depicted in Fig. 7, we distinguish between two different kinds of buffers depending on their capacity.

In the case of an unbounded buffer, the incoming customers can always be accommodated within the buffer. The specific syntax restriction requires that, in order for an AEI to be classified as an unbounded buffer for n classes of customers, it must have a behavior equivalent to the following one:

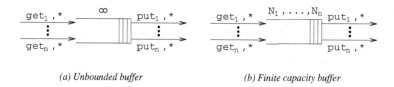

(a) Unbounded buffer                    (b) Finite capacity buffer

**Fig. 7.** Graphical representation of the buffers

$\text{UnboundedBuffer}(\text{integer } h_1, \ldots, h_n; \text{void}) =$
    choice
    {

        $<\text{get}_1, *>.\text{UnboundedBuffer}(h_1 + 1, \ldots, h_n),$

        $\vdots$

        $<\text{get}_n, *>.\text{UnboundedBuffer}(h_1, \ldots, h_n + 1),$
        $\text{cond}(h_1 > 0) \Rightarrow <\text{put}_1, *>.\text{UnboundedBuffer}(h_1 - 1, \ldots, h_n),$

        $\vdots$

        $\text{cond}(h_n > 0) \Rightarrow <\text{put}_n, *>.\text{UnboundedBuffer}(h_1, \ldots, h_n - 1)$
    }

with: $h_1, \ldots, h_n$ initially set to nonnegative integers; $\text{get}_1, \ldots, \text{get}_n$ being input interactions attached to output interactions of arrival processes, fork processes, join processes, or service processes; $\text{put}_1, \ldots, \text{put}_n$ being output interactions attached to input interactions of fork processes with buffer, join processes with buffers, or service processes with buffer; $\text{get}_i$ being an input or-interaction if the customers of class $i$ belong to a finite population and come directly from their arrival processes.

If the buffer capacity is finite, instead, then the incoming customers can be accommodated only if the buffer capacity is not exceeded. The specific syntax restriction requires that, in order for an AEI to be classified as a finite capacity buffer for $n$ classes of customers, where the customers of class $i$ can occupy up to $N_i$ positions in the buffer, it must have a behavior equivalent to the following one:

$\text{FiniteCapBuffer}(\text{integer}(0..N_1) \, h_1, \ldots, \text{integer}(0..N_n) \, h_n; \text{void}) =$
    choice
    {

        $\text{cond}(h_1 < N_1) \Rightarrow <\text{get}_1, *>.\text{FiniteCapBuffer}(h_1 + 1, \ldots, h_n),$

        $\vdots$

        $\text{cond}(h_n < N_n) \Rightarrow <\text{get}_n, *>.\text{FiniteCapBuffer}(h_1, \ldots, h_n + 1),$
        $\text{cond}(h_1 > 0) \Rightarrow <\text{put}_1, *>.\text{FiniteCapBuffer}(h_1 - 1, \ldots, h_n),$

        $\vdots$

        $\text{cond}(h_n > 0) \Rightarrow <\text{put}_n, *>.\text{FiniteCapBuffer}(h_1, \ldots, h_n - 1)$
    }

with the remaining constraints equal to those for the unbounded buffers, except for the fact that now the initial values of $h_1, \ldots, h_n$ cannot exceed the corresponding capacities.

It is worth observing that the buffers outlined above do not make any assumption about the order in which the customers of the same class are taken from the buffer with respect to the order in which they arrive at the buffer. Therefore, from the point of view of the four average performance indices introduced in Sect. 3.1, such buffers can be used to support any queueing discipline with noninterruptable service, like FCFS, LCFS, SIRO, and NP. On the contrary, the buffers above cannot be used to describe those queueing disciplines in which the service of a customer can be interrupted (PP, LCFS-PR), or can be divided into several rounds (RR, PS), or can immediately take place (IS).

To conclude, for the sequential compiler system of Sect. 2 we observe that PB is an unbounded buffer for two classes of customers.

## 4.5   Fork Processes

A fork process handles the splitting of each request of the customers of a certain class into several subrequests to be served in parallel by different service centers. As depicted in Fig. 8, we distinguish between two different kinds of fork processes depending on the presence or the absence of a buffer — modeled by another AEI — where the customers can wait before being split.

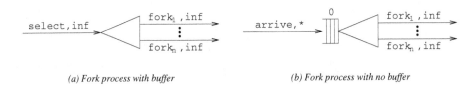

(a) Fork process with buffer                    (b) Fork process with no buffer

**Fig. 8.** Graphical representation of the fork processes

In the case of a fork process equipped with a buffer, the description of the fork process starts with the selection of the next customer to be split from the buffer. The specific syntax restriction requires that, in order for an AEI to be classified as a fork process equipped with a buffer, where the subrequests are forwarded to n different forks or service centers, it must have a behavior equivalent to the following one:

ForkProcWithBuffer(void; void) =
   <select, inf>.<fork$_1$, inf>.....<fork$_n$, inf>.ForkProcWithBuffer()

with: select being an input interaction attached to the output interaction of a buffer; fork$_1$, ..., fork$_n$ being output interactions attached to input interactions of buffers (not related to join processes), fork processes with no buffer, or service processes with no buffer; the fork actions possibly having specific priority levels and specific weights if the related destinations are service processes with no buffer.

In the case of a fork process with no buffer, instead, the description of the fork process starts with the arrival of the next customer to be split directly from an arrival process, a fork, a join, or a service center. The specific syntax restriction requires that, in order for an AEI to be classified as a fork process with no buffer, where the subrequests are forwarded to n different forks or service centers, it must have a behavior equivalent to the following one:

ForkProcNoBuffer(void; void) =
<arrive, *>.<fork$_1$, inf>.....<fork$_n$, inf>.ForkProcNoBuffer()

with arrive being an input interaction — or an input or-interaction if the customers belong to a finite population and come directly from their arrival processes — attached to an output interaction of an arrival process, a fork process, a join process, or a service process and the remaining constraints equal to those for the fork processes equipped with a buffer.

## 4.6  Join Processes

A join process handles the merging of the subrequests of the customers of a certain class after they have been served in parallel by different service centers. As depicted in Fig. 9, we distinguish between two different kinds of join processes depending on the presence or the absence of buffers — modeled by other AEIs — where the subrequests can wait before being merged.

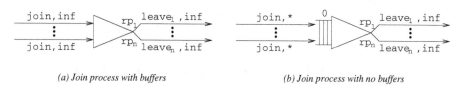

(a) Join process with buffers            (b) Join process with no buffers

**Fig. 9.** Graphical representation of the join processes

In the case of a join process equipped with buffers, the description of the join process starts with the selection of the next subrequests to be merged from the buffers. The specific syntax restriction requires that, in order for an AEI to be classified as a join process equipped with buffers, where the subrequests are forwarded by several different joins or service centers and the result of the merging has a set of n different finite population arrival processes, forks, joins, or service centers as destinations chosen according to the intraclass routing probabilities $rp_1, \ldots, rp_n$, it must have a behavior equivalent to the following one:

JoinProcWithBuffer(void; void) =
    <join, inf>.JoinProcWithBuffer'()
JoinProcWithBuffer'(void; void) =
    choice
    {
        <choose$_1$, inf(1, rp$_1$)>.<leave$_1$, inf>.JoinProcWithBuffer(),

        $\vdots$

        <choose$_n$, inf(1, rp$_n$)>.<leave$_n$, inf>.JoinProcWithBuffer()
    }

with: `join` being an input and-interaction attached to the output interaction of each buffer; $leave_1, \ldots, leave_n$ being output interactions attached to input interactions of arrival processes for finite populations, buffers, fork processes with no buffer, join processes with no buffers, or service processes with no buffer; the destination choice actions omitted if there is only one possible destination; the departure actions possibly having specific priority levels and specific weights if the related destinations are service processes with no buffer; the departure actions omitted if the related destinations are arrival processes for unbounded populations; $leave_i$ being an output or-interaction if destination $i$ is an arrival process for a finite population.

In the case of a join process with no buffers, instead, the description of the join process starts with the arrival of the subrequests to be merged directly from a join or a service center. The specific syntax restriction requires that, in order for an AEI to be classified as a join process with no buffers, with the same characteristics as in the previous example, it must have a behavior equivalent to the following one:

```
JoinProcNoBuffer(void; void) =
    <join, *>.JoinProcNoBuffer'()
JoinProcNoBuffer'(void; void) =
    choice
    {
        <choose₁, inf(1, rp₁)>.<leave₁, inf>.JoinProcNoBuffer(),
        ⋮
        <chooseₙ, inf(1, rpₙ)>.<leaveₙ, inf>.JoinProcNoBuffer()
    }
```

with `join` being an input and-interaction attached to output interactions of join processes or service processes and the remaining constraints equal to those for the join processes equipped with buffers.

## 4.7   Service Processes

A service process is a server for customers of different classes, whose service times follow a phase-type distribution. As depicted in Fig. 10, we distinguish between two different kinds of service processes depending on the presence or the absence of a buffer — modeled by another AEI — where the customers can wait before being served.

In the case of a service process equipped with a buffer, the description of the service process starts with the selection of the next customer to be served from the buffer. As an example, the behavior of an AEI, which acts as a service process equipped with a buffer that serves customers of $n$ different classes, where each class $i$ has priority $prio_i$ to be selected, probability $prob_i$ to be selected among the classes with the same priority, exponentially distributed service time with rate $\mu_i$, and a set of $d_i$ different finite population arrival processes, forks, joins, or service centers as destinations chosen according to the intraclass routing probabilities $rp_{i,1}, \ldots, rp_{i,d_i}$, respectively, must be equivalent to the following one:

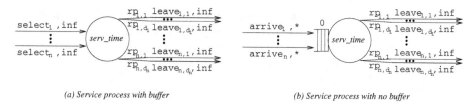

(a) Service process with buffer          (b) Service process with no buffer

**Fig. 10.** Graphical representation of the service processes

```
ServProcWithBuffer(void; void) =
    choice
    {
        <select₁, inf(prio₁, prob₁)>.ServProcWithBuffer'₁(),

        ⋮

        <selectₙ, inf(prioₙ, probₙ)>.ServProcWithBuffer'ₙ()
    }
ServProcWithBuffer'ᵢ(void; void) =
    <serveᵢ, μᵢ>.ServProcWithBuffer''ᵢ()
ServProcWithBuffer''ᵢ(void; void) =
    choice
    {
        <chooseᵢ, inf(1, rpᵢ,₁)>.<leaveᵢ,₁, inf>.ServProcWithBuffer(),

        ⋮

        <chooseᵢ, inf(1, rpᵢ,dᵢ)>.<leaveᵢ,dᵢ, inf>.ServProcWithBuffer()
    }
```

with: $select_1, \dots, select_n$ being input interactions attached to the output interactions of a buffer; $leave_{1,1}, \dots, leave_{n,d_n}$ being output interactions attached to input interactions of arrival processes for finite populations, buffers, fork processes with no buffer, join processes with no buffers, or service processes with no buffer. The specific syntax restriction requires that, in order for an AEI to be classified as a service process equipped with a buffer, its behavior and interactions must be equivalent to the previous ones, with: the exponentially timed actions possibly replaced for certain classes of customers by terms describing more general phase-type distributions where $ServProcWithBuffer''_i()$ is substituted for each occurrence of stop; the destination choice actions omitted for those classes of customers for which there is only one possible destination; the departure actions possibly having specific priority levels and specific weights if the related destinations are service processes with no buffer; the departure actions omitted if the related destinations are arrival processes for unbounded populations; the departure actions being output or-interactions if the related destinations are arrival processes for finite populations.

In the case of a service process with no buffer, instead, the description of the service process starts with the arrival of the next customer to be served directly from arrival processes, forks, joins, or service centers. As an example, the behavior of an AEI, which acts as a service process with no buffer that serves customers of $n$ different classes, where each class $i$ has the same characteristics as in the previous example, must be equivalent to the following one:

```
ServProcNoBuffer(void; void) =
    choice
    {
        <arrive₁, *>.ServProcNoBuffer'₁(),

            ⋮

        <arriveₙ, *>.ServProcNoBuffer'ₙ()
    }
ServProcNoBuffer'ᵢ(void; void) =
    <serveᵢ, μᵢ>.ServProcNoBuffer''ᵢ()
ServProcNoBuffer''ᵢ(void; void) =
    choice
    {
        <chooseᵢ, inf(1, rpᵢ,₁)>.<leaveᵢ,₁, inf>.ServProcNoBuffer(),

            ⋮

        <chooseᵢ, inf(1, rpᵢ,dᵢ)>.<leaveᵢ,dᵢ, inf>.ServProcNoBuffer()
    }
```

with: $arrive_1, \ldots, arrive_n$ being input interactions attached to output interactions of arrival processes, fork processes, join processes, or service processes; $leave_{1,1}, \ldots, leave_{n,d_n}$ being output interactions attached to input interactions of arrival processes for finite populations, buffers, fork processes with no buffer, join processes with no buffers, or service processes with no buffer. The specific syntax restriction requires that, in order for an AEI to be classified as a service process with no buffer, its behavior and interactions must be equivalent to the previous ones, with the arrival actions being input or-interactions if the related customers belong to a finite population and come directly from their arrival processes, and the remaining constraints similar to those for the service processes equipped with a buffer.

It is worth observing that the service processes above allow for classes of customers with different service priorities (NP) and with specific service frequencies among classes with the same service priority (variants of SIRO). This is realized in two different ways for the two kinds of service processes. For the service processes equipped with a buffer, the service priorities and the service frequencies are expressed through the priority levels and the weights associated with the immediate selection actions. This is not possible in the case of the service processes with no buffer, because the arrival actions are passive, hence their priority levels and weights are reactive, i.e. their scope is limited to passive actions of the same type, whereas the arrival actions for different classes of customers have different types. This drawback is overcome by expressing the service priorities and the service frequencies through the priority levels and the weigths of the immediate output interactions of the arrival processes, fork processes, join processes, and service processes that forward customers to the service processes without buffer.

The case of a service center composed of several identical and independent servers is regulated by an additional specific syntax restriction. It requires first of all that the service processes constituting the multi-server service center are instances of the same AET with the same individual service time distribution and the interactions attached to the same AEIs. Three cases then arise. In the first case, the service processes share a buffer, from which they take all of their customers. In this case, the $put_1, \ldots, put_n$ actions of the buffer must be output or-interactions. In the second case, the service processes have no buffer and receive some of their customers directly from arrival processes for unbounded populations, fork processes, join processes, or service processes. Similarly to the previous case, the output interactions of the upstream arrival processes for un-bounded populations, fork processes, join processes, or service processes that are related to the multi-server service center, must be output or-interactions. In the third case, the service processes have no buffer and receive some of their customers from arrival processes for finite populations. For each such upstream arrival process, the action among $deliver_1, \ldots, deliver_n$ that is related to the multi-server service center must be replaced in the specification of the arrival process by as many alternative copies of it as there are service processes in the multi-server service center.

To conclude, for the sequential compiler system of Sect. 2 we observe that SC is a service process equipped with a buffer, which serves two different classes of customers — returning to the unbounded populations to which they belong — according to two different hypoexponential distributions.

## 4.8   Translating AEIs into QN Basic Elements

Given an Æmilia specification that satisfies both the general and the specific syntax restrictions introduced in the previous sections, the translation of its constituent AEIs into their corresponding QN basic elements is carried out by applying a set of functions that provide the attributes that label the resulting QN basic elements, as depicted in Fig. 6, 7, 8, 9, and 10.

There are two groups of functions. The functions of the first group play a documental role and are subsequently used to assemble the QN basic elements according to the attachments declared in the Æmilia specification. The functions of the first group are *qnbe*, *name*, *input*, and *output*. When applied to an AEI, *qnbe* determines whether it is an arrival process for an unbounded population or a single customer belonging to a finite population, a buffer with unlimited or finite capacity, a fork process with or without buffer, a join process with or without buffers, or a service process with or without buffer. As an example, for the sequential compiler system of Sect. 2 we have:

$$qnbe(PG_1) = \text{arrival process for an unbounded population}$$
$$qnbe(PG_2) = \text{arrival process for an unbounded population}$$
$$qnbe(PB) = \text{unbounded buffer}$$
$$qnbe(SC) = \text{service process equipped with a buffer}$$

The other three functions, instead, associate the name of the AEI with the corresponding QN basic element and label the incoming and outgoing arrow-headed arcs of the QN basic element with the corresponding input and output interactions of the AEI, respectively. As an example:

$$name(\text{PG}_1) = \text{PG}_1$$
$$name(\text{PG}_2) = \text{PG}_2$$
$$name(\text{PB}) = \text{PB}$$
$$name(\text{SC}) = \text{SC}$$
$$input(\text{PG}_1) = \emptyset$$
$$input(\text{PG}_2) = \emptyset$$
$$input(\text{PB}) = \{<\texttt{get\_prog}_1, *>, <\texttt{get\_prog}_2, *>\}$$
$$input(\text{SC}) = \{<\texttt{select\_prog}_1, \texttt{inf}>, <\texttt{select\_prog}_2, \texttt{inf}>\}$$
$$output(\text{PG}_1) = \{<\texttt{deliver\_prog}, \texttt{inf}>\}$$
$$output(\text{PG}_2) = \{<\texttt{deliver\_prog}, \texttt{inf}>\}$$
$$output(\text{PB}) = \{<\texttt{put\_prog}_1, *>, <\texttt{put\_prog}_2, *>\}$$
$$output(\text{SC}) = \emptyset$$

| |
|---|
| $pt\_distr(\texttt{stop}) = \emptyset$ |
| $pt\_distr(<\texttt{phase}, \lambda>.E) = hypoexp(exp(\lambda), pt\_distr(E))$ |
| $pt\_distr(\texttt{choice}$ |
| $\{$ |
| $\quad <\texttt{branch}_1, \texttt{inf}(1, \texttt{w}_1)>.E_1,$ |
| $\quad \vdots$ |
| $\quad <\texttt{branch}_n, \texttt{inf}(1, \texttt{w}_n)>.E_n$ |
| $\})\qquad = hyperexp(\frac{\texttt{w}_1}{\texttt{w}_1 + \ldots + \texttt{w}_n}, pt\_distr(E_1);$ |
| $\qquad\qquad\qquad \vdots$ |
| $\qquad\qquad\qquad \frac{\texttt{w}_n}{\texttt{w}_1 + \ldots + \texttt{w}_n}, pt\_distr(E_n))$ |
| $pt\_distr(A(\underline{e})) = pt\_distr(E) \qquad \text{if } A(\underline{x}; \underline{y}) = E$ |

**Table 3.** Recursive definition of function $pt\_distr$

The functions of the second group are $int\_arr\_time$, $capacity$, $queueing\_disc$, $serv\_time$, and $intra\_routing\_prob$:

- Function $int\_arr\_time$ indicates the phase-type distribution governing the interarrival times of the arrival processes. In the case of an AEI acting as an arrival process for an unbounded population of customers (resp. for a single customer belonging to a finite population), $int\_arr\_time$ is the result of the application of function $pt\_distr$ of Table 3 to the term equivalent to `UnboundedPopArrProc()` (resp. `SingleCustArrProc()`), with each occurrence of the term equivalent to `UnboundedPopArrProc'()` (resp. `SingleCustArrProc'()`) replaced by `stop`. As an example:

$$int\_arr\_time(\text{PG}_1) = exp(\lambda_1)$$
$$int\_arr\_time(\text{PG}_2) = exp(\lambda_2)$$

- Function *capacity* determines the capacity of the buffers. In the case of an AEI acting as an unbounded buffer, the application of *capacity* yields $\infty$. In the case of an AEI acting as a finite capacity buffer for n classes of customers, where the customers of class i can occupy up to $N_i$ positions in the buffer as specified by the parameters of the AEI behavior, the application of *capacity* yields $N_1, \ldots, N_n$. As an example:

$$capacity(\text{PB}) = \infty$$

- Function *queueing_disc* defines the queueing discipline of the buffers based on the priority levels of the input interactions of the service processes to which the buffers are attached. If all the input interactions of the service process to which a buffer is attached have the same priority level, then the application of *queueing_disc* to the buffer yields FCFS, otherwise NP. As an example:

$$queueing\_disc(\text{PB}) = \text{FCFS}$$

- Function *serv_time* establishes the phase-type distribution governing the service times of the service processes. In the case of an AEI acting as a service process equipped with a buffer (resp. with no buffer) for n classes of customers, *serv_time* for class i is the result of the application of function *pt_distr* of Table 3 to the term equivalent to `ServProcWithBuffer`$'_i$`()` (resp. `ServProcNoBuffer`$'_i$`()`), with each occurrence of the term equivalent to `ServProcWithBuffer`$''_i$`()` (resp. `ServProcNoBuffer`$''_i$`()`) replaced by `stop`. As an example:

$$serv\_time(\text{SC}, 1) = hypoexp(exp(\mu_1), exp(\mu_p), exp(\mu_c), exp(\mu_o), exp(\mu_g))$$
$$serv\_time(\text{SC}, 2) = hypoexp(exp(\mu_1), exp(\mu_p), exp(\mu_c), exp(\mu_g))$$

- Function *intra_routing_prob* reports the intraclass routing probabilities for the customers of a certain class leaving an arrival process, a join process, or a service process. It is simply derived from the weights of the choice actions of the QN basic element from which the customers of the considered class depart. It is worth observing that, in the case of a join process or a service process, this function returns a value also for a destination given by an arrival process for an unbounded customer population, and that, for a complete graphical representation of the considered QN basic element, such a value must label the join process or service process despite of the absence of the related outgoing arrow-headed arc. As an example:

$$intra\_routing\_prob(\text{PG}_1, 1, \text{PB}) = 1$$
$$intra\_routing\_prob(\text{PG}_2, 2, \text{PB}) = 1$$
$$intra\_routing\_prob(\text{SC}, 1, -) = 1$$
$$intra\_routing\_prob(\text{SC}, 2, -) = 1$$

We conclude by showing in Fig. 11 the QN basic elements associated with the AEIs constituting the sequential compiler system.

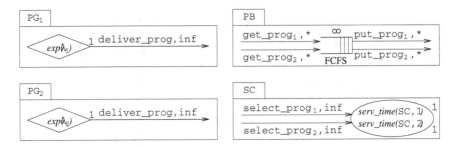

**Fig. 11.** QN basic elements of `SeqCompSys`

## 4.9   Attachment Driven Composition of QN Basic Elements

Given an Æmilia specification that satisfies both the general and the specific syntax restrictions introduced in the previous sections, once each of its constituent AEIs has been mapped to its corresponding QN basic element, the translation is completed by connecting the resulting QN basic elements according to the attachments declared in the Æmilia specification. Graphically, this amounts to superposing the arrow-headed arcs of the QN basic elements corresponding to interactions attached to each other. The obtained QN is closed if there are no arrival processes, in which case the QN population is given by the summation of the initial number of customers in each buffer.

It is worth observing that the specific syntax restrictions ensure the correct composition of the QN basic elements obtained from the translation of the AEIs declared in the Æmilia specification, because the restrictions impose that:

- The input interactions of an arrival process for a finite population cannot be attached to output interactions of other arrival processes, buffers, and fork processes.
- The output interactions of an arrival process cannot be attached to input interactions of other arrival processes for finite populations, buffers related to join processes, and join processes with no buffers.
- The input interactions of a buffer cannot be attached to output interactions of other buffers.
- The output interactions of a buffer cannot be attached to input interactions of arrival processes for finite populations and other buffers.
- The output interactions of a fork process cannot be attached to input interactions of arrival processes for finite populations, buffers related to join processes, and join processes with no buffers.
- The input interactions of a join process cannot be attached to output interactions of arrival processes and fork processes.
- Suitable or-interactions are used in the case of arrival processes for finite populations as well as multi-server service centers.
- Suitable and-interactions are used in the case of join processes.

We conclude by showing in Fig. 12 the QN associated with the Æmilia specification of the sequential compiler system of Sect. 2.

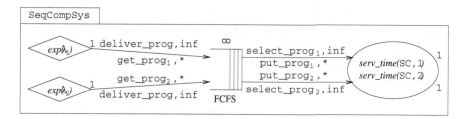

**Fig. 12.** QN associated with `SeqCompSys`

## 5   A Practical Methodology

When tackling the construction of a software system, at the SA design level there are two main issues related to the system performance. First, the designer may need to choose among several alternative SAs for the system under study, with the choice being driven especially by performance considerations. Second, for a specific SA of the system under study, the designer may want to understand whether its performance can be improved and, if so, it would be desirable for the designer to have some diagnostic information that guide the modification of the SA itself. In this section we show how these two issues can be addressed in practice by employing a methodology based on the translation of Æmilia specifications into QN models, which allows for a quick prediction, improvement, and comparison of the performance of different SAs for the system under study.

Before illustrating the methodology, it is worth recalling that the use of an ADL like Æmilia in the methodology is due to the fact that Æmilia comes equipped with an analysis machinery that supports both functional verification and performance evaluation, together with some SA level checks. On the other hand, the use of QNs in the methodology is motivated by their capability of providing performance indices both at their constituent service center level and at the overall network level. Another advantage is that the local performance indices can be interpreted back on the components of the architectural specification and used as a feedback to ameliorate the performance of the architectural specification.

The methodology focuses on the four average performance measures mentioned in Sect. 3.1, which will be computed for groups of software components forming a QN service center:

-  The throughput is a measure of the productivity of the service centers, so it can provide information about those components that are bottlenecks, i.e. those components that are responsible for degrading the system performance.
-  The utilization is the fraction of time during which a service center is being used. In software component terms, this amounts to the fraction of time during which the code of a group of components is being executed, so it supplies useful information, which may be exploited at deployment time, about the relative usage of computational resources by different software components.

- The mean number of customers present in a service center is an indicator
  to be used for a reasonable dimensioning of buffers and data repositories in
  general, in order to avoid performance degradation due to code execution
  blocking (under-sized buffers) and waste of memory (over-sized buffers).
- The mean response time is the time spent on average by a customer within
  a service center. In software component terms, this essentially amounts to
  the expected running time of a group of software components for a complete
  execution of their code. In other terms, it is a measure of the quality of
  service perceived by a generic user of the software system.

The four average performance measures considered above, although generally
useful for the feedback they quickly provide, are not necessarily connected in
a specific way to the performance requirements of the system under study. In
addition to that, as we shall see they are usually computed after applying some
approximations at the Æmilia specification level or at the QN level. As a consequence, the methodology must be complemented by an additional phase, in
which the exact Æmilia specification of the chosen SA is checked against the
specific performance requirements.

The various phases of the methodology are depicted in Fig 13. Given a set of
(functional and performance) requirements characterizing the software system
under study, the designer can devise multiple alternative SAs that should meet
the requirements. Such SAs are typically expressed in an informal way, e.g. in
natural language or through box-and-line diagrams (phase 1). Then the designer
works on each SA separately.

First of all, since the SA must be analyzed, its informal description must be
converted by the designer into a component-oriented formal representation supporting both functional verification and performance evaluation. This is carried
out by the designer using Æmilia (phase 2).

The Æmilia specification produced for the SA does not necessarily satisfy the
syntax restrictions that make it possible to translate the specification into a QN
model. In such a case, the original Æmilia specification must be approximated
with another Æmilia specification that meets both the general restrictions and
the specific restrictions, so that it can be converted into a QN (phase 3). The
approximation must be conducted in a way that every original AEI becomes
an arrival process, a buffer with a noninterruptable queueing discipline, a fork
process, a join process, or a service process, with the appropriate attachments.
This may require that the behavior of some AEI is modified. This happens
e.g. when some scheduling algorithm based on PP, LCFS-PR, RR, PS, or IS
is adopted within an AEI, which needs to be approximated with a noninterruptable discipline. [4] In addition, the approximation may require adding new
AEIs or deleting existing AEIs. This is the case e.g. when an AEI contains several alternative exponentially timed actions, which means that the AEI is the
combination of several components running in parallel that must therefore be

---

[4] According to the results mentioned at the end of Sect. 3.1, this approximation may
be exact with respect to the four average performance indices of interest.

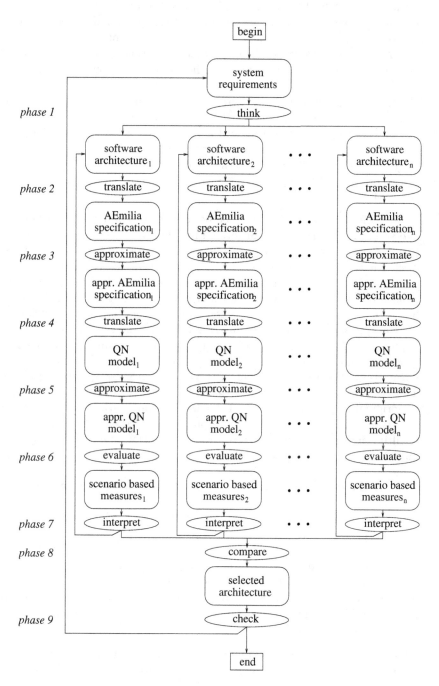

**Fig. 13.** Phases of the methodology

represented separately. The approximation is justified at this level of abstraction by the fact that we are more interested in getting a quick indication about the performance of the SA, rather than in its precise evaluation.

The Æmilia specification is then automatically translated into a QN based performance model, in accordance with the guidelines provided in Sect. 3.1 (phase 4).

The QN model obtained for the SA is not necessarily product form, which may hamper a quick computation of the four average performance measures of interest at the component level as well as at the overall system level. In such a case, the original QN model must be approximated with another QN model that hopefully is product form, with the approximation aiming at transforming every service center of the QN into a QS M/M/1 or a QS M/M/$m$ with possibly variable arrival rates (phase 5):

- Finite, nonzero capacity buffers must be transformed into unbounded buffers, and similarly NP must be transformed into FCFS. This is not a problem at this stage as we are more interested in finding a reasonable size and queueing discipline for the buffers, rather than working with a size and a queueing discipline fixed a priori. However, zero capacity buffers cannot be approximated as seen before, because their performance would be significantly altered.
- Since we are considering only noninterruptable, nonprioritized queueing disciplines, phase-type distributed interarrival times and service times must be approximated with exponentially distributed interarrival times and service times having the same expected values as the original ones, respectively.
- For each multi-class service center, the classes must be approximated with a single class whose service time distribution is the convex combination of the original (exponential) service time distributions, with the coefficients being given by the interclass routing probabilities of the original classes. The resulting hyperexponential service time distribution must then be approximated with an exponential service time distribution with the same expected value. [5]
- As far as the arrival processes are concerned, we recall that the overall arrival rate for an unbounded customer population (represented by a single arrival process) is constant, whereas the overall arrival rate for a finite customer population (represented by several arrival processes) is variable. Such overall arrival rates convey useful information to be exploited when computing the interclass routing probabilities needed for the approximation of multi-class service centers with single-class service centers. We also recall that the total arrival rate for a service center having several external arrivals is the sum of the overall arrival rates of the different populations of customers that can get to the service center.

Although the perturbation of the four average performance measures introduced by the approximations above cannot easily be quantified, it is worth reminding

---

[5] If all the classes have the same (exponential) service time distribution, then the overall service time distribution coincides with the original one and no further approximation is needed.

that, as observed in [37], QN models are in general robust, i.e. their approximate analysis is in any case useful to get some indications about the performance of the systems they represent. With respect to the architectural level of abstraction, the approximations above are justified in the framework of the proposed methodology by the fact that we are more interested in getting a quick feedback about how to improve the average performance of a specific SA or making a rapid comparison of the average performance of architectural alternatives, rather than in a precise performance evaluation. This is conducted anyhow, but only in the last phase of the methodology, in order to make sure that the exact Æmilia specification of the best architectural design, selected with respect to the four average performance indices possibly after some approximations, actually meets the specific performance requirements.

The QN model for the SA is subsequently evaluated in order to compute the throughput, the utilization, the mean number of customers, and the mean response time for each service center, as well as the corresponding measures for the overall QN, in different scenarios (phase 6):

- Such an evaluation preliminarily requires the parameterization of the QN and the characterization of its workload. Since the Æmilia specifications are already parameterized and their translation into QN models preserves the parameterization, the QN model for the SA is parameterized by construction. As far as the characterization of the workload is concerned, we have to include in the Æmilia specification suitable arrival processes for those service centers with external arrivals and to establish the number of customers initially present in each buffer.
- The evaluation of the QN then proceeds in accordance with some scenarios of interest, which are derived by playing with the arrival rates and the service rates. As an example, the four average performance measures can be computed under light and heavy load, by making the interrivals rates vary from small values to values close to those of the service rates (without violating stability), or by changing the numbers of customers initially in the buffers from small values (close to zero) to large values (close to the buffer capacities). As another example, it is useful to assess how the four average performance measures vary in the case in which all the service centers have service rates of the same order of magnitude, in the case in which there is one service center whose service rate is some orders of magnitude smaller than the service rates of the other service centers, and in the more general case in which the rates of all the service centers range in an interval between a minimum rate and a maximum rate that are some orders of magnitude apart.
- The evaluation of the QN can be accomplished on the basis of the selected scenarios in three different ways. The most convenient way is symbolic analysis, which is possible only if the QN is open and product form and has a simple topology. In this case the four average performance measures are expressed through a suitable combination of the formulas at the end of Sect. 3.1, which is particularly desirable at the architectural level of design, as usually

the actual values of the arrival rates and the service rates are not known yet in this early stage. If the QN is product form but it is not open or it has not a simple topology, then the four average performance measures are calculated after solving the traffic equations or by applying some algorithm like MVA, which require the specification of the values of the arrival rates, the service rates, and the intraclass routing probabilities. In this case, the specification of the parameter values will be driven by the selected scenarios. If the QN is not product form, as may happen in the case in which some buffers have zero capacity or there are forks and joins, then we resort to approximation algorithms, which again require the scenario driven specification of the parameter values.

Once the values of the four average performance indices for the SA are available in the selected scenarios, they are interpreted back on the Æmilia specification of the SA at the level of the groups of components forming the QN service centers (phase 7). On the basis of such a component-oriented feedback, the designer can make some modification on the SA to improve its performance and return to phase 2, or proceed with the next phase.

When the predict-improve cycle is terminated for every SA devised for the system under study, all the alternative SAs are compared on the basis of the four average performance measures in different scenarios, in order to single out the best one (phase 8). Of course, the scenario driven comparison should be fair, which means that all the alternative SAs should be given comparable workloads in each scenario. In addition, we note that the outcomes of the comparison in different scenarios may be different. In this case, the best SA must be selected by taking into account the frequency with which every considered scenario can arise in practice.

Finally, the chosen SA is checked against the specific performance requirements of the system under study (phase 9). As explained at the beginning of this section, this is needed because the four average performance measures used to choose among the alternative SAs are not necessarily connected in a specific way to the performance requirements, so we do not know whether the best SA selected on the basis of the four average performance measures actually meets the performance requirements. Moreover, we have to take into account that the Æmilia specification or the QN model of the chosen SA might have been approximated in the previous phases, while now we have to consider the exact Æmilia specification of the chosen SA. The check of such an exact Æmilia specification can be accomplished by formally specifying the performance requirements through reward structures and temporal logic formulas [14,22,5]. If the outcome of the check is positive, then the application of the methodology terminates, otherwise the designer has to reconsider the performance requirements — as they may turn out to be impossible to meet — and apply the methodology again.

# 6   Comparing Three Different Compiler Architectures

The compiler shown in Table 2, whose QN model is reported in Fig. 12, examines one source program at a time, i.e. it is a completely sequential compiler. In this section we consider two different architectures realizing a pipeline compiler and a concurrent compiler, respectively, and we apply the methodology described in Sect. 5 to compare the three alternative architectures. This requires specifying the pipeline compiler and the concurrent compiler in Æmilia, building their associated QN models as described in Sect. 4, and computing the four average performance measures on the three QN models in some scenarios of interest.

## 6.1   Æmilia Specification of the Pipeline Compiler

The architecture for the pipeline compiler allows the various compilation phases to work on different programs. This is achieved by splitting the various phases into different AETs — one for the lexer, one for the parser, one for the type checker, one for the code optimizer, and one for the code generator — and by providing each such AET with its own buffer.

The pipeline compiler system, which includes the arrival sources for the two classes of programs, is graphically represented in Fig. 14, while its Æmilia specification is given in Tables 4, 5, and 6. Each compilation phase is modeled by a specific AET. In addition, there are two further AETs that model unbounded FCFS buffers accepting one class of programs — for the optimizer — or two classes of programs — for all the other compilation phases. The declared AEIs and their attachments ensure that the compilation phases are combined in the correct order and that each phase is provided with its own buffer, so making it possible the simultaneous compilation of several programs at different stages. PipeCompSys is the output of phase 2 of the methodology for the pipeline architecture. Since it satifies all the syntax restrictions of Sect. 4, it is also the output of phase 3.

## 6.2   QN Model of the Pipeline Compiler

In order to carry out phase 4 for the pipeline architecture, we apply the functions defined in Sect. 4.8 to the AEIs of PipeCompSys, thus obtaining their corresponding QN basic elements. In particular, the service time of each class of programs within each service process is exponentially distributed as follows:

$$serv\_time(\mathtt{L}, 1) = serv\_time(\mathtt{L}, 2) = exp(\mu_1)$$
$$serv\_time(\mathtt{P}, 1) = serv\_time(\mathtt{P}, 2) = exp(\mu_p)$$
$$serv\_time(\mathtt{C}, 1) = serv\_time(\mathtt{C}, 2) = exp(\mu_c)$$
$$serv\_time(\mathtt{O}) = exp(\mu_o)$$
$$serv\_time(\mathtt{G}, 1) = serv\_time(\mathtt{G}, 2) = exp(\mu_g)$$

By connecting the QN basic elements according to the attachments, we then obtain the QN model depicted in Fig. 15, where the actions labeling the arrows have been omitted for the sake of readability. Note that the QN structure closely resembles the structure of the graphical description in Fig. 14, making it easier

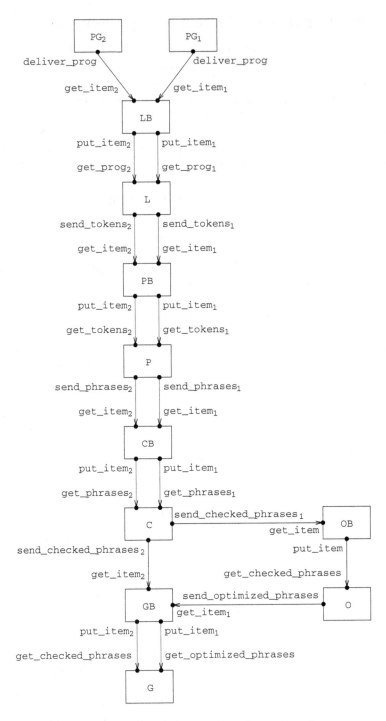

**Fig. 14.** Graphical description of PipeCompSys

```
ARCHI_TYPE                  PipeCompSys(rate λ₁, λ₂, μₚ, μₚ, μ_c, μₒ, μ_g)
  ARCHI_ELEM_TYPES

    ELEM_TYPE               ProgGenT(rate λ)
      BEHAVIOR              ProgGen(void; void) =
                              <generate_prog, λ>.<deliver_prog, inf>.ProgGen()
      INPUT_INTERACTIONS
      OUTPUT_INTERACTIONS UNI deliver_prog

    ELEM_TYPE               OneClassBufferT(integer h)
      BEHAVIOR              OneClassBuffer(integer h; void) =
                              choice
                              {
                                <get_item, *>.OneClassBuffer(h + 1),
                                cond(h > 0) ⇒ <put_item, *>.
                                                OneClassBuffer(h − 1)
                              }
      INPUT_INTERACTIONS   UNI get_item
      OUTPUT_INTERACTIONS  UNI put_item

    ELEM_TYPE               TwoClassesBufferT(integer h₁, h₂)
      BEHAVIOR              TwoClassesBuffer(integer h₁, h₂; void) =
                              choice
                              {
                                <get_item₁, *>.TwoClassesBuffer(h₁ + 1, h₂),
                                <get_item₂, *>.TwoClassesBuffer(h₁, h₂ + 1),
                                cond(h₁ > 0) ⇒ <put_item₁, *>.
                                                TwoClassesBuffer(h₁ − 1, h₂),
                                cond(h₂ > 0) ⇒ <put_item₂, *>.
                                                TwoClassesBuffer(h₁, h₂ − 1)
                              }
      INPUT_INTERACTIONS   UNI get_item₁; get_item₂
      OUTPUT_INTERACTIONS  UNI put_item₁; put_item₂

    ELEM_TYPE               LexerT(rate μ₁)
      BEHAVIOR              Lexer(void; void) =
                              choice
                              {
                                <get_prog₁, inf>.<recognize_tokens, μ₁>.
                                  <send_tokens₁, inf>.Lexer(),
                                <get_prog₂, inf>.<recognize_tokens, μ₁>.
                                  <send_tokens₂, inf>.Lexer()
                              }
      INPUT_INTERACTIONS   UNI select_prog₁; select_prog₂
      OUTPUT_INTERACTIONS  UNI send_tokens₁; send_tokens₂
```

**Table 4.** Textual description of PipeCompSys — first part

| | |
|---|---|
| ELEM_TYPE | ParserT(rate $\mu_p$) |
| BEHAVIOR | Parser(void; void) = |
| | choice |
| | { |
| | $<$get_tokens$_1$, inf$>$.$<$parse_phrases, $\mu_p>$. |
| | $<$send_phrases$_1$, inf$>$.Parser(), |
| | $<$get_tokens$_2$, inf$>$.$<$parse_phrases, $\mu_p>$. |
| | $<$send_phrases$_2$, inf$>$.Parser() |
| | } |
| INPUT_INTERACTIONS | UNI get_tokens$_1$; get_tokens$_2$ |
| OUTPUT_INTERACTIONS | UNI send_phrases$_1$; send_phrases$_2$ |
| ELEM_TYPE | CheckerT(rate $\mu_c$) |
| BEHAVIOR | Checker(void; void) = |
| | choice |
| | { |
| | $<$get_phrases$_1$, inf$>$.$<$check_phrases, $\mu_c>$. |
| | $<$send_checked_phrases$_1$, inf$>$.Checker(), |
| | $<$get_phrases$_2$, inf$>$.$<$check_phrases, $\mu_c>$. |
| | $<$send_checked_phrases$_2$, inf$>$.Checker() |
| | } |
| INPUT_INTERACTIONS | UNI get_phrases$_1$; get_phrases$_2$ |
| OUTPUT_INTERACTIONS | UNI send_checked_phrases$_1$; send_checked_phrases$_2$ |
| ELEM_TYPE | OptimizerT(rate $\mu_o$) |
| BEHAVIOR | Optimizer(void; void) = |
| | $<$get_checked_phrases, inf$>$. |
| | $<$optimize_phrases, $\mu_o>$. |
| | $<$send_optimized_phrases, inf$>$.Optimizer() |
| INPUT_INTERACTIONS | UNI get_checked_phrases |
| OUTPUT_INTERACTIONS | UNI send_optimized_phrases |
| ELEM_TYPE | GeneratorT(rate $\mu_g$) |
| BEHAVIOR | Generator(void; void) = |
| | choice |
| | { |
| | $<$get_optimized_phrases, inf$>$. |
| | $<$generate_code, $\mu_g>$.Generator(), |
| | $<$get_checked_phrases, inf$>$. |
| | $<$generate_code, $\mu_g>$.Generator() |
| | } |
| INPUT_INTERACTIONS | UNI get_optimized_phrases; get_checked_phrases |
| OUTPUT_INTERACTIONS | |

**Table 5.** Textual description of PipeCompSys — second part

```
ARCHI_TOPOLOGY

   ARCHI_ELEM_INSTANCES PG₁ : ProgGenT(λ₁);
                        PG₂ : ProgGenT(λ₂);
                        LB : TwoClassesBufferT(0, 0);
                        L : LexerT(μ₁);
                        PB : TwoClassesBufferT(0, 0);
                        P : ParserT(μₚ);
                        CB : TwoClassesBufferT(0, 0);
                        C : CheckerT(μ𝒸);
                        OB : OneClassBufferT(0);
                        O : OptimizerT(μₒ);
                        GB : TwoClassesBufferT(0, 0);
                        G : GeneratorT(μ𝗀);

   ARCHI_INTERACTIONS

   ARCHI_ATTACHMENTS    FROM PG₁.deliver_prog TO LB.get_item₁;
                        FROM PG₂.deliver_prog TO LB.get_item₂;
                        FROM LB.put_item₁ TO L.get_prog₁;
                        FROM LB.put_item₂ TO L.get_prog₂;
                        FROM L.send_tokens₁ TO PB.get_item₁;
                        FROM L.send_tokens₂ TO PB.get_item₂;
                        FROM PB.put_item₁ TO P.get_tokens₁;
                        FROM PB.put_item₂ TO P.get_tokens₂;
                        FROM P.send_phrases₁ TO CB.get_item₁;
                        FROM P.send_phrases₂ TO CB.get_item₂;
                        FROM CB.put_item₁ TO C.get_phrases₁;
                        FROM CB.put_item₂ TO C.get_phrases₂;
                        FROM C.send_checked_phrases₁ TO OB.get_item;
                        FROM C.send_checked_phrases₂ TO GB.get_item₂;
                        FROM OB.put_item TO O.get_checked_phrases;
                        FROM O.send_optimized_phrases TO GB.get_item₁;
                        FROM GB.put_item₁ TO G.get_optimized_phrases;
                        FROM GB.put_item₂ TO G.get_checked_phrases

END
```

**Table 6.** Textual description of `PipeCompSys` — third part

to interpret at the architectural description level the performance results that will be obtained at the QN level.

## 6.3  Æmilia Specification of the Concurrent Compiler

The architecture for the concurrent compiler consists of two sequential compilers operating in parallel and taking the programs from a shared buffer. Its graphical representation is shown in Fig. 16, while its Æmilia description is reported in Table 7. The difference with respect to `SeqCompSys` is that in `ConcCompSys` there

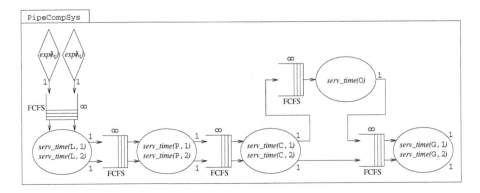

**Fig. 15.** QN associated with `PipeCompSys`

are two instances of `SC` and the output interactions of the buffer are declared to be or-interactions, thus forwarding programs to either of the two instances of `SC`. It is easy to see that `ConcCompSys` satisfies all the syntax restrictions of Sect. 4.

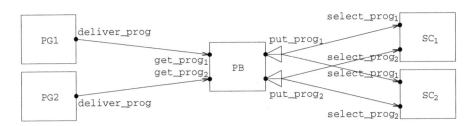

**Fig. 16.** Graphical description of `ConcCompSys`

### 6.4   QN Model of the Concurrent Compiler

The QN for `ConcCompSys` is shown in Fig. 17, where once again the action labeling the arrows have been omitted for simplicity. Differently from the QN for `SeqCompSys`, now we have a service center with two servers.

### 6.5   Analysis of the Sequential Compiler

We now return to the sequential architecture and we evaluate it with respect to the four average performance measures in a given set of scenarios of interest. Let us concentrate on a specific scenario in this set, which is characterized by certain actual values for the numeric parameters of `SeqCompSys` denoted by $\lambda_{seq,1}$, $\lambda_{seq,2}$, $\mu_{seq,1}$, $\mu_{seq,p}$, $\mu_{seq,c}$, $\mu_{seq,o}$, and $\mu_{seq,g}$. Before proceeding with phase 6, we observe that the QN model associated with `SeqCompSys`, which is shown in Fig. 12, is

```
ARCHI_TYPE                    ConcCompSys(rate λ₁, λ₂, μ₁, μₚ, μ𝒸, μₒ, μ𝗀)
  ARCHI_ELEM_TYPES

    ELEM_TYPE                 ProgGenT(rate λ)
      BEHAVIOR                ProgGen(void; void) =
                                <generate_prog, λ>.<deliver_prog, inf>.ProgGen()
      INPUT_INTERACTIONS
      OUTPUT_INTERACTIONS UNI deliver_prog

    ELEM_TYPE                 ProgBufferT(integer h₁, h₂)
      BEHAVIOR                ProgBuffer(integer h₁, h₂; void) =
                                choice
                                {
                                  <get_prog₁, *>.ProgBuffer(h₁ + 1, h₂),
                                  <get_prog₂, *>.ProgBuffer(h₁, h₂ + 1),
                                  cond(h₁ > 0) -> <put_prog₁, *>.ProgBuffer(h₁ − 1, h₂),
                                  cond(h₂ > 0) -> <put_prog₂, *>.ProgBuffer(h₁, h₂ − 1)
                                }
      INPUT_INTERACTIONS  UNI get_prog₁; get_prog₂
      OUTPUT_INTERACTIONS OR put_prog₁; put_prog₂

    ELEM_TYPE                 SeqCompT(rate μ₁, μₚ, μ𝒸, μₒ, μ𝗀)
      BEHAVIOR                SeqComp(void; void) =
                                choice
                                {
                                  <select_prog₁, inf>.<recognize_tokens, μ₁>.
                                    <parse_phrases, μₚ>.<check_phrases, μ𝒸>.
                                    <optimize_code, μₒ>.<generate_code, μ𝗀>.SeqComp(),
                                  <select_prog₂, inf>.<recognize_tokens, μ₁>.
                                    <parse_phrases, μₚ>.<check_phrases, μ𝒸>.
                                    <generate_code, μ𝗀>.SeqComp()
                                }
      INPUT_INTERACTIONS  UNI select_prog₁; select_prog₂
      OUTPUT_INTERACTIONS

  ARCHI_TOPOLOGY

    ARCHI_ELEM_INSTANCES  PG₁ : ProgGenT(λ₁);
                          PG₂ : ProgGenT(λ₂);
                          PB : ProgBufferT(0, 0);
                          SC₁, SC₂ : SeqCompT(μ₁, μₚ, μ𝒸, μₒ, μ𝗀)

    ARCHI_INTERACTIONS

    ARCHI_ATTACHMENTS     FROM PG₁.deliver_prog TO PB.get_prog₁;
                          FROM PG₂.deliver_prog TO PB.get_prog₂;
                          FROM PB.put_prog₁ TO SC₁.select_prog₁;
                          FROM PB.put_prog₁ TO SC₂.select_prog₁;
                          FROM PB.put_prog₂ TO SC₁.select_prog₂;
                          FROM PB.put_prog₂ TO SC₂.select_prog₂
END
```

**Table 7.** Textual description of ConcCompSys

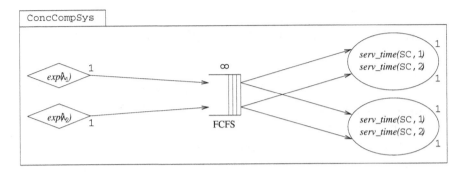

**Fig. 17.** QN associated with `ConcCompSys`

closely related to a QS M/M/1. To transform it into a QS M/M/1, we perform phase 5 as follows:

- The two arrival processes are merged into a single arrival process with arrival rate $\lambda_{\text{seq}} = \lambda_{\text{seq},1} + \lambda_{\text{seq},2}$. We observe that the probability that an incoming program belongs to class 1 (resp. 2) is $\lambda_{\text{seq},1}/\lambda_{\text{seq}}$ (resp. $\lambda_{\text{seq},2}/\lambda_{\text{seq}}$).
- The hypoexponential service time for the first class of programs is approximated with an exponential service time with rate $\mu_{\text{seq},1}$ such that $\mu_{\text{seq},1}^{-1} = \mu_{\text{seq},1}^{-1} + \mu_{\text{seq},p}^{-1} + \mu_{\text{seq},c}^{-1} + \mu_{\text{seq},o}^{-1} + \mu_{\text{seq},g}^{-1}$.
- The hypoexponential service time for the second class of programs is approximated with an exponential service time with rate $\mu_{\text{seq},2}$ such that $\mu_{\text{seq},2}^{-1} = \mu_{\text{seq},1}^{-1} + \mu_{\text{seq},p}^{-1} + \mu_{\text{seq},c}^{-1} + \mu_{\text{seq},g}^{-1}$.
- The two classes of programs are merged into a single class, whose hyperexponential service time is approximated with an exponential service time with rate $\mu_{\text{seq}}$ such that $\mu_{\text{seq}}^{-1} = (\lambda_{\text{seq},1}/\lambda_{\text{seq}}) \cdot \mu_{\text{seq},1}^{-1} + (\lambda_{\text{seq},2}/\lambda_{\text{seq}}) \cdot \mu_{\text{seq},2}^{-1}$.

Denoted by $\rho_{\text{seq}} = \lambda_{\text{seq}}/\mu_{\text{seq}}$ the traffic intensity of the resulting QS M/M/1 approximating the open QN model for the sequential architecture, and assumed $\rho_{\text{seq}} < 1$, phase 6 is conducted symbolically by employing the first group of formulas at the end of Sect. 3.1. The results of the evaluation are reported in Table 8.

| | |
|---|---|
| Compiler throughput: | $\overline{X}_{\text{seq}} = \lambda_{\text{seq}}$ |
| Compiler utilization: | $\overline{U}_{\text{seq}} = \rho_{\text{seq}}$ |
| Mean number of programs in the compiler: | $\overline{N}_{\text{seq}} = \rho_{\text{seq}}/(1 - \rho_{\text{seq}})$ |
| Mean compilation time: | $\overline{R}_{\text{seq}} = 1/[\mu_{\text{seq}} \cdot (1 - \rho_{\text{seq}})]$ |

**Table 8.** Symbolic evaluation for the sequential architecture

## 6.6   Analysis of the Pipeline Compiler

As far as the evaluation of the pipeline architecture is concerned, after denoting by $\lambda_{\text{pipe},1}$, $\lambda_{\text{pipe},2}$, $\mu_{\text{pipe},1}$, $\mu_{\text{pipe},p}$, $\mu_{\text{pipe},c}$, $\mu_{\text{pipe},o}$, and $\mu_{\text{pipe},g}$ the actual values for the numeric parameters of PipeCompSys that characterize a certain scenario, we note that the application of phase 5 to the QN of Fig. 15 simply boils down to merging the two arrival processes into a single arrival process with arrival rate $\lambda_{\text{pipe}} = \lambda_{\text{pipe},1} + \lambda_{\text{pipe},2}$. The multi-class service processes for the lexer, the parser, the checker, and the generator are trivially converted into single-class service processes with service rates $\mu_{\text{pipe},1}$, $\mu_{\text{pipe},p}$, $\mu_{\text{pipe},c}$, and $\mu_{\text{pipe},g}$, respectively, as the two classes of programs have the same service rate in each of the four multi-class service processes.

The resulting open QN model, which is used in phase 6, is product form and is symbolically evaluated by decomposing it into five QSs M/M/1 with the appropriate arrival rates. In particular, at equilibrium the arrival rate for the lexer, the parser, the checker, and the generator is $\lambda_{\text{pipe}}$, while the arrival rate for the optimizer is $\lambda_{\text{pipe},1}$. As a consequence, the probability that a program leaving the checker enters the optimizer (resp. the generator) is $\lambda_{\text{pipe},1}/\lambda_{\text{pipe}}$ (resp. $\lambda_{\text{pipe},2}/\lambda_{\text{pipe}}$). Another consequence is that the traffic intensity for the lexer, the parser, the checker, and the generator is $\rho_{\text{pipe},j} = \lambda_{\text{pipe}}/\mu_{\text{pipe},j}$ where $j \in \{1, p, c, g\}$, while the traffic intensity for the optimizer is $\rho_{\text{pipe},o} = \lambda_{\text{pipe},1}/\mu_{\text{pipe},o}$. Assuming that the QN is stable, which means that each of its service centers is stable, i.e. $\lambda_{\text{pipe}} < \min(\mu_{\text{pipe},1}, \mu_{\text{pipe},p}, \mu_{\text{pipe},c}, \mu_{\text{pipe},o} \cdot (\lambda_{\text{pipe}}/\lambda_{\text{pipe},1}), \mu_{\text{pipe},g})$, we symbolically derive the four average performance indices both for the various compilation phases and for the overall pipeline compiler, as reported in Table 9.

| | |
|---|---|
| Phase $j$ throughput: | $\overline{X}_{\text{pipe},j} = \lambda_{\text{pipe}}$ for $j \in \{1, p, c, g\}$ |
| | $\overline{X}_{\text{pipe},o} = \lambda_{\text{pipe},1}$ |
| Phase $j$ utilization: | $\overline{U}_{\text{pipe},j} = \rho_{\text{pipe},j}$ |
| Mean number of programs in phase $j$: | $\overline{N}_{\text{pipe},j} = \rho_{\text{pipe},j}/(1 - \rho_{\text{pipe},j})$ |
| Mean duration of phase $j$: | $\overline{R}_{\text{pipe},j} = 1/[\mu_{pipe,j} \cdot (1 - \rho_{\text{pipe},j})]$ |
| Compiler throughput: | $\overline{X}_{\text{pipe}} = \overline{X}_{\text{pipe},g}$ |
| Compiler utilization: | $\overline{U}_{\text{pipe}} = 1 - \prod_j (1 - \overline{U}_{\text{pipe},j})$ |
| Mean number of programs in the compiler: | $\overline{N}_{\text{pipe}} = \sum_j \overline{N}_{\text{pipe},j}$ |
| Mean compilation time: | $\overline{R}_{\text{pipe}} = \frac{\lambda_{\text{pipe},1}}{\lambda_{\text{pipe}}} \cdot \sum_j \overline{R}_{\text{pipe},j} + \frac{\lambda_{\text{pipe},2}}{\lambda_{\text{pipe}}} \cdot \sum_{j \neq o} \overline{R}_{\text{pipe},j}$ |

**Table 9.** Symbolic evaluation for the pipeline architecture

## 6.7   Analysis of the Concurrent Compiler

We denote by $\lambda_{\text{conc},1}$, $\lambda_{\text{conc},2}$, $\mu_{\text{conc},1}$, $\mu_{\text{conc},p}$, $\mu_{\text{conc},c}$, $\mu_{\text{conc},o}$, and $\mu_{\text{conc},g}$ the actual values for the numeric parameters of ConcCompSys with respect to a certain scenario. The QN model associated with `ConcCompSys`, which is shown in Fig. 17, can easily be transformed into a QS M/M/2 by performing phase 5 as in the case of `SeqCompSys`.

Denoted by $\rho_{conc} = \lambda_{conc}/(2 \cdot \mu_{conc})$ the traffic intensity of the resulting QS M/M/2 approximating the open QN model for the concurrent architecture, and assumed $\rho_{conc} < 1$, phase 6 is conducted symbolically by employing the second group of formulas at the end of Sect. 3.1 with $m = 2$. The results of the evaluation are reported in Table 10.

| | |
|---|---|
| Compiler throughput: | $\overline{X}_{conc} = \lambda_{conc}$ |
| Compiler utilization: | $\overline{U}_{conc} = 2 \cdot \rho_{conc}/(1 + \rho_{conc})$ |
| Mean number of programs in the compiler: | $\overline{N}_{conc} = 2 \cdot \rho_{conc}/(1 - \rho_{conc}^2)$ |
| Mean compilation time: | $\overline{R}_{conc} = 1/[\mu_{conc} \cdot (1 - \rho_{conc}^2)]$ |

**Table 10.** Symbolic evaluation for the concurrent architecture

## 6.8 Comparison of the Three Architectures

Due to the simplicity of the three architectures, for each of them phase 7 is skipped altogether. So, we can finally compare the sequential architecture, the pipeline architecture, and the concurrent architecture on the basis of the four average performance indices that we have symbolically computed (phase 8). In order to perform a fair comparison, we assume that in every scenario the compilation phases have the same duration for the three architectures, i.e. $\mu_{seq,j} = \mu_{pipe,j} = \mu_{conc,j} \equiv \mu_j$ for all $j \in \{1, p, c, o, g\}$. On the contrary, the three arrival rates $\lambda_{seq}$, $\lambda_{pipe}$, and $\lambda_{conc}$ can freely vary provided that they preserve the frequency of each class of programs, i.e. $\lambda_{seq,c}/\lambda_{seq} = \lambda_{pipe,c}/\lambda_{pipe} = \lambda_{conc,c}/\lambda_{conc} \equiv p_c$ for all $c \in \{1, 2\}$.

We focus on two different scenarios and we concentrate only on the mean number of programs that are compiled per unit of time, as analogous results can be derived for the other three average performance indices. In the first scenario, we assume that the three architectures undergo to a light workload. In this case, the specific architecture does not really matter, as the relations among the three throughputs directly depend on the relations among the three arrival rates: $\overline{X}_{t_1} \mathcal{R} \overline{X}_{t_2}$ if and only if $\lambda_{t_1} \mathcal{R} \lambda_{t_2}$, with $t_1, t_2 \in \{seq, pipe, conc\}$ and $\mathcal{R} \in \{<, =, >\}$.

In the second scenario, instead, we assume that the three architectures undergo to a heavy workload. This means that the values of the three arrival rates are such that all the architectures work close to their maximum throughputs, which can be derived from the corresponding stability conditions. In the case of the sequential architecture, $\lambda_{seq}$ is close to $\overline{X}_{seq,max} = \mu_{seq}$, with $\mu_{seq}^{-1} = p_1 \cdot \sum_j \mu_j^{-1} + p_2 \cdot \sum_{j \neq o} \mu_j^{-1}$. In the case of the pipeline architecture, $\lambda_{pipe}$ is close to

$\overline{X}_{\text{pipe,max}} = \min(\mu_1, \mu_{\text{p}}, \mu_{\text{c}}, \mu_{\text{o}}/p_1, \mu_{\text{g}})$. In the case of the concurrent architecture, $\lambda_{\text{conc}}$ is close to $\overline{X}_{\text{conc,max}} = 2 \cdot \mu_{\text{conc}}$, with $\mu_{\text{conc}}^{-1} = p_1 \cdot \sum_j \mu_j^{-1} + p_2 \cdot \sum_{j \neq \text{o}} \mu_j^{-1}$. In this scenario, for an accurate comparison it is worth considering the three following sub-scenarios:

- In the first sub-scenario, the five compilation phases have approximatively the same average duration, i.e. $\mu_1 \cong \mu_{\text{p}} \cong \mu_{\text{c}} \cong \mu_{\text{o}} \cong \mu_{\text{g}} \equiv \mu$. In this case $\overline{X}_{\text{seq,max}} \cong (4 + p_1)^{-1} \cdot \mu$, $\overline{X}_{\text{pipe,max}} \cong \mu$, and $\overline{X}_{\text{conc,max}} \cong 2 \cdot (4 + p_1)^{-1} \cdot \mu$. It follows that:

$$\overline{X}_{\text{pipe,max}}/\overline{X}_{\text{seq,max}} \cong 4 + p_1$$
$$\overline{X}_{\text{pipe,max}}/\overline{X}_{\text{conc,max}} \cong 2 + 0.5 \cdot p_1$$
$$\overline{X}_{\text{conc,max}}/\overline{X}_{\text{seq,max}} \cong 2$$

Therefore, in this sub-scenario, the pipeline architecture outperforms — in terms of mean number of programs compiled per unit of time — the sequential architecture (resp. the concurrent architecture) of a factor that ranges between 4 and 5 (resp. between 2 and 2.5) depending on the frequency of the programs of class 1. In addition, we see that the concurrent architecture outperforms the sequential architecture of a factor 2. We conclude that in this sub-scenario the pipeline architecture is the architecture of choice.

- In the second sub-scenario, there is one compilation phase, say lexical analysis, whose average duration is several orders of magnitude greater than the average duration of the other phases, i.e. $\mu_1 \ll \mu_j$ for all $j \in \{\text{p}, \text{c}, \text{o}, \text{g}\}$. In this case $\overline{X}_{\text{seq,max}} \cong \mu_1$, $\overline{X}_{\text{pipe,max}} = \mu_1$, and $\overline{X}_{\text{conc,max}} \cong 2 \cdot \mu_1$. It follows that:

$$\overline{X}_{\text{pipe,max}}/\overline{X}_{\text{seq,max}} \cong 1$$
$$\overline{X}_{\text{conc,max}}/\overline{X}_{\text{pipe,max}} \cong 2$$
$$\overline{X}_{\text{conc,max}}/\overline{X}_{\text{seq,max}} \cong 2$$

We conclude that in this sub-scenario, in which one of the five phases is a bottleneck, splitting the various phases among different components operating in parallel brings no advantage, and the architecture of choice is the concurrent one.

- In the third sub-scenario, the average durations of the five compilation phases range between a minimum value and a maximum value that are several orders of magnitude apart, i.e. $\mu_{\text{min}} \leq \mu_j \leq \mu_{\text{max}}$ for all $j \in \{1, \text{p}, \text{c}, \text{o}, \text{g}\}$ with $\mu_{\text{min}} \ll \mu_{\text{max}}$. In this case $(4 + p_1)^{-1} \cdot \mu_{\text{min}} \leq \overline{X}_{\text{seq,max}} \leq (4 + p_1)^{-1} \cdot \mu_{\text{max}}$, $\overline{X}_{\text{pipe,max}} = \mu_{\text{min}}$, and $2 \cdot (4 + p_1)^{-1} \cdot \mu_{\text{min}} \leq \overline{X}_{\text{conc,max}} \leq 2 \cdot (4 + p_1)^{-1} \cdot \mu_{\text{max}}$. It follows that:

$$(4 + p_1) \cdot (\mu_{\text{min}}/\mu_{\text{max}}) \leq \overline{X}_{\text{pipe,max}}/\overline{X}_{\text{seq,max}} \leq 4 + p_1$$
$$(4 + p_1) \cdot (\mu_{\text{min}}/\mu_{\text{max}})/2 \leq \overline{X}_{\text{pipe,max}}/\overline{X}_{\text{conc,max}} \leq (4 + p_1)/2$$
$$2 \leq \overline{X}_{\text{conc,max}}/\overline{X}_{\text{seq,max}} \leq 2$$

which generalizes the results of the previous two sub-scenarios, showing that the concurrent architecture is always twice as faster as the sequential one, and that the pipeline architecture is not always better than the other two, as $(4 + p_1) \cdot (\mu_{\text{min}}/\mu_{\text{max}})$ and $(4 + p_1) \cdot (\mu_{\text{min}}/\mu_{\text{max}})/2$ can be less than 1 because so is $\mu_{\text{min}}/\mu_{\text{max}}$.

# 7   Conclusion and Future Perspectives

In this paper we have presented a methodology for the prediction, the improvement, and the comparison of typical average performance indices of alternative architectural designs developed for a software system. The methodology relies on the SPA based ADL called Æmilia, which provides a textual and graphical environment in which architectural descriptions can be developed in an easy and controlled way, and on QNs, which are structured performance models equipped with fast solution algorithms for computing typical average performance measures and allow such performance measures to be interpreted back at the SA description level. The combined use of Æmilia and QNs is made possible by a suitable translation, which can be applied to a reasonably wide class of Æmilia specifications satisfying certain syntax restrictions and has a complexity linear in the number of software components declared in the Æmilia specifications. The methodology and the translation have been illustrated on a scenario-based comparison of a sequential SA, a pipeline SA, and a concurrent SA for a compiler system.

As far as future work is concerned, first we would like to provide an automated support for our methodology. This will be accomplished by implementing the translation of Æmilia specifications into QN models as well as the solution of QN models in the architectural assistant module of the Æmilia-based software tool TwoTowers 3.0 [12]. Second, we would like to integrate our methodology within the software development cycle, both upstream and downstream. On the one hand, we would like to develop a translation from notations used in the software engineering practice, like e.g. UML, to our framework, in order to hide as much as possible all the formal details with which the typical designer may not be familiar. On the other hand, we would like to be able to generate code that is guaranteed to possess the performance requirements proved at the SA level. In this respect, a critical issue to address is taking into account the impact on the software performance of the hardware architecture and operating system on which the software system will be deployed.

# References

1. M. Ajmone Marsan, G. Balbo, G. Conte, S. Donatelli, and G. Franceschinis, *"Modelling with Generalized Stochastic Petri Nets"*, John Wiley & Sons, 1995.
2. A. Aldini and M. Bernardo, *"A General Deadlock Detection Approach for Software Architectures"*, to appear in Proc. of the *12th Int. Formal Methods Europe Symp. (FME 2003)*, LNCS, Pisa (Italy), 2003.
3. F. Aquilani, S. Balsamo, and P. Inverardi, *"Performance Analysis at the Software Architectural Design Level"*, in Performance Evaluation 45:205-221, 2001.
4. F. Baccelli, W.A. Massey, and D. Towsley, *"Acyclic Fork-Join Queueing Networks"*, in Journal of the ACM 22:248-260, 1989.
5. C. Baier, B. Haverkort, H. Hermanns, and J.-P. Katoen, *"Automated Performance and Dependability Evaluation Using Model Checking"*, in *Performance Evaluation of Complex Systems: Techniques and Tools*, LNCS 2459:261-289, 2002.

6. S. Balsamo, *"Product Form Queueing Networks"*, in *Performance Evaluation: Origins and Directions*, LNCS 1769:377-401, 2000.
7. S. Balsamo, M. Bernardo, and M. Simeoni, *"Combining Stochastic Process Algebras and Queueing Networks for Software Architecture Analysis"*, in Proc. of the *3rd Int. Workshop on Software and Performance (WOSP 2002)*, ACM Press, pp. 190-202, Roma (Italy), 2002.
8. S. Balsamo, V. De Nitto Personè, and R. Onvural, *"Analysis of Queueing Networks with Blocking"*, Kluwer, 2001.
9. S. Balsamo, L. Donatiello, and N. van Dijk, *"Bounded Performance Analysis of Parallel Processing Systems"*, in IEEE Trans. on Parallel and Distributed Systems 9:1041-1056, 1998.
10. F. Baskett, K.M. Chandy, R.R. Muntz, and G. Palacios, *"Open, Closed, and Mixed Networks of Queues with Different Classes of Customers"*, in Journal of the ACM 22:248-260, 1975.
11. H. Beilner, J. Mäter, and C. Wysocki, *"The Hierarchical Evaluation Tool HIT"*, in Proc. of the *7th Int. Conf. on Modelling Techniques and Tools for Computer Performance Evaluation (TOOLS 1994)*, LNCS 794, Wien (Austria), 1994.
12. M. Bernardo, *"TwoTowers 3.0: Enhancing Usability"*, to appear in Proc. of the *11th Int. Symp. on Modeling, Analysis and Simulation of Computer and Telecommunication Systems (MASCOTS 2003)*, IEEE-CS Press, Orlando (FL), October 2003 (http://www.sti.uniurb.it/bernardo/twotowers/).
13. M. Bernardo, *"Symbolic Semantic Rules for Producing Compact STGLA from Value Passing Process Descriptions"*, to appear in ACM Trans. on Computational Logic, 2003.
14. M. Bernardo and M. Bravetti, *"Performance Measure Sensitive Congruences for Markovian Process Algebras"*, in Theoretical Computer Science 290:117-160, 2003.
15. M. Bernardo, P. Ciancarini, and L. Donatiello, *"Architecting Families of Software Systems with Process Algebras"*, in ACM Trans. on Software Engineering and Methodology 11:386-426, 2002.
16. M. Bernardo, L. Donatiello, and P. Ciancarini, *"Stochastic Process Algebra: From an Algebraic Formalism to an Architectural Description Language"*, in *Performance Evaluation of Complex Systems: Techniques and Tools*, LNCS 2459:236-260, 2002.
17. M. Bernardo and F. Franzè, *"Exogenous and Endogenous Extensions of Architectural Types"*, in Proc. of the *5th Int. Conf. on Coordination Models and Languages (COORDINATION 2002)*, LNCS 2315:40-55, York (UK), 2002.
18. M. Bernardo and F. Franzè, *"Architectural Types Revisited: Extensible And/Or Connections"*, in Proc. of the *5th Int. Conf. on Fundamental Approaches to Software Engineering (FASE 2002)*, LNCS 2306:113-128, Grenoble (France), 2002.
19. J.P. Buzen, *"Computational Algorithms for Closed Queueing Networks with Exponential Servers"*, in Comm. of the ACM 16:527-531, 1973.
20. K.M. Chandy and C.H. Sauer, *"Computational Algorithms for Product Form Queueing Networks"*, in Comm. of the ACM 23:573-583, 1980.
21. W.-M. Chow, E.A. MacNair, and C.H. Sauer, *"Analysis of Manufactoring Systems by the Research Queueing Package"*, in IBM Journal of Research and Development 29:330-342, 1985.
22. G. Clark, S. Gilmore, J. Hillston, and M. Ribaudo, *"Exploiting Modal Logic to Express Performance Measures"*, in Proc. of the *11th Int. Conf. on Modeling Techniques and Tools for Computer Performance Evaluation (TOOLS 2000)*, LNCS 1786:247-261, Schaumburg (IL), 2000.

23. E.M. Clarke, O. Grumberg, and D.A. Peled, *"Model Checking"*, MIT Press, 1999.
24. W.R. Cleaveland and O. Sokolsky, *"Equivalence and Preorder Checking for Finite-State Systems"*, in Handbook of Process Algebra, Elsevier, pp. 391-424, 2001.
25. A.E. Conway and N.D. Georganas, *"RECAL - A New Efficient Algorithm for the Exact Analysis of Multiple-Chain Closed Queueing Networks"*, Journal of the ACM 33:786-791, 1986.
26. R.G. Franks, A. Hubbard, S. Majumdar, J.E. Neilson, D.C. Petriu, J.A. Rolia, and C.M. Woodside, *"A Toolset for Performance Engineering and Software Design of Client-Server Systems"*, in Performance Evaluation 24:117-135, 1995.
27. R.G. Franks and C.M. Woodside, *"Performance of Multi-level Client-server Systems with Parallel Service Operations"*, in Proc. of the *1st Int. Workshop on Software and Performance (WOSP 1998)*, ACM Press, pp. 120-130, Santa Fe (NM), 1998.
28. E. Gelenbe, *"Queueing Networks with Negative and Positive Customers"*, in Journal of Applied Probability 28:656-663, 1991.
29. N. Götz, U. Herzog, and M. Rettelbach, *"Multiprocessor and Distributed System Design: The Integration of Functional Specification and Performance Analysis Using Stochastic Process Algebras"*, in Proc. of the *16th Int. Symp. on Computer Performance Modelling, Measurement and Evaluation (PERFORMANCE 1993)*, LNCS 729:121-146, Roma (Italy), 1993.
30. H. Hermanns, *"Interactive Markov Chains"*, LNCS 2428, 2002.
31. J. Hillston, *"A Compositional Approach to Performance Modelling"*, Cambridge University Press, 1996.
32. R.A. Howard, *"Dynamic Probabilistic Systems"*, John Wiley & Sons, 1971.
33. K. Kant, *"Introduction to Computer System Performance Evaluation"*, McGraw-Hill, 1992.
34. L. Kleinrock, *"Queueing Systems"*, Wiley, 1975.
35. S.S. Lavenberg, *"Computer Performance Modeling Handbook"*, Academic Press, 1983.
36. S.S. Lavenberg and C.H. Sauer, *"Approximate Analysis of Queueing Networks"*, in [35], pp. 173-221.
37. E.D. Lazowska, J. Zahorjan, G. Scott Graham, and K.C. Sevcik, *"Quantitative System Performance: Computer System Analysis Using Queueing Network Models"*, Prentice Hall, 1984.
38. R. Milner, *"Communication and Concurrency"*, Prentice Hall, 1989.
39. M.K. Molloy, *"Performance Analysis using Stochastic Petri Nets"*, in IEEE Trans. on Computers 31:913-917, 1982.
40. R. Nelson and A. Tantawi, *"Approximate Analysis of Fork-Join Synchronization in Parallel Queues"*, in IEEE Trans. on Computers 37:739-743, 1988.
41. M.F. Neuts, *"Matrix-Geometric Solutions in Stochastic Models – An Algorithmic Approach"*, John Hopkins University Press, 1981.
42. H.G. Perros, *"Queueing Networks with Blocking"*, Oxford University Press, 1994.
43. D.E. Perry and A.L. Wolf, *"Foundations for the Study of Software Architecture"*, in ACM SIGSOFT Software Engineering Notes 17:40-52, 1992.
44. M. Reiser and S.S. Lavenberg, *"Mean-Value Analysis of Closed Multichain Queueing Networks"*, in Journal of the ACM 27:313-322, 1980.
45. J.A. Rolia and K.C. Sevcik, *"The Method of Layers"*, in IEEE Trans. on Software Engineering 21:682-688, 1995.
46. M. Shaw and D. Garlan, *"Software Architecture: Perspectives on an Emerging Discipline"*, Prentice Hall, 1996.

47. C. Smith, *"Performance Engineering of Software Systems"*, Addison-Wesley, 1990.
48. W.J. Stewart, *"Introduction to the Numerical Solution of Markov Chains"*, Princeton University Press, 1994.
49. Simulog Corp., *"The QNAP2 Reference Manual"*, 1989.
50. K.S. Trivedi, *"Probability and Statistics with Reliability, Queueing, and Computer Science Applications"*, John Wiley & Sons, 2001.
51. P.D. Welch, *"The Statistical Analysis of Simulation Results"*, in [35], pp. 267-329.
52. C.M. Woodside, J.E. Neilson, D.C. Petriu, and S. Majumdar, *"The Stochastic Rendezvous Network Model for Performance of Synchronous Client-Server-like Distributed Software"*, in IEEE Trans. on Computers 44:20-34, 1995.

# Software Architecture and Dependability

Valérie Issarny[1] and Apostolos Zarras[2]

[1] INRIA, Domaine de Voluceau, B.P. 105, 78 153 Le Chesnay Cédex, France,
`Valerie.Issarny@inria.fr`
[2] Computer Science Department, University of Ioannina, Greece,
`zarras@cs.uoi.gr`

**Abstract.** Dependable systems are characterized by a number of attributes including: reliability, availability, safety and security. For some attributes (namely for reliability, availability, safety), there exist probability-based theoretic foundations, enabling the application of *dependability analysis techniques*. The goal of dependability analysis is to forecast the values of dependability attributes, based on certain properties (e.g. failure rate, MTBF, etc.) that characterize the system's constituent elements.

Nowadays, architects, designers and developers build systems based on an architecture-driven approach. They specify the system's software architecture using Architecture Description Languages or other standard modeling notations like UML. Given the previous, we examine what we need to specify at the architectural level to enable the automated generation of models for dependability analysis. In this paper, we further present a prototype implementation of the proposed approach, which relies on UML specifications of dependable systems' software architectures. Moreover, we exemplify our approach using a case study system.

## 1 Introduction

To characterize a system as a dependable one, it must be trustworthy. In other words, the users of the system must be able to rely on the services it provides. The less the system fails in providing correct service the more dependable it is. A system failure is the manifestation of a fault, which leads the system into an erroneous state. Building dependable systems amounts in building systems that do not fail, or building systems whose failure can be tolerated. In order to achieve the previous there are several techniques that have been proposed. These techniques can be classified into the following categories [22]:

- Fault prevention techniques, aiming at the avoidance of fault creation within the system.
- Fault tolerance techniques aiming at the provision of correct service, despite the presence of faults.
- Fault removal techniques, whose main objective is to reduce the presence of faults in the system.

M. Bernardo and P. Inverardi (Eds.): SFM 2003, LNCS 2804, pp. 259–285, 2003.
© Springer-Verlag Berlin Heidelberg 2003

- Fault forecasting techniques, whose goal is to analyze and estimate the number of faults in the system and their consequences.

Developing dependable systems relies on a software development process that consists of a set of typical engineering work-flows. This set of work-flows is usually performed in an iterative manner. Namely, the work-flows we consider are:

- The requirements elicitation work-flow.
- The analysis and design work-flow.
- The implementation work-flow.
- The test work-flow.
- The deployment work-flow.

The development process further comprises work-flows that aim at managing the execution of the engineering work-flows. The previous consist of several tasks for managing workers (i.e., architects, designers, developers), the activities performed by those workers and the artifacts produced after the execution of the activities. Applying fault prevention, fault removal, fault tolerance and fault forecasting techniques requires introducing corresponding activities in the engineering work-flows of the software development process. Moreover, using the aforementioned techniques has also implications on the management work-flows.

Fault prevention involves applying specific design methodologies and construction rules. Consequently, there are activities to be added in the analysis and design work-flow and in the implementation work-flow. The management work-flows must further contain activities that constraint the workers participating in the aforementioned engineering work-flows to apply the fault prevention activities introduced in the engineering work-flows.

Fault tolerance techniques consist of: error recovery and error compensation techniques. Error recovery aims at taking the system from an erroneous state to an error-free state, while error compensation involves enhancing the system with redundant entities so as to be able to deliver correct service from an erroneous state. Based on the previous, the analysis and design work-flow must include activities that introduce fault detectors, fault notifiers, redundancy management, logging and recovery elements in the architecture of the dependable system. The implementation work-flow must contain activities that deal with the integration of the previous elements with the rest of the system's entities. Finally, the deployment work-flow must contain activities for properly deploying redundant elements on hardware nodes.

Fault removal techniques are composed of three basic steps: verification, diagnosis and correction. The verification step aims at checking whether the system's behavior is coherent with the system's expected behavior. If it is not, the other two steps must be performed. In general, during the verification step a number of constraints are checked against the system's actual behavior. The constraints may be either generic in that they are required for many different families of systems (dead-lock freedom, absence of starvation, absence of memory leaks), or specific to the particular system. System-specific constraints are deduced from the users' functional requirements on the system (e.g., the system is able to successfully execute specific scenarios). Verification may be either static, or dynamic. In static verification, the constraints on the system behavior are checked against a model of the system (e.g., model checking techniques). Static verification techniques involve introducing specific activities in the analysis and design work-flow for building the system model in terms of a formalism like PROMELA [14], FSP [27], etc. Dynamic verification amounts in testing the runtime behavior of the system using random or deterministic test cases. Naturally, dynamic verification imposes performing specific activities in the testing work-flow.

By definition [22], dependability is a quite wide concept, which is characterized by a number of attributes including *reliability, availability, security* and *safety*. Depending on the system, our interest is usually narrowed into some of those attributes. The goal of fault forecasting is to estimate-predict the values of dependability attributes, based on certain properties (e.g., failure rate, MTBF, service rate, etc.) that characterize the system's constituent elements. From now on, we refer to fault forecasting techniques as dependability analysis techniques. Reliability analysis, for instance, aims at calculating the probability that the system provides correct service for a particular time period. Traditional techniques for dependability analysis rely on specifying constraints describing either what it means for the system to provide error-free service (Block Diagrams), or what it means for the system to provide erroneous service (Fault Trees). More sophisticated analysis techniques require modeling the system's failure and repair behavior using state space models.

Regarding the software development process, dependability analysis requires specifying related properties (e.g., failure rate, MTBF) characterizing the elements that make up the system. Consequently, we need to enhance the analysis and design work-flow to include such activities. Moreover, we have to enhance the deployment work-flow with activities that allow achieving the previous for the nodes used for executing the system's elements. Finally, constraints for error-free or erroneous service delivery and state space models must be specified during the analysis and design work-flow. The values of the properties that characterize the system's constituent elements may be assumed, or they may be based on measures gathered during the testing work-flow of a previous iteration.

In this paper, we present an approach for automating the previous activities. More specifically, in Section 2, we present general concepts related to the specification of software architectures and the dependability analysis of systems at the architectural level. Then, in Section 3, we examine what we need to specify at the architectural level to enable the automated generation of models for dependability analysis and how to generate them from architectural descriptions. Section 4 presents a prototype implementation of the proposed approach, which relies on UML to specify the architecture of dependable systems. In Section 5, we give details related to a case study we use for the assessment of the solution we propose. Finally, in Section 6, we summarize with our contribution and the future perspectives of this work.

# 2  Software Architecture and Dependability Analysis

As we mentioned in Section 1, our main goal is to facilitate the generation of constraints and state space models for the dependability analysis of systems, from the systems' architectural descriptions. Specifying software architectures involves using a notation. Architecture Description Languages (ADLs) are notations enabling the rigorous specification of the structure and behavior of software systems.

ADLs come along with tools supporting the analysis and the construction of software systems, whose architecture is specified using them. Several ADLs have been proposed so far (e.g., ASTER[17], CONIC [28], C2 [40], DARWIN [26], DCL [4], DURRA [5], RAPIDE [24], SADL [33], UNICON [38], WRIGHT [2]); they are more or less based on the same principles [7, 15, 30]. In particular, the architecture of software systems is specified using *components*, *connectors* and *configurations*.

Before getting into the semantics of components, connectors and configuration, it should be noted that ADLs are widely known and used in academia, but their use in the industry is quite limited. Industrials, nowadays, prefer using object-oriented notations for specifying the architecture of their software systems. UML, in particular, is becoming an industrial standard notation for the definition of a family of languages (i.e., UML profiles) for modeling software systems. However, there is a primary concern regarding the imprecision of the semantics of UML.

One way to increase the impact of ADLs in the real world and decrease the ambiguity of UML is to define an ADL that provides a set of core extensible UML-based language constructs for the specification of components, connectors and configurations. This core set of extensible constructs shall further facilitate future attempts for mapping existing ADLs into UML.

## 2.1  Components

A *component* is a unit of data or computation and the basic features that characterize it are its interface, type and properties.

A component *interface* describes a number of interaction points between the component and the rest of the architecture. All of the ADLs mentioned above support this particular feature. However, several syntactic and semantic differences have been observed between them. In ASTER, for instance, an interface defines a set of operations; components export interfaces to the environment and import interfaces from other architectural elements. In CONIC, an interface defines a set of entry and exit ports that are typed. In DARWIN, CONIC's successor, an interface specifies services required from and provided by a component. In DCL, components are called *modules*. A module is a group of actors, i.e., a group of processing elements that communicate through asynchronous point-to-point message passing [1]. A module description comprises request rules, which prescribe the module's interface. A component interface in C2 defines two kinds of interaction points, named top and bottom ports. Ports are used by a particular component to accept requests from, and issue requests to, components that reside either above, or below it (the architecture is topologically structured). A component interface in UNICON defines a number of interaction points, called players. Players are typed entities. The type of a player can be out of a limited set of predefined types. In WRIGHT, a component interface defines input and output ports. Pretty similar is the way interaction points are defined in DURRA. In RAPIDE, the points of interaction can be either services required from or provided by a component, or events generated by a component. Finally, in SADL, an interface is just a point of interaction.

A component *type* is a template used to instantiate different component instances into a running configuration. All of the ADLs mentioned above distinguish between component types and instances. Types are usually extensible. Sub-typing (e.g., in C2, ASTER) is a typical method used to define type extensions. In DARWIN and RAPIDE, types are extended through parameterization.

Component *properties* characterize the component's observable behavior (which may include erroneous behavior). In WRIGHT, behavior is described in CSP [12, 13]. In RAPIDE, partially ordered sets of events (posets) are used to describe component behavior. In the very first version of DARWIN, properties were described in CCS [32]; in the latest version, properties are described in pi-calculus, which extends the semantics of CCS with means that allow specifying the dynamic instantiation of processes [31]. In DCL, the behavior of a module is deduced by the behaviors of the actors that constitute the module. An extension of the basic ACTORS formalism is used to describe the behavior of actors [3] within a software architecture. Finally, in ASTER, temporal logic is used to describe properties. Similarly, in SADL, the authors propose using Temporal Logic of Actions (TLA) [21] for the specification of component properties.

## 2.2   Connectors

A connector is an architectural element that models the interaction protocols among components. Its basic features are again its interface, type, and properties.

Some ADLs do not consider connectors as first-order architectural elements (e.g., CONIC, DARWIN, RAPIDE). For the other ADLs, a connector specification is similar to a component specification. In WRIGHT and UNICON, for instance, a connector interface is a set of interaction points, named roles. In DURRA, a connector is called channel and its interface is defined in the very same way as a component interface. In C2 and SADL, connector interfaces are described using the same syntax as the one used to describe component interfaces. In DCL, connectors are again groups of actors, called *protocols*. Protocols define a set of roles describing the way interaction takes place among modules. In all ADLs, except for UNICON, connector types are extensible. The formalism used for the specification of component properties is further used for the specification of connector properties.

## 2.3   Configurations

A configuration is the assembly of components and connectors. It is described in terms of associations (usually called bindings) between points of interaction. Several ADLs either assume or provide means to describe *constraints* for a particular configuration.

Constraints may simply describe restrictions on the way components are bound. In DARWIN, for instance, only bindings between required and provided services are allowed. In ASTER, the types of the interfaces that are bound should match. Some ADLs allow specifying constraints on the behavior of the overall configuration. In ASTER, for example, we can specify dependability requirements for a particular configuration. RAPIDE also allows specifying constraints on the behavior of a particular configuration. Constraints may also relate to the (dynamic) evolution of a particular configuration. In DURRA and RAPIDE, for example, it is possible to describe conditions under which a configuration changes into another one.

## 2.4   ADLs and Dependability Analysis

Pioneer work on the dependability analysis of software systems at the architectural level includes Attribute-Based Architectural Styles (ABAS) [25]. In general, an architectural style includes the specification of: types of basic architectural elements (e.g., pipe and filter) that can be used for specifying a software architecture, constraints on the use of these types, and patterns describing the data and control interaction between them.

An ABAS is an architectural style, which additionally provides modeling support for the analysis of a particular quality attribute. Dependability attributes (i.e., reliability, availability, safety) are among the quality attributes for which we can define ABASs. More specifically, an ABAS includes the specification of:

- *Quality attribute measures* characterizing the quality attribute (e.g., the probability that the system correctly provides a service for a given duration).
- *Quality attribute stimuli*, i.e., events affecting the value of the quality attribute measures (e.g., failures).
- *Quality attribute properties*, i.e., architectural properties affecting the value of the quality attribute measures (e.g., faults, redundancy).
- *Quality attribute models*, i.e., traditional models that formally relate the above elements (e.g., a state space model that predicts reliability based on the failure rates and the redundancy used).

In [20], the authors introduce the Architecture Tradeoff Analysis Method (ATAM) where the use of an ABAS is coupled with the specification of a set of scenarios that constitutes a *service profile*. ATAM has been applied for analyzing quality attributes like performance, availability, modifiability, and real-time. In all these cases, quality attribute models (e.g., state-space models, queuing networks, etc.) are manually built given the specification of a set of scenarios and an ABAS-based architectural description of a system. However, in [20], the authors recognize the complexity of the aforementioned task; the development of quality analysis models requires about 25% of the time spent for applying the whole method. ATAM is a promising approach for doing things right. However, it needs to be enriched for facilitating the specification of quality models.

One solution to the previous lies on the automated generation of quality attribute models from architectural descriptions. Note that there is no unique way to model systems. A model is built based on certain assumptions. Thus, the model generation procedures should be customizable. Customization is done according to the assumptions, made by the developer for the quality stimuli and properties, affecting the value of the particular quality attribute that is assessed. While this paper concentrates on dependability quality attributes, the interested reader may refer to [43] for details regarding the case of performance.

# 3   ABAS for Automated Dependability Analysis of Software Architectures

As already mentioned in the introduction, dependability is characterized by a number of attributes including reliability, availability, safety, security. For reliability, availability and safety, there exist probability-based theoretic foundations, enabling *dependability analysis*. In this section, we define an ABAS that facilitates dependability analysis regarding these attributes [42].

To perform dependability analysis, we have to specify a service profile, i.e., a set of scenarios, describing how the system provides a particular service. A scenario (e.g., a UML collaboration or sequence diagram) specifies the interactions among a set of component and connector instances, structured as prescribed by the configuration of the system. Scenarios are associated with the values of the dependability measures that the system's users require (these values are gathered during the requirements elicitation). Moreover, the definitions of the base architectural elements are associated with dependability measures, properties, and stimuli, as detailed below.

## 3.1   Dependability Measures, Stimuli, and Properties

The basic reliability measure we use is the probability that the system provides correct service for a given time period. Similarly, the availability measure we consider is the probability that the system provides correct service at a given moment in time. For safety, a typical measure is the probability that there will be no catastrophic failure for a given time period. Hence, safety analysis is reliability analysis regarding only catastrophic failures.

A scenario may fail if instances of components, nodes[3], and connectors used in it, fail because of faults causing errors in their state. The manifestations of

---

[3] An architectural component is assumed to be associated with a set of nodes on top of which it executes. For primitive components the associated set contains one node, while for composite components, it may contain more than one node

errors are failures. Hence, faults are the basic *properties*, associated with components/connectors/nodes, which affect the dependability measures. Failures are the *stimuli*, associated with components/connectors/nodes, causing changes in the value of the dependability measures. According to [22], faults and failures are further characterized by the features given in Tables 1 and 2. Different combinations of the values of these features can be used to customize properly the generation of dependability models, which is detailed in Section 3.2.

| Features | Range | Associated Architectural Element |
|---|---|---|
| domain | time/value | Component/Connector/Node |
| perception | consistent/inconsistent | |

**Table 1.** Dependability Stimuli: Specification of Failures

| Features | Range | Associated Architectural Element |
|---|---|---|
| nature | intention/accident | Component/Connector/Node |
| phase | design/operational | |
| causes | physical/human | |
| boundaries | internal/external | |
| persistence | permanent/temporary | |
| arrival-rate | Real | |
| active-to-benign | Real | |
| benign-to-active | Real | |
| disappearance | Real | |

**Table 2.** Dependability Properties : Specification of Faults

Another property of the base architectural elements that affects dependability measures is redundancy. Redundancy schemas can be specified using the base architectural constructs defined in Section 2. More specifically, a redundancy schema is a composite component that encapsulates a configuration of redundant architectural elements, which behave as a single fault tolerant unit. According to [23], a redundant schema is characterized by the following features: the kind of mechanism used to detect errors, the way the constituent elements execute towards serving incoming requests, the confidence that can be placed on the results of the error detection mechanism and the number of component and node faults that can be tolerated. The features characterizing a redundancy schema are summarized in Table 3. A repairable redundancy schema is characterized by additional features (e.g., repair-rate).

## 3.2   Dependability Models

The dependability properties, stimuli and measures can be formally related using Block Diagrams (BDs), Fault Trees (FTs) and state space models [34, 11, 35].

| Features | Range | Associated Architectural Element |
|---|---|---|
| error-detection | vote/comp./acceptance | Component |
| execution | parallel/sequential | |
| confidence | absolute/relative | |
| service-delivery | continuous/suspended | |
| no-comp-faults | Integer | |
| no-node-faults | Integer | |

**Table 3.** Redundancy Property

A BD represents graphically a constraint for providing a service S. Hereafter, we call such a constraint, *constraint-to-succeed*. The BD consists of a set of system components that need to be operational to provide S (i.e., the components participating in a scenario that describe how the system provides S). Every component C in the BD is characterized by certain dependability measures. The reliability (resp. availability) measure for C is the probability that C provides correct service for a time period T (resp. time instance t). The safety measure for C is the probability that there is no catastrophic failure of C during a time period T. Components are connected using serial or M-out-of-N parallel connections. If we connect N components using serial connections, all of them must be operational to provide S. On the other hand, if we connect them using an M-out-of-N parallel connection, at least M components out of the set must be operational to provide S. The overall system reliability (resp. availability, safety) is obtained through simple combinatorial calculations involving the reliability (resp. availability, safety) measures of the individual components that belong to the BD.

Taking an example, suppose that providing a service for a time period T requires using components C1, C2 and C3. The corresponding constraint-to-succeed can be specified as a logical formula, $C1 \wedge C2 \wedge C3$, consisting of the conjunction of three predicates. Predicates $C1$, $C2$, $C3$ are true if components C1, C2, C3 are operational and false otherwise. The BD that graphically represents the constraint-to-succeed is shown in Figure 1(a). According to that BD, C1 is connected in serial with C2, which is further connected in serial with C3. The overall reliability is the probability that the $C1 \wedge C2 \wedge C3$ constraint holds:

$$BD.reliability \quad = P(C1 \wedge C2 \wedge C3)$$
$$P(C1 \wedge C2 \wedge C3) = C1.reliability * C2.reliability * C3.reliability$$

Suppose now that providing a service S for a time period T requires using either components C1, C2 or C1, C3. Again, the constraint-to-succeed can be described as a logical formula, $C1 \wedge (C2 \vee C3)$. The corresponding BD is given in Figure 1(b). C2 and C3 are connected with a 1-out-of-2 parallel connection forming a new block, which is connected in serial with C1. The overall reliability is the probability that the $C1 \wedge (C2 \vee C3)$ constraint holds:

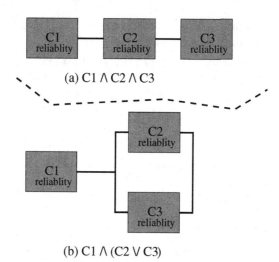

(a) C1 ∧ C2 ∧ C3

(b) C1 ∧ (C2 ∨ C3)

**Fig. 1.** Example of a Block Diagram.

$$BD.reliability \quad = P(C1 \wedge (C2 \vee C3))$$
$$P(C1 \wedge (C2 \vee C3)) = C1.reliability * C2.reliability+$$
$$C1.reliability * C3.reliability-$$
$$C1.reliability * C2.reliability * C3.reliability$$

So far, we calculate the dependability measures of a particular system as a function of the dependability measures that characterize the components of this system. However, we can further think of dependability measures as a function of the probability that the system fails. To calculate the probability of system failure we have to identify and model what should happen for the system to fail. The previous can be achieved using FTs [34, 11, 35]. FTs and BDs are equivalent in the sense that the values of the dependability measures obtained are the same. Moreover, having a BD, we can easily generate automatically an equivalent FT, and conversely. However, BDs and FTs enable modeling the system from different perspectives, depending on which one is more convenient for the worker in charge of the dependability analysis.

An FT visualizes a constraint, which describes undesired stimuli (i.e., failures) that lead to system failure. Hereafter, we call such a constraint, *constraint-to-fail*. The overall system failure is called the top-event. Undesired events are connected with AND and OR gates. AND gates connect events whose subsequent or concurrent occurrence triggers the top-event. OR gates connect events whose alternative occurrence triggers the top-event. Every event is characterized by the probability of its occurrence ($P_{occur}$).

Taking an example, suppose that providing a service S requires using components C1, C2 and C3, then a failure of any of them leads to system failure. The aforementioned constraint can be described as a logical formula, $FC1 \vee FC2 \vee FC3$. Predicates $FC1$, $FC2$, $FC3$ are true if components C1, C2, C3, respectively, have failed and false otherwise. The resulting FT, shown in Figure 2(a), depicts an OR gate that takes as input the failure events of C1, C2, C3 and has as output the failure of the overall system. The reliability in this case is:

$$FT.reliability \qquad = 1 - P(FC1 \vee FC2 \vee FC3)$$
$$P(FC1 \vee FC2 \vee FC3) = FC1.P_{occur} + FC2.P_{occur} + FC3.P_{occur} -$$
$$FC1.P_{occur} * FC2.P_{occur} -$$
$$FC1.P_{occur} * FC3.P_{occur} -$$
$$FC2.P_{occur} * FC3.P_{occur} +$$
$$FC1.P_{occur} * FC2.P_{occur} * FC3.P_{occur}$$

Suppose now that S requires using component C1 and either component C2, or component C3. Then, a failure of both C2 and C3 leads to system failure. Alternatively, a failure of C1 leads to system failure. The previous can be specified as a logical formula, $FC1 \vee (FC2 \wedge FC3)$. Figure 2(b) gives the corresponding FT. The reliability in this case is:

$$FT.reliability \qquad = 1 - P(FC1 \vee (FC2 \wedge FC3))$$
$$P(FC1 \vee (FC2 \wedge FC3)) = FC2.P_{occur} * FC3.P_{occur} + FC1.P_{occur} -$$
$$FC2.P_{occur} * FC3.P_{occur} * FC1.P_{occur}$$

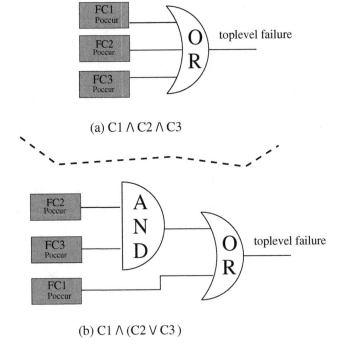

(a) C1 ∧ C2 ∧ C3

(b) C1 ∧ (C2 ∨ C3 )

**Fig. 2.** Example of a Fault Tree.

The techniques we presented until now, rely on static descriptions of either the components we need for correct service provisioning (i.e., BDs), or the failures that lead to an overall system failure (i.e., FTs). Although those techniques are quite easy to apply, they do not cover cases where we have to model dynamic aspects of the system that affect the values of the dependability measures. For example, the dependability analysis of systems with transient faults involves modeling that those faults disappear with a certain rate. Similarly, the dependability analysis of systems with intermittent faults requires modeling the way those faults activate (if an intermittent fault is active the service is not correctly provided) and passivate (if an intermittent fault is passive the service is correctly provided despite the presence of the fault), during the lifetime of the system. In other words, we have to model the failure behavior of the components and connectors that make up the system. In the case of repairable systems, we have to further model how faulty architectural elements eventually become operational, and conversely. Another issue that we can not model with BDs and FTs is the occurrence of dependent failures.

Modeling and analyzing the failure and repair behavior of systems relies on state space models [34, 11, 6, 10]. A state space model consists of a set of transitions between states of the system. A state describes a situation where either the system operates correctly, or not. In the latter case, the system is said to be in a *death state*. The state of the system depends on the states of the architectural elements that constitute it. Hence, a state can be seen as a composition of sub-states, each one representing the situation of an architectural element. A state is constrained by the range of all possible situations that may occur. A transition is characterized by the rate by which the source situation changes into the target situation. If, for instance, the difference between the source and the target situation is the failure of a component, the transition rate is the faulty component's failure rate. If, on the other hand, the difference between the source and the target situation is the repair of a component, the transition rate is the component's repair rate. The mathematical model that is employed for calculating reliability and availability based on a state space model, involves solving a system of first order differential equations.

Taking an example, suppose that in order to provide a service S we have to use components C1, C2 and C3. Moreover, suppose that C1, C2 and C3 have permanent faults. The state space model that specifies the failure behavior of the system is given in Figure 3; it consists of four states representing the following situations:

**State 1** C1, C2, C3 are operational.
**State 2** C1 failed, C2, C3 are operational (death state).
**State 3** C2 failed, C1, C3 are operational (death state).
**State 4** C3 failed, C1, C2 are operational (death State).

The state space model comprises transitions from state 1 to states 2, 3, 4 characterized by the failure rates of C1, C2, C3, respectively.

Let $P(t) = [p_1(t), p_2(t), p_3(t), p_4(t)]$ be a vector that gives the probabilities that the system is in states 1, 2, 3, 4, respectively. The system of differential equations that can be used to calculate those probabilities is the following: $P'(t) = P(t) * A$ where A is a matrix that can be easily calculated from the state space model as follows: For every transition from state i to state j, set A(i, j) equal to the transition rate. The value of every diagonal element A(i, i) is set to the negated sum of the non-diagonal i row elements of the matrix.

$$A = \begin{vmatrix} -\sum(A(0,i))_{i=1\ldots3} & C1.failure\_rate & C2.failure\_rate & C3.failure\_rate \\ 0 & 0 & 0 & 0 \\ 0 & 0 & 0 & 0 \\ 0 & 0 & 0 & 0 \end{vmatrix}$$

Assuming that $P(0) = [1, 0, 0, 0]$, and that the failure rates of C1, C2, C3 are constant we have the following solution for $P(t)$:

$$P(t) = P(0) * e^{A*t}$$

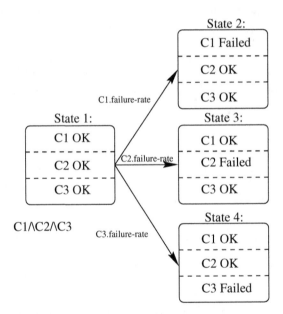

**Fig. 3.** Example of a state space model.

### 3.3    Automated Generation of State Space Models from Architectural Descriptions

The specification of large state-space models is often too complex and error-prone. The approach proposed in [19] alleviates this problem. In particular, instead of specifying all possible state transitions, the authors propose specifying the state range of the system, a death-state constraint, and transition rules between sets of states of the system.

The state range consists of a set of variables whose values describe a possible state situation. For example, a system that consists of a redundancy schema of three redundant components may be in 4 states. In each state $i : [0..3]$, $3 - i$ redundant components are operational. Then, the state range is defined as a single variable $numOfOperational : [0..3]$ whose value specifies the number of operational components.

A transition rule may state that: if the system is in a state where more than 1 component are operational (e.g., $numOfOperational > 1$), then the system may get into a state where the number of operational components is reduced by one (e.g., $numOfOperational = numOfOperational - 1$). Given the previous information, a complete state space model can be generated using the algorithm described in [19]. Briefly, the algorithm takes as input an initial state (e.g., the state 0 where $numOfOperational = 3$) and recursively applies the transition rules. During a recursive step and for a particular transition rule, the algorithm produces a transition to a state derived from the initial one. If the death-state (e.g., $numOfOperational <= 1$) constraint holds for the resulting state, the recursion stops.

State range definitions, transitions rules and death constraints can be automatically generated from architectural descriptions embedding the specification of dependability stimuli and properties, by following the steps below.

First, a state range definition for each scenario *scen* belonging to a given service profile is generated. The state of a scenario is composed of the states of the component and connector instances used within the scenario and the state of nodes on top of which the component instances execute. If a component is composite, its state is composed of the states of the constituent elements. The state range for the scenario consists of a set of variables, each one of which corresponds to a component/connector/node. The values of a variable depend on the kind of faults that may cause failures. At this point, the generation procedure is customized accordingly. In the case of permanent faults for instance, a component/connector/node may be either in an operational, or in a failed state. Hence, the corresponding state range variable may take two possible values OPERATIONAL or FAILED. In the case of intermittent faults, a component/connector/node may be in an operational state, or it may be in a failed-active or in a failed-benign state. Consequently, the corresponding state range variable may take three values OPERATIONAL, FAILED-ACTIVE, FAILED-BENIGN. The values of a state range variable further depend on the kind of redundancy used (take for instance the example we gave above with the 3 redundant components). Again, the generation procedure is customized accordingly.

After generating the state range definition for a scenario *scen*, the step that follows comprises the generation of transition rules for components/connectors/-nodes used in the scenario. These rules depend on the kinds of faults of the corresponding architectural element. For instance, for permanent faults, the rules follow the pattern given in Table 4. What is left at this point is to generate the definition of the initial state of the scenario, and the definition of the death state constraint. The initial state is a state where all of the elements used in the

| Architectural Element | Rule |
|---|---|
| Component | For all instances of primitive components, $c$:<br><br>– If *scen* is in a state where $c$ is in an OPERATIONAL state $st$, then *scen* may get into a state $st'$ where $c$ is FAILED. The rate of these transitions is equal to the arrival rates of the faults that cause the failure of $c$, *c.Faults.arrival-rate* (see Table 2).<br><br>For all instances of composite components, $c$:<br><br>– If *scen* is in a state $st$ where $c$ is OPERATIONAL, then *scen* may get into a state $st'$ where $c$ is FAILED due to a failure of a constituent element $c'$. The rate of these transitions is equal to the arrival rates of the faults that cause the failure of $c'$, *c'.Faults.arrival-rate*.<br><br>For all instances of composite components $rc$, representing a redundancy schema of $k$ components:<br><br>– If *scen* is in a state $st$ where $rc$ is OPERATIONAL, and the number of failed redundant component instances is $fc$, then *scen* may get into a state $st'$ where the number of failed components of $rc$ is $fc + l$. The difference between $st$ and $st'$ is $l$ redundant component instances of the same type $t$, which in $st$ were OPERATIONAL and in $st'$ are FAILED. This rule captures failure dependencies among redundant component instances of the same type. These components are used in the same conditions and with the same input. Hence, if one of them fails due to a design or an operational fault, all of them will fail. |
| Connector | For all instances of primitive connectors, see the case of primitive components. For all instances of composite connectors, see the case of composite components. |
| Node | We assume that nodes fail independently from each other. Hence, for all nodes in *scen*:<br><br>– If *scen* is in a state $st$ where a node $n$ is in an OPERATIONAL state, then *scen* may get into a state $st'$ where $n$ is in a FAILED state.<br>– Moreover, in $st'$, all instances of components $c$ deployed on $n$ are in a FAILED state.<br>– Finally, in $st'$ all instances of redundancy schemas $rc$, built out of $m$ components deployed on $n$, have $fc + m$ failed components and $fn + 1$ failed nodes.<br><br>The rate of these transitions is equal to the arrival rate of the faults that caused the failure of $n$, *n.Faults.arrival-rate*. |

**Table 4.** Transition Rules for Permanent Faults

scenario are operational. A scenario is in death state if any of the architectural elements used in it is not operational. Hence, the death state constraint consists of the disjunction of base predicates, each one of which defines the death state constraint for an individual element used in the scenario. More specifically, the base predicate for a component, connector, or a node, states that the value of the corresponding state range variable is FAILED. The base predicate for a redundancy schema is the disjunction of two predicates. The first one states that the number of failed redundant component instances is greater than the number of component faults that can be tolerated. Similarly, the second one states that the number of failed redundant nodes is greater than the number of node faults that can be tolerated.

## 4    A Developer-Oriented Environment for Dependability Analysis

The ideas proposed so far for dependability analysis at the architectural level are realized in the prototype implementation of a developer-oriented environment [43, 36]. As we already discussed in Section 2, UML is an emerging industrial standard for modeling the architecture of software systems. Consequently, our environment relies on an already existing UML modeling tool. More specifically, we use the Rational Rose tool[4] for the specification of software architectures.

However, we further mentioned the fact that the semantics of UML are imprecise compared to the ones of the ADLs we examined in Section 2. Consequently, we proposed defining an ADL that extends the standard UML semantics towards dealing with this lack of precision. To define ADL components, connectors, and configurations in relation to standard UML model elements, we undertook the following steps: (i) identify standard UML element(s), whose semantics are close to the ones needed for the specification of ADL components, connectors and configurations; (ii) if the semantics of the identified element(s) do not exactly match the ones needed for the specification of components, connectors, and configurations, extend them properly and define a corresponding UML stereotype(s)[5]; (iii) If the semantics of the identified element(s) match exactly, adopt the element(s) as a part of the core ADL language constructs.

As discussed in the literature [9, 29], various UML modeling elements may be used to specify an ADL component. The most popular ones are the Class, Component, Package, and Subsystem elements. From our point of view, the UML Component element is semantically far more concrete compared to an ADL component, as it specifically corresponds to an executable software module. The UML Class element is often considered as the basis for defining architectural

---

[4]  `http://www.rational.com`. Notice that the use of the Rational Rose tool was mainly motivated by pragmatic consideration that is the ownership of a license and former experience with this tool. However, our specific developments may be integrated within any extensible, UML-based tool that processes XMI files.

[5]  A UML stereotype is a UML element whose base class is a standard UML element. Moreover, a stereotype is associated with additional constraints and semantics.

components. However, a UML class does not directly support the hierarchical composition of systems. It is true that the definition of a UML Class may be composite, consisting of a number of constituent classes. However, the class specification can not contain the interrelationships among the constituent classes. Consequently, if an ADL composite component is mapped into a UML class, its definition may comprise a set of constituent components for which we have no means to describe the way they are connected through connectors. Technically, to achieve the previous we would need to define a Package containing the UML class definitions and a static structure diagram showing how they are connected. However, packages cannot be instantiated or associated with other packages. Hence, they are not adequate for specifying ADL components. This leads us to use the UML Subsystem element to model ADL components. A UML Subsystem is a subtype of both the UML Package and Classifier element. Hence, it may be instantiated multiple times, and associated with other subsystems. Precisely, we define an ADL component as a stereotyped UML Subsystem, that may provide and require standard UML interfaces. The ADL component stereotype is characterized by a property, named *"composite"*, which may be true or false, depending on whether or not a component is built out of other components and connectors. Moreover, the ADL component stereotype is associated with the dependability features identified in Tables 1, 2 and 3.

The natural choice for specifying ADL connectors in UML is by stereotyping the standard UML Association element. A connector role corresponds to an association end. Moreover, the distinctive feature of a connector is a non-empty set of interfaces, named *"Interfaces"*, representing the specific parts of components' functionality playing the roles. Each interface out of the set must be provided by at least one associated component. Equally, each interface out of the set must be required by at least one associated component. The ADL Connector stereotype is further characterized by the dependability features identified in Tables 1 and 2.

So far, we considered connectors as associations representing communication protocols. However, we must not ignore the fact that, in practice, connectors are built from architectural elements, including components and more primitive connectors. Taking CORBA for example, a CORBA connector can be seen as a combination of functionalities of the ORB and of CORBA services (i.e., COSs). Hence, it is necessary to support hierarchical composition of connectors. At this point, we face a technical problem: UML Associations can not be composed of other model elements. However, there exists a standard UML element called Refinement defined as *"a dependency where the clients are derived by the suppliers"* [37]. The refinement element is characterized by a property called mapping. The values of this property describe how the client is derived by the supplier. Hence, to support the hierarchical composition of connectors, we define a stereotype, whose base class is the standard UML Refinement element and is used to define the mapping between a connector and a composite component that realizes the connector.

By definition, a configuration specifies the assembly of components and connectors. In UML, the assembly of model elements is specified by a model. The corresponding semantic element of a model is the standard UML Model element, defined as *"an abstraction of a modeled system specifying the system from a certain point of view and at a certain level of abstraction...the UML Model consists of a containment hierarchy where the top most package represents the boundary of the modeled system"* [37]. Hence, a configuration is actually a UML model, consisting of a containment hierarchy where the top-most package is a composite ADL component. The given definition of configuration is weak in that it enables the description of any architectural configuration provided it complies with the well-formedness rules associated with the component and connector elements. This results from our concern of supporting the description of various architectural styles, which possibly come along with specific ADLs as is the case with the C2 style [30]. Constraints that are specific to a style are introduced through the definition of a corresponding extension of the ADL configuration element, possibly combined with extensions of the ADL component and connector stereotypes.

The Rational Rose tool allows the definition of user specific add-ins that facilitate the specification and use of stereotyped elements and their associated features. Given the aforementioned facility, we implemented an add-in that eases the specification of architectural descriptions using the stereotypes mentioned above. Moreover, we use an already existing add-in, which enables generating XMI textual specifications of architectures specified graphically using the Rational Rose tool; these textual specifications serve as input to tools for dependability and performance analysis [43].

The generation of the XMI textual specifications for dependability analysis relies on the automated procedure we described in Section 3 (the procedure and the tools we use for the case of performance are detailed in [43]). The specific tool we use for dependability analysis is SURE-ASSIST [6]. The tool is properly customized to accept as input the textual specifications we generate. Then, it calculates reliability bounds. The tool was selected because it is highly rated among other reliability tools [10] and because it is available for free. However, the automated support provided by our environment for dependability analysis can be coupled with any other tool that accepts as input state space models.

## 5    The Developer-Oriented Environment in Action

To illustrate the use of our environment for dependability analysis, we employ an example taken from a case study we investigated in the context of the DSoS IST project[6]. The case study is a travel agent system (TA). TA offers services for flight, hotel, and car reservations. It consists of the integration of different kinds of existing systems supporting air companies, hotel chains, and car rental companies. Figure 4 gives a screen shot of the actual architecture of the TA as

---

[6] http://www.newcastle.research.ec.org/dsos

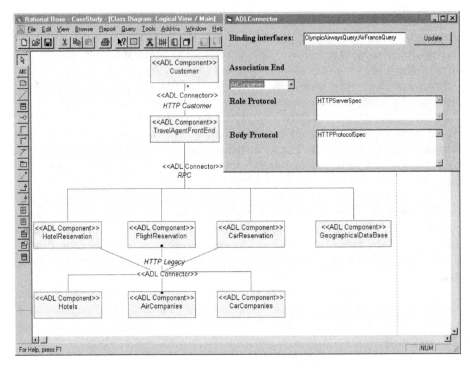

**Fig. 4.** The Architecture of the Travel Agent system.

specified using the UML modeling tool, which we customized. The TA comprises the *TravelAgentFrontEnd* component, which serves as a GUI for potential customers wanting to reserve tickets, rooms, and cars. The TA further includes the *HotelReservation, FlightReservation, CarReservation* components, which accept as input individual parts of a customer request for hotel, ticket and car reservation, and translate them into requests for services provided by specific hotel, air company and car company components. The set of the hotel components is represented by the Hotels composite component. Similarly, the sets of air company and car company components are represented by the *AirCompanies* and *CarCompanies* composite components. Two different kinds of connectors are used in our architecture. The HTTP connectors (e.g., see Figure 4) represent the interaction protocol among customers and the TA front end component, and among components translating requests and existing component systems implementing Web servers. The RPC connector represents the protocol used among the front end component and the components that translate requests. Note that multiparty connectors abstract complex connector realizations, which may actually be refined into various protocols, depending on the intended behavior. For instance, the RPC connector may be refined into a number of bi-party connectors as well as into a complex transactional connector.

The dependability measure we are interested in is reliability. However, the goal of the analysis is not to obtain precise values of the reliability measure since this would require to precisely model the Internet. The previous is considered, in general, as rather unrealistic [8]. For that reason, we concentrate on comparing different scenarios towards improving the design of our system, while assuming certain invariants for modeling issues related to the Web. Our objective is to try to improve the reliability of TA while keeping the cost of the required changes in the TA system low.

The scenario shown in Figure 5 as a UML collaboration diagram, is a typical use case of TA. This scenario constitutes the basic service profile used for the reliability analysis, i.e., the provided scenario is processed for the automatic generation of the state space model analyzed by the SURE-ASSIST tool. According to the scenario, one or more customers use an instance, *ta*, of the *TravelAgent-FrontEnd* to request the reservation of a flight ticket, a hotel room and a car. The *ta* component instance breaks down such a request into 3 separate requests. The first one relates to the flight ticket reservation and is sent to an instance, *fr*, of the *FlightReservation* component. The *fr* component instance uses this request to generate a new set of requests, each one of which is specific to an air company that collaborates with the TA system. The set of specific requests is finally sent to an instance, *ac*, of the *AirCompanies* composite component, which represents the current set of collaborating air companies. Similarly, the second and the third requests are related to the hotel and the car reservations, respectively. These requests are sent to instances of the *HotelReservation* and *CarReservation* components, which reproduce them properly and send them to the current sets of collaborating hotels and car companies.

The component instances used in the scenario may fail to give answers to customers. Component failures are manifestations of design faults. We assume that these faults are accidental, created by the component developers. Moreover, component faults are all permanent and their arrival rates vary depending on the type of the components. More specifically, the fault arrival rates for the components that represent component systems supporting hotels, air companies and car companies are much smaller compared to the faults arrival rates of the rest of the components that make up the TA system. The reason behind this is that the component systems supporting hotels, air companies and car companies have already been in use and their implementations are quite stable. On the other hand, the TA front end and reservation components are still under development. The nodes used in our scenario may fail because of permanent faults. HTTP and RPC connectors may also fail, however, in this case it is more pragmatic to assume that we deal with temporary faults, which may disappear with a certain rate. The arrival rates of node faults are much smaller than the arrival rates of component faults. This holds similarly for the RPC connector. On the contrary, the HTTP connector is expected to be quite unreliable, with a failure rate greater than that of the components used in the TA. For illustration, Figure 5 shows the detailed specification of the reliability stimuli and properties that are given for the *FlightReservation* component.

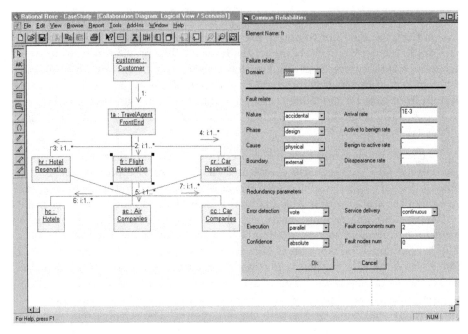

**Fig. 5.** A generic scenario for TA

By taking a closer look at the architecture of the TA system, we can deduce that some sort of redundancy is used. In particular, the *Hotels*, *AirCompanies* and *CarCompanies* components are composite, consisting of $k$ components that represent the dependable systems supporting hotels, air companies and car companies. The reservation components request from them, room, ticket and car reservations. For the scenario to be successful, we need answers from at least one hotel, one air company, and one car company. Hence, *Hotels*, *AirCompanies*, and *CarCompanies* can be seen as ad hoc redundancy schemas with the following properties: the execution of redundant elements is parallel (*Redundancy.execution = parallel*), the number of component and node faults that can be tolerated is $k - 1$ (*Redundancy.no-comp-faults* and *Redundancy.no-node-faults = k − 1*).

To further improve the architecture regarding the provided reliability, we designed three additional redundancy schemas. The first one contains $n$ different versions of the *HotelReservation* component. Upon the instantiation of the schema, $n$ component instances are created, one of each version. These instances execute in parallel and are deployed on $n$ different nodes. The second schema contains $n$ versions of the *FlightReservation* component, the instances of which are also deployed on the $n$ nodes, on top of which the instances of the *Hotel-Reservation* component execute. Finally, the last schema contains $n$ versions of the *CarReservation* component, the instances of which are also deployed on the nodes used to execute the instances of the *HotelReservation* component. At runtime, a customer request is broken down by the instance of the *TravelAgentFrontEnd* component into individual requests for flight ticket, hotel room and car reservation. Each one of these requests is replicated and sent to all the redundant instances of the corresponding reservation component. Each instance of the reservation component translates the request into specific requests for the corresponding available component systems and sends them. When the instance of the *TravelAgentFrontEnd* starts receiving offers for flight tickets, hotel rooms and cars, it removes identical reply messages and combines them into replies that are returned to the customer. We tried our scenario for $n = 1, 2, 3$ redundant versions. Given the aforementioned scenario, three complete state space models were generated and analytically solved. The results obtained are summarized in Figure 6. For further detail about the scenario, including complexity of the generated state space models, the interested reader is referred to [43].

The main observation we make is that the reliability of TA does increase. However, the improvement when we use redundant versions is certainly not spectacular. The explanation for this is simple. In our scenario, the most unreliable element used is the HTTP connector. This is the main source causing the reliability measure to have small values. Any improvement in the rest of the architectural elements used shall not cover this problem, which unfortunately can not be easily alleviated. Hence, using multiple versions does not bring much gain. However, the good news are that regarding the cost of using multiple versions, we do not lose much. The elements for which we produced multiple versions just translate TA specific requests into component systems' specific requests. Since the functionality of these components is quite simple, re-implementing them differently (e.g., using different developers) is not a complex, neither a time-consuming task. Note here that the fact that the functionality of the redundant components is simple does not mean that there can be no bugs in their implementation. Actually, mistakes in the mapping of TA requests into component systems' specific requests can be quite often. Furthermore, the cost of developing multiple versions is low since we did not really use any strong synchronization among the different versions.

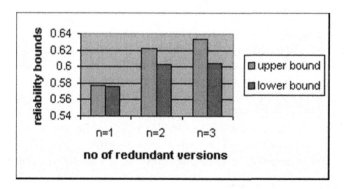

**Fig. 6.** Results produced by the reliability analysis of TA

# 6    Conclusion

Work in the software architecture domain primarily focuses on the standard (as opposed to exceptional) behavior of the software system. However, it is crucial from the perspective of system dependability to also account for failure occurrences, which impacts all the phases of the software development process, from the requirements elicitation phase to the deployment phase. In the context of the research activities of the INRIA ARLES research group[7], we have more specifically concentrated on solutions assisting the design and analysis of dependable distributed software systems.

## 6.1    Assisting the Analysis of Dependable Systems

In this paper, we presented automated support for the dependability analysis of software systems at the architectural level. The overall design and realization of the resulting development environment is guided by the needs of its current and potential users, imposing the simplification of certain important and inevitable development activities related to the quality analysis and assurance of dependable systems. The quality analysis of systems is traditionally based on methods and tools that have a strong formal basis. We believe that the proposed environment brings everyday developers closer to such methods and tools. The environment relies on an architecture description language for the specification of dependable systems architectures, which is defined based on UML, a standard and widely accepted notation for modeling software. Our environment further provides a certain level of automation that eases the development of traditional quality models from architectural descriptions. The associated prototype has been used in the context of the DSoS IST project for the quality analysis of the Travel Agent system. Part of the analysis was presented here in the form of demonstrating examples. We further used the basic ideas of our environment in the context of the C3DS IST[8] project for the performance and reliability analysis of workflow-based dependable systems [41].

## 6.2    Assisting the Design of Dependable Systems

From the perspective of the system's design, failures may be handled through the integration within the system architecture of components and connectors that provide fault tolerant capabilities. Practically, this means that failures are handled by an underlying fault-tolerant mechanism (e.g., transparent replication management) at the middleware level. Such fault tolerance support must further be coupled with application-specific fault tolerance that relies at least on an exception handling mechanism, which enables the software developer to specify the actions to be undertaken under the occurrence of application-specific and underlying runtime exceptions. We have then carried out research in the

---

[7] http://www-rocq.inria.fr/arles

[8] http://www.newcastle.research.ec.org/c3ds/

two following complementary directions towards assisting the architecting of dependable systems:

(i) Systematic aid in the development of middleware architectures for dependable systems;
(ii) Architecture-based exception handling.

The use of middleware is the current practice for developing distributed systems. Developers compose reusable services provided by proprietary or standard middleware infrastructures to deal with non-functional requirements. However, developers still have to design and implement middleware architectures combining available services in a way that best fits the application's requirements. In order to ease this task, we have customized the environment discussed in this paper with the following features [18]: (i) an ADL for modeling middleware architectures, (ii) a repository populated with architectural descriptions of middleware services, and (iii) automated support for composing middleware architectures out of available services according to target non-functional properties whose quality may be assessed both qualitatively and quantitatively.

As previously raised, it is necessary to complement fault tolerance support provided by the underlying middleware architecture, with support for exception handling. We have, thus, proposed a solution to architecture-based exception handling [16], which enhances exception handling implemented within components and connectors. Our solution lies in: (i) extending the ADL so as to enable the specification of required changes to the architecture in the presence of failures, and (ii) associated runtime support for enabling resulting dynamic reconfigurations.

## 6.3   Perspectives

The above results have been proven successful for assisting the architecting of dependable distributed systems that are closed, i.e., systems whose components depend on a single administrative domain and are known at design time. However, future distributed systems will increasingly be open, which raises new issues for making them dependable. In this context, we are undertaking research in the following directions:

(i) Architecting open distributed systems in a way that accounts for mobility, which requires support for the dynamic composition and quality assessment of architecture instances;
(ii) Design of fault tolerance mechanisms for open distributed systems considering that the systems span multiple administrative domains and hence cannot accommodate locking-based solutions as, e.g., enforced by transactional processing [39].

In general, the above calls for new solutions that allow the development of dependable systems that are highly dynamic and hence requires the integration of adaptive runtime support aimed at enforcing dependability.

# References

[1]  G. Agha. *Actors: A Model of Concurrent Computation.* MIT Press, 1986.

[2]  R. Allen and D. Garlan. Formalizing Architectural Connection. In *Proceedings of the 16th International Conference on Software Engineering*, pages 71–80. IEEE, 1994.

[3]  M. C. Astley. *Customization and Composition of Distributed Objects: Policy Management in Distributed Software Architectures.* PhD thesis, University of Illinois, 1999.

[4]  M. C. Astley and G. Agha. Customization and Composition of Distributed Objects: Middleware Abstractions for Policy Management. In *Proceedings of the 6th International Symposium on the Foundations of Software Engineering*, pages 1–9. ACM-SIGSOFT, November 1998.

[5]  M. Barbacci, C. Weinstock, D. Doubleday, M. Gardner, and R. Lichota. DURRA: A Structure Description Language for Developing Distributed Applications. *Software Engineering Journal*, pages 83–94, March 1993.

[6]  R. Butler and W. Ricky. The SURE Approach to Reliability Analysis. *IEEE Transactions on Reliability*, 41(2):210–218, June 1992.

[7]  P. C. Clements. A Survey of Architecture Description Languages. In *Proceedings of the 8th International Workshop on Software Specification and Design*, March 1996.

[8]  S. Floyd and V. Paxson. Difficulties in Simulating the Internet. *ACM/IEEE Transactions on Networking*, 2001.

[9]  D. Garlan, J. Kompanec, and P. Pinto. Reconciling the Needs of Architectural Description with Object-Modeling Notations. In *Proceedings of the 3rd International Conference on the Unified Modeling Language (UML-00)*, 2000.

[10]  R. Geist and K. Trivedi. Reliability Estimation of Fault Tolerant Systems : Tools and Techniques. *IEEE Computer*, 23(7):52–61, July 1990.

[11]  R. Glass. *Software Reliability Guidebook.* Prentice-Hall, 1979.

[12]  C.A.R. Hoare. An Axiomatic Basis for Computer Programming. *Communication of the ACM*, 12(10):576–583, October 1969.

[13]  C.A.R. Hoare. *Communicating Sequential Processes.* Prentice-Hall, 1985.

[14]  G. J. Holzmann. The SPIN Model Checker. *IEEE Transactions on Software Engineering*, 23(5):279–295, 1997.

[15]  V. Issarny. Configuration-Based Programming Systems. In *Proceedings of SOFSEM'97: Theory and Practice of Informatics*, pages 183–200. Springer-Verlag, November 1997.

[16]  V. Issarny and J-P. Banâtre. Architecture-based Exception Handling. In *Proceedings of the 34th Hawaii International Conference on System Sciences*, 2001.

[17]  V. Issarny, C. Bidan, and T. Saridakis. Achieving Middleware Customization in a Configuration-based Development Environment: Experience with the Aster Prototype. In *Proceedings of the 4th International Conference on Configurable Distributed Systems*, pages 207–214. IEEE, 1998.

[18]  V. Issarny, C. Kloukinas, and A. Zarras. Systematic Aid for Developing Middleware Architectures. *Communications of the ACM (CACM)*, 45(6):53–58, 2002.

[19]  S. C. Johnson. Reliability Analysis of Large Complex Systems Using ASSIST. In *Proceedings of the 8th Digital Avionics Systems Conference*, pages 227–234. AIAA/IEEE, 1988.

[20]  R. Kazman, S. J. Carriere, and S. G. Woods. Toward a Discipline of Scenario-Based Architectural Engineering. *Annals of Software Engineering*, 9:5–33, 2000.

[21] L. Lamport. The Temporal Logic of Actions. *ACM Transactions on Programming Languages and Systems*, 16(3):872–923, May 1994.

[22] J-C. Laprie. Dependable Computing and Fault Tolerance : Concepts and Terminology. In *Proceedings of the 15th International Symposium on Fault-Tolerant Computing (FTCS-15)*, pages 2–11, 1985.

[23] J.-C. Laprie, J. Arlat, C. Beounes, and K. Kanoun. Definition and Analysis of Hardware and Software Fault-Tolerant Architectures. *IEEE Computer*, 23(7):39–51, 1990.

[24] D. C. Luckham and J. Vera. An Event-Based Architecture Definition Language. *IEEE Transactions on Software Engineering*, 21(9):717–734, Sept 1995.

[25] M. Klein and R. Kazman and L. Bass and Carriere, S. J. and M. Barbacci and H. Lipson. Attribute-based architectural styles. In *Proceedings of the 1st IFIP Working Conference on Software Architecture (WICSA-1)*, pages 225–243, 1999.

[26] J. Magee, N. Dulay, and J. Kramer. Structuring Parallel and Distributed Programs. In *Proceedings of the 1st International Conference on Configurable Distributed Systems*, March 1992.

[27] J. Magee, J. Kramer, and D. Giannakopoulou. Behavior Analysis of Software Architectures. In *Proceedings of the 1st IFIP Working Conference on Software Architectures (WICSA-1)*, pages 35–49, 1999.

[28] J. Magee, J. Kramer, and M. Sloman. Constructing Distributed Systems in CONIC. *IEEE Transactions on Software Engineering*, 16(5):663–675, June 1989.

[29] N. Medvidovic, D. S. Rosenblum, J. E. Robbins, and D. F. Redmiles. Modeling Software Architectures in the Unified Modeling Language. *ACM Transactions on Software Engineering and Methodology*, (to appear).

[30] N. Medvidovic and R. Taylor. A Classification and Comparison Framework for Software Architecture Description Languages. *IEEE Transactions on Software Engineering*, 26(1):70–93, 2000.

[31] R. Milner. *A Calculus of Communicating Systems*. Cambridge University Press, 1980.

[32] R. Milner. *Communicating and Mobile Systems: the pi-calculus*. Springer-Verlag, 1999.

[33] M. Moriconi, X. Qian, and A. Riemenschneider. Correct Architecture Refinement. *IEEE Transactions on Software Engineering*, 21(4):356–372, April 1995.

[34] G. Myers. *Software Reliability - Principles and Practices*. John Wiley and Sons, 1976.

[35] NASA. Reliability Block Diagrams and Reliability Modeling. Technical report, NASA Glenn Research Center, May 1995. http://www-osma.lerc.nasa.gov/rbd/rbdtut.html.

[36] K. Nguyen and V. Issarny. Demonstration of Support for Architectural Design for Dependable SoS. CSDA2 report. Available at URL: http://www.newcastle.research.ec.org/dsos/deliverables.

[37] OMG. UML Semantics 1.3, 1997.

[38] M. Shaw, R. Deline, D. Klein, T. Ross, D. Young, and G. Zelesnik. Abstractions for Software Architecture and Tools to Support Them. *IEEE Transactions on Software Engineering*, 21(4):314–335, 1995.

[39] F. Tartanoglu, V. Issarny, A. Romanovsky, and N. Levy. *Architecting Dependable Systems*, volume 2677 of *LNCS*, chapter Dependability in the Web Services Architecture. Springer-Verlag, 2003.

[40] R. N. Taylor, N. Medvidovic, K. M. Anderson, E. J. Whitehead, J. E. Robbins, K. A. Nies, P. Oreizy, and D. L. Dubrow. A Component and Message Based Ar-

chitectural Style for GUI Software. *IEEE Transactions on Software Engineering*, 22(6):390–406, July 1996.

[41] A. Zarras and V. Issarny. Automating the Performance and Reliability Analysis of Enterprise Information Systems. In *Proceedings of the 16th IEEE International Conference on Automated Software Engineering (ASE'01)*, 2000.

[42] A. Zarras, C. Kloukinas, and V. Issarny. *Architecting Dependable Systems*, volume 2677 of *LNCS*, chapter Quality Analysis of Dependable Systems: A Developer Oriented Approach. Springer-Verlag, 2003.

[43] A. Zarras, C. Kloukinas, V. Issarny, and K. Nguyen. *Initial Results on Architectures and Dependable Mechanisms for Dependable SoSs*, IC2 report An Architecture-based Environment for the Development of DSoS. Available at URL: http://www.newcastle.research.ec.org/dsos/deliverables.

# Author Index